Unbound Feet

Unbound Feet

A Social History of Chinese
Women in San Francisco

Judy Yung

UNIVERSITY OF CALIFORNIA PRESS

Berkeley / Los Angeles / London

University of California Press
Berkeley and Los Angeles, California

University of California Press, Ltd.
London, England

Library of Congress Cataloging-in-Publication Data

Yung, Judy.
    Unbound feet : a social history of Chinese women in San Francisco / Judy Yung.
        p.   cm.
    Includes bibliographical references and index.
    ISBN 0-520-08866-2 (alk. paper).—ISBN 0-520-08867-0 (pbk. : alk. paper)
    1. Chinese American women—California—San Francisco—History. 2. Women
Immigrants—California—San Francisco—History. 3. San Francisco (Calif.)—Social
conditions.   I. Title.
F869.S39C595 1995
979.4'61004951—dc20   94-40397

Printed in the United States of America
9 8 7 6 5 4 3 2 1

To my mother and
in memory of my father

The world can not move without women's sharing in the movement. China compressed the feet of her women and thereby retarded the steps of her men.

Frances Ellen Harper

Contents

Terminology and Transliterations

 For political reasons, I use the term *Asian American* instead of *Oriental* and do not hyphenate *Chinese American* even when used as an adjective. During the 1960s, Chinese and Japanese Americans came to recognize *Oriental* as a derogatory name that connotes exoticism and inferiority. The term *Asian American* became the preferred name in recognition of the group's common history of oppression, geographical origins, and political destiny. The hyphen was eliminated because it inferred that Chinese Americans have split identities, that somehow they are not fully American like everyone else. For the same reason and to be consistent, I do not use the hyphen when referring to any ethnic American group.

 I call the first generation to come to the United States *immigrants* and their children who were born in the United States *second generation* or *American-born Chinese*. When referring to both groups, I use either *Chinese in America* or *Chinese Americans*, especially when I need to differentiate them from Chinese people in China. For example, when comparing women in China and Chinese women in America, I use *Chinese women* for the former group and *Chinese American women* for the latter. *Overseas Chinese* is used instead of *Chinese Americans* when the reference point is in China.

 In regard to racial and ethnic terms, I use what is generally preferred by the groups themselves: *black, Asian American, Native American,* and *Chicano.* Depending on the time period under discussion, I use either *Mexican* or *Chicano; racial minority* or *Third World; minority women* or *women of color.* In a racial context, I generally use *white* instead of *European American.* Otherwise, I try to be ethnic specific in identifying the group by using *Italian American, German American, Jewish*

American, etc. The term *America* should be understood as an abbreviated form of *United States of America*. To be *Americanized* is to become acculturated but not necessarily assimilated into American life. To avoid the trap of associating the dominant white group with everything that is American, *Western* is preferred over *American* when the reference is to cultural practices; thus, Western dress, not American dress.

Following standard practice, I use the Pinyin romanization system for Chinese proper nouns, except in cases where the names have been commonly spelled in a different romanization system. For common words and phrases in the Cantonese dialect or direct quotes from Cantonese-speaking persons, I use the Cantonese spelling.

When using a person's Chinese name, I follow Chinese practice by giving the surname (family name) first, followed by the given name, without an intervening comma. For example, in the name Tom Yip Jing, Tom is the surname, and Yip Jing, the given name. Without meaning to be disrespectful, I generally use the person's given name instead of his or her last name whenever I refer to that individual more than once in the text. Since many Chinese Americans share the same surname, I adopted this practice to avoid confusion. The appearance of *Shee* in a woman's name indicates that she is married. For example, a woman with the maiden name of Law who married into the Low family would thenceforth be known as Law Shee Low.

Finally, although it is standard practice to indicate spelling and grammatical errors in quoted passages by the use of "[*sic*]," I chose to forgo doing so in many instances in order to remain faithful to the exact wording and style of speech, and to avoid interrupting the flow of the conversation.

Acknowledgments

The making of *Unbound Feet*—from its initial conception as a dissertation topic over ten years ago, through the laborious research, analysis, and writing phases, and finally to completion as a published book—would not have been possible without the generous support and assistance of many individuals and institutions. The research could not have been carried out without the help of Chester Chan, Gordon Chang, Barbara Ige, David W. Lee, Franklin Lee, Sharon Owyang, Col. William Strobridge, Wang Xing Chu, Shelley Wong, Angela Chang of the Gum Moon Women's Residence, Rosemary Chan of the Square and Circle Club, Yeeling Fong of the International Institute of San Francisco, Teresa Wu of the Chinese YWCA, Wei Chi Poon of the Asian American Studies Library at the University of California, Berkeley, Waverly Lowell of the National Archives in San Bruno, and the staffs of the San Francisco Public Library, Bancroft Library at the University of California, Berkeley, the Labor Archives and Research Center, San Francisco State University, Interlibrary Loan Department at McHenry Library at the University of California, Santa Cruz, and the Hoover Institution on War, Revolution, and Peace at Stanford University. Special thanks go to Sucheng Chan for sharing her data from the 1900 and 1910 manuscript censuses; Peggy Pascoe for her copious notes from the case files of Cameron House; Philip P. Choy for his personal copy of the Chinese YWCA board minutes and staff reports; and Him Mark Lai for use of his private collection on Chinese American history.

As oral history forms the core of this study, I am especially grateful to the many Chinese American women who entrusted me with their life stories and the men who provided me with their insights of San Francisco Chinatown: June Chan, Rena Jung Chung, Richard Koch Dare,

Marietta Chong Eng, Alice Sue Fun, Maggie Gee, May Lew Gee, Gladys Ng Gin, Penny Chan Huey, Bessie Hung, Ruth Chan Jang, Jew Law Ying, Francis Jong, Florence Chinn Kwan, Clara Lee, Ira Lee, Jane Kwong Lee, Lim P. Lee, Louise Schulze Lee, Lucy Lee, Mickey Lee, Stanley Lee, Sue Ko Lee, Law Shee Low, Eva Lowe, May Mock, Helen Pon Onyett, Edwin Owyang, Fred Schulze, Charlotte Sexton, Martha Taam, Dora Lee Wong, Helen Hong Wong, Wong Shee Chan, Wong Wee Ying, Margaret Woo, Jessie Lee Yip, and Alice Fong Yu.

For their expert and technical assistance, I wish to acknowledge Chris Huie for the photo reproductions, Ellen Yeung for translations from Chinese into English, Wang Xing Chu for typing the Chinese glossary, Gary Kawaguchi for inputting the 1920 census data, and the staffs at the Word Processing Center, University of California, Santa Cruz, for setting the statistical tables and at the University of California Press for guiding the publication process.

Many of my colleagues did close readings of early drafts of this study and gave me helpful suggestions for improving the text. I want to thank Tomás Almaguer, Bettina Aptheker, Michael Cowan, John Dizikes, Dana Frank, Marge Frantz, Gail Hershatter, Elaine H. Kim, Ann Lane, Susan Mann, Franklin Ng, Forrest Robinson, Mary P. Ryan, Ronald Takaki, and Ling-chi Wang. The book also benefited from the critical comments of publisher reviewers, including Mari Jo Buhle, Roger Daniels, Ramón Gutiérrez, and Valerie Matsumoto. For guiding my thinking and giving me incisive, critical feedback through every stage of this book, I am especially grateful to Him Mark Lai, Ruthanne Lum McCunn, Peggy Pascoe, and William Wei.

Last but not least, my greatest thanks go to Sandy Lee for her sisterly support and encouragement, and to Smokey for being such an affectionate furball throughout this project.

Research for this book was supported by an American Fellowship from the American Association of University Women Educational Foundation, a U.C. Affirmative Action Dissertation Year Fellowship from the Graduate Division of the University of California, Berkeley, and faculty research funds granted by the University of California, Santa Cruz.

Introduction

For years I assumed that my parents were among the first generation to come to the United States—my father in 1921, and my mother later, in 1941—and that I was a second-generation Chinese American, born and raised in San Francisco. Only after I began researching Chinese American women's history and my own family history did I discover that I was really the third generation on my father's side and the fourth generation on my mother's side. How this came about is a history lesson in itself, a lesson that I believe offers insights into Chinese immigration patterns and the different experiences of Chinese women from those of men.

Political upheavals and conditions of poverty at home drove many young men from the Pearl River delta in Southeast China to immigrate to the United States after gold was discovered in California. Among them were my maternal great-grandfather, Chin Lung (a.k.a. Chin Hong Dai) and my paternal grandfather, Tom Fat Kwong. Both came alone without their families in search of a better livelihood: Chin Lung in 1882, Tom Fat Kwong in 1911. Because of cultural restrictions, economic considerations, and immigration laws that specifically excluded them, few Chinese women came to the United States on their own or to join their husbands during these years.

Chin Lung immigrated right before the passage of the Chinese Exclusion Act of 1882, which barred the further entry of Chinese laborers. He was hardworking and rather resourceful. Within six years he had learned to speak English and saved enough money—sacking rice at the Sing Kee store in San Francisco Chinatown and, later, engaging in tenant farming with fellow villagers in the Sacramento–San Joaquin Delta—to go home and marry.[1] In this way, he was luckier than most other Chinese laborers, who never made enough to return home and instead lived a bachelor existence in Chinatown enclaves devoid of traditional family life. There were few Chinese women in America for them to marry, and antimiscegenation laws prohibited intermarriage between whites and Chinese.

In 1888 Great-Grandfather returned to China and married Leong Kum Kew (a.k.a. Leong Shee), but he could not bring her back with him to the United States because the Chinese Exclusion Act also barred wives of Chinese laborers. Only family members of U.S. citizens, merchants, and diplomats were exempt. Upon his return, therefore, Chin Lung invested wisely in the Sing Kee store in order to establish merchant status; he was finally able to send for my great-grandmother in 1893. While he continued to farm in the Sacramento Delta on hundreds of acres of leased land, amassing a fortune growing potatoes with borrowed credit and hired help, Great-Grandmother stayed in San Francisco Chinatown, where she gave birth to five children, two girls and three boys. The oldest child was my grandmother Chin Suey Kum, born in 1894. Even though she had status and the means to live well, Great-Grandmother, who had bound feet, found life in America inconvenient, alienating, and harried. Her domestic life was quite different from her husband's public life. With Chin Lung off pursuing exciting activities such as building a fortune in farming and participating in community politics, she remained sequestered at home, raising their children with the help of a *mui tsai* (domestic slave girl). So unhappy was she in America that in 1904 she packed up and returned to China with all of her children. Chin Lung chose to remain in the United States and make periodic trips home to visit.

Although their five children were all American-born citizens and had the right to return, only the boys were encouraged to do so. Traditional gender roles and the lack of economic and political power on the part of Chinese women denied both daughters that option. It was considered proper that all of the sons return and establish families in the United States while both daughters be married into wealthy families in China. Grandmother was wed to Jew Hing Gwin, a prominent herb doctor. They had seven children, my mother, Jew Law Ying, being the eldest. Unfortunately, the family hit hard times when Grandfather succumbed to opium and lost the entire family fortune. Grandaunt Chin Suey Ngon's situation was equally tragic, for her husband died only a few months after their wedding. Once married, by U.S. law both Grandmother and

Great-Grandfather Chin Lung and family in San Francisco, 1903. *From left to right:* Suey Kum, Suey Ngon, Wing, Leong Shee, Chin Lung, Foo, Wah, and *mui tsai* Ah Kum. (Judy Yung collection)

Grandaunt forfeited the right to return to the United States. Only with the support of her brother and by lying about her marital status was Grandaunt able to return to America in 1920.[2]

Meanwhile, on the paternal side of my family, Grandfather Tom Fat Kwong had managed to be smuggled across the U.S. border sometime before 1911. He farmed in Redwood City, California, for a few years and served in World War I. This military duty could have allowed him to legalize his status and send for the wife, daughter, and two sons who he had left behind in China. Before he had a chance to do so, though, he was killed by a car while bicycling home one dark night. His sudden death cut off the only viable source of income for his family in China. So my father, being the eldest son, found another way to immigrate to the United States: in 1921, with money borrowed from relatives, he purchased the necessary documents and passage to come as Yung Hin Sen, the "paper son" of Yung Ung, an established merchant in Stockton, California.[3] For the next fifteen years he worked hard as a houseboy, gardener, and cook, finally saving enough money to repay his debts and return to China to marry. He was by then thirty-three years old. The marriage to my mother was arranged by Chin Lung himself, at the suggestion of his eldest daughter-in-law, Wong Shee Chan, who had befriended my father in San Francisco.

My mother told me, "Everyone said coming to Gold Mountain would be like going to heaven."[4] But although she was a daughter of a U.S. citizen, immigration as a derivative citizen through the mother was not legally permissible. And so she agreed to marry my father. After they married, my father returned to the United States alone because Chinese laborers still did not have the right to bring their wives into the country. Only after five more years of hard work and saving was he able to buy a few nominal shares in a Chinatown business, establish merchant status, and send for my mother and my eldest sister, Bak Heong, born after he had returned to America.

Just as Great-Grandmother had warned her, however, the promise of Gold Mountain proved elusive for my mother as well. My father remained a laborer all his life, working as a janitor while my mother sewed into the night for garment sweatshops. They had to really struggle to eke out a living and raise us six children. Later, when I compared my mother's life with that of Chin Lung's other grandchildren, who were fortunate to have been born and raised in America, I saw how much harsher her life turned out to be because of the racist and sexist restrictions that were placed on Chinese immigrant women. And I wondered how many other Chinese women suffered similar consequences for no fault of their own?

It was in the quest for answers to my own identity as a Chinese American woman—answers that I could not find in any history textbook—that I felt a need to study Chinese American women's history. How and why did Chinese women come to America? What was their life like in America? How did their experiences compare and contrast to those of Chinese men, European women, and other women of color, and what accounted for the differences? If life in America was as harsh for them as it was for my great-grandmother and mother, how did they cope? What cultural strengths did they draw from, and what strategies did they devise to adapt themselves to this new and often hostile land? Were things easier for their American-born daughters? What difference did their lives make to their families, community, and the larger society?

As I attempted to write a social history of Chinese American women and provide a viable framework by which to understand how gender perceptions, roles, and relationships changed because of these women's work, family, and political lives in America, it became evident to me that current race and feminist theories were inadequate for this purpose, since they generally fail to integrate race, gender, and class as equally important categories of historical analysis. Race theorists tend to explain the Asian American experience in light of race and class oppression, but overlook gender; feminist scholars tend to examine women's subordination in terms of gender and, at times, class, but ignore differences among women based on race.[5] The growing scholarship on women of color is beginning to correct these incomplete approaches by looking simultaneously at race, class, and gender in explaining women's oppression and diverse life histories, but these studies often focus strictly on black-white race relations, ignoring other racial groups such as Asian American women.[6] Only Evelyn Nakano Glenn includes Asian American women in any significant way in her analysis of the triple oppression faced by women of color in the labor force.[7]

Nevertheless, the questions that these studies on women of color raise are applicable to my study of Chinese American women: Did immigration, work, and family life in America oppress Chinese women or liberate them? How were Chinese women affected by the racial and sexual division of labor under capitalism? Did the segregation of their paid and unpaid labor to the private (domestic) sphere reinforce their economic dependency on men and consequently their subordinate role within the family? And, in keeping with current scholarship that challenges the notion of homogeneous womanhood,[8] how did women respond differently to their allotted role in life? What was the extent of gender conflict within the Chinese American community, and of class and generational differences among Chinese women themselves? By addressing these same questions, I explore the intersection of race, class, and gender in the lives of Chinese American women, but only within a socioeconomic context. As a historian, I need to also ask: What sociohistorical forces were at play that can explain social change for Chinese American women in the first half of the twentieth century?

Analyzing the life stories of Chinese women has led me to conclude that their experiences have been as much a response to economic, social, and political developments in China as in the United States. Faced with discriminatory exclusion from American life throughout most of their history, Chinese Americans remained attached to homeland politics and highly influenced by developments there—including women's emancipation—until the 1940s, when Chinese exclusion ended and diplomatic relations between the United States and China broke off. Without doubt, economic opportunities outside the home, albeit limited, during the period under study did give Chinese women, both immigrant and American-born, some economic leverage as well as broadening their social and political consciousness. As they took on jobs in garment factories, sales and clerical work, and defense industries during World War II, they gained a degree of economic independence and social mobility. But of equal importance—and this was particularly true for a significant number of educated, middle-class women—their views on gender roles and relations changed owing to the influences of Chinese nationalism, Christianity, and acculturation into American life. The former two factors had a greater impact on immigrant women. Chinese nationalists who saw modernization as the answer to resisting Western imperialism advocated women's emancipation from footbinding, ignorance, and confinement within the domestic sphere. Protestant missionary women, intent on reforming urban society and "rescuing" female victims of male abuse, advocated the same in Chinatown. The third factor, acculturation, had more of a bearing on American-born women. Through church, school, and the popular media, the second generation was encouraged to challenge traditional gender roles at home and discrimination outside, to shape a new cultural identity and lifestyle for themselves. As will be shown, all three factors, to some degree, influenced Chinese American women to reevaluate their gender roles and relationships, to move into the public sphere and become more involved in labor, social, and political issues in their community. But it was not until World War II, with its labor shortages and China's changing relationship to the United States as an ally, that racial and gender barriers were lowered to allow Chinese American women a degree of socioeconomic and political mobility.

To lend symbolic significance to this study, I have chosen to organize it around the theme of footbinding. Widely practiced in China from the twelfth century to the beginning of the twentieth century, footbinding involved tightly wrapping the feet of young girls with bandages until the arches were broken, the toes permanently bent under toward the heel, and the whole foot compressed to a few inches in length. Despite the excruciating pain that it caused, parents continued to subject their daughters to this crippling custom because bound feet were considered an asset in the marriage market, a sign of gentility and beauty. So difficult was it to walk far unassisted that it also kept women from "wandering," thus reinforcing their cloistered existence and ensuring their chastity.[9] Although footbinding was not widely practiced in America (only merchant wives who immigrated before 1911, when the new government in China outlawed footbinding, had bound feet), it is still applicable to this study as a symbol of women's subjugation and subordination.[10]

Thus, as applied in Chapter 1, "Bound Feet: Chinese Women in the Nineteenth Century," footbinding represents the cloistered lives of most Chinese women in nineteenth-century San Francisco. Whether prostitute, *mui tsai*, or wife, they were doubly bound by patriarchal control in Chinatown and racism outside. Confined to the domestic sphere and kept subordinate to men, these women led lives in America that were more inhibiting than liberating. In Chapter 2, "Unbound Feet: Chinese Immigrant Women, 1902–1929," the metaphor is further extended as a measure of social change for Chinese American women. Here we look at Chinese immigrant women's efforts to take advantage of their new circumstances in America to reshape gender roles and relationships—in essence, to unbind their socially restricted lives with the support of Chinese nationalist reformers and Protestant missionary women. Chapter 3, "First Steps: The Second Generation, 1920s," explores attempts by American-born Chinese women to take the first steps toward challenging traditional gender roles at home and racial discrimination in the larger society. While some openly rebelled as flappers, most accommodated the limitations imposed on them by creating their own bicultural identity and lifestyle, although within the parameters of a segregated social existence, and waited for better opportunities. In Chapter 4, "Long Strides: The Great Depression, 1930s," we see how both generations of Chinese women in San Francisco stood more to gain than lose by the depressed economy. Ironically, because of past discrimination, they were able to take long strides toward improving their socioeconomic status, contributing to the sustenance of their families, tackling community issues, and joining the labor movement. Finally, Chapter 5, "In Step: The War Years, 1931–1945," delineates how Chinese women—by joining the armed services, working alongside other Americans in the defense factories, and giving generously of their time, money, and energies to the war effort in both China and the United States—came to fall in step with the rest of their community as well as the larger society.

This outline of the progression of social changes in the lives of Chinese American women is not to suggest that their status moved only in a linear direction, because they did experience setbacks along the way; rather, it suggests that their lives were constantly changing in response to conditions within a specific sociohistorical context. Moreover, although Chinese nationalism, Christianity, and acculturation encouraged resistance to multiple forms of oppression, they also extracted a heavy price from Chinese women, calling on them to put aside feminist concerns for the sake of national unity and to go against their cultural heritage in favor of Western values. In response, Chinese women took the pragmatic course, shifting their behavior as needed to adapt and survive in America. The well-being of their families, community, and country always came first, but that did not mean passing up opportunities along the way to improve their own situation as well. Nor did women easily give up their traditional modes of thought and behavior. Like other immigrant women, mothers chose to continue or change their traditional ways according to what suited their new lives in modern America, while daughters chose to fuse selective aspects of both cultures into a new bicultural identity and lifestyle.[11]

I chose San Francisco, known as Dai Fow (the Big City) to Chinese Americans, as the focal point of this study because it has served as the port of entry for most Chinese immigrants throughout their history. As such, the city has the oldest, and until recently the largest, Chinese population in the United States (now exceeded by New York), as well as the richest depository of archival materials on Chinese American women. It also provides a diverse range of women to interview, many of whom can still recall life for themselves and their mothers in San Francisco during the early 1900s. Their experiences, of course, are not representative of all Chinese American women, many of whom led very different lives in other urban centers and rural communities during this same time period. But because of San Francisco's significance as an economic, political, and cultural center in Chinese American history, it is an important and logical place to start in documenting the social history of Chinese American women. I hope, though, that this study will inspire further research on Chinese women in other parts of the country where they have also settled.

I settled on the years from 1902 to 1945 as the pivotal period of social change for Chinese women in San Francisco for a number of reasons. The year 1902 marks the first time that the issue of women's emancipation was publicly aired in San Francisco Chinatown. This was done by Sieh King King, an eighteen-year-old student from China and an ardent reformer, who, in a historic speech before a large Chinatown crowd, denounced footbinding and advocated equality between the sexes. The year 1945 marks the end of World War II and the turning point for Chinese American women in terms of improved racial and gender relations and increased socioeconomic opportunities. In between these benchmark years, both immigrant and American-born Chinese women learned to challenge and accommodate race, class, and gender oppression in their lives, to make the most of the socioeconomic opportunities and historical circumstances of this time period, and to define their ethnic identity and broaden their gender role as Chinese American women.

Uncovering and piecing together the history of Chinese American women has not been an easy task. There are few written records to begin with, and what little material does exist on the subject is full of inaccuracies and distortions. Thus, I have had to draw from a unique but rich variety of primary sources: government documents and census data, the archives of Christian and Chinese women's organizations, Chinese- and English-language newspapers, oral histories, personal memoirs, and photographs. Taken together, these sources, I believe, provide an alternative and more accurate view of Chinese American women than has existed before, for they show definitively that these women were not passive victims but active agents in the making of their own history. At the same time, I am well aware that these sources are biased, telling us more about the experiences of educated, middle-class women than of illiterate, working-class women; of the American-born than of the immigrant woman; of the exceptional achiever than of the ordinary homemaker. Mindful of this skewed representation, I have tried to compensate by qualifying my descriptions of Chinese women's lives and using oral histories of common, everyday women whenever available.

Government reports and census data, although often biased and inaccurate, provided important quantitative data with which to measure the socioeconomic progress of Chinese American women throughout the period under study. For example, the 1900, 1910, and 1920 unpublished manuscript censuses for San Francisco—which list Chinese women as household members, giving their age, marital status, country of birth, year of immigration, literacy, and occupation—helped to create a comparative picture of family structure, the prostitution trade, Chinese women's ability to read and write, and their occupational concentrations. The published census reports for 1940 and 1950, together with local survey reports by the Community Chest of San Francisco and the California State Relief Administration, provided additional important socioeconomic data for the 1930s and 1940s. The immigration files at the National Archives were invaluable in helping me trace the immigration experience of my own family as well as that of Chinese immigrant women in general.

Missionary journals and case files from the Presbyterian and Methodist mission homes told harrowing stories about the plight of prostitutes, *mui tsai*, and abused women who sought the help of Protestant missionaries. On the whole, they gave a general, though oftentimes sensationalized, picture of the oppressed lives of these women as recorded from the perspective of missionaries seeking to rescue and "civilize" them. But individual cases, such as Wong Ah So's story in Chapter 2, also described the socioeconomic conditions in China and Chinatown that led to the enslavement and mistreatment of Chinese women, as well as the process by which they were rescued and then "rehabilitated." These records also revealed a spirit of resilience, resistance, and autonomy among those who chose to seek or accept the help and services of the mission homes. In addition, articles written by American-born Chinese women in Christian publications provided insights into the cultural dilemma faced by women of that period.

Digging into the archives of Chinese women's organizations, such as the Chinese YWCA and Square and Circle Club (both of which are still active in San Francisco today), yielded written records of social conditions, activities, and perspectives of Chinese immigrant and American-born women. Founded in 1916, the Chinese YWCA was created solely to serve Chinese women in San Francisco. Its records and scrapbooks offered substantial evidence of the extent to which women benefited from the organization's educational programs, social clubs, social services, and community projects. The Square and Circle Club was organized in 1924 by seven American-born Chinese women committed to community service. Its scrapbooks revealed the influence of acculturation on the lives of the second generation. Still another important scrapbook, this one belonging to Sue Ko Lee, a member of the former Chinese Ladies' Garment Workers' Union, provided the workers' view of the first labor strike in which Chinese women participated in large numbers.

San Francisco newspapers, in English as well as Chinese, were crucial sources because they chronicled the activities and documented the views of Chinese American women. From the *San Francisco Chronicle* and *San Francisco Examiner* came numerous articles about the changing role of Chinese American women, including ones on Sieh King King's famous speech dealing with women's rights; on Tye Leung Schulze, the first Chinese woman to vote; and on the active participation of women in Chinese nationalist causes. Of the four Chinese daily newspapers in San Francisco during the period under study, the *Chung Sai Yat Po* (literally, "Chinese American daily newspaper") provided the best coverage on

Chinese immigrant women. Its inclusion of women's issues, activities, and occasional writings—untapped until now—provided a rare insider's view of the lives of Chinese American women. In terms of periodicals that addressed the second generation, both the *Chinese Digest* and the *Chinese Press* were extremely useful in documenting the views and activities of Chinese women during the Depression and World War II years.

Oral histories, despite the drawbacks of faulty or selective memory and retrospective interpretations, added life and credence to this study, allowing women from the bottom up to tell their own history. Indeed, in the absence of writings by Chinese women, life history narratives offer us the only access to their personal experiences, thoughts, and feelings. I was fortunate to have at my disposal over 350 interviews of Chinese American women from the following collections: Chinese Women of America Research Project, Chinese Culture Foundation of San Francisco; History of Chinese Detained on Angel Island Project, Chinese Culture Foundation of San Francisco; Southern California Chinese American Oral History Project, Chinese Historical Society of Southern California, Los Angeles; and historian Him Mark Lai's private collection. Another rich source of first-hand accounts was the Survey of Race Relations, an oral history project that includes interviews with over 200 Chinese Americans conducted in the 1920s. These voices ring with an immediacy and truth not found in retrospective interviews.

In addition, I personally contacted and interviewed twenty-six elderly Chinese women and six men, all of whom had lived most of their lives in San Francisco. I wanted to learn from the women themselves what life was like for them in San Francisco during the first half of the twentieth century. From the men I wanted to hear their recollections of family and community life, particularly during the Great Depression and World War II years. Many of the women were related either to me or to acquaintances of mine. Some I had come to know through my job as a public librarian, my previous research for the book *Chinese Women of America*, and my involvement in the Chinese Historical Society of America. Their ages ranged from sixty to one hundred years old, with the majority in their seventies and eighties at the time of the interviews. Six of the women were first generation; twenty-one were American-born. Among them were seamstresses, clerks, waitresses, housewives, and professionals (teachers, nurses, and politicians). My status as an insider (as a second-generation Chinese American woman born and raised in San Francisco Chinatown) and local historian and writer with a proven track record facilitated access to their life stories. I interviewed most of the women alone in their homes, usually for two hours at a stretch. A few of the interviews required repeated sessions and as much as six hours to complete; five were conducted in the Cantonese dialect. Once trust and rapport had been established and the women understood I was trying to write their history for the next generation as well as to set the historical record straight, I found them quite willing to discuss in detail their life histories and views on race, class, and gender issues. Regardless of their educational background, they were articulate, opinionated, and forthright in their responses to my questions, which I asked in a quasi-chronological and topological order. In my line of questioning, transcription, translation, editing, and selection of passages to include in this book, I have tried to stay true to the spirit and content of their stories as told to me. When necessary, I have corroborated questionable details in their stories against information from other interviews and whatever documentary evidence was at my disposal. As used in this book, oral histories served as one important source of evidence, attesting to the hopes, fears, struggles, and triumphs of women when faced with limitations as well as opportunities.

Though aware of the illiteracy and silence imposed on most Chinese women, I had still hoped to find primary writings or personal memoirs by Chinese American women. For the 1902–45 period, the only such published work is Jade Snow Wong's *Fifth Chinese Daughter*, an autobiography about the cultural conflicts of a second-generation Chinese woman growing up in San Francisco Chinatown.[12] In the process of interviewing my subjects, however, I uncovered the following unpublished writings: two autobiographical essays, one by Lilly King Gee Won about her family's involvement in Dr. Sun Yat-sen's revolutionary movement, the other by Tye Leung Schulze about her escape from an arranged marriage and subsequent marriage to a German American immigration inspector; a manuscript by Dr. Margaret Chung about her life as a physician and volunteer in World War II; an unpublished autobiography by Jane Kwong Lee about her immigration to the United States in 1922 and her subsequent involvement as a community worker in San Francisco Chinatown; and the private letters of Flora Belle Jan, a Chinese American flapper and writer. Together, they represent a significant contribution to the scarce published writings by Chinese American women in the pre–World War II period. It is my intention to have a selection of them published in the near future, along with immigration documents, journalistic articles, and oral histories conducted in conjunction with this book.

To further embellish the text, I have included photographs from a number of public archives and private collections. Photographs add a rich, visual dimension to this study and provide us with further insight into the hopes and aspirations, immigration and acculturation patterns, family and work life, and social activism of Chinese American women. Moreover, depending on who the photographer was and the circumstances in which the photographs were taken, they also reveal how Chinese American women were viewed by outsiders as opposed to insiders. As a series of images for comparison and contrast, photographs taken at different time periods can also serve as effective markers of social change.

Considering the myriad influential factors at play, my belated discovery of my true generational status and family history should not be surprising. For decades, anti-Chinese immigration laws discouraged the immigration of Chinese women and retarded the development of family life. Because of anti-Chinese sentiment, life under exclusion in America necessitated a pact of silence among Chinese immigrants about their past. And until recently, racial minorities and women were generally excluded from written American history. Only since the civil rights movement, the establishment of ethnic studies programs on college campuses, and the current interest in cultural diversity have studies such as this one been possible.

As the only in-depth study so far on Chinese American women, *Unbound Feet* fills the information void and restores Chinese women's rightful place in ethnic, women's, and American history, acknowledging their indomitable spirit and significant contributions. More important, by showing how Chinese American women were able to move from bound lives in the nineteenth century to unbound lives by the end of World War II despite the multiple forms of oppression they faced, this study adds to the growing scholarship on women of color and the ongoing debate about the workings and eradication of race, gender, and class oppression. Although Chinese American women have still not achieved full equality, the important strides they made during a period of great social change warrant careful study. It is my hope that *Unbound Feet* will contribute to a more accurate and inclusive view of women's history, and to a more complex synthesis of our collective past.

CHAPTER I

Bound Feet

Chinese Women in the Nineteenth Century

The absence of talent in a woman is a virtue.
A Chinese proverb

Feet are bound not to make them beautiful as a curved bow, but to restrain the women when they go outdoors.
Nü'er-Ching (Classic for Girls)

When Great-Grandmother Leong Shee arrived in San Francisco on the vessel *China* on April 15, 1893, she had with her an eight-year-old girl named Ah Kum. When asked by the immigration inspector who the girl was, she said that Ah Kum was her daughter. The story she told was that she had first immigrated to the United States with her parents, was married to Chong Sung of Sing Kee Company in 1885, gave birth to Ah Kum in 1886, and then returned to China with the daughter in 1889. When asked what she remembered of San Francisco, she replied in Chinese, "I do not know the city excepting the names of a few streets, as I have small feet and never went out." Thirty-six years later, when she was interrogated for a departure certificate, she denied ever saying any of this.[1]

Great-Grandmother most likely had to make up the story in order to ger her *mui tsai*, Ah Kum, into the United States. By law, merchant wives and daughters were allowed, but not domestic slave girls. Yet having Ah Kum was as much a status symbol as a real help for Leong Shee. Allowing Ah Kum to accompany his wife was probably one of the concessions Great-Grandfather Chin Lung had made to entice her to join him in America. While Chin Lung continued to farm in the Sacramento–San Joaquin Delta, Great-Grandmother chose to live above the Sing Kee store at 808 Sacramento Street, where she gave birth to five children in quick succession. Even with Ah Kum's help, Great-Grandmother found life in America difficult. Unable to go out because of her bound feet, Chinese beliefs that women should not be seen in public, and perhaps fear for her own safety, she led a cloistered but busy life. Being frugal, she took in sewing to make extra money. As she told my mother many years later, "Ying, when you go to America, don't be lazy. Work hard and you will become rich. Your grandfather grew potatoes, and although I was busy at home, I sewed on a foot-treadle machine, made buttons, and weaved loose threads [did finishing work]."[2]

Great-Grandmother's secluded and hard-working life in San Francisco Chinatown was typical for Chinese women in the second half of the nineteenth century. Wives of merchants, who were at the top of the social hierarchy in Chinatown, usually had bound feet and led bound lives. But even women of the laboring class—without bound feet—found themselves confined to the domestic sphere within Chinatown. Prostitutes, who were at the bottom of the social order, had the least freedom and opportunity to change their lives. Whereas most European women found immigration to America a liberating experience, Chinese women, except in certain situations, found it inhibiting. Their unique status in America was due to the circumstances of their immigration and the dynamic ways in which race, class, gender, and culture intersected in their lives.

Passage to Gold Mountain

Few women were in the first wave of Chinese immigrants to America in the mid–nineteenth century. Driven overseas by conditions of poverty at home, young Chinese men—peasants from the Pearl River delta of Guangdong Province (close to the ports of Canton and Hong Kong)—immigrated to Gold Mountain in search of a better livelihood to support their families. They were but a segment of the Chinese diaspora and a sliver of the international migration of labor caused by the global expansion of European capitalism, in which workers, capital, and technology moved across national borders to enable entrepreneurs to exploit natural resources and a larger market in undeveloped countries.[3] According to one estimate, at least 2.5 million Chinese migrated overseas during the last six decades of the nineteenth century, after China

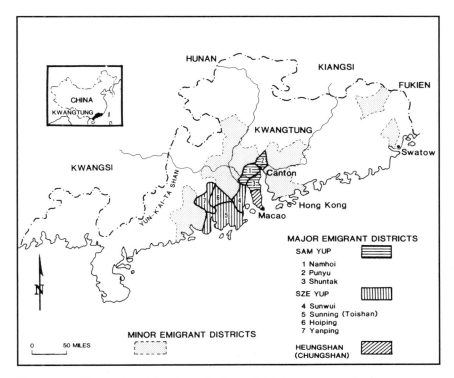

Kwangtung (Guangdong) Province: Emigrant Districts. SOURCE: Sucheng Chan, *This Bittersweet Soil: The Chinese in California Agriculture, 1860–1910* (Berkeley and Los Angeles: University of California Press, 1986), p. 19.

was defeated in the Opium Wars (1839–42; 1856–60) and forced open by European imperialist countries to outside trade and political domination.[4] Except for the 250,000 Chinese who were coerced into slave labor in the "coolie trade" that operated from 1847 to 1874, most willingly answered the call of Western capitalists, immigrating to undeveloped colonies in the Americas, the West Indies, Hawaii, Australia, New Zealand, Southeast Asia, and Africa to live, work, and settle.

Peasants in the Pearl River delta in southeast China were particularly hard hit by imperialist incursions. Aside from suffering increased taxes, loss of land, competition from imported manufactured goods, and unemployment, they also had to contend with problems of overpopulation, repeated natural calamities, and the devastation caused by the Taiping Rebellion (1850–64), the Red Turban uprisings (1854–64), and the ongoing Punti-Hakka interethnic feud. Because of their coastal location and their long association with the sea and contact with foreign traders, they were easily drawn to America by news of the gold rush and by labor contractors who actively recruited young, able-bodied men to help build the transcontinental railroad, reclaim swamplands, develop the fisheries and vineyards, and provide needed labor for California's growing agriculture and light industries. Steamship companies and creditors were also eager to provide them with the means to travel to America.[5] Like other immigrants coming to California at this time, Guangdong men intended to strike it rich and return home.[6] Thus, although more than half of them were married, most did not bring their wives and families. In any case, because of the high costs and harsh living conditions in California, the additional investment required to obtain passage for two or more, and the lack of job opportunities for women, it was cheaper and safer to keep the family in China and support it from across the sea.

The absence of women set the Chinese immigration pattern apart from that of most other immigrant groups. In 1850, there were only 7 Chinese women, versus 4,018 Chinese men, in San Francisco.[7] Five years later, women made up less than 2 percent of the total Chinese population in America.[8] As merchant Lai Chun-chuen explained in response to the anti-Chinese remarks of California Governor John Bigler:

> It is stated that "too large a number of the men of the Flowery Kingdom have emigrated to this country, and that they have come alone, without their families." We may state among the reasons for this that the wives and families of the better families of China have generally compressed feet; they live in the utmost privacy; they are unusual to winds and waves; and it is exceedingly difficult to bring families upon distant journies over great oceans. Yet a few have come; nor are they all. And further, there have been several injunctions warning the people of the Flowery land not to come here, which have fostered doubts; nor have our hearts found peace in regard to bringing families.[9]

Patriarchal cultural values, financial considerations, and anti-Chinese legislation prevented most Chinese women from becoming part of the early stream of immigrants to America. Confucian ideology, which had governed social conduct in China for nearly 2,000 years, dictated that women remain subordinate to men and confined to the domestic sphere. The "Three Obediences" prescribed that a Chinese woman obey her father at home, her husband after marriage, and her eldest son when widowed. The "Four Virtues" required of her were propriety in behavior, speech, demeanor, and household duties. Separate spheres for men and women were clearly defined. As a popular saying put it, "Men are the masters of external affairs, women the mistresses of domestic affairs"; in other words, men ruled the country, while women stayed home to manage the household and raise the children. Education was thus important for sons but not for daughters. Rather, Chinese proverbs claimed, "The absence of talent in a woman is a virtue," since "A woman too well educated is apt to create trouble."[10] And because it was the son—not the daughter—who stayed within the family, worked for its honor and prosperity, continued the family lineage, and fulfilled the duties of ancestral worship, so it was that daughters—rarely sons—were sold, abandoned, or drowned during desperate times.[11]

Neither men nor women had a choice in the selection of their spouses, but women were further disadvantaged in that they had no right to divorce or remarry should the arranged marriage prove unhappy or the husband die. Men, but not women, were also permitted to commit adultery, divorce, remarry, practice polygyny, and discipline their spouses as they saw fit. According to a Chinese proverb, "A woman married is like a horse bought; you can ride them or flog them as you like." Widows without sons could not inherit property, and women could not participate in politics or public activities. Their proper place was in the home, where their sexuality could be regulated and controlled. Further, the practice of footbinding ensured that women did not "wander" too far outside the household gate, let alone go abroad. In fact, until 1911 the emigration of women was illegal according to Chinese law.

In practice, only the scholar-gentry, merchant, and landowner classes could afford to bind their daughters' feet and keep their women cloistered and idle. But even gentry women were known to venture out of their chambers to steal away to the mountains, attend women's gatherings, and accompany their husbands on business trips. It was also common for peasant women in the rice-growing and silk-rearing districts of Guangdong Province to work both inside and outside the home. Within the household women were expected to care for family members, provide moral training for the children, observe customs and holidays, do the household chores of cleaning, washing, and cooking, and bring in extra income by handicraft work such as spinning, weaving, and sewing. They also worked outside the home gathering fuel and herbs, fetching water, doing the wash, picking mulberry leaves, tea leaves, or cotton, guarding the crops, gathering the harvest, hulling rice or threshing wheat, raising geese and other livestock, gardening, and marketing. Some also hired out as domestic servants or manual laborers.[12] Although they enjoyed more freedom of movement than well-to-do women, even this relatively active work kept them close to home and controlled by men. Women's wages were generally lower than men's, and any monies earned by women went immediately into the family coffers.

New studies of women's diverse roles in China have led to a reassessment of their presumed status as passive victims. One exceptional group of women were the *zishunü* of the Shunde, Nanhai, and Panyu districts, who practiced the *shuqi* custom of "combing up the hair" as a sign of confirmed spinsterhood. Their labor was essential in the sericulture industry—rearing silkworms, tending mulberry trees, spinning silk threads, and weaving—and allowed these women to enjoy economic independence and freedom of movement. They did not practice footbinding and openly resisted marriage by returning to their natal home to live after the wedding, purchasing a secondary wife to take their place, and joining sisterhoods in which they vowed celibacy. It is likely that some were also lesbians.[13] Hakka women in Guangdong Province also did not practice footbinding and were known for being independent-minded, even domineering, having proven themselves capable of hard labor and self-support in the absence of their husbands. They were also known for their courage and military prowess. Many fought side by side with men against the Qing government in the Taiping Rebellion.[14] For most other women, however, work seldom resulted in greater independence or leverage. They were still subordinate to men, depending on them to protect and provide for them.

Thus, when their men went overseas to America, most Chinese women (following the Confucian teaching, "A woman's duty is to care for the household, and she should have no desire to go abroad") remained at home, attended to their children and in-laws, and awaited the return of their husbands. This was not an easy task, considering that the separation could extend anywhere from ten years to a lifetime, depending on when finances would allow the husband a visit home or a final return. In the meantime, family members and fellow villagers tried to ensure that the women remained chaste. The harsh punishment meted out by villagers on No Name Woman in Maxine Hong Kingston's *The Woman Warrior* for bearing an illegitimate child while her husband was overseas was not unusual.[15] Cantonese folk rhymes tell of the conflicting feelings involved in being a *gamsaanpo* (wife of a Gold Mountain man) or, more appropriately, a *sausaanggwai* (grass widow):

> O, just marry all the daughters to men from Gold Mountain:
> All those trunks from Gold Mountain—

You can demand as many as you want!
O, don't ever marry your daughter to a man from Gold Mountain:
Lonely and sad—
    A cooking pot is her only companion![16]

If you have a daughter, don't marry her to a Gold Mountain man.
Out of ten years, he will not be in bed for one.
The spider will spin webs on top of the bedposts,
While dust fully covers one side of the bed.[17]

Although other groups of women, such as Italian women, were similarly discouraged from traveling abroad by cultural constraints during this period, Chinese women were further hindered by economic and political barriers.[18] Few Chinese women had the resources to travel to America on their own, and many were discouraged from doing so by the inhospitable conditions in that far-off land. Although enterprising capitalists needed Chinese labor to help them exploit the western frontier, they had no use for women. Indeed, the presence of women and families, it was felt, would only stabilize the Chinese work force, causing them to demand higher wages and better working conditions. Nor did the American ideals of life, liberty, and the pursuit of happiness apply equally to people of color. Treated as a reserve army of low-wage workers, the Chinese were tolerated only as long as their labor was needed. Anti-Chinese prejudice, discriminatory laws, and outright violence ensured that the Chinese remained subordinate to the dominant white society and that they did not bring their women and families to settle in America.[19]

Although initially welcomed to California as valuable labor and investors in an expanding economy, Chinese immigrants quickly became the targets of white miners, workers, and politicians when the gold ran out and economic times turned sour. In 1852 a Foreign Miners' Tax, which accounted for more than half of the tax revenues collected in California until its repeal in 1870, was imposed, affecting primarily Chinese miners. Special taxes were also levied on Chinese fishermen, laundrymen, and brothel owners. Other local ordinances, which did not specifically name the Chinese but which obviously were passed to harass and deprive them of a livelihood, included the cubic-air law, which prohibited residence in rooms with less than 500 cubic feet of air per person; the sidewalk ordinance, which made it a misdemeanor for any person to carry baskets across the shoulders; and the queue ordinance, which required that the hair of every male prisoner in the city jails be cut to within an inch of the scalp. Laws were also passed by the California legislature that denied Chinese basic civil rights, such as the right to immigrate, give testimony in court, be employed in public works, intermarry with whites, and own land. Negatively stereotyped as coolie labor, immoral and diseased heathens, and unassimilable aliens, the Chinese were driven out of the better-paying jobs in the mines, factories, fishing areas, and farmlands. They were generally not allowed to live outside Chinatown, and their children were barred from attending white schools.[20]

But racial prejudice, segregation, and discriminatory laws against the Chinese were evidently not enough to assuage popular discontent over the economic upheavals caused by the growing pains of industrial capitalism. It was not unusual for Chinese to be robbed and murdered with impunity, but during depression years when the unemployment rate was high, entire Chinese communities suffered unprecedented racial hatred and physical violence. On a number of these occasions in the 1870s and 1880s, Chinese settlements throughout the American West were attacked by bloodthirsty mobs out to loot, lynch, burn, and drive the Chinese out. In the Los Angeles riot of 1871, unarmed Chinese were shot down in cold blood. Others were hauled out of buildings, beaten, and murdered while their homes were looted. In 1885 the massacre of Chinese miners at Rock Springs, Wyoming, claimed twenty-eight Chinese lives and caused $147,000 in property damage. All of the shacks belonging to the Chinese were set on fire, and stragglers were shot as they emerged. Federal troops had to be called in to protect the survivors.[21]

The most damaging blow to Chinese immigration and settlement proved to be the Chinese Exclusion Act of 1882, passed by a Congress under siege from white labor and politicians at the height of the anti-Chinese movement. The act suspended the immigration of Chinese laborers to the United States for ten years. It was renewed in 1892 for another ten years, and in 1904 extended indefinitely. The Exclusion Acts were strictly enforced until they were repealed in 1943.[22] It was the first time in American history that a specific group of people was excluded on the basis of race and class. In the interest of diplomatic and trade relations between China and the United States, Chinese officials, students, teachers, merchants, and travelers were exempted by treaty provisions—and therein lay the loophole through which Chinese, including women, were able to continue coming after 1882. Although the number of Chinese immigrants dropped sharply—only 92,411 entered during the Exclusion period (1882–1943), as compared to 258,210 prior to the 1882 act—Chinese immigration was not totally stopped.[23] As my maternal great-grandfather and father did, Chinese immigrants who could pool enough money to become partners in import-export businesses were able to attain merchant status and so send for their wives and children. Many others who had merchant or U.S. citizenship status would falsely report a number of sons (rarely daughters) in China, thereby creating "paper son" slots that were then sold to fellow villagers who desired to immigrate.

The class bias of the Exclusion Act applied to women as well as men. Wives of laborers, although not specifically mentioned in the act, were barred by implication. The ambiguity was settled two years later in the separate cases of *In re Ah Quan* and *Case of the Chinese Wife [Ah Moy]*. Both women were married to Chinese laborers who were bringing them back with them after a visit to China. While their husbands, who possessed the proper certificate indicating prior residence in the United States, were allowed to reenter, the two women were barred because they were of the laboring class (by virtue of their husbands' status) and were entering the United States for the first time.[24]

Chinese women could enter only if they qualified as one of the exempt classes; even this right, however, had to be won through the judiciary. Chung Toy Ho and Gue Lim, both merchant wives, were initially denied admission on the grounds that they did not hold merchant's certificates. Their successful appeals established the right for merchant wives to join their husbands in the United States. As Judge Matthew Deady of the Circuit Court for the District of Oregon ruled in the case of *Chung Toy Ho*,

> My conclusion is that under the treaty and statute, taken together, a Chinese merchant who is entitled to come into and dwell in the United States is thereby entitled to bring with him, and have with him, his wife and children. The company of the one, and the care and the custody of the other, are his by natural right; he ought not to be deprived of either, unless the intention of Congress to do so is clear and unmistakable.[25]

The Exclusion Act severely limited the number of Chinese women who could come to America, keeping a crack open mainly for the privileged few—the wives and daughters of merchants. But in fact, rigorous enforcement of the act, along with the implementation of anti-Chinese measures regulating prostitution such as the Page Law of 1875, kept even those Chinese immigrant women with legitimate claims out of the country and made immigration to America an ordeal for any woman who tried to enter. Immigration officials apparently operated on the premise that every Chinese woman was seeking admission on false pretenses and that each was a potential prostitute until proven otherwise. Only women such as my great-grandmother who had bound feet and a modest demeanor were considered upper-class women with "moral integrity." As one immigration official wrote in his report, "There has never come to this port, I believe, a bound footed woman who was found to be an immoral character, this condition of affairs being due, it is stated, to the fact that such women, and especially those in the interior, are necessarily confined to their homes and seldom frequent the city districts." Furthermore, he wrote, "The present applicant No. 14418 is a very modest appearing woman whose evident sincerity, frankness of expression and generally favorable demeanor is very convincing."[26] Most other women, however, were detained for inordinate lengths of time and cross-examined like criminals. Under such trying circumstances, women suffered humiliation and, often, the added expense of legal fees in order to obtain release and appeal adverse decisions. They also ran the risk of being barred for a number of other reasons: lack of proper documentation, having a contagious disease, or discrepancies in their testimonies. As a result, the numbers of Chinese women in the United States remained low throughout the nineteenth century, never exceeding the 5,000 mark, or 7 percent of the total Chinese population (see appendix table 1); the scarcity of women supported Chinese prostitution, which was rampant until the 1880s; and merchant wives predominated as the favored class of Chinese immigrant women throughout the Exclusion period.

Bound Lives in Old Chinatown

A good number of the Chinese women who came to the United States in the nineteenth century—despite the social, economic, and political barriers—settled in San Francisco: 654, or 37 percent of all Chinese women in the country, lived in San Francisco in 1860; 2,136, or 47 percent, in 1900. But they were still grossly outnumbered by men, who on the average made up 95 percent of the total Chinese population during these years. While women from such European areas as Ireland, Scandinavia, and Bohemia immigrated to the United States on their own for economic reasons, few Chinese women came alone.[27] Most had either been sold into prostitution or domestic slavery, or they were coming to join their husbands. To a large degree, the legacy of bound feet, bound lives, continued for these women in San Francisco. Not only were their lives as circumscribed and socially restricted as in China, but alienation and anti-Chinese hostilities in a foreign land compounded the difficulties they faced. Speaking no English, having no independent means of support, and insulated within Chinatown from alternative views of gender roles, they continued to abide by the patriarchal values of their homeland, maintaining a subordinate role to men and confining their activities to the domestic sphere. In this sense, their early settlement in America was similar to that of Jewish mothers and Italian women, whose cultures also dictated that they remain within the house, isolated from the larger society.[28] Regardless of social status—whether prostitute, *mui tsai*, or wife—Chinese women were considered the property of men and treated as such.

As in China, Chinese women stayed close to home and appeared as little as possible in public. Indeed, the predominantly male and relatively lawless society of mid-nineteenth-century San Francisco contributed to their sheltered existence. Moreover, the Chinese kinship system, which formed the buttress for patriarchal control in Chinatown, successfully kept them outside the power structure: only men could be members of the clan and district associations that governed Chinatown, or of the trade guilds and tongs (secret societies) that regulated both legal and illicit businesses. Footbinding, practiced only among the merchant wives, was not necessary to stop Chinese women in San Francisco from "wandering"; their physical and social mobility was effectively bound by patriarchal control within Chinatown and racism as well as sexism outside.

Migration from the preindustrial household economy of China to the industrialized, urban society of San Francisco had little effect on the socioeconomic status of most Chinese women. During the same period, Arab, Jewish, and Irish immigrant women, for example, often became more independent through outside employment and exposure to American ideas of individuality and women's rights.[29] Chinese women, confined within the home and within Chinatown, did not have these same opportunities. Even as San Francisco experienced an economic boom following the gold rush, growing to become a major commercial and industrial center by the end of the century, Chinese women found themselves at the lowest rung of a labor market stratified by race and gender. While white men dominated the better-paying jobs in the professional and skilled trades, Chinese men concentrated in three low-wage industries (cigars, woolen goods, and boots and shoes), engaged in Chinatown enterprises that serviced their own community, or did menial work as domestic servants and laundrymen.[30] Although a few white women found work as schoolteachers and clerks or kept boarders, the majority competed with Chinese laborers for jobs as garment workers, laundresses, and domestic servants. Because of the scarcity of well-paying jobs, a number of white women also turned to prostitution. Unlike on the East Coast, where European immigrant women filled the ranks of factory workers, in San Francisco women were kept locked out of the city's expanding manufacturing economy. In 1870, out of 1,223 manufacturing establishments, only 5 employed women. By 1885, although the total number of manufacturers had more than doubled, the number employing women had only increased to 13.[31] All the while, Chinese women fared poorly. In 1885, a municipal report on Chinatown found, only two women were employed in the factories.[32] Most Chinese women either did piecework at home for subcontractors—sewing, washing, rolling cigars, and making slippers and brooms—or worked as prostitutes, receiving no wages for their services. While women earned fifty cents a day sewing, Chinese men earned one dollar a day as factory workers—both far below the standard wage for white men of two dollars per day in the early 1880s.[33]

Given these conditions, there was little opportunity for Chinese immigrant women to change their subordinate gender role and socioeconomic status in nineteenth-century San Francisco. Yet there was heterogeneity in their class backgrounds, life experiences, and the ways in which they utilized and adapted their culture and knowledge to sustain themselves in the new world. Starting from the bottom up, a closer examination of the gender roles of Chinese prostitutes, *mui tsai*, and immigrant wives within the context of race, class, and gender dynamics in the nineteenth century will help to illuminate their history and diversity; it will also point to the extent of social change in the lives of Chinese women who came after them in the 1902–45 period.

THE RISE OF CHINESE PROSTITUTION

The scarcity of women in the American West, the suspension of social and moral restraints, and the easy access to wealth during the early years of the gold rush attracted women from different parts of the world. The first prostitutes to arrive were women from Mexico, Peru, and Chile; these were followed by women from France and other European countries, as well as women from American cities such as New York and New Orleans.[34] According to one writer in 1851, "To sit with you near the bar or a card table, a girl charges one ounce [of gold; $16] an evening . . . and if you wanted anything more from these nymphs, you had to pay 15 to 20 ounces [$240 to $320]."[35] In contrast, a woman working as a domestic servant made $50 to $75 per month. Consequently, many women, particularly those with only a rudimentary education and few marketable skills, drifted into prostitution as a matter of economic survival or profit.[36]

Whereas the majority of white prostitutes came to San Francisco as independent professionals and worked for wages in brothels, Chinese prostitutes were almost always imported as unfree labor, indentured or enslaved. Most were kidnapped, lured, or purchased from poor parents by procurers in China for as little as $50 and then resold in America for as much as $1,000 in the 1870s.[37] One young woman testified in 1892:

> I was kidnapped in China and brought over here [eighteen months ago]. The man who kidnapped me sold me for four hundred dollars to a San Francisco slave-dealer; and he sold me here for seventeen hundred dollars. I have been a brothel slave ever since. I saw the money paid down and am telling the truth. I was deceived by the promise I was going to marry a rich and good husband, or I should never have come here.[38]

Upon arrival in San Francisco many such Chinese women, usually between the ages of sixteen and twenty-five, were taken to a barracoon, where they were either turned over to their owners or stripped for inspection and sold to the highest bidder. Few women could read the terms of service in the contracts they were forced to sign with thumbprints. A typical contract read:

> An agreement to assist the woman, Ah Ho, because coming from China to San Francisco she became indebted to her mistress for passage. Ah Ho herself asks Mr. Yee Kwan to advance for her six hundred and thirty dollars, for which Ah Ho distinctly agrees to give her body to Mr. Yee for service of prostitution for a term of four years. There shall be no interest on the money. Ah Ho shall receive no wages. At the expiration of four years, Ah Ho shall be her own master. Mr. Yee Kwan shall not hinder or trouble her. If Ah Ho runs away before her time is out, her mistress shall find her and return her, and whatever expense is incurred in finding and returning her, Ah Ho shall pay. On this day of agreement Ah Ho, with her own hands, has received from Mr. Yee Kwan six hundred and thirty dollars. If Ah Ho shall be sick at any time for more than ten days, she shall make up by an extra month of service for every ten days' sickness. Now this agreement has proof—this paper received by Ah Ho is witness. Tung Chee [dated 1873].[39]

In principle, these contracts were similar to those signed by the large number of white migrants recruited to the American colonies in the seventeenth and eighteenth centuries. In exchange for passage, they agreed to work without wages for a period of four to seven years. At the end of their indenture, they were promised new clothes, tools, seed, arms, provisions, and land. Until the Alien Contract Labor Law of 1885 forbade the importation of workers under contract, indentured servants were protected by law from breach of contract and flagrant abuse.[40] The same was not true for Chinese prostitutes like Ah Ho. As she later probably realized, the allowable ten days of absence in her contract were insufficient to cover failings due to menstrual periods, illness, or pregnancy; thus, such contracts could be extended indefinitely. Nor did she have access to legal protection. Most Chinese prostitutes were subjected to such physical and mental abuse that few could outlive their contract terms of four to six years.[41] As Lucie Cheng Hirata points out in her definitive article on Chinese prostitution, "In reality, . . . the contract system offered very little advantage over the outright sale or slave system and was, in a number of ways, more brutal because it raised false hopes."[42]

A selected number of young women were sold to wealthy Chinese in San Francisco or outlying rural areas as concubines or mistresses and sequestered in comfortable quarters. As long as they continued to please their owners, they were pampered and well cared for. But if they failed to meet their masters' expectations, they could be returned to the auction block for resale. The remainder of the women either were sold to parlor houses that served well-to-do Chinese or white gentlemen or ended up in cribs catering to a racially mixed, poorer clientele.[43]

Parlor houses were luxurious rooms on the upper floors of Chinatown establishments that were furnished with teakwood and bamboo, Chinese paintings, and cushions of embroidered silk. Here, anywhere between four and twenty-five Chinese courtesans, all richly dressed and perfumed, were made available to a select clientele. The "exotic" atmosphere, the relatively cheap rates, and the rumor that Chinese women had vaginas that ran "east-west" instead of "north-south" attracted many white patrons.[44] Other parlor house women, known as "sing-song girls," whose livelihoods depended on their abilities to sing, converse, drink, and flatter, were available for hire as well. According to one newspaper account, Chinese clients paid for the company of these women at the theater, followed by an elaborate dinner with friends.[45] Another newspaper account stated that no Chinese banquet was complete without their presence: "They sing, they play, they light and hold the pipes, and after the banquet is finished they join in the games. For a few hours of such work they get from $3 to $5 each."[46] Savings from this money, as well as the jewelry and rich gifts the women often received from their clients, were sometimes enough for them to buy back their freedom or to send money home to support their families. Those redeemed by wealthy clients were considered fortunate. The majority "were there to be fondled or misused, one day loaded with jewels, then next day to be stripped and sold to the highest bidder, if it were the desire of her master."[47]

In contrast, the cribs—considered the end of the line—were shacks no larger than twelve by fourteen feet, often facing a dimly lit alley, where prostitutes hawked their wares to poor laborers, teenage boys, sailors, and drunkards for as little as twenty-five cents. The cribs were sparsely furnished with a washbowl, a bamboo chair or two, and a hard bed covered with matting. The women took turns enticing customers through a wicket window with plaintive cries of "Two bittee lookee, flo bittee feelee, six bittee dooee!" Harshly treated by both owners and customers and compelled to accept every man who sought their business, most women succumbed to venereal disease.[48] Once hopelessly diseased, they were discarded on the street or locked in a room to die alone.[49] Thus, Chinese prostitutes in San Francisco, exploited as they were for their bodies by men who had control over their fates and livelihoods, were the archetype of female bondage and degradation.

Various studies of the manuscript schedules of the U.S. population censuses indicate that a high percentage of the Chinese female population in San Francisco worked as prostitutes: from 85 to 97 percent in 1860; 71 to 72 percent in 1870; and 21 to 50 percent in 1880.[50] There were reasons for these high percentages. Race and class dynamics created the need for Chinese prostitutes in America, while gender and class made poor Chinese daughters the victims of an exploitative labor system controlled by unscrupulous men denied gainful employment in the larger labor market. Certain sectors of the American capitalist economy called for a mobile male labor force unencumbered by women and families. Chinese cultural values and American immigration policies that discouraged the immigration of women resulted in a skewed sex ratio that, when combined with anti-Chinese prejudice and antimiscegenation attitudes (institutionalized in 1880 when California's Civil Code was amended to prohibit the issuance of a marriage license to a white person and a "Negro, Mulatto, or Mongolian"),[51] forced most Chinese immigrants to live a bachelor's existence. Stranded in America until they could save enough money to return home, both married and single Chinese men found it difficult to establish conjugal relations or find female companionship. Some married other women of color—black, Mexican, or Native American; a few cohabited with white women; but the majority sought sexual release in brothels.[52] The demand for Chinese prostitutes by both Chinese and white men intersected with an available supply of young women sold into servitude by impoverished families in China. What resulted was the organized trafficking of Chinese women, which proved immensely profitable for the tongs that came to control the trade in San Francisco.

According to Lucie Cheng Hirata's calculations, brothel owners made an annual net profit of $2,500 on each prostitute, a figure that dwarfed the $500 average annual income of other occupations open to the Chinese. Owners also profited from the sewing and other subcontracting work that prostitutes were forced to do whenever they had free time. And owners were not the only ones who profited from the women: procurers in China, importers who accompanied the women to San Francisco, immigration officials, highbinders and policemen paid to protect the business, landlords who charged brothel owners exorbitant rents, tongs that collected a weekly tax on each woman, and opium dealers and gambling houses all reaped the economic benefits of prostitution. The Hip Yee Tong, which reportedly started the traffic in 1852, imported six thousand women and netted $200,000 profit from the trade between 1852 and 1873.[53] So competitive and lucrative was the trade that violent tong wars often erupted over possession of a single woman. In 1875, for example, two tongs battled it out with knives, daggers, clubs, and hatchets after a Suey Sing Tong member was assassinated by a Kwong Dock Tong member over possession of Kum Ho, a prostitute. According to one sensationalistic account, "The highbinders fought hand to hand. Skulls split and abdomens ripped." Nine of the fifty fighters suffered serious injuries before the police dared to intervene.[54] As late as 1897, when the Chinese Society of English Education joined efforts with the Chinese Six Companies[55] to stop Chinese prostitution, they were sent the following death warrant:

> Lately, having learned that the Chinese Society of English Education has retained an attorney to prevent girls imported for immoral purposes from landing and made efforts to deport them to China, in consequence of which there is a great loss of our blood-money. As you are all Christianized people, you should do good deeds, but if you keep on going to the Custom-house trying to deport girls brought here for immoral purposes

from China, and trying to prevent them from landing, your lives of your several people are not able to live longer than this month.

Your dying day is surely on hand.

Your dying day is surely on hand.

The dying men's names are as follows: Dear Wo, Lee Hem, Ong Lin Foon, Chin Fong, Chin Ming Sek, Hoo Yee Hin.[56]

Because of their value as property, Chinese prostitutes were closely guarded and harshly punished for any infractions. They also had no political rights and limited access to legal recourse within or outside the Chinese community; resistance was thus difficult. Their one consolation was the knowledge that they were fulfilling their filial duty: their sacrifice was helping to save their family from starvation. In this sense, their circumstances were no better or worse than those of prostitutes in China, where girls sold into prostitution for the same reasons were relegated to the lowest, or "mean," class and treated as slaves for life.[57] In America, though, Chinese prostitutes lacked the support of family ties and suffered the added burden of racism. White hoodlums, when they were in the mood, "stole the earnings of the slave girls, and stormed the houses wherein the latter were on display and compelled them to submit to frightful abuses."[58] Chinese prostitutes were also discriminated against monetarily, earning less for their services than their white counterparts. The infamous Atoy, who commanded the highest price among Chinese prostitutes, charged one ounce of gold; her white peers were able to charge as much as twenty ounces. In the cribs, a Chinese woman could be had for fifty cents, while sex with a white woman in an equivalent situation cost twice as much.[59] And whereas a white prostitute could leave the profession at will, relocate to escape stringent law enforcement in certain parts of the city, marry, or try to find other employment, Chinese women, because of their race and indentured status, enjoyed none of these options.

Discrimination against Chinese prostitutes, as well as prostitutes from Latin American countries, was most apparent at the institutional level. Both groups of women were ghettoized and, in accordance with the racial prejudice of the day, consistently singled out for moral condemnation and legal suppression, even though white prostitution was more prevalent. Latino women who had been brought as indentured labor from Mexico, Panama, and Chile to work in the cantinas and fandango parlors at the foot of Telegraph Hill were forced to accept all comers at cheap prices. Vilified as shameless, lewd *greaseritas*, they were by day robbed and subjected to criminal attacks by the same men who bought their services at night. Confined to Little Chile—which after 1865 became a major nucleus of the notorious Barbary Coast—they had little opportunity to learn English or the social graces needed to secure work in the more respectable parlor houses outside their ghetto.[60]

The treatment of Chinese women paralleled that of the Latino women. Sensational stories of the cruelties of the Chinese prostitution trade and of the rescue operations of missionaries appeared in books, magazines, and newspapers.[61] It was said that Chinese women were "reared to a life of shame from infancy" and that "not one virtuous Chinawoman has been brought to this country."[62] They were also accused of disseminating vile diseases capable of destroying "the very morals, the manhood and the health of our people . . . ultimately destroying whole nations."[63] Overall, local ordinances against prostitution were more strictly enforced in the Chinese quarter. In response, the *California Police Gazette* commented:

> It is a pity officers could not find some better employment than prosecuting these poor Chinese slaves. Do they not know that these poor serfs are *obliged* to do as they do? The officers do not pitch into WHITE females who pursue the same course. Oh no, they could not do that. Their *pleasures* and *interests* would be interfered with.[64]

In 1865, the San Francisco Board of Supervisors passed an "Order to Remove *Chinese* Women of Ill-Fame from Certain Limits in the City" (emphasis added). A year later, the California state legislature approved "An Act for the Suppression of *Chinese* Houses of Ill-Fame" (emphasis added). Although the acts succeeded in confining Chinese prostitution to certain geographical areas and closing down some of the Chinese brothels, they did not end the prostitution trade. The state then proceeded in 1870 to pass "An Act to Prevent the Kidnapping and Importation of Mongolian, Chinese, and Japanese Females for Criminal or Demoralizing Purposes," thus making it illegal for ships to bring in women of questionable character.[65]

As economic conditions worsened after the 1873 depression, public sentiment continued to mount against the Chinese. In 1875 Congress stepped in and passed the Page Law, forbidding the entry of "Oriental" contract laborers, prostitutes, and criminals. The enforcement process, which involved the stringent screening of women in Hong Kong by the American consul, succeeded in reducing not only the number of prostitutes but also the overall number of Chinese immigrant women.[66] Between 1876 and 1882, the number of Chinese women entering the

United States declined relative to the previous seven-year period by 69 percent. The numbers were further reduced by the Chinese Exclusion Act: from an annual average of 298 between 1860 and 1882 to an annual average of 61 between 1882 and 1904, the year the Exclusion Act was extended indefinitely.[67] By making it more difficult for Chinese women to immigrate and by successfully reducing their numbers, the laws inadvertently increased the demand and raised the value of prostitutes, but still did not stop the lucrative trade.

As hopeless and pathetic as this picture of enslavement appeared, Chinese prostitutes found a number of escape avenues. As in China, they were sometimes redeemed and married, mostly to Chinese laborers who had saved enough money to afford a wife. A few successfully ran away with lovers despite the heavy bounty often placed on the man's head by the owner. Others escaped their sordid reality through insanity or suicide by swallowing raw opium or drowning themselves in the bay—an honorable act of protest and vengeance by Chinese cultural standards. But being in America accorded them additional avenues of resistance. A few went to the police for protection. Some women, like Mah Ah Wah and Yoke Qui, two women detained by the authorities upon arrival, were able to escape prostitution by refusing to accept bail, claiming that they had been imported for immoral purposes against their will. Both were remanded to China.[68]

A small number of prostitutes were also able to rise to the rank of madam. Ah Toy, the best-known Chinese woman in nineteenth-century popular literature, was among the first to do so. According to one account, Ah Toy immigrated alone from Hong Kong in 1849 at the age of twenty "to better her condition."[69] Early writings describe her as being tall, well built, English-speaking, and having bound feet. As the Frenchman Albert Benard de Russailh put it in 1851, "The Chinese are usually ugly, the women as well as the men; but there are a few girls who are attractive if not actually pretty, for example, the strangely alluring Achoy, with her slender body and laughing eyes."[70] She soon became infamous as the most successful Chinese courtesan in the city. White miners were known to line up around the block and pay an ounce of gold ($16) just "to gaze on the *countenance* of the charming Ah Toy."[71] Within a year or two of her arrival she became a madam—owner of a number of Chinese prostitutes on Pike Street (now Walter U. Lum Place)—and a well-known personality in the courtroom, where she appeared a number of times to sue those clients who had paid her with brass filings instead of gold and to protest the control of Chinese prostitutes through taxation by certain Chinatown leaders. Important personages attended her tea parties, and it was said that as early as 1850 she influenced Chinese residents to participate in the celebration of California's admission into the union. During the Vigilance Committee's investigation of Chinese prostitution, Ah Toy was spared, reportedly because one of her lovers was the Vigilante brothel inspector, John A. Clarke. In 1857 she sold her house, packed her belongings, and retired to China, announcing to journalists that she had no intention of returning. In March 1859, however, it was reported that she had been arrested in San Francisco for keeping a "disorderly house." She was not heard of again until 1928, when her death was announced in the local newspapers. She reportedly had been living in Santa Clara County since 1868, first with her husband and then, when he died in 1909, with her brother-in-law. Last seen selling clams to visitors in Alviso, she died just three months short of her hundredth birthday.[72]

Based on available published accounts of Chinese prostitution, free agents and madams such as Ah Toy were likely few and far between. One other known exception is Suey Hin, who at a certain point owned fifty girls of various ages. According to a newspaper account, Suey Hin was born in Shandong Province and sold by her father when five years old for a piece of gold. She was later resold in San Francisco for three "handfuls" of gold when she was twelve. For ten years she worked as a prostitute until she and a "poor washerman" who loved her saved $3,000— enough to buy back her freedom so they could get married. Three years later, her husband became sick and died. As she said, "I didn't have anything but just myself, and I had to live, and I could not live on nothing." So she returned to China, bought her first eight girls, and smuggled them into the country under the guise of being native-born daughters. In 1898 she converted to Christianity and freed the last of her seven slaves, returning one who had originally been kidnapped back to her family in China and promising to find Christian husbands for the others.[73] Suey Hin and Atoy's stories point to the complex class and gender relationships within Chinatown. Men were not the only ones who exploited Chinese prostitutes for profit. When given the opportunity, Chinese women promoted themselves from the rank of oppressed to oppressor, preying on younger women in a vicious circle of traffic and procurement.[74]

The most viable option open to Chinese prostitutes was two Protestant mission homes that singled them out for rescue and rehabilitation beginning in the 1870s; for in their view, "Of all the darkened and enslaved ones, the Chinese woman's fate seems the most pitiful."[75] Inspired by the Social Gospel Movement, missionary women were intent on establishing female moral authority in the American West and rescuing female victims of male abuse. They saw Chinese women as the ultimate symbol of female powerlessness, as exemplified in their domestic confinement, sexual exploitation, and treatment as chattel. Unable to work effectively among Chinatown bachelors and spurned by white prostitutes, they found their calling among Chinese prostitutes and *mui tsai*. In turn, some Chinese prostitutes, calculating their chances in an oppressive environment with few options for improvement, saw the mission homes as a way out of their problems.[76]

Soon after Rev. Otis Gibson organized the Women's Missionary Society of the Methodist Episcopal Church on the Pacific Coast in 1871 expressly "to elevate and save the souls of heathen women," Jin Ho became the first Chinese woman to seek refuge there. She had escaped from a brothel and attempted to drown herself rather than endure a life of slavery. Rescued by a passing black boatman, Jin Ho asked to see a "Jesus man" and was taken to Rev. Gibson. After a year in the Methodist home, she was baptized and married to a Chinese Christian. Other runaway prostitutes also sought refuge in the home, and at any one time an average of twenty women were provided housing and clothing, taught reading and writing, and given sewing to do to meet incidental expenses. Of the first seventy-five Chinese inmates, ten requested to return to China, fifteen were baptized, and seventeen married (seven to Chinese Christians). The others either supported themselves independently by sewing or continued to live at the Methodist home.[77]

Many more Chinese women sought refuge at the Presbyterian Mission Home, which took a more aggressive stance against prostitution. As superintendent of the home from 1877 to 1897, Margaret Culbertson devised the technique of rescue work, whereby brothels were raided with the assistance of the police whenever a Chinese girl or woman sent word for help. According to Donaldina Cameron, who succeeded Culbertson, approximately 1,500 girls were rescued in this way during the first thirty years of the home's existence.[78] Because of the high value placed on prostitutes, owners went to great expense to recover their "property," hiring highbinders to retrieve the women or paying legal fees to file criminal charges against the women on trumped-up charges of larceny. Once rescued, the women often had to be guarded in the home and defended in court. As inmates, the women were subjected to strong doses of Christian doctrine and a regimented life of constant activity, the combination of which was meant to instill "virtue" in them. The day started at 7 A.M. with roll call and morning prayer, followed by breakfast, an hour of housework, then classes, dinner, prayer meeting, study session, and bedtime. Promptness at mealtimes was required, as was written permission to leave the premises. Women were assigned household chores, taught Chinese and English, trained for industrial or domestic employment, and encouraged to work for wages either sewing in the Mission Home or serving as domestic workers outside the institution. Some—particularly those assigned to the home by the courts—resented the restrictions and austerity of the Mission Home and chose to return to their former status. Others opted to return to China. A significant number, however, agreed to marry Chinese Christians and begin life anew in America.[79]

Protestant missionaries provided an important service in rescuing Chinese prostitutes from a wretched life of enslavement. Indeed, they were the only ally abused Chinese women had in the late nineteenth century, and it was largely thanks to their efforts that Chinese prostitution declined by the turn of the century. Yet their work also had a damaging effect on the Chinese community and on the moral psyche of the rescued women. In their zeal to rescue and transform Chinese women into their own image, missionary women often manipulated the law and the press to serve their ulterior motives. In the process, they not only infringed on the civil rights of an already disenfranchised population, but also helped to perpetuate negative stereotypes of the Chinese, thus adding fuel to anti-Chinese sentiment and legislation. This effect was ironic, considering that Protestant missionaries were the one group that consistently opposed the Chinese Exclusion laws. Their efforts were also flawed by an unyielding belief in the superiority of Victorian cultural values, to the point of self-righteous condescension. Rescued women were often pressured into adopting gender roles that emphasized female purity, piety, and Christian home life. Because missionary women strongly believed that the Christian home should center on the moral authority of the wife and not the patriarchal control of the husband, they worked hard to turn Chinese women against traditional Chinese marriages and family life, alienating the Chinese community and subjecting the women to cultural conflict and social ostracism as a result. Moreover, by choosing to focus only on transforming the gender role of wives, excluding husbands in the process of change, they further alienated the men and jeopardized the long-term efficacy of their work.

But as Peggy Pascoe's study on missionary rescue homes recounts so well, Chinese women who sought help from the mission homes were neither powerless victims nor entirely free agents, but women who lived in a world with many constraints and few opportunities. Recognizing that the Mission Home offered them a chance to change their circumstances, they went there with their own hidden agendas. A number of entrants to the Presbyterian Mission Home between 1874 and 1880 were prostitutes who wanted the protection of home officials in order to marry suitors of their choice. Other women used the Mission Home as a temporary refuge from male abuse, to escape arranged marriages, or to gain leverage in a polygynous marriage. Although they were genuinely grateful for the services of the Mission Home, many did not convert to Christianity or end up mirroring the Victorian ideals of womanhood. Rather, as Pascoe's study points out, Chinese wives came to shape a new set of gender relations in their Chinese American marriages.[80]

THE PIVOTAL STATUS OF *MUI TSAI*

Not far from the reaches of prostitution were *mui tsai*—girls who were brought from China to work as domestic servants in affluent Chinese homes or brothels, or young daughters of prostitutes who worked in this capacity in brothels. Although John W. Stephens, in his study of the manuscript censuses, estimates that only 2 percent of Chinese women were listed as "young servants" in the 1870 census, their presence and role were more significant than that.[81] The *mui tsai* system, a cultural carryover from China, was generally regarded by the Chinese as a form of charity for impoverished girls. The term itself comes from the Cantonese dialect and means "little sister." Under this age-old system, poor parents would sell a young daughter into domestic service, usually stipulating in a deed of sale that she be freed through marriage when she turned eighteen. Meanwhile, the girl received no wages for her labor, was not at liberty to leave of her own free will, and had no legal recourse for complaint should she be mistreated, raped, or forced into an unhappy marriage. In China, Hong Kong, and Malaysia, where the system continued until the 1940s, girls sold to rich and benevolent owners supposedly benefited from the system. Well fed, clothed, and sheltered, they were known to establish long-lasting affectionate relationships with their mistresses. Many *mui tsai*, however, did not fare as well. Treated as "work horses," they had to take care of children not much younger than themselves, perform heavy household chores, and often suffer the sexual advances of their masters or the physical abuses of their mistresses.[82] Their hard lives paralleled that of European female indentured servants, who made up one-third of the indentured population in antebellum America. Like *mui tsai*, these women were on call twenty-four hours a day and responsible for a wide range of domestic chores and child care.[83] But whereas they were protected by law from flagrant abuse and breach of contract, *mui tsai* enjoyed no such protection. There was no guarantee that their contracts would be honored—that they would obtain freedom through marriage when they came of age. Indeed, depending on the family's economic situation, a *mui tsai* could be resold into prostitution for a handsome sum.

Some *mui tsai* who immigrated with merchant families later fulfilled their role as bond servants in America and were then freed for marriage. I believe that is what happened in the case of my great-grandmother's *mui tsai*, Ah Kum. However, in the absence of other details about Ah Kum's life in America, the life story of Quan Laan Fan, who immigrated as a *mui tsai* in the 1880s, serves as a better example. In an oral history interview in 1974, Laan Fan explained that when she was seven, her family's litter of pigs died and the family went into debt.[84] Her parents then sold her to Quan Seung's family, with whom she lived a comfortable life. Seung was the second wife of Wong, a Gold Mountain man, and because she did not have bound feet like the first wife, she was chosen to join him in America. "Seung wanted me to come over to be their errand girl. That's how I came to America," said Laan Fan.

Immigration to America put an end to Laan Fan's comfortable life. Wong owned a grocery store on Washington Street near Ross Alley in San Francisco, and it became Laan Fan's job to fetch meals from there daily for her mistress. "Everyday I would go and bring our meals back from the store," she recalled. "Just the two of us would eat together [Seung and herself]. We didn't have to cook. I'd go out by myself at nine o'clock in the morning to get our daytime meal and at four o'clock for the evening meal." This was no easy task for a girl. "The pot had three layers to it," Laan Fan said. "Two layers were for *soong* [main dishes] and the third layer was for rice. Sometimes, I'd have another pot for soup which I carried home or else it was included in the big pot. I was so short, I dragged the pot home everyday until I wore a hole in it!" She also rolled cigarettes at home for income, sending most of the money she earned to her mother in China, keeping some for clothes and shoes. She was allowed to study Chinese and English with teachers from the Baptist Church. Then, at eighteen or nineteen, she was married to Sam. Although he was much older than she, and poor, the marriage endured. They first tried growing flowers in nearby Belmont, but then moved back to San Francisco, where she worked as a telephone operator in Chinatown to help support their family of eight children.

The outcome of Quan Laan Fan's life fulfilled the original intent of the *mui tsai* system. Both she and her family gained by the sale; she was well treated by Seung's family and was properly married off, albeit to an old man, when she came of age. Yet newspaper accounts and missionary records typically painted a different picture of the fates of *mui tsai*. According to these sources, brothel owners often purchased young girls from China with the intention of using them first as domestic servants and then as prostitutes when they became older, thus maximizing their investment. Wu Tien Fu, rescued by Protestant missionaries in 1894, was such a *mui tsai*:[85]

> I was six when I came to this country in 1893. My worthless father gambled every cent away, and so, left us poor. I think my mother's family was well-to-do, because our grandmother used to dress in silk and satin and always brought us lots of things. And the day my father took me, he fibbed and said he was taking me to see my grandmother, that I was very fond of, you know, and I got on the ferry boat with him, and Mother was crying, and I couldn't understand why she should cry if I go to see Grandma. She gave me a new toothbrush and a new washrag in a blue bag when I left her. When I saw her cry I said, "Don't cry, Mother, I'm just going to see Grandma and be right back." And that worthless father, my own father, imagine, had every inclination to sell me, and he sold me on the ferry boat. Locked me in the cabin while he was negotiating my sale. And I kicked and screamed and screamed and they wouldn't open the door till after some time, you see, I suppose he had made his bargain and had left the steamer. Then they opened the door and let me out and I went up and down, up and down, here and there, couldn't find him.

She was later taken to San Francisco and resold to a brothel, where she worked as a *mui tsai*:

> [My owner] used to make me carry a big fat baby on my back and make me to wash his diapers. And you know, to wash you have to stoop over, and then he pulls you back, and cry and cry. Oh, I got desperate, I didn't care what happened to me, I just pinched his cheek, his seat, you know, just gave it to him. Then of course I got it back. She, his mother, went and burned a red hot iron tong and burnt me on the arm.

Fortunately for Tien Fu, someone reported her situation to Donaldina Cameron at the Presbyterian Mission Home, who subsequently rescued her and brought her to live at the home. She told about the rescue:

They described me much bigger than I was so when they came they didn't recognize me. And then the woman who had reported to the mission said, "Why didn't you take her? She's the girl." They said, "She looked too small," and then they came back again. But even then, they weren't sure that I was the one, so they undressed me and examined my body and found where the woman had beaten me black and blue all over. And then they took me to the home. Oh, it was in the pouring rain! I was scared to death. You know, change from change, and all strangers, and I didn't know where I was going. Away from my own people and in the pouring rain. And they took me, a fat policeman carried me all the way from Jackson Street, where I was staying, to Sacramento Street to the mission, Cameron House. So I got my freedom there.

With the help of a benefactor, H. C. Coleman of Morristown, New Jersey, Tien Fu was able to attend the Stevens' School in Germantown, Pennsylvania, for four years, and the Toronto Bible School for another two years. She saved enough money to return to China, but, unable to find her family, she returned and devoted the rest of her life to the goals of the Mission Home, assisting Donaldina Cameron in rescues, interpreting for her in court, and taking charge of the nursery department. She never married but remained Cameron's constant companion even after she retired from mission work in 1951. When Tien Fu passed away in 1975, she was buried beside Cameron, who had predeceased her in 1968.

As in China, *mui tsai* were pivotal in defining women's social status in Chinatown. At best, a *mui tsai* could hope to be married to a man who would provide for her; at worst, she could be resold into prostitution. Until she became of marrying age, she was at the mercy of her owners, who could abuse her at will. In this sense, merchant wives, who held control over the fate of their *mui tsai*, were in a position similar to that of Chinese madams vis-à-vis their slave girls. As it was for prostitutes, life for *mui tsai* in America proved to be a double-edged sword. Far away from China, they lacked the protection and support of family and kin, but there were more avenues of escape available to them. Along with the Mission Homes, the Society for the Prevention of Cruelty to Children looked after their interests and offered them help.[86] The lack of accurate statistics makes it difficult to gauge the number of *mui tsai* in San Francisco or their outcomes. Given the small number of merchant families that could afford *mui tsai*, and the large number of prostitutes, the nineteenth century probably saw more Wu Tien Fus than Quan Laan Fans. After all, it was more profitable for owners of *mui tsai* to satisfy the demand for prostitutes than for wives.[87] Nevertheless, like organized prostitution, the *mui tsai* system had all but vanished by the 1920s thanks to the efforts of missionary women and Chinese social reformers intent on modernizing Chinatown—this in a country, it should be noted, where slavery had been abolished in 1865 and contract labor in 1885.

THE SHELTERED LIVES OF IMMIGRANT WIVES

Between 1870 and 1880, the percentage of Chinese women in San Francisco who were prostitutes had declined from 71 to 50 percent, while the percentage of women who were married had increased from approximately 8 to 49 percent, most likely owing to the enforcement of antiprostitution measures, the arrival of wives from China, and the marriage of ex-prostitutes to Chinese laborers. The number of wives continued to rise after the passage of the Chinese Exclusion Act of 1882, when merchant wives became the prime category of female immigrants from China. By the turn of the century, married women made up 62 percent of the Chinese female population in San Francisco.[88]

Within the patriarchal structure of San Francisco Chinatown, immigrant wives occupied a higher status than *mui tsai* and prostitutes, but they too were considered the property of men and constrained to lead bound lives. Members of the merchant class, capitalizing on miners' and labor crews' need for provisions and services, were among the first Chinese to come to California. They were also the only Chinese who were allowed to and who could afford to bring their wives and families, or to establish second families in America.[89] In the absence of the scholar-gentry class, which chose not to emigrate, the merchant class became the ruling elite in Chinatown, and their families formed the basis for the growth of the Chinese American population and the formation of the middle class.

Referred to as "small-foot" or "lily-feet" women in nineteenth-century writings because of their bound feet, most merchant wives led the cloistered life of genteel women. They generally had servants and did not need to work for wages or be burdened by the daily household chores of cooking, laundering, and cleaning. Rather, they spent their leisure hours prettying up or creating needlework designs, to be used as presents to distant relatives or as ornamentation for their own apparel and that of family members. Sui Seen Far, a noted California writer in the late nineteenth century, described their lives this way:

The Chinese woman in America lives generally in the upstairs apartments of her husband's dwelling. He looks well after her comfort and provides all her little mind can wish. . . . She seldom goes out, and does not receive visitors until she has been a wife for at least two years. Even then, if she has no child, she is supposed to hide herself. After a child has been born to her, her wall of reserve is lowered a little, and it is proper for cousins and friends of her husband to drop in occasionally and have a chat with "the family."

Now and then the women visit one another. . . . They laugh at the most commonplace remark and scream at the smallest trifle; they examine one another's dresses and hair, talk about their husbands, their babies, their food; squabble over little matters and make up again; they dine on bowls of rice, minced chicken, bamboo shoots and a dessert of candied fruits.[90]

At least one merchant wife in San Francisco Chinatown did not view her life so positively, though. "Poor me!" she told a white reporter. "In China I was shut up in the house since I was 10 years old, and only left my father's house to be shut up in my husband's house in this great country. For seventeen years I have been in this house without leaving it save on two evenings."[91] To pass her time, she worshiped at the family altar, embroidered, looked after her son, played cards with her servant, or chatted with her Chinese neighbors. Periodically, her hairdresser would come to do her hair, or a female storyteller would come to entertain her. Her husband had also provided her with a European music box and a pet canary. Only through her husband, servant, hairdresser, and female neighbors was she able to maintain contact with the outside world.

Despite her wealth, she envied other women "who are richer than I, for they have big feet and can go everywhere, and every day have something new to fill their minds." This woman, however, as she was well aware, was still only a piece of property to her husband, always fearful of being sold "like cows" if her husband tired of her, or of having her son taken from her and sent back to China to the first wife. Also, as she herself pointed out, she had few avenues of escape. Chinatown was governed by the laws of China, and the Mission Home could provide her with only a temporary refuge. "I am too old for any man to desire in marriage, too helpless in the ways of making money to support myself, too used to the grand living my husband provides to be deprived of it."

In fact, however, such women of leisure were but a small proportion of immigrant wives in the late nineteenth century. Most wives were married to Chinese laborers who, having decided to settle in America, had saved enough money to send for a wife or to marry a local Chinese

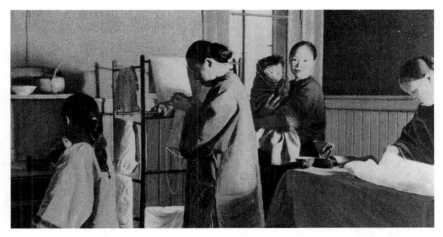

Women doing laundry, San Francisco, 1890s. (Charles Weidner photo, Judy Yung collection)

woman—most likely a former prostitute or American-born. As it was for other working-class immigrant women, life for this group of wives was marked by constant toil, with little time for leisure. Undoubtedly, they were the seamstresses, shirtmakers, washerwomen, gardeners, fisherwomen, storekeepers, and laborers listed in the manuscript census. Even those listed as "keeping house" most likely also worked for wages at home or took in boarders to supplement their husbands' low wages.[92] In addition to their paid work, they were burdened with child care and domestic chores, which they had to perform in crowded housing arrangements. According to the San Francisco Health Officer's Report for 1869–70, "Their mode of living is the most abject in which it is possible for human beings to exist. The great majority of them live crowded together in rickety, filthy and dilapidated tenement houses like so many cattle."[93] Five years later, the writer B. E. Lloyd noted in *Lights and Shades of San Francisco*, "A family of five or six persons will occupy a single room, eight by ten feet in dimension, wherein all will live, cook, eat, sleep, and perhaps carry on a small manufacturing business."[94] In 1880 the city's Board of Health condemned Chinatown as "a cancer-spot, which endangers the healthy and prosperous condition of the city of San Francisco."[95]

Like peasant women in China, working-class wives in San Francisco could freely go out to work, worship at the temple, or shop in the Chinatown stores that provided for all their needs. But they did not travel

Shopping in San Francisco Chinatown, 1890s. (Courtesy of Philip P. Choy)

far from home or mingle with men. Even when they spent an occasional evening at the Chinese opera, they would sit in a separate section from the men. Nor did they linger long in the streets, so threatened were they by the possibility of racial and sexual assaults. As reported in the *Daily Alta California*:

> Last evening, at the fire on Dupont street, a crowd of Waverly Place loafers, and thieves, and roughs, who were being kept back from the fire by the police, amused themselves by throwing a Chinawoman down in the muddy street and dragging her back and forth by the hair for some minutes. The poor female heathen was rescued from their clutches at last by officer Saulsbury, and taken to the calaboose for protection. He also arrested one of her assailants, who was pointed out by the woman, but as she could not testify against him [Chinese could not legally testify against whites] he was dismissed on his arrival at the calaboose.[96]

The safety of Chinese women could not be assured even in the company of white missionaries. According to the testimony of Rev. W. C. Pond:

> Under the protection of American ladies they [Chinese girls from the Methodist mission] went out, one afternoon to walk. When at some distance from home, they were set upon by a gang of men and boys, pelted, and then, as I understand, struck, their clothes rent, their ear-rings torn from their ears, and when an Irish woman (God bless her!) gave them refuge, her house was stoned.[97]

As it became more difficult to import Chinese prostitutes, Chinese women found themselves the targets of kidnappers, sometimes in broad daylight, to be sold into prostitution. During one week in February 1898, eight such kidnappings occurred.[98]

Unlike in China, where three generations often lived under the same roof, the typical family structure in San Francisco Chinatown was nuclear, including a married couple, the husband about nine years older than the wife, and one or two children.[99] The family, however, remained a patriarchal, economic unit. Within this structure, the husband worked outside the home for wages, while the wife stayed home to perform unpaid housework and child care as well as paid piecework for subcontractors. Since the husband was the chief wage earner and the representative of the family on the outside, the wife was dependent on him for subsistence and protection and thus remained in a subordinate role. In this sense, their respective roles and gender relations were no different from those in preindustrial China. But the absence of the mother-in-law, the scarcity of women, and the couple's common goal to survive in a new and often hostile land were different circumstances that did begin to affect gender roles and relationships.

One of the advantages for women who immigrated to America was the chance to remove themselves from the rule of the tyrannical mother-in-law, the one position that allowed women in China any power.[100] Not only was the daughter-in-law freed from serving her in-laws, but she was also freed of competition for her husband's attention and loyalty and given full control over managing the household. Because of the small number of Chinese women, wives in America were valued and accorded more respect by their men (although there were still incidences of wife abuse). In addition, most Chinese men, because of their low socioeconomic status, could not afford a concubine or mistress, much less a wife. Thus, having a wife was a status symbol to be jealously guarded. Women physicians who attended Chinese wives and children had "much to say of the kindness and indulgence of Chinese husbands, their sympathy and consideration towards their wives in pregnancy and childbirth and their willingness to spend money for pretty clothes for them."[101] This same indulgence is also evident in photographs taken in the 1890s that show Chinese families in the streets of Chinatown or at the park.[102]

Wives were also more valued in America because they were essential helpmates in the family's daily struggle for socioeconomic survival. As it was for European immigrants, the family's interest was paramount, and all members worked for its survival and well-being. A Chinese wife's earnings from sewing, washing, or taking in boarders could mean the difference between having pork or just bean paste with rice for dinner, or between life and death for starving relatives back in China. It was also her duty to cook and prepare the Chinese meals and special foods for certain celebrations, to maintain the family altar, to make Chinese clothing and slippers for the family, to raise the children to be "proper Chinese," and to provide a refuge for the husband from the hostile world outside. Thus, even while the family was a site of oppression for Chinese women in terms of the heavy housework and child care responsibilities and possibly wife abuse, it was also a source of empowerment. Wives ran the household and raised the children; they also played an important role in the family economy and in maintaining Chinese culture and family life as a way of resisting cultural onslaughts from the outside.

As Protestant women gained a foothold in bringing Christianity, Western ideas, and contact with the outside world into Chinatown homes, Chinese wives became more aware of their bound lives. They also became an important link between the Chinese family and the larger society and an influential factor in the education and socialization of Chinese American children. Convinced that there was little hope of redeeming the Chinese unless the women were converted to Christianity and Americanized, missionary women visited Chinese homes regularly to give lessons on the Bible and American domestic and sanitary practices, often while the women worked—"one woman making paper gods, another overalls, another binding shoes."[103] According to one missionary report in 1887, the visiting list was eighty-five families long, including one hundred children, thirty-six "little-footed" women, fifteen "little-footed" girls, and about twenty-eight slave girls.[104] Mothers, one observer noted, were particularly interested in having missionaries provide their children with an education:

> The most encouraging features in visiting from house to house in Chinatown are, first, the great love the mothers have for their children, their anxiety to have them learn English, and their pride in the progress made in reading, writing, spelling and singing, and the desire to help the teacher in her work, evidenced by collecting the children to be taught, and scolding them when inattentive or sulky.[105]

These visits won few converts, but some mothers were persuaded to educate their daughters and discontinue the practice of binding their feet, and a small number of women also began to venture out of the home to attend church functions. Abused wives also found their way to the mission homes. Records of the Presbyterian Mission Home indicate that a number of "runaway wives" came asking for help when they were threatened with being sold, subjected to beatings, or just unhappy with their husbands. In one case, Lan Lee, who had continually been beaten by her husband and threatened with murder, was assisted by the Presbyterian mission in winning a divorce on the grounds of extreme cruelty in 1893.[106] Slowly, Chinese women were becoming aware of legal rights in America, rights that European women already knew how to take advantage of.

UNBOUND LIVES OF EXCEPTIONAL WOMEN

There were exceptional Chinese women in nineteenth-century San Francisco who did not live oppressive lives under the control of men or other women. The unbound lives of Maria Seise, Mary Tape, and Lai Yun Oi, for instance, provide important insight into the possibilities for social change among Chinese immigrant women. All three immigrated as single women on their own, and, in contrast to the restrictive lives of their peers, all three were self-sufficient, exercised freedom of choice, and were to a large extent in control of their own lives.

Maria Seise was probably the first Chinese woman to immigrate to California (preceding Ah Toy by one year), and she remained self-supporting throughout her life. She arrived in San Francisco aboard the *Eagle* with the Charles V. Gillespie household in 1848. Gillespie, an enterprising New York trader, was returning from a stay in Hong Kong with three Chinese servants, two men and Maria Seise. According to the records of Bishop Ingraham of the Trinity Episcopal Church in San Francisco, who baptized her in 1854, Maria Seise ran away from her home in Canton at an early age to avoid being sold into slavery by her parents. Upon arrival in Macao she worked for a Portuguese family, adopting their dress and Roman Catholic faith. She later married a Portuguese sailor, who left on a voyage and never returned. Destitute, she then worked as a servant for an American family and in 1837 went with them to the Sandwich Islands (now Hawaii). Upon her return to China six years later she found employment with the Gillespies, accompanying them to San Francisco in 1848. She became, according to the church records,

> a companion [to Mrs. Gillespie,] enjoying her fullest confidence. She has acquired a sufficient knowledge of the English language to enable Mr. Wyatt to instruct and examine her for confirmation and no shadow of doubt as to her preparation and fitness for assuming these responsibilities existed in his mind, or in that of the lady with whom she lived, who knelt at her side to receive the rite at the same time.[107]

The two Chinese male servants soon left for the gold fields, but, according to one source, Maria Seise stayed with the Gillespies, who settled on a large tract of land in the vicinity of Chinatown.[108]

Although Chinese men did not hesitate to speak up and use the courts and diplomatic channels to fight discrimination whenever possible, there were not many Chinese women like Ah Toy who had the resources—English language facility, finances, and adeptness—to do the same on their own behalf. Mary Tape was one of the few. Brought up in an orphanage in Shanghai, she immigrated to America with missionaries at the age of eleven and lived for five years at the Ladies' Relief Society outside Chinatown. She later married Joseph Tape, a Chinese American expressman and interpreter for the Chinese consulate. Mary Tape spoke English and was thoroughly Westernized in dress and lifestyle. According to a newspaper reporter, she was also a self-taught photographer, artist, and telegrapher, as well as the mother of four musically accomplished children.[109] In 1884, when their daughter Mamie Tape was denied entry into the neighborhood school outside Chinatown because "the association of Chinese and white children would be very demoralizing mentally and morally to the latter,"[110] Mary and Joseph Tape took the Board of Education to court (*Tape v. Hurley*). The lower court ruled that all children, regardless of race, had the right to a public school education—a ruling that was upheld by both state and federal courts; but the school district circumvented the ruling by establishing a separate school for Chinese children in Chinatown. Enraged, Mary Tape wrote the board a scathing letter of protest, which read in part:

> I see that you are going to make all sorts of excuses to keep my child out off the Public Schools. Dear sirs, Will you please to tell me! Is it a disgrace to be Born a Chinese? Didn't God make us all!!! What right! have you to bar my children out of the school because she is a chinese Descend. . . . You have expended a lot of the Public money foolishly, all because of a one poor little Child. Her playmates is all Caucasians ever since she could toddle around. If she is good enough to play with them! Then is she not good enough to be in the same room and studie with them? . . . It seems no matter how a Chinese may live and dress so long as you know they Chinese. Then they are hated as one. There is not any right or justice for them. . . . May you Mr. Moulder, never be persecuted like the way you have persecuted little Mamie Tape. Mamie Tape will never attend any of the Chinese schools of your making! Never!!! I will let the world see sir What justice there is When it is govern by the Race prejudice men![111]

As an outspoken woman able to stand up for her rights, Mary Tape was a rarity among Chinese women in nineteenth-century San Francisco. Fortunate to have had an education, a liberal upbringing, financial resources, and a supportive husband, she was an early example of an emancipated Chinese American woman.

Like Maria Seise, Ah Toy, and Mary Tape, Lai Yun Oi immigrated as a single woman on her own. Her story is unusual in that she came as a widow in the late 1870s or early 1880s and was able independently to make her fortune in America even though she spoke no English and had few marketable skills. As her grand-nephew the historian Him Mark Lai recalled her story, Lai Yun Oi was originally from the Nanhai district, where women who were employed in the sericulture industry were more independent than most other women in China. They did not practice footbinding and often followed the *shu qi* custom of refusing to marry.[112] It was therefore not surprising that Lai Yun Oi chose not to stay at her husband's home and village after he died, which would have been the "proper" thing to do. Instead she went to seek work in Canton and then followed a fellow clansman on his way to New York. She finally decided to settle alone in San Francisco, where she worked as a *dai kum* (a woman who escorts young brides in the traditional Chinese wedding ceremony), supplementing her income by doing needlework at home and providing hairdressing services to women in Chinatown. Living frugally and investing wisely in businesses in New York and San Francisco, Lai Yun Oi was able to return to Canton, invest in a tailor shop and a few buildings there, and retire comfortably while still in her mid-fifties.[113]

My great-grandmother Leong Shee did not come from the same liberal background as Lai Yun Oi; nor was she as educated and influenced by missionary women as Maria Seise or Mary Tape. For Chinese women like her, immigration to America was not a liberating experience; their lives were doubly bound by American and Chinese ideologies that emphasized the inferiority of the Chinese race and the subordination of women, on one hand, and economic conditions that nurtured prostitution and the exploitation of female labor, on the other. But Great-Grandmother, because of her class background, an understanding husband, and a domineering personality, was able to do something about her unhappy circumstances: she chose to leave America and return home with all her children. It was back in China that Great-Grandmother, encouraged by the liberal ideology of the 1911 Revolution, became an emancipated woman. She unbound her feet, converted to Christianity, and became educated and active in the local Church of Christ. Moreover, she invested her husband's money wisely in property and business ventures, had a two-story house with indoor plumbing built for herself in Macao, purchased four *mui tsai* to serve her and her family, and lived to the ripe age of ninety-four.

Even at this early stage of their history, Chinese women were adapting to life in Gold Mountain with mixed results. Although most of them lived bound lives, remaining confined to the domestic sphere and subordinate to men, their important roles as producers (wage earners) and reproducers (childbearers as well as homemakers) in a predominantly male and pervasively racist land elevated their value as scarce commodities and essential helpmates to their men. Others, most notably prostitutes and *mui tsai*, suffered considerable abuse in America but found new options opened to them, through the assistance of missionary women and what legal rights were available to them at the time. Nonetheless, as in the case of my great-grandmother, it took the additional influence of Chinese nationalism and its inherent feminist ideology, combined with increased economic opportunities and the continued support of Protestant women, before Chinese immigrant women could become "new women" in the modern era of the twentieth century.

CHAPTER 2

Unbound Feet

Chinese Immigrant Women, 1902–1929

No nation can rise above the level of its home and the key to elevating home-life is to raise the status of women.
Mrs. E. V. Robbins
Occidental Board of Foreign Missions, 1902

Without educating women, we can't have a strong nation; without women's rights, our nation will remain weak.
Qiu Jin
revolutionary heroine, 1906

From the beginning, social change for Chinese women in San Francisco was tied to the nationalist and women's movements in China. This became evident on the afternoon of November 2, 1902, when Sieh King King, an eighteen-year-old student from China and an ardent reformer, stood before a Chinatown theater full of men and women and "boldly condemned the slave girl system, raged at the horrors of foot-binding and, with all the vehemence of aroused youth, declared that men and women were equal and should enjoy the privileges of equals."[1] Her talk and her views on women's rights were inextricably linked with Chinese nationalism and the 1898 Reform Movement, which advocated that China emulate the West and modernize in order to throw off the yoke of foreign domination. Beginning with the Opium War (1839–1842), China had suffered repeated defeats at the hands of Western imperialist powers and been forced to yield to their demands for indemnities and extraterritorial rights. Fearing the further partitioning of China and possibly national extinction, reformers and revolutionaries alike were advocating social, economic, and political changes for their country along the lines of the Western model. Elevating the status of women to the extent that they could become "new women"—educated mothers and productive citizens—was part of this nationalist effort to strengthen and defend China against further foreign encroachment.[2]

Sieh King King, whose talk was sponsored by the Baohuanghui (Protect the Emperor Society), a reform party that advocated restoring the deposed emperor and establishing a constitutional monarchy in China, expounded on exactly this point. China was oppressed from within by feudal practices and from without by Western imperialism, she said. The country was weak because for centuries it had bound the feet of women and kept them ignorant, effectively barring them from work and public affairs. The solution, she concluded, lay in establishing schools for the 200 million women in China so that they could develop their intellect, engage in professions, and contribute to the well-being of their families and the prosperity of their country on the same footing as men.[3]

Sieh King King's sentiments on women's emancipation actually had roots in China, even before the arrival of Westerners. As early as the seventeenth century, women of the gentry class were becoming educated and asserting themselves as literary talents. Their rising visibility as writers and publishers of their own works sparked controversy, leading male scholars like Mao Qiling, Yuan Mei, Yu Zhengxie, and Li Ruzhen to denounce sexist practices such as footbinding and the double standards of chastity. In the 1850s, the Taiping rebels, who sought to liberate China from Manchu rule, abolished footbinding, prostitution, arranged marriages, and polygyny and allowed women to fight in the army, own land, and be educated. But it wasn't until foreign missionaries gained a foothold in China after the Opium War that women's emancipation was advanced through the establishment of anti-footbinding societies and schools for girls, institutions that became an integral part of the modernization platform of the Reform Movement led by Kang Youwei.[4]

Although Chinese reformers and Protestant missionaries differed in their ultimate goals—reformers sought national salvation, while Christians sought religious conversion—they shared a common strategy, namely social reform, of which women's emancipation played a central role. While reformers understood that China could not be saved as long as half its population remained underutilized, missionaries saw the remaking of Chinese women in their image as the key to converting and civilizing all of China. For these reasons, both groups worked for women's emancipation, not only in China, but also in Chinese communities such as San Francisco Chinatown. Their overlapping programs

included education and equal rights for women and an end to footbinding, female slavery, and polygyny. Regardless of the reformers' respective motives, Chinese women in both China and the United States
directly benefited from their combined efforts, which encouraged them
to unbind their feet and their lives, to free themselves of patriarchal oppression.

Sieh King King herself was an embodiment of feminist ideology stemming from both Western Christianity and Chinese nationalism. A daughter of a liberal-minded merchant, Sieh King King grew up and attended
a missionary school in the treaty port of Shanghai, where she and other
reformers were heavily influenced by Western contact and ideas. Even
before emigrating as a student to the United States, where she hoped
to further her education, she had developed a national reputation as a
patriot and an orator. According to one newspaper account, in 1901 she
delivered a stirring speech before thousands of people in Shanghai in
which she protested the treaty forced upon the Chinese government that
granted Russia special rights in Manchuria.[5] Although missionary efforts
resulted in few religious conversions, ideas of women's emancipation did
capture the imagination of women such as Sieh King King, who argued
that an improvement in women's conditions would make for stronger
families and ultimately a stronger China. Unlike in the West, in China
the argument for improving women's lot was always put in terms of how
it would benefit the Chinese race and nation, rather than how it would
benefit women as individuals.[6] Because this line of thinking was in keeping with traditional Chinese thought and practice—that the collective
good took precedence over individual needs—it was more effective than
Western feminist ideology in gaining wide support for women's emancipation in China as well as in San Francisco Chinatown.

Although it is difficult to measure the real impact of Sieh King King's
speech about women's emancipation on her audience without hearing
from the audience itself, newspaper reporters did note that women listened "like zealots" and men "with every sign of approval."[7] And later
that evening, at a banquet held in Sieh King King's honor, women would
be allowed for the first time to sit in the main banquet hall and enjoy
the same food as the men.[8] A year later, Sieh King King gave another
"eloquent and inspiring speech" in which she again "expounded her
views on the role of Chinese women and the need to abolish outdated
Chinese customs and emulate the West," this time to an exclusively female audience of two hundred.[9] After that, she was not mentioned again
in the local English- or Chinese-language newspapers.[10] But what she

advocated on behalf of Chinese women—unbound feet, education, equal rights, and public participation—remained at the heart of social change for Chinese women for the next three decades. The cause of women's rights would be raised during each epoch of China's continuing fight against feudalism and imperialism—through the 1911 Revolution, the 1919 May Fourth cultural revolution, and the War of Resistance Against Japan (1937–1945)—when the country was in need of the services of all its citizens. With each national crisis, the hold of patriarchy over the lives of Chinese women would loosen.[11]

What happened to women in China had a direct impact on Chinese women in the United States. Beginning in the early twentieth century, not only were new immigrants bringing a different set of cultural baggage with them in regard to women's roles, but political developments in China remained in general more meaningful to Chinese immigrants who had been barred from participation in mainstream American society. Aware that the racial oppression and humiliation they suffered in America was due in part to China's weak international status and inability to protect its citizens abroad, Chinese immigrants kept nationalist sentiment alive, focusing their attention and energies on helping China become a stronger and more modern country, even as they worked to change their unfavorable image and treatment in America. As reported in the local press, Chinese women were becoming "new women" in the homeland, and Chinese women in America were encouraged to do likewise.[12] But aside from Chinese nationalism, the reform work of Protestant missionary women and the Chinese women's entry into the urban economy also helped to advance women's cause in San Francisco Chinatown.

Journey to Gold Mountain

At the time of Sieh King King's speech, China was still suffering under the stranglehold of Western imperialism and the inept rule of the Manchus. China's defeat in the Sino-Japanese War (1894–95) and the Boxer Rebellion (1900) resulted in further concessions of extraterritorial rights and war indemnities to the imperialist powers, including Japan, Germany, Russia, France, England, and the United States. China's subjugation, by adding to the humiliation and economic burden of an overtaxed Chinese population, only strengthened the resolve of nationalists to modernize their country and rid China of both foreign domination and Manchu rule. But even after Sun Yat-sen's Tong-menghui (United Covenant League) succeeded in overthrowing the Qing dynasty in 1911, the problems of foreign control, internal dissension, and economic deterioration persisted. Political and social upheavals continued unabated as warlords, and then Nationalists, Communists, and Japanese, fought for control of China.[13] Life for the ordinary Chinese remained disrupted; survival was precarious. Oppressed by the competition of imported foreign commodities, inflation, heavy taxes, increased rents, and rampant banditry, peasants could not hope to make enough money to meet their expenses. A common saying at the time was "The poor man who faces two swords—heavy farm rent and high interest—has three roads before him: to run away at night, hang himself, or go to jail."[14] Consequently, many able-bodied peasants in Southeast China continued to emigrate overseas where kinfolk had already settled. Despite the Chinese Exclusion Acts and anti-Chinese hostilities, a good number went to America, the Gold Mountain, by posing as members of the exempt classes or by smuggling themselves across the borders.

Chinese immigration declined drastically during the Exclusion period (1883–1943; see appendix table 2). Since many Chinese in the United States were also returning to China (90,299 between 1908 and 1943), the Chinese population in the United States dropped significantly, from 105,465 in 1880 to 61,639 in 1920.[15] By 1900 the industrial revolution was over, the American West had been conquered, and Chinese labor was no longer being recruited. Many Chinese continued to disperse eastward to cities, where they could find work and where their presence was better tolerated. By 1910, 40.5 percent of the Chinese in the United States were concentrated in cities with populations above 25,000; by 1920, the percentage had increased to 66 percent. Most worked in ethnic enterprises in Chinatowns, as domestic servants for European American families, or opened small laundries, grocery stores, and restaurants in out-of-the-way places. Others found seasonal employment in agriculture or in canneries.[16] Those who had the economic means got married and started families or sent for their wives and children from China.[17]

Although there was a precipitous drop in the immigration of Chinese women to the United States following the passage of the Chinese Exclusion Act, their numbers began increasing steadily after 1900. A number of reasons explain this increase despite the effort to keep Chinese and their families out of the country. Conditions at home were worsening and becoming unsafe for family members left behind by overseas Chinese. These deteriorating conditions, combined with the lowering of cultural restrictions against women traveling abroad, encouraged increasing numbers of Chinese women to emigrate overseas to join their husbands or to pursue educational and employment opportunities on their own. Unlike in the nineteenth century, when there were no gainful jobs for them in America, they now had an economic role to play in the urban economy or in their husbands' small businesses. Only immigration legislation continued to limit the numbers of women (as well as dictate who could come at all).[18]

Most Chinese women entered the country as merchant wives, the class most favored by immigration legislation throughout the Exclusion period. Until 1924, wives of U.S. citizens were also admissible. But the passage of the Immigration Act of 1924, which was aimed primarily at curbing immigration from eastern, southern, and central Europe, dealt Asian immigration a deadly blow when it included a clause that barred any "alien ineligible to citizenship" admittance. By law, this group included the Chinese, Japanese, Koreans, and Asian Indians. On May 25, 1925, the U.S. Supreme Court ruled that Chinese merchant wives were still admissible because of treaty obligations; the Chinese wives of U.S. citizens, however, being themselves ineligible for citizenship, were not. Alarmed by what this interpretation would mean for their future in America, American-born Chinese fought back through the organized efforts of the Chinese American Citizens Alliance. Arguing persuasively that every male American citizen had the right to have his wife with him, that it was inhumane to keep husbands and wives separated, and that aliens (merchants) should not be entitled to more rights under the immigration laws than U.S. citizens, they moved Congress to amend the 1924 act in 1930 to permit the entry of Chinese alien wives of U.S. citizens—but only those who were married prior to May 26, 1924.[19] Another way for Chinese women to come to the United States was as daughters of U.S. citizens. In this case, however, they were allowed entry only if they claimed derivative citizenship through the father (not the mother), and they had to be unmarried.[20] A few women also came as students, one of the classes exempted from exclusion. But Chinese female students amounted to only about thirty annually in the 1910s and several dozens annually in the 1920s.[21]

Even those with the legal right to immigrate sometimes failed to pass the difficult interrogations and physical examinations required only of Chinese immigrants.[22] Aware of the intimidating entry procedures, many were discouraged from even trying to immigrate. Many Chinese Americans shared the sentiments of Pany Lowe, an American-born Chinese man who was interviewed in 1924:

> Sure I go back to China two times. Stay ten or fifteen months each time. I do not want to bring my wife to this country. Very hard get her in. I know how immigration inspector treat me first time when I come back eighteen years old. . . . My father have to go to court. They keep me on boat for two or three days. Finally he got witness and affidavit prove me to be citizen. They let me go, so I think if they make trouble for me they make trouble for my wife. . . . I think most Chinese in this country like have their son go China get married. Under this new law [Immigration Act of 1924], can't do this. No allowed marry white girl. Not enough American-born Chinese to go around. China only place to get wife. Not allowed to bring them back. For Chinaman, very unjust. Not human. Very uncivilized.[23]

American immigration laws and the process of chain migration also determined that most Chinese women would continue to come from the rural villages of Guangdong Province, where traditional gender roles still prevailed. Wong Ah So and Law Shee Low, both of whom immigrated in 1922, serve as examples of Guangdong village women who came as obedient daughters or wives to escape poverty and for the sake of their families. Jane Kwong Lee, who also came to the United States in 1922, was among the small number of urbanized "new women" who emigrated on their own for improved opportunities and adventure. Together, these three women's stories provide insights into the gender roles and immigration experiences of Chinese women in the early twentieth century.

"I was born in Canton [Guangdong] Province," begins Wong Ah So's story, "my father was sometimes a sailor and sometimes he worked on the docks, for we were very poor."[24] Patriarchal cultural values often put the daughter at risk when poverty strikes: from among the five children (two boys and three girls) in the family, her mother chose to betroth her, the eldest daughter, to a Gold Mountain man in exchange for a bride price of 450 Mexican dollars.

> I was 19 when this man came to my mother and said that in America there was a great deal of gold. Even if I just peeled potatoes there, he told my mother I would earn seven or eight dollars a day, and if I was willing to do any work at all I would earn lots of money. He was a laundryman, but said he earned plenty of money. He was very nice to me,

and my mother liked him, so my mother was glad to have me go with him as his wife.[25]

Out of filial duty and economic necessity, Ah So agreed to sail to the United States with this laundryman, Huey Yow, in 1922: "I was told by my mother that I was to come to the United States to earn money with which to support my parents and my family in Hongkong."[26] Sharing the same happy thoughts about going to America as many other immigrants before her, she said, "I thought that I was his wife, and was very grateful that he was taking me to such a grand, free country, where everyone was rich and happy."[27]

Huey Yow had a marriage certificate prepared and told her to claim him as her husband to the immigration officials in San Francisco, although there had been no marriage ceremony. "In accordance to my mother's demands I became a party to this arrangement," Ah So admitted later. "On my arrival at the port of San Francisco, I claimed to be the wife of Huey Yow, but in truth had not at any time lived with him as his wife."[28]

Law Shee Low (Law Yuk Tao was her given name before marriage), who was a year younger than Wong Ah So, was born in the village of Kai Gok in Chungshan District, Guangdong Province.[29] Economic and political turmoil in the country hit her family hard. Once well-to-do, they were reduced to poverty in repeated raids by roving bandits. As Law recalled, conditions became so bad that the family had to sell their land and give up their three servants; all four daughters had to quit school and help at home.

> My grandmother, mother, and an aunt all had bound feet, and it was so painful for them to get around. When they got up in the morning, I had to go fetch the water for them to wash up and carry the night soil buckets out. Every morning, we had to draw water from the well for cooking, for tea, and for washing. I would help grandmother with the cooking, and until I became older, I was the one who went to the village marketplace every day to shop.

Along with one other sister, Law was also responsible for sweeping the floor, washing dishes, chopping wood, tending the garden, and scrubbing the brick floor after each rainfall. In accordance with traditional gender roles, none of her brothers had to help. "They went to school. It was work for girls to do," she said matter-of-factly.

As in the case of Wong Ah So, cultural values and economic necessity led her parents to arrange a marriage for Law with a Gold Mountain man. Although aware of the sad plight of other women in her village who were married to Gold Mountain men—her own sister-in-law had gone insane when her husband in America did not return or send money home to support her—Law still felt fortunate: she would be going to America with her husband.

> I had no choice; we were so poor. If we had the money, I'm sure my mother would have kept me at home. . . . We had no food to go with rice, not even soy sauce or black bean paste. Some of our neighbors even had to go begging or sell their daughters, times were so bad. . . . So my parents thought I would have a better future in Gold Mountain.

Her fiancé said he was a clothing salesman in San Francisco and a Christian. He had a minister from Canton preside over the first "modern" wedding in his village. Law was eighteen and her husband, thirty-four. Nine months after the wedding, they sailed for America.

Jane Kwong Lee was born in the same region of China (Op Lee Jeu village, Toishan District, Guangdong Province) at about the same time (1902). But in contrast to Law Shee Low and Wong Ah So, she came from a higher-class background and emigrated under different circumstances. Her life story, as told in her unpublished autobiography, shows how social and political conditions in China made "new women" out of some like herself. Like Law and Ah So, Jane grew up subjected to the sexist practices of a patriarchal society. Although her family was not poor, her birth was not welcomed.

> I was the second daughter, and two girls in a row were one too many, according to my grandparents. Girls were not equal to boys, they maintained. Girls, after they married, belonged to other families; they could not inherit the family name; they could not help the family financially no matter how good they were at housework. In this atmosphere of emotional depression I was an unwanted child, and to add to the family sadness the weather seemed to be against me too. There was a drought, the worst drought in many years, and all the wells dried up except one. Water had to be rationed. My long (youngest) uncle went out to get the family's share daily. The day after I was born, the man at the well gave him the usual allotment, but my uncle insisted on obtaining one more scoop. The man asked why and the answer was, "We have one more mouth." Then, and only then, the villagers became aware that there had been a baby born in their midst. My grandparents were ashamed of having two granddaughters consecutively and were reluctant to have their neighbors know they had one more person in their family. They wanted grandsons and hoped for grandsons in the future. That is why they named me "Lin Hi," meaning "Link Young Brother." They believed in good

Wedding portrait of Law Shee Low and husband Low Gun (a.k.a. Low Gar Chong), Heungshan (now Zhongshan) District, Guangdong Province, China, 1921. (Courtesy of Law Shee Low)

omens and I did not disappoint them. My brother was born a year and a half later.[30]

Compared to Law's hard-working childhood, Jane lived a carefree life, playing hide-and-seek in the bamboo groves, catching sparrows and crabs, listening to ghost stories, and helping the family's *mui tsai* tend the vegetable garden. It was a life punctuated by holiday observances and celebrations of new births and marriages as well as the turmoil of family illnesses and deaths, droughts and floods, political uprisings and banditry.

Like Law, Jane came from a farming background. Her grandfather was successful in accumulating land, which he leased out to provide for the family. Her uncle and father were businessmen in Australia; their remittances made the difference in helping the family weather natural disasters and banditry and provided the means by which Jane was able to acquire an education at True Light Seminary in Canton. Social reforms and progressive views on women's equality at the time also helped to make her education possible:

Revolution was imminent. Progress was coming. Education for girls was widely advocated. Liberal parents began sending their daughters to school. My long [youngest] aunt, sixth aunt-in-law, godsister Jade and cousin Silver went to attend the True Light Seminary in Canton. Women's liberation had begun. It was the year 1911—the year the Ching [Qing] Dynasty was overthrown and the Republic of China was born.[31]

Her parents were among the liberal ones who believed that daughters should be educated if family means allowed it. Her father had become a Christian during his long sojourn in Australia, and her mother was the first in their village to unbind her own feet. From the age of nine, Jane attended True Light, a boarding school for girls and women sponsored by the Presbyterian Missionary Board in the United States. She completed her last year of middle school at the coeducational Canton Christian College. It was during this time that she adopted the Western name Jane. By then, "the Western wind was slowly penetrating the East and old customs were changing," she wrote.[32]

The curriculum stressed English and the three R's—reading, writing, and arithmetic—but also included classical Chinese literature. In addition, students had the opportunity to work on the school journal, learn Western music appreciation, and participate in sports—volleyball, baseball, and horseback riding. The faculty, all trained in the United States, exposed students to Western ideas of democracy and women's emancipation. During her last year in school, Jane, along with her classmates, was swept up by the May Fourth Movement, in which students agitated for political and cultural reforms in response to continuing foreign domination at the end of World War I:

> The 21 demands from Japan stirred up strong resentment from the students as well as the whole Chinese population. We boycotted Japanese goods and bought only native-manufactured fabrics. We participated in demonstration parades in the streets of Canton. Student delegates were elected to attend student association discussion meetings in Canton; once I was appointed as one of two delegates from our school. Our two-fold duty was to take part in the discussions and decisions and then to convince our schoolmates to take active parts in whatever action was decided. It was a year of turmoil for all the students and of exhaustion for me.[33]

By the time she graduated from middle school, Jane had decided she wanted to become a medical doctor, believing "it would give me not only financial independence, but also social prestige."[34] Her only other choices at the time were factory work or marriage. But further education seemed out of the question because her father's remittances from

Australia could no longer support the education of both Jane and her younger brother. Arguing that graduates trained in American colleges and universities were drawing higher salaries in China than local graduates, Jane convinced her mother to sell some of their land in order to pay her passage to the United States. Her mother also had hopes that she would find work teaching at Chinese schools in America and be able to send some of her income home. In 1922, Jane obtained a student visa and sailed for the United States, planning to earn a doctorate and return home to a prestigious academic post. Her class background, education, and early exposure to Western ideas would lead her to a different life experience in America than Law Shee Low and Wong Ah So, who came as obedient wives from sheltered and impoverished families.

Detainment at Angel Island

Like thousands of immigrants before them, Law Shee Low, Wong Ah So, and Jane Kwong Lee had to pass immigration inspection upon their arrival in America. In contrast to the frightening but relatively brief stay of European immigrants at Ellis Island in New York Harbor, most Chinese immigrant women experienced humiliation and despair during their extended detainment at the Port of San Francisco owing to the strict implementation of the Chinese Exclusion laws. Prior to the building of the Angel Island Immigration Station in 1910, Chinese immigrants were housed in a dilapidated wooden shed at the Pacific Mail Steamship Company wharf. The testimony of Mai Zhouyi, a missionary from Canton and wife of a Chinese merchant, describes the ordeal of detainment suffered by Chinese immigrant women. Locked in the shed for over forty days pending investigation of her right to land, she spoke out against the inhumane treatment she received there at a public gathering in Chinatown following her release:

All day long I faced the walls and did nothing except eat and sleep like a caged animal. Others—Europeans, Japanese, Koreans—were allowed to disembark almost immediately. Even blacks were greeted by relatives and allowed to go ashore. Only we Chinese were not allowed to see or talk to our loved ones and were escorted by armed guards to the wooden house. Frustrated, we could only sigh and groan. Even the cargo was picked up from the docks and delivered to its destination after custom duties were paid. Only we Chinese were denied that right. How can it be that they look upon us as animals? As less than cargo? Do they think we Chinese are not made of flesh and blood? That we don't have souls? Human beings are supposed to be the superior among all creatures. Should we allow ourselves to be treated like cargo and dumb animals?[35]

Her sentiments echo those of European immigrants who experienced Ellis Island as the "Island of Tears," of bars, cages, and callous brutality on the part of immigration officials. As Fannie Kligerman, who had fled the pogroms in Russia, recalled:

> It was like a prison. They threw us around. You know that children don't know anything. They would say, "Stay here. Stay there." And you live through it, you just don't fight back. And when it came to food we never had fresh bread, the bread was always stale. Where they got it, we don't know. . . . Everybody was sad there. There was not a smile on anybody's face. Here they thought maybe they wouldn't go through. There they thought maybe my child won't go through. There was such a sadness, no smile any place. . . . Just so much sadness there that you have to cry.[36]

Whereas most European immigrants remember the confusion of being quickly processed through the cursory physical, mental, and legal examinations, and the brief moment of fear at possibly being refused entry for reasons of health, morals, or finances, Chinese immigrants who passed through Angel Island have more haunting memories of being locked up in the "wooden building" for weeks and months, the fearful interrogation sessions where they were asked hundreds of questions regarding their past, and the frustration and humiliation of being treated as criminals for nothing more than the simple desire to enter the promised land. Ellis Island was an island not just of tears but also of hope for most European immigrants; for Chinese immigrants, however, Angel Island (nicknamed the "Ellis Island of the West" by immigration authorities) was a prison to men and women alike.[37]

Jane Kwong Lee's status as a student spared her the agony of Angel Island. Along with other first-class passengers who were members of the exempt classes, she had her papers inspected aboard ship and was allowed to land immediately.[38] In contrast, after their ship docked in San Francisco Bay, Law Shee Low and Wong Ah So were separated from their husbands and taken to Angel Island for physical examination and interrogation.

Like hundreds of other Chinese before her, Law had an unfavorable first impression of America via Angel Island.[39] Unaccustomed to disrobing before male doctors and presenting stool samples in a test for parasitic diseases, Chinese women suffered personal humiliation during the physical examination. "Those with hookworms had to go to the hospital," said Law. "Liver fluke was incurable, but hookworm was. There was a new bride who had liver fluke and was deported." After the physical examination, Law remembers being locked up indefinitely in the women's barracks with a dozen other Chinese women to await interrogation.

> It was like being in prison. They let us out for meals and then locked us up again when we came back. They brought us knitting things but we didn't know how. They were willing to teach us but we weren't in the mood. We just sat there all day and looked out the windows. . . . We didn't even care to go out to eat, the food was so bad. . . . The bean sprouts was cooked so badly you wanted to throw up when you saw it. There was rice but it was cold. I just took a few spoonfuls and left. Same food all the time. We began craving for salted fish and chicken. We wanted preserved bean paste. Their food was steamed to death; smelled bad and tasted bad. The vegetables were old and the beef was of poor quality and fatty. They must have thought we were pigs.

Fortunately for Law, her husband sent her some *dim sum* (Chinese savory pastries), fresh fruit, and Chinese sausages, which she gladly shared with other women in the barracks. "The Western woman we called Ma [Deaconess Katharine Maurer, appointed by the Women's Home Missionary Society of the Methodist Episcopal Church to tend to the needs of Chinese women at Angel Island] delivered it. Called our names. Searched it first for fear of coaching notes [to help her during her interrogation]," Law explained.

Finally, after ten days of waiting, Law was called to appear before the Board of Special Inquiry. Following the advice of the other women, she drank a few mouthfuls of cold water to control the fear within her.

> One woman who was in her fifties was questioned all day and then later deported, which scared all of us. She said they asked her about [life in China:] the chickens and the neighbors, and the direction the house faced. How would I know all that? I was scared. Fortunately, they didn't ask me all that. Just when I got married. When the interpreter asked me whether I visited my husband's ancestral home during the wedding, I said no because I was afraid he was going to ask me which direction the house faced like the woman told me and I wouldn't know. Evidently, their father [her husband] had said yes. So when they asked me again and I said no, their father, who was being interrogated at the same time the second time around, said, "*Choy!* You went back; why don't you say so?" The Westerner [immigration officer] hit the table with his hand [in ob-

jection] and scared me to death. So when he slapped the table, I quickly said, "Oh, I forgot. I did pass by [in the wedding sedan chair] but I didn't go in." So they let me land. But when they led me back to the barracks, I thought I would be deported so I cried. Later at 4 P.M., they called me to get on the boat to go to San Francisco and the others happily helped me gather my things together to leave.

Compared to others, Law's interrogation was unusual in that her husband was allowed to sit in and the process was concluded in one day. "It could have been because this church lady helped us," she suggested. It was generally known that a supporting letter from Donaldina Cameron of the Presbyterian Mission Home often helped get cases landed.

For many other Chinese immigrants, the ordeal at Angel Island was much more agonizing and prolonged. Because affidavits and records had to be reviewed and the testimonies given by immigrants and their witnesses corroborated, even the most expeditious case generally took at least a week. According to one study of procedures at Angel Island, "Each applicant is asked from two or three hundred questions to over a thousand. The records of the hearing generally runs in length from twenty to eighty typewritten pages, depending on the nature of the case."[40] In contrast, European immigrants at Ellis Island were asked a total of twenty-nine questions. In all the Chinese cases, the burden of proof rested on the detainee to show that he or she was not an inadmissible alien. For those who failed the interrogation—usually because of discrepancies in their answers to detailed questions relating to their family history or village life in China—appeals to the Commissioner of Immigration in Washington, D.C., led to additional expenses and extended stays at Angel Island of another six months to a year. According to the testimony of an immigration inspector who was assigned to the Angel Island Immigration Station from 1929 to 1940, "More than 75 percent passed the interrogation at Angel Island. Of those that were denied here, there was always an appeal to Washington and probably only 5 percent of those denied were ever really deported."[41] These statistics were similar in the experience of European immigrants at Ellis Island, where in general only 2 percent of them were deemed "undesirable aliens" and deported. But statistics do not reveal the different process that only Chinese immigrants were subjected to, a process different not only in degree but also in kind.

The disparate responses of Chinese men and women confronted by this harsh treatment reveal their respective gender roles as defined by their home culture and then adapted to their new environment at Angel Island. While the men passed the time actively—reading Chinese newspapers, playing sports outdoors in a fenced-in area, listening to Chinese phonograph records, and gambling or debating among themselves—the women sat around and waited quietly, some occupying their time with needlework. A few took advantage of the weekly walks outside under the watchful eyes of a guard. Whereas the men organized a Self-Governing Association for mutual assistance and to protest conditions at Angel Island, the women did not organize and seemed unable to voice objections to their harsh treatment. Their one defender and friend was Methodist Deaconess Katharine Maurer, known as the "Angel of Angel Island." Assigned to work among the Chinese detainees beginning in 1912, she shopped for the women, provided them with needlework materials, taught them the Bible and English, wrote letters, organized holiday programs for them, and administered to their various needs.[42] Men were able to vent their anger and frustrations by carving poems into the barrack walls, many of which are still visible today. Women, deprived of education, were less literate, and although some remember seeing lines of poetry on the barrack walls, most could not express themselves in writing.[43] One Chinese woman who was illiterate resorted to memorizing the coaching information on her family background by putting it into song.[44]

As women waited for the ordeal to pass, many shared the sentiments of a Mrs. Jew, who was detained on Angel Island the same year as Law Shee Low and Wong Ah So:

> There wasn't anything special about it. Day in, day out, the same thing. Every person had to be patient and tell herself, "I'm just being delayed, it doesn't matter." I never even bathed. I kept thinking each day that I would be ready to leave and as each day went by, I just waited. I didn't eat much, nor move around much, so I never perspired. I had no clothes to wash. . . . I kept thinking, "Had I known it was like this, I never would have wanted to come!"[45]

Confined in the barracks together for indefinite sentences, women maintained a pragmatic attitude and bonded in an effort to cope with the situation. They chatted with one another, shared whatever food they had, dressed one another's hair, consoled those who had failed the interrogation, and accompanied one another to the bathroom after hearing stories of women who had hung themselves there. When asked who comforted the women when they became depressed, Law replied:

Who was depressed? There were two women who had been there for three months. They didn't cry; didn't seem to care. They even sang sometimes and joked with the man who came in to do the cleaning. Whenever this foreign woman offered to take us out for walks, usually on Fridays, just the two would go. They were two friends and very happy and carefree. They had little going for them, but they managed to struggle on.[46]

Although sobbing was often heard in the women's barracks and there were known cases of suicide, this cultural attribute of "making do" helped many Chinese women through detainment at Angel Island. When finally granted permission to land, immigrant women like Law Shee Low and Wong Ah So tried to put Angel Island behind them as they began their new lives in America.

"New Women" in the Modern Era of Chinatown

The San Francisco Chinatown that Law Shee Low, Wong Ah So, and Jane Kwong Lee came to call home was different from the slum of "filth and depravity" of bygone days. After the 1906 earthquake and fire destroyed Chinatown, Chinese community leaders seized the opportunity to create a new "Oriental City" on the original site. The new Chinatown, in stark contrast to the old, was by appearance cleaner, healthier, and more modern with its wider paved streets, brick buildings, glass-plated storefronts, and pseudo-Chinese architecture. Dupont Street (now Grant Avenue), lined with bazaars, clothing stores, restaurants, newspaper establishments, grocery stores, drugstores, bookstores, and meat and fish markets, became the main business thoroughfare for local residents and a major tourist attraction by the time of the Panama-Pacific International Exposition in 1915.[47] But behind the facade of the "Oriental City," hastily built with tourism and business in mind, was a ghetto plagued by overcrowding, substandard housing, and poor sanitation. Dwelling units for bachelors were constructed above, below, and behind shops in crowded quarters and often with poor lighting and ventilation.[48] There were so few Chinese families then that little thought was given to their housing needs.

Aside from the change in physical appearance, Chinatown was also socially transformed by life under Exclusion. Internal economic and political strife mounted as the Chinese community—kept out of the professions and trades, and isolated within a fifteen-block area of the city—developed its own economic infrastructure, political parties, and social institutions. Merchant associations, trade guilds, and tongs fought over control of the distribution and commercial use of Chinatown's limited space and economic resources, often engaging in bloody warfare in the period from the 1880s to the 1920s. At the same time, strife developed among political factions that disagreed on the best strategy to save China. The Zhigongtang (the American counterpart of the Triad Society in China) favored restoring the Ming emperor; the Baohuanghui advocated a constitutional monarchy; and the Tongmenghui (forerunner of the Guomindang) saw a democratic republic as the answer to China's future. In an effort to establish order in the community, nurture business, and protect the growing numbers of families, the merchant elite and middle-class bourgeoisie established new institutions: Chinese schools, churches, a hospital, newspapers, and a flurry of organizations such as the Chinese Chamber of Commerce, Chinese American Citizens Alliance, Chinatown YMCA and YWCA, Christian Union, and Peace Society.[49] Many of these new social groups also formed alliances with outside law enforcement agents and moral reformers to eliminate gambling, prostitution, and drugs in an effort to clean up Chinatown's image. Their work was met with strong resistance from the tongs that profited by these vice industries, but the progressive forces eventually won out. As reported in the community's leading newspaper, *Chung Sai Yat Po (CSYP)*,[50] soon after the 1911 Revolution in China, queues and footbinding were eliminated, tong wars and prostitution reduced, and more of Chinatown's residents were dressing in Western clothing and adopting democratic ideas. Arriving in San Francisco Chinatown at this juncture in time gave immigrant women such as Wong Ah So, Law Shee Low, and Jane Kwong Lee unprecedented opportunities to become "new women" in the modern era of Chinatown.

DECLINE IN PROSTITUTION

Fortunately for Wong Ah So, prostitution was already on the decline by the time she arrived in San Francisco, thanks to the efforts of Chinese nationalists, Protestant missionaries, and those who supported the social purity movement. As her case demonstrates, Chinese women brought to the United States as prostitutes at this time continued to suffer undue hardships but benefited from the socio-historical forces intent on eliminating prostitution in the city. Moreover, it reveals the inner workings of the Chinese prostitution trade, the complicit role of Chinese madams in the illegal business, and the coping mechanisms Chinese prostitutes devised to deal with their enslavement.

Upon landing, Ah So's dreams of wealth and happiness vanished when she found out that her husband, Huey Yow, had in fact been paid $500 by Sing Yow, a madam, to procure her as a slave.

> When we first landed in San Francisco we lived in a hotel in Chinatown, a nice place, but one day, after I had been there for about two weeks, a woman came to see me. She was young, very pretty, and all dressed in silk. She told me that I was not really Huey Yow's wife, but that she had asked him to buy her a slave, that I belonged to her, and must go with her, but she would treat me well, and I could buy back my freedom, if I was willing to please, and be agreeable, and she would let me off in two years, instead of four if I did not make a fuss.[51]

For the next year, Ah So worked as a prostitute for Sing Yow in various small towns. She was also forced to borrow $1,000 to pay off Huey Yow, who was harassing her and threatening her life. Then, seeking higher profits, Sing Yow betrayed her promise and sold Ah So to another madam in Fresno for $2,500. "When I came to America," Ah So's story continues, "I did not know that I was going to live a life of slavery, but understood from women with whom I talked in Hongkong that I was to serve at Chinese banquets and serve as an entertainer for the guests. I was very miserable and unhappy. My owners knew this and kept very close watch over me, fearing that I might try to escape."[52]

Meanwhile, her family in China continued to write her asking for money. Even as her debts piled up and she became ill, she fulfilled her filial obligation by sending $300 home to her mother, enclosed with a letter that read in part:

> Every day I have to be treated by the doctor. My private parts pain me so that I cannot have intercourse with men. It is very hard. . . . Next year I certainly will be able to pay off all the debts. Your daughter is even more anxious than her mother to do this. As long as your daughter's life lasts she will pay up all the debts. Your daughter will do her part so that the world will not look down upon us.[53]

In another letter to her mother, aside from reconfirming her commitment to fulfill the responsibilities of a filial daughter, Ah So also expressed the desire to "expiate my sin" by becoming a Buddhist nun—the correct move by traditional moral standards.[54] She had indeed internalized the social expectations of virtuous Chinese women, putting these values to good use in helping herself cope with her present, desperate situation.

But before Ah So could realize her wish, help arrived. One evening at a tong banquet where she was working, she was recognized by a friend of her father's, who sought help from the Presbyterian Mission Home on her behalf. Ten days later, Ah So was rescued and placed in the care of Donaldina Cameron. As she wrote, "I don't know just how it happened because it was all very sudden. I just know that it happened. I am learning English and to weave, and I am going to send money to my mother when I can. I can't help but cry, but it is going to be better. I will do what Miss Cameron says."[55] A year later, after learning how to read Chinese and speak English and after becoming a Christian, Ah So agreed to marry Louie Kwong, a merchant in Boise, Idaho.

Her connections to Cameron and the Presbyterian Mission Home did not end there, though. A few years later, Ah So wrote to complain about her husband and to ask Cameron for advice. Louie Kwong had joined the Hop Sing Tong, refused to educate his own daughters (by a previous marriage), had struck her and refused to pay her old boarding fees in the Mission Home, and, worst of all, threatened to send for a concubine from China because she had not borne him a son.[56] This complaint to Cameron about her husband shows that she had evidently changed her attitude regarding traditional gender roles. In support, Cameron promptly sent a Chinese missionary worker to investigate the matter. It must have helped because five years later, in another letter to Cameron dated December 28, 1933, Ah So wrote about being happily married and "busy, very busy" raising her husband's three daughters, their own two sons and a daughter, plus an adopted daughter and a brother-in-law's ten-year-old son. Ah So had made it back to China only to find that her mother had died and entrusted her with the lives of her two younger brothers and two younger sisters. "I am very grateful and thankful to God that my husband is willing to care for these smaller brothers and [unmarried] sister and help them," she wrote. With the closing assurance that "the girls and I are getting along fine," she enclosed a photograph of herself with her husband and enlarged family.[57]

Wong Ah So's story harks back to the plight of the many Chinese women who were brought to the United States as prostitutes to fill a specific need in the Chinese bachelor society. By the 1920s, however, the traffic had gone underground and was on the decline. In 1870, the peak year of prostitution, 1,426 or 71 percent of Chinese women in San Francisco were listed as prostitutes. By 1900 the number had dropped

Wong Ah So, husband Louie Kwong, and family in 1933. (*Missionary Review of the World;* Judy Yung collection)

to 339 or 16 percent; and by 1910, 92 or 7 percent. No prostitutes could be found in the 1920 census,[58] although English- and Chinese-language newspaper accounts and the records of the Presbyterian Mission Home indicate that the organized prostitution of Chinese women in San Francisco continued through the 1920s. The last trial of a prostitution ring occurred in 1935,[59] in which damaging testimony by two courageous Chinese prostitutes—Leung Kwai Ying and Wong So—led to the conviction of Wong See Duck, a hardware merchant and longtime dealer in prostitution, and his three accomplices. The Exclusion Acts and other antiprostitution legislation passed in the late nineteenth century had succeeded in stemming the traffic, but not eradicating it. Even the earthquake and fire of 1906, which destroyed Chinatown, did not wipe out prostitution, for brothels were reopened in the new buildings. As law enforcers stepped in to curb the trade, prices escalated and ingenious methods were devised to circumvent the law. After the earthquake, prostitutes sold for $3,000, and the services of lawyers hired to keep them in the possession of their owners averaged $700 a case. By the 1920s, the price of a young Chinese woman in her teens had risen to as much as $6,000 to $10,000 in gold.[60]

To bypass immigration restrictions, women were coached to enter the country disguised as U.S. citizens or wives of U.S. citizens. One newspaper account reported that they came with "red certificates," a document issued to American-born Chinese females who had departed for China between 1880 and 1884. Although immigration inspectors suspected that these certificates—which were never marked "Canceled"—were being reused by women assuming bogus identities, they could not prove it, especially when an abundance of Chinese witnesses was on hand to vouch for the women's identities.[61] Still another newspaper account stated that American-born Chinese men were being paid to bring in "wives" when they returned from visits to China.[62] Other women reportedly came in disguised as theatrical performers, gained entry by bribing immigration officials, or were smuggled in as stowaways or across the Canadian or Mexican border. As the importation of women became more difficult, local sources were tapped, and the kidnapping of young women and the sales of *mui tsai* into prostitution increased.

Public opposition to prostitution and other social vices, spurred by female moral reformers and Chinese nationalist leaders, was on the rise in the early 1900s and contributed greatly to the demise of the trade. In 1900, Donaldina Cameron took over as superintendent of the Presbyterian Mission Home. The youngest daughter of Scottish sheep ranchers, Cameron was born in 1867, two years before her parents moved from New Zealand to California. At the age of twenty-five, after breaking off an engagement, she found her calling at the Presbyterian Mission Home, assisting matron Margaret Culbertson in her rescue work. Deeply religious, maternal, and committed to Victorian moral values, Cameron seemed the perfect choice for the job. Called *lo mo* (mother) by her young charges and *fan gwai* (foreign devil) by her critics in the Chinese community, she became well known for her rescue work. Numerous accounts describe in vivid detail the dangerous raids led by Cameron, who was credited with rescuing hundreds of Chinese slavegirls during her forty years of service at the Mission Home. Following the tradition established by Culbertson, Cameron provided a home for the rescued women, educated them, trained them in job skills, and inculcated them with Victorian moral values. The goal was to regroom them to enter society as Christian women. While some women chose to return to China under Christian escort, others opted to enter companionate marriages, pursue higher education, or become missionary workers.[63] Indeed, the Mission Home's goal was best expressed in a drama devised and presented by Cameron and her staff at a national jubilee held at the home in 1920:

> "The Pictured Years" showed the Chinese work under that militant Saint, Miss Culbertson, and also under Miss Cameron and Miss Higgins. Realistic scenes of rescue work in the cellars and on the roofs of the Chinese quarter were thrillingly presented; . . . the days of the exodus, after the earthquake and during the great fire of 1906; a prune-picking scene, prettily staged, showing the latest experience of our Chinese girls; and the climax—a tableau of a Christian Chinese family (the wife and mother a former ward of the Board), with the daughter in University cap and gown.[64]

Such was the ideal transformation that Cameron as the benevolent white mother wanted for her Chinese "harvest of waifs gathered from among an alien and heathen people," as she herself described them.[65] Yet she was also known for defending Chinese women against stereotyping, sensationalization, and ideas of racial determinism. Although some historians have criticized Cameron for her patronizing attitude and the regimented way in which she ran the Mission Home, those who knew and worked with her have only a high regard for her work among the Chinese.[66]

While Cameron and the Presbyterian Mission took the leadership role and credit for rescuing Chinese prostitutes, they did not work alone. They sought and received the cooperation of immigration and juvenile authorities, law enforcement agents, lawyers, the judicial system, and both the English- and Chinese-language presses, as well as civic-minded groups and individuals. Dramatic newspaper accounts of rescue raids helped to keep the antiprostitution campaign alive while at the same time promoting the Protestant women's crusade for moral reform. The celebrated case of Kum Quey was one such well-publicized story that shows not only Cameron's uncanny skills at rescue work, but also the extent of public support that was needed to free one Chinese girl from slavery.

According to popular accounts, Kum Quey was first rescued by Cameron from a brothel in Baker Alley and was living in the Mission Home when her owner and a constable from San Jose came to arrest her on trumped-up charges of grand larceny. Suspecting foul play, Cameron accompanied Kum Quey to Palo Alto and insisted on staying with her in jail while she awaited trial. Early that morning, three men broke into the jail cell, overpowered Cameron, and abducted Kum Quey. The men got a judge to hold an impromptu trial on a country road in their favor, and then forced Kum Quey into marrying one of them. Meanwhile, with the help of a Palo Alto druggist, a network of informants, and the cooperation of a policeman, Cameron caught up with the party in San Francisco and had one of the abductors arrested. Her retelling of the abduction, well covered in the local newspapers, incensed private citizens as well as Stanford University students. They condemned the affair and the complicity of local officials at a town hall meeting, raised funds for Kum Quey's cause, and stormed the local jail in protest.

Through her Chinese contacts, Cameron found out that Kum Quey had come to the United States two years before as one of seventy "Oriental maidens" for the Omaha Exposition but instead was put to work in a Chinatown brothel. With this new information in hand, Cameron solicited the help of immigration authorities. During the trial Kum Quey defied her owner's instructions, admitting instead that she had entered the United States illegally and been forced into prostitution. Not giving up, the abetting constable slipped out of the courtroom and attempted to run off with Kum Quey, but was successfully pursued and apprehended by an immigration officer and a private citizen. The court gave Kum Quey into Cameron's guardianship, and a San Jose grand jury later indicted the judge, constable, and abductors involved in the crime. And so happily ended the story of Kum Quey.[67]

The developments in the Kum Quey case were followed closely in *CSYP*. Edited by the Presbyterian minister Ng Poon Chew, the newspaper was influential in molding public opinion against Chinese prostitution in the context of its overall advocacy of the modernization of China and social reform in Chinatown. Numerous editorials in *CSYP* argued that *mui tsai* and prostitutes were signs of Chinese decadence in the eyes of Westerners and should be eradicated. Those involved in the prostitution trade were told to search their consciences and mend their ways. With the establishment of shelters for prostitutes rescued by missionaries and through the efforts of both the American and Chinese governments to suppress prostitution, "your profits will suffer and your reputation [will be] ruined," admonished one editorial.[68] Attempts were also made by middle-class institutions such as the Chinese consulate, Chinese Six Companies, Chinese Society of English Education, Chinese Students Alliance, Chinese American Citizens Alliance, and Chinese Cadet Corps to discourage if not stop the prostitution trade in Chinatown. All opponents had to put their lives at risk in the face of the overwhelming power of tongs in Chinatown, specifically the secret societies that had the most to lose from the demise of prostitution.[69]

By the early 1900s, however, the nation's purity crusade had reached the West Coast.[70] After the 1906 earthquake, Catholic, Protestant, and Jewish moral reformers joined efforts to mount an all-out attack against prostitution and commercialized vice in San Francisco. The American Purity Federation even threatened to seek a national boycott of the upcoming Panama-Pacific International Exposition if the city failed to clean up its image. In the atmosphere of progressivism that had gripped the entire nation, there rose a public outcry against venereal diseases and the international trafficking of white slavery—"the procuring, selling, or buying of women with the intention of holding or forcing them into a life of prostitution."[71] Melodramatic stories of innocent white women who had been tricked and forced into a brutal life of prostitution—not unlike the situation of Chinese prostitutes—drew the passionate ire of humanitarians and purity reformers committed to correcting sexual mores in the nation.[72] Their efforts culminated in the 1910 passage of the White Slave Traffic Act (also known as the Mann Act after its author, Congressman James R. Mann), which in effect outlawed the interstate and international trafficking in women.

As there were few convictions, and as the act did not address voluntary prostitution, individual states next stepped in with the enactment of "red-light" abatement laws, which sought to prosecute the brothel owners. Prostitution was finally curtailed in San Francisco after the California legislature passed the Red-Light Abatement Act in 1913. The first raid and test case under this act was a Chinese brothel at Dupont and Bartlett Alley owned by Woo Sam. The prosecution was upheld by both the U.S. District Court and the California Supreme Court in 1917, and after that, local police closed almost all brothels in the city, including those in Chinatown.[73] With the advent of World War I, further legislation was passed to wipe out the remaining traces of prostitution that had gone underground, this time in the interest of protecting the health of American soldiers. Public Law No. 12, signed into law by President Woodrow Wilson in 1917, authorized the secretary of war to arrest any prostitutes operating within five miles of a military camp. So many women were arrested as a result that prison and health facilities in San Francisco became seriously overcrowded. The antiprostitution measure continued to be enforced after the war, effectively shutting down the red-light district in San Francisco, including Chinatown, for good.[74] Any other traces of Chinese prostitution were left in the hands of Donaldina Cameron and Jack Manion, the police sergeant assigned to head the Chinatown detail in 1921, to finish off.[75]

By 1920, the ratio of Chinese males to females in San Francisco had dropped from 6.8 to 1 in 1910 to 3.5 to 1, and there were visible signs of family life. The Methodist Mission records showed fewer rescues and more attention being paid to abused wives, daughters, and orphans. By 1930, the sex ratio had declined further, to 2.8 to 1, and the Presbyterian Mission redirected its program to the growing numbers of neglected children. Wong Ah So—a direct beneficiary of the community's reform climate and the efforts of Protestant missionary women—was among the last to be rescued, Christianized, and married to a Chinese Christian. As the presence of wives and families increased and commercialized vices associated with a bachelor society declined, Chinese immigrant men shed their sojourner identities, and Chinatown assumed a new image as an upstanding community and major tourist attraction.

IMMIGRANT WIVES AS INDISPENSABLE PARTNERS

Immigrant wives like Law Shee Low also found life in America better than in China. They did not find streets paved with gold, but, practically speaking, they at least had food on the table and hope that through their hard work conditions might improve for themselves and their families. Although women were still confined to the domestic sphere within the borders of Chinatown, their contributions as homemakers, wage earners, and culture bearers made them indispensable partners to their husbands in their struggle for economic survival. Their indispensability, combined with changing social attitudes toward women in Chinatown, gave some women leverage to shape gender arrangements within their homes and in the community.

By the time Law arrived in 1922, women's roles and family life in San Francisco Chinatown had changed considerably relative to the nineteenth century. U.S. census sources provide an important quantitative view of that change. After steadily decreasing in numbers since 1890, the Chinese female population in San Francisco increased 22 percent between 1910 and 1920, primarily because of the immigration of wives and the birth of daughters. At the same time, the Chinese sex ratio in San Francisco dropped from 553.3 males per 100 females in 1900 to 349.2 in 1920 (see appendix table 3). Whereas most Chinese women in nineteenth-century San Francisco had been single, illiterate, and prostitutes, the 1920 manuscript census for the city indicates that 63 percent of Chinese women were married, only 28 percent were illiterate, and there were no prostitutes (see appendix tables 4 and 5). These figures attest to a new pattern of life in Chinatown. More men were becoming settlers and establishing families; and the community was heeding the call among social reformers to educate the women and eradicate prostitution.[76]

The manuscript censuses also indicate that fewer Chinese women were employed in 1920 (12 percent) as compared to 1910 (17 percent) and 1900 (31 percent) and that most of the employed women were seamstresses who worked at home (see appendix table 6). As was true in the previous two decades, in 1920 the majority of Chinese husbands worked as merchants, grocers, or business managers—occupations lucrative enough that these men could afford wives in America (see appendix table 7). Overall, however, more women probably worked for pay than were registered in the censuses. Indeed, except for wives of merchants and business managers, most women had to work for pay in order to supplement their husbands' low incomes.[77] Like European immigrant women, some ran boarding houses. Others helped in family businesses or did handwork at home for pay. Because such work was not considered "gainful labor" by census takers, though, they were not accounted for in the censuses. Moreover, language and cultural barriers most likely contributed to the inaccurate recording of census information on the Chinese population.

In 1910, a total of 521 families (76 percent of all families) had a nuclear structure: a married couple and an average of 3.5 children (as compared to 1.5 children in 1880). Although there were no three-generation families living under one roof in 1880, there were thirty such households in 1910. Thirty-seven households also included a mother-in-law. In 1880, 20 percent of the households had an average of two to three boarders. The 1910 census showed that 22 percent of the households with a female present had an average of 3.8 boarders, and 15 percent had an average of 2.5 relatives living in the household. These statistics show an increased tendency for families to take in boarders or relatives most likely out of economic necessity, for mutual kin support, or in compliance with work benefits accorded employees. In the absence of servants (only three households reported servants), it was most likely the wife who had to clean and cook for everyone else—no simple matter considering the living conditions then. For example, the Lee household, listed at 846 Clay Street in 1910, had a total of nineteen residents: a male head, who was listed as a grocer; his wife, who was listed as unemployed; their two children; two male relatives and one lodger, who apparently worked in the grocery store; and twelve other lodgers, who were listed variously as porters, laundrymen, janitors, farm workers, or fishermen. The wife, Lee Shee Jung, must have done all the housework for the entire household and the cooking for at least her immediate family and the three household members who worked for her husband—all without the assistance of any servants.

With the exception of twenty-one households (3 percent of the total), all of the families lived within the borders of Chinatown, which ran five blocks north and south between Sacramento and Broadway Streets and two blocks east and west between Stockton and Kearny Streets. Law Shee Low joined these families when she arrived in 1922. Her sheltered life in San Francisco Chinatown is typical of that of most immigrant wives, who by all appearances presented a submissive image in public but ruled at home. Their husbands continued to be the chief breadwinners, to control the purse strings, and to be the women's points of connection to the outside world. But, in the absence of the mother-in-law, immigrant wives held the reins in the household, maintaining the integrity of their families in an alien and often hostile land. With few exceptions, they were hard working, frugal, tolerant, faithful and respectful to their husbands, and self-sacrificing toward their children. As such, they were model wives in the traditional sense, but in America, they were also indispensable partners to their husbands in their efforts to establish and sustain family life.

Once released from Angel Island, Law moved into a one-room tenement apartment in Chinatown with her husband, where she lived, worked, and gave birth to eleven children, eight of whom survived. Owing to racial discrimination and economic constraints, they had little choice but to accept the poor, crowded housing conditions in Chinatown, which had been hurriedly built after the 1906 earthquake to accommodate bachelors, not families.[78]

> We rented a room on Stockton Street for eleven dollars a month. We did everything in that one room: sleep, eat, and sit. We had a small three-burner for cooking. There was no ice box, and my husband had to shop for every meal. We did not use canned goods and things like that. We ate only Chinese food. There was no hot water, and we would all hand wash our clothes. We used to dry them on the roof or in the hallways. That's what happens when you are poor. It was the same for all my neighbors. We were all poor together.[79]

Living in Chinatown encouraged the continuation of Chinese cultural practices and provided a sense of security and cultural sustenance for immigrants like Law. At the same time, however, it impeded their acculturation into American society.[80] Compared to Chinese women who lived outside Chinese communities, women in San Francisco Chinatown continued to speak Chinese only, eat Chinese food, dress in Chinese clothing, and maintain Chinese customs much longer. Although by the 1920s most of them wore their hair in short, pageboy cuts or in marcelled waves and walked in Western shoes with low heels, many, like Law, still wore Chinese clothing—colorful shirts with high collars and flared sleeves that stopped at the elbows, and lightly gathered skirts that fell below the knees.[81]

Since their first responsibility was to their families, immigrant wives like Law found themselves housebound, with no time to take advantage of English classes offered by the churches or to engage in leisure activities outside the home. While her husband worked in a restaurant that catered to black customers on the outskirts of Chinatown, Law stayed home and took in sewing. The only other job opened to women like her was shrimp peeling, which earned them half as much as sewing.[82] Like other immigrant women who followed traditional gender roles, Law believed that "nice Chinese ladies always stay home and take care of the house chores, children, and husband."[83] This arrangement was also preferred by employers, who made larger profits when they could pass overhead costs such as space, lighting, equipment, electricity, and supplies on to employees working at home.

> At first someone from the Low family clan brought me things to sew by the dozens and taught me how to do the seams and how to gather. This one teacher I had specialized in baby clothes with beautiful decorations, embroidered pockets and all. He taught me well, and I made over two dozen pieces a day. The pay was over a dollar a dozen.[84]

Even working twelve hours a day, her husband was bringing home only $60 a month, barely enough to cover rent and food. As she had one child after another, it was easier for her to stay home and sew, even though increasing numbers of women were working in Chinatown sewing factories that paid more than home work. When her husband didn't have time to do the shopping, she would pay to have groceries delivered. "That way with children at home, you didn't have to go out and waste time," she explained. "They would deliver pork and vegetables, and you could then cook it." When asked whether she felt imprisoned, she replied,

> There was no time to feel imprisoned; there was so much to do. We worked like crazy. We had to cook, wash the clothes and diapers by hand,

the floors, and sew whenever we had a chance to sit still. . . . Who had time to go out? It was the same for all my neighbors. We were all good, obedient, and diligent wives. All sewed; all had six or seven children.

Large families, which added to the burden of immigrant wives, were the norm in the 1920s. The Chinese birth rate in San Francisco was twice as high as the city-wide rate because of cultural values that favored large families and sons as well as the lack of knowledge of birth control among Chinese women. According to Law:

> Many had ten or more children. One had nine daughters and was still trying for a son. We didn't want that many, but we didn't know about birth control. Even if we didn't want it, we didn't have the money to go see the doctor. The midwife wanted us to have more babies. But even the midwife had a bad time because no one could afford to pay her. It was $25 a baby.

Law wasn't even aware that she was pregnant when she had the first of three miscarriages at home. The Chinese infant mortality rate was also high: 71 per 1,000 live births in 1929, compared to the city-wide rate of 49 per 1,000.[85] As was common for poor families in those days, all of Law's children were born at home with the help of neighbors or the local midwife. "Who could afford to go to the hospital?" she said. Only when one of her children caught pneumonia did she and her husband make use of the hospital, but by then to no avail. Their son was only three years old when he died. "He was a good boy. . . . I cried for a few years; it was so tragic," she recalled sadly. "We didn't have any money, and we didn't know better."

Although they had more girls (seven) than boys (one survived), her husband was more than willing to provide for them all regardless of sex. "He liked children," Law observed.

> Other men would beat their children and kick them out of the house. He wasn't like that. Other men would scold their wives for having girls. One woman who had four children told me her husband would drag her out of bed and beat her because she didn't want to have any more children. We heard all kinds of sad stories like that, but my husband never picked on me like that.

Fortunately for Law, her husband turned out to be cooperative, supportive, and devoted. Until he developed a heart condition in the 1950s, he remained the chief breadwinner, first cooking at a restaurant, then picking fruit in Suisun, sewing at home during the depression, and fi-

nally working in the shipyards during World War II. Although he refused to help with housecleaning or child care, he did all the shopping,
cooked the rice, and hung out the wash. In Law's estimation of him as
a husband,

> He wasn't bad. He did care about me. When he was afraid I wasn't eat-
> ing, he would tell me to eat more. He was just a bit stubborn. . . . When
> he was first unemployed, he went and played Chinese dominoes one night.
> When he came back in the early morning, I said to him when he pre-
> sented me with a chicken, "I don't want to eat your chicken; I don't like
> you to gamble." So he stopped going and went back to sewing. . . . I
> heard there was a building known as the Empress Building in Chinatown,
> where the wives beat the husbands if they were unemployed or did some-
> thing wrong. But it wasn't so in our building.

He also asked a "Jesus woman" to come teach her English. But after her
first baby, Law couldn't afford the time to study and told her not to come
anymore.

It was not until her children were older that Law went out to work
in the sewing factories and to the Chinese movies on Saturdays, but she
still did not leave the confines of Chinatown. Prior to that, she went out
so seldom that one pair of shoes lasted her ten years. Because they were
poor, she was especially frugal. She gave most of her earnings to her husband (since he did the shopping), made her own clothes and those of
her children, and managed to send periodic remittances home to her
family. The neighbors in her building were all from the same area of
Guangdong Province, and they became lifelong friends. They often chatted, and occasionally—three or four times a year—they would go out to
visit friends in the evening or go shopping together. So insular was her
life in Chinatown that to this day, Law still does not speak English or
dare go outside Chinatown alone. And she still continues to wear Chinese clothing.

Marxist feminists like Heidi Hartmann would characterize Law Shee
Low's life as oppressive. Because of the sexual division of labor at home
and in the workplace, women like Law remained confined to the domestic sphere and in a subordinate position vis-à-vis men.[86] But from
Law's vantage point, although her life was hard, it was not "oppressive."
She may have been restricted to the domestic sphere and stuck in low-
wage work, but she was not subordinate or totally dependent on her husband. Because she also contributed to the family income, bore the responsibility of running the household, and provided cultural sustenance,
their relationship was interdependent. As far as she was concerned, the

family's well-being was of prime importance. Given the extra measure of racism that put Chinese at a disadvantage in the labor market, what counted between her and her husband was not economic equality, but the adequacy of overall family income.

Nor did she regard her housework and child care duties as a form of exploitation. Although doubly burdened by wage labor and household responsibilities, immigrant wives like Law were taught to regard the home as their domain and to rule it proudly with an iron fist. Most were strict with their children, demanding unquestioning obedience, adherence to traditional gender roles, and the continued observance of folk religion, Chinese language and food, and the celebration of annual festivals such as Chinese New Year, Ching Ming, Dragon Boat, Girls' Day, Mid-Autumn, and Winter Solstice. Preparations were time-consuming, but Chinese women took their role as culture bearer seriously and did not shirk their duties regardless of how hectic their lives were. Providing a cultural refuge became an important way for Chinese women to instill ethnic pride in their children and help their families resist the cultural assaults and racist denigration inflicted by the dominant society. Indeed, their daily struggle to improve the quality of life for themselves and their families was in itself an act of resistance.[87] Although their family life exacted a heavy toll on their personal lives, it also served to sustain them. In this sense, family for them was a site of both oppression and resistance.[88] Working hard had meaning for Chinese women because it enabled them to fulfill their filial obligations as well as provide a better future for their children. Many women shared Law's pragmatic views about life in America:

> It took a lot of hard work, sweat, and tears, but for the sake of the children, it was all worth it in the end. . . . My kids have been good to me. They always remember my birthday. They chip in for my rent, electricity, insurance, everything; and they give me spending money. Thank God and thank heaven![89]

Abused wives who were less fortunate than Law found new avenues of resistance through the help of Chinese reformers, Protestant missionary women, and, in some cases, even the American legal system. *CSYP*, representing both the nationalist and Protestant perspectives, consistently supported women's emancipation, printing numerous editorials and articles that condemned "barbaric" practices such as footbinding, polygamy, slavery, and arranged marriages and advocated women's education and rights. "For centuries we have erred in teaching our women to be obedient . . . to not even step out into the courtyard but remain in their lonely quarters as captive prisoners. . . . Women with bound feet, weakened bodies, and undeveloped intelligence cannot attain equality with men," one editorial stated.[90] The newspaper was also an important disseminator of information about resources for women in the community, as it often covered talks by social reformers on women issues, followed the efforts of Protestant organizations to improve conditions for Chinese women, and announced educational classes for girls and women.[91]

Although most immigrant wives like Law did not read the Chinese newspapers, they were affected by public opinion as filtered through their husbands, neighbors, and the social reformers. Law noted that after the 1911 Revolution it was no longer considered "fashionable" to have bound feet, concubines, or *mui tsai* in China or in Chinatown. And as housebound as Law was, she was aware of the mission homes that rescued prostitutes, helped abused women, and provided education for children and immigrant women. Although Law never had cause to seek their help, a number of her peers used them to settle domestic disputes, usually in their favor.

Missionary records provide both a quantitative and qualitative picture of the nature and outcomes of these domestic problems. The Methodist Mission Home handled a total of twenty-three domestic cases involving Chinese women between 1903 and 1913, while the Presbyterian Mission Home had seventy-eight such cases between 1923 and 1928.[92] Although many of the cases stemmed from physical abuse, wives also came to the mission homes for help because their husbands smoked opium, drank excessively, practiced adultery or polygamy, or were negligent in providing for the family. In one case, a mother and her seventeen-year-old daughter sought help at the Methodist Home when they discovered that the prospective groom already had a wife and family in China. The home was able to help the daughter get out of the marriage and return to China.[93] Ex-residents of the mission homes, such as Wong Ah So, sought later help from the homes when problems arose in their marriages, often owing to cultural clashes in gender roles. There were also cases of widows who had been robbed of their inheritances, mistreated, or threatened by their husbands' relatives. One twenty-year-old widow had all her jewelry taken and was about to be sold into prostitution when missionary workers stepped in to protect her. She later married an interpreter, and the couple chose to return to China. In another case, a widow came to the home with her daughter seeking protection from her husband's relatives, who were demanding $500 cash and possession of the daughter before they would allow the woman to remarry.[94]

In most cases of family quarrels or mistreatment, missionary workers attempted to mediate by counseling the husbands and persuading them to agree to mend their ways. One husband accused of beating his wife promised to do better and then, by way of compliance, rented a room for her near the Methodist Mission Home. Another couple reconciled only after the husband signed an agreement stipulating that he would give up opium, treat his family more kindly and provide for them, and send the children to the Presbyterian Mission Home or to their grandmother should the wife die. If marital relations failed to improve, the homes would then temporarily house the wife and children at the husband's expense, help the woman find employment, and, if necessary, file on her behalf for divorce. Missionary workers did not regard arranged marriages as legitimate, so they had few qualms about breaking them up and encouraging women to remarry in the Western tradition. Annulments were also sought when undesirable arranged marriages involved minors. Here again can be seen the imposition of moral values on the part of missionary women that clashed with traditional Chinese views on marriage. While such intervention was likely resented by most Chinese in the community, it did provide a way out for Chinese women in abusive situations.

Whereas divorce was increasing in the white middle class by the 1920s, it remained rare among Chinese American women. No woman was listed as divorced in the 1900 or 1920 manuscript censuses for San Francisco. Only one woman was listed as such in 1910—a twenty-year-old immigrant who resided at the Presbyterian Mission Home. Between 1867 and 1929, the divorce rate rose 2,000 percent in the United States, and by the end of the 1920s more than one in every six marriages ended in court.[95] For Chinese Americans, the divorce rate in 1920 was only five times as great as that in 1890. Most of these cases were filed by missionary women on behalf of rescued prostitutes or abused wives.[96] Chinese women such as Mrs. Chan Sung Chow Bow, who filed for divorce on her own, were exceptional. According to newspaper accounts, she sued for divorce in 1921 because her husband gambled and refused to take her out, "telling her that movies and other amusement places were intended for men and not for women." As she argued, that might be all right in China, where they were married in 1911, but it was not acceptable in San Francisco, where she observed that "as many women as men attend the movies and other places of amusement."[97] Yet another woman knew how to take advantage of this legal option when she wrote Donaldina Cameron in 1923, asking, "Let me enter your Home and study English [because] I am going to divorce with my husband for the sake of free from repression."[98] Even with the help of Protestant missionaries, it was not an easy decision for Chinese women to file for divorce. As Mrs. Hsieh Gin, a long-time resident of Chinatown, recalled, "In 1929, there was one divorced woman in Chinatown, and she was a marked woman. Men made nasty remarks to her while women even refused to talk to her."[99] The Chinese community may have been willing to support women's emancipation, but it was not ready to condone divorce.

INTO THE PUBLIC SPHERE: WAGE WORK

Although housebound because of cultural constraints and child care responsibilities, immigrant women like Law Shee Low were still able to achieve a degree of socioeconomic mobility and to some extent reshape gender relations. But as the anthropologist Michelle Zimbaldist Rosaldo once argued, women remain oppressed, lacking value and status, as long as they are confined to the private sphere, cut off from other women and the social world of men. One way women could gain power and a sense of value was by transcending domestic limits and entering the men's world.[100] In some ways, this framework is applicable to Chinese immigrant women like Jane Kwong Lee, who did indeed attain social mobility and status after she entered the public sphere as a wage earner and social activist. Nevertheless, as feminist critics of the public/private dichotomy have pointed out, female devaluation has no one cross-cultural cause. Other related factors, such as class, race, sexuality, institutional setting, place, and time, need to be acknowledged as well.[101] In Jane's situation, her class and educational background facilitated her entry into the public sphere, but she still encountered difficulties owing to institutional racism and sexism.

Compared to Wong Ah So and Law Shee Low, Jane Kwong Lee had an easier time acclimating to life in America. Not only was she educated, Westernized, English-speaking, and unencumbered by family responsibilities, but she also had the help of affluent relatives who provided her with room and board, financial support, and important contacts that enabled her eventually to strike out on her own. B. S. Fong's family, with whom she stayed, lived in a three-bedroom unit over a Chinatown storefront. Jane had her own bedroom. During the first few weeks after her arrival she was taken shopping, to restaurants and church, to visit relatives, and introduced to a group of young women who took her hiking. Arriving in the middle of a school semester, she was unable to enroll in a college, so she decided to look for a job to support herself.

In spite of her educational background and qualifications, she found that only menial jobs and domestic service were open to her. "At heart I was sorry for myself; I wished I were a boy," she wrote in her autobiography. "If I were a boy, I could have gone out into the community, finding a job somewhere as many newcomers from China had done."[102] But as a Chinese woman, she had to bide her time and look for work appropriate for her race and gender. Thus, until she could be admitted to college, and during the summers after she enrolled at Mills College, Jane took whatever jobs were open to Chinese women. She tried embroidery work at a Chinatown factory, sorting vegetables in the wholesale district, working as a live-in domestic for a European American family, peeling shrimp, sorting fruit at a local cannery, and sewing flannel nightgowns at home. Finding all of these jobs taxing and low-paying, she did not stay long at any of them; but she came away with a better appreciation of the diligence and hard work that immigrant women applied to the limited jobs open to them. She described one job at a Chinese-owned cannery:

> We worked in rows alongside immigrant women from Italy and other European countries. First we sorted cherries. I liked cherries so much, I just ate, ate, and ate. Then we sorted apricots. That was easy. After apricots, we had to open peaches. I was so slow at it I hardly made any money. With cherries and apricots, I could make a dollar a day, but with peaches, I couldn't keep up with the women who worked very fast and made almost ten dollars a day because they were used to doing field work in China.[103]

Here she acknowledged the class difference between herself and peasant women from China, knowing full well that while she could leave these jobs and move on to something better, they often did not have the same option.

As was true for European immigrant women, the patterns of work for Chinese women were shaped by the intersection of the local economy, ethnic traditions, their language and job skills, and family and child care needs, but in addition, race was an influential factor.[104] At the time of Jane's arrival, San Francisco was experiencing a period of growth and prosperity. Ranked the eighth largest city in the country, it was the major port of trade for the Pacific Coast and touted as the financial and corporate capital of the West. Jobs were plentiful in the city's three largest economic sectors—domestic and personal service, trade and transportation, and manufacturing and mechanical industries—but they were filled according to a labor market stratified by race and gender. Native-born white men occupied the upper tier, consisting largely of white-collar professional and managerial positions; foreign-born white men dominated the middle tier, which included the metal and building trades and small merchants; and minority men were concentrated in the bottom tier as laborers, servants, waiters, teamsters, sailors, and longshoremen. In a similar racial scaling, native-born white women occupied the professional, manufacturing, trade, and transportation sectors; white immigrant women, the domestic and transportation sectors; and minority women, personal and domestic services. Within this occupational hierarchy, most Chinese could find work only in the bottom tier. Chinese men worked chiefly as laborers, servants, factory workers in cigar and garment shops, laundrymen, and small merchants, while Chinese women, handicapped further by gender, worked primarily in garment and food-processing factories for low piece-rate wages.[105]

The majority of Chinese factory women were employed in the garment industry, which had been dominated by Chinese men since the 1870s. But as competition from Eastern seaboard manufacturers with superior equipment and labor resources cut into the margin of profit and lowered wages, the ranks of male operators shrank, and garment factories began looking to Chinese women as a source of cheap labor. As early as 1906, a Chinese sewing factory advertised jobs for thirty women workers in *CSYP*. Still, it wasn't until women's emancipation took hold in China that they began to leave the home to work in Chinatown factories.[106] After World War I, Chinese immigrant women came to dominate the trade, working in Chinatown sweatshops that contracted work from white manufacturers. By 1930, there were over three hundred Chinese women employed in forty-six shops, sewing ladies' and male workers' garments for substandard wages and without the benefit of a labor organization.[107]

According to an Industrial Welfare Commission investigation in 1922, Chinese women operated power machines and did handwork, pressing, and finishing for piece rates that fluctuated between factories and depended on the complexity of the task at hand. Aprons ranged from $0.60 to $1.75 a dozen, and nightgowns from $1.10 to $1.50 a dozen. Coveralls were $0.45 a dozen, while shirts and overalls were $1.00 a dozen. Those making buttonholes earned $0.30 a shirt, while those sewing on buttons made $0.18 a dozen. Based on the reported weekly earnings of women who did similar piece-rate work at home, we can calculate that the wages of garment workers averaged $31 a month.[108] In contrast, Chinese houseboys averaged $80 a month, and Chinese cooks, $95 a month in 1926.[109] As no time records were kept and there was no set pay period, and as women worked on an irregular schedule that revolved around family responsibilities, it was impossible for the Industrial Welfare Commission investigator to determine whether state minimum wages were being paid, though it was obvious that the eight-hour law was being violated. There was at least one indication of dual wages: one woman told the investigator that she earned 10 cents less per dozen sewing on fancy buttons than the men. With inadequate child care services in the community, most worked with their children close by or had their babies strapped to their backs. Women took breaks whenever family duties called. In the investigator's opinion, sanitary provisions were inadequate, particularly ventilation and lighting, but the toilet facilities were fairly clean.[110]

Unlike the situation for Jewish women in the New York garment industry, Chinese women remained trapped in this seasonal, low-wage occupation with no opportunity for upward mobility. The garment industry in both New York and San Francisco operated under the same contracting system, in which manufacturing firms farmed out work orders to contractors who produced the clothing with the help of sweatshop labor paid on a piece-rate basis. Jewish and Chinese contractors who set up small sewing factories in their respective ethnic enclaves drew their cheap labor from a network of kin and *landsleit* (same geographic origins) connections. Whereas both Jewish men *and* women were recruited to the trade in New York, only Chinese women were available and willing to do garment work in San Francisco by the 1920s. Although Jewish women worked at a disadvantage because of the sexual division of labor (in which women are given the harder and less profitable tasks to perform) and dual wages (in which women are paid less than men for the same work), they had more options than Chinese women to change their circumstances. Jewish daughters could be promoted from low-paying, unskilled jobs to better-paying, skilled jobs within a factory, move on to work for larger factories outside the ghetto, and organize to improve conditions in the workplace.[111] Chinese immigrant women, lacking the same language skills and political consciousness and further hindered by racism, often could not avail themselves of the same opportunities.

Immigrant women who worked outside Chinatown in the 1920s also experienced discrimination on the basis of race as well as gender and cultural differences. The records of the Chinese YWCA provide three concrete examples of the extent of this discrimination. In one large cigar factory that employed fifty to sixty Chinese to strip tobacco, one-third of whom were women, Chinese workers worked in a separate room from non-Chinese workers and were paid only half the minimum wage. According to the YWCA worker who investigated the situation, "This group of Chinese did not speak any English and had no knowledge of a minimum wage law, nor did they know of provisions for piece rate." In a similar case, a fruit preserve factory that employed a large number of non-English-speaking Chinese women continued to pay the women at the old rate, while English-speaking European workers who knew about the raise in the minimum wage and demanded such were paid at a higher rate. In the third case, Chinese immigrant women employed at a glacé fruit factory contracted sugar poisoning because the employer had not printed warnings in Chinese of job-related dangers.[112]

Given these circumstances, for Jane Kwong Lee, being Chinese and a woman was a liability in the job market, but because she spoke English, was educated, and had good contacts among middle-class Chinese Christians, she was better off than most other immigrant women. She eventually got a scholarship at Mills College and part-time work teaching Chinese school and tutoring Chinese adults in English at the Chinese Episcopal Church in Oakland. After earning her bachelor's degree in sociology, she married, had two children, and returned to Mills, where she received a master's degree in sociology and economics in 1933. She then dedicated herself to community service, working many years as coordinator of the Chinese YWCA and as a journalist and translator for a number of Chinatown newspapers.

Most immigrant women, however, because of their limited skills and economic needs, had no choice but to take menial jobs. Wong Shee Chew, whose husband was injured in a tong battle in 1918, supported her two sons single-handedly by laboring in a cannery from 6 A.M. to 8 P.M., six days a week. She also peeled shrimp and sewed garments on the side.[113]

Margaret Leong Lowe, a widow with three children, embroidered flowers and sewed evening gowns to support her family. She said,

> I worked about six days a week. Sometimes I bring home work. I never go to somebody's house. I haven't got time. Sometimes the next door neighbor comes over to my house to talk a little bit. Sunday? Same work

at home. Take three children to Sunday church. I be mother, I be father. I had to make money and take care of children. . . . I worked fifty-two years. Seventy-two years old stopped. I worked my whole life.[114]

For women who worked outside the home, it was not an easy task juggling the double responsibilities of homemaker and wage earner. But as long as there were jobs for them and working outside paid more than home work, women were compelled to become factory laborers out of economic necessity. The piece-rate system and flexible schedule in some ways worked to the advantage of both employers and employees. The latter gained by being able to work whatever hours they could depending on family duties, while the former profited by paying women at piece rates they set. Against the backdrop of a cramped and unsanitary working environment, a grueling pace of work, and downward pressure on wages, this system also accounted for the unstructured work style, personal autonomy, and congenial atmosphere that made garment work more bearable to both Jewish and Chinese women. As the Industrial Welfare Commission investigator observed in 1922:

> Most of the women drift into the factory from ten to eleven in the morning. They return home when the children are due, around luncheon and at three in the afternoon before they go to the Chinese school. They give them their bread and butter or whatever corresponds to it in Chinese. Children who were in the plant frequently needed the mothers' attention and there was cessation of work very often when we came into a workroom. Sometimes the power was shut off, so that no one missed anything of our business. There was stoppage too when a worker felt the need of a cup of tea, the tea caddy being a feature of several places.[115]

Joining the labor market proved to be a double-edged sword for Chinese immigrant women: on the one hand, their earnings helped some to support their families and elevate their socioeconomic status; on the other hand, they became exploited laborers in the factory system, adding work and stress to their already burdensome family life.[116] As immigrants and women of color, they were relegated to the lowest rungs of the labor market. On the positive side, however, working outside the home offered women social rewards—a new sense of freedom, accomplishment, and camaraderie. As was true for Jewish women who worked in the neighborhood garment shop, Chinese women developed long-lasting relationships with their employers and with fellow employees who shared a common past, culture, geographic origin, and concern for one another's well-being. The sewing factory was more than just a workplace.

It was an arena for social interactions, where women could learn from one another, share problems, support one another, bicker and make up, and pass the time with storytelling and jokes, gossip and news, and singing while they worked. As one study pointed out, "It is apparent that some go to work in factories merely for a pastime so that they can mingle in groups and pass the time away quicker."[117] Working outside the home also meant that Chinese women were no longer confined to the home; they were earning money for themselves or the family, and they were making new acquaintances and becoming exposed to new ideas. Some used their earnings to send remittances back to their families in China, while others invested in jewelry and property. As Jane Kwong Lee observed, having money to spend made the women feel more liberated in America than in China: "They can buy things for themselves, go out to department stores to choose their own clothes instead of sewing them."[118] Once released from the confines of the home and exposed to the outside world, they also became more socially aware, and some were even drawn to community activism.

INTO THE PUBLIC SPHERE: COMMUNITY WORK

For working-class women like Law Shee Low, family and work responsibilities consumed all their time and energy, leaving little left over for self-improvement or leisure activities, and even less for community involvement. This was not the case for a growing group of educated, middle-class women who, inspired by Christianity, Chinese nationalism, and Progressivism, took the first steps toward community activism in Chinatown. Prominent among these early leaders and activists were the wives and daughters of merchants and Protestant ministers.

Chinese women's efforts to organize for self-improvement and community service paralleled those of the white and black women's club movements, although Chinese women's clubs developed much later and followed a different course in certain respects. While white and black women started their clubs in the early and late nineteenth century, respectively, the first major Chinese women's club in America—the Chinese Women's Jeleab [Self-Reliance] Association—did not appear until 1913. As Gerda Lerner points out, women's organizations usually got going only after a sizable group of educated, middle-class women with some leisure emerged.[119] Given their later arrival and smaller numbers in America, Chinese women were slower than white and black women in developing the necessary leadership for organized activity. The organizational structure of these women's clubs was similar, though, since black and Chinese women patterned their clubs after those of white women. Indeed, one of the reasons black and Chinese women's clubs formed in the first place was that both groups were excluded from white women's clubs. Middle-class values such as support for education, socioeconomic mobility, and community improvement formed the basis for most women's organizations, but white women were more interested in self-improvement and gender equality, black women in racial equality, and Chinese women in national salvation for China.[120] The driving force behind Chinese immigrant women's entry into the public sphere was the well-being of their family, community, and nation.

The Protestant churches were the first to encourage Chinese women's participation in organized activities outside the home, as evidenced by the small but visible number of Chinese women who attended Sunday services, English classes, meetings, outings, and Christmas programs sponsored by churches in the early 1900s. At a time when respectable women were still seldom seen in public, these regular outings were often the only occasion on which women left their homes. This point was made in a *San Francisco Chronicle* interview with Foo Tai, "a Christianized Chinese woman." According to the reporter, Foo Tai spent her day at home cooking, sewing, and caring for her baby while her husband worked outside as a cook. An educated woman, she seldom went out *except* to attend church meetings as president of the Chinese Women's Society of the Baptist Mission or to shop at the local stores.[121] A number of other churches helped organize similar Chinese women's societies to encourage involvement in Christian activities. Members of the (Congregational) Mothers and Daughters Society, (Presbyterian) Circle of the King's Daughters, and (Methodist) Missionary Society met regularly to have lunch or socialize, and paid dues to help support the work of Bible women in their home villages in China.[122]

Chan Fuk Tai, an educated woman who was married to a pharmacist, also seldom went out except to teach Bible study, Chinese language, and embroidery to Chinese girls at the Baptist church. According to her daughter Dora Lee Wong, it was the one chance she had to mingle with other Chinese women, many of whom were the wives of Chinese ministers. "And she had quite a large class of students—girls who came from well-to-do merchant families," Dora added.[123] The church thus provided educated, middle-class women such as Foo Tai and Chan Fuk Tai entry into the public sphere, an opportunity to interact with other women of like mind, and a means to develop leadership skills. Indeed,

Chinese women committed to the Christian cause were among the earliest women leaders in the community to organize events on behalf of women, the church, and national salvation. For example, Mrs. Ng Poon Chew (a.k.a. Chun Fah), who was brought up and educated at the Presbyterian Mission Home, was indispensable to her husband in his role as minister, *CSYP* editor, and champion for civil rights and Chinese nationalism. She was also actively involved in the establishment of the Chinese YWCA in 1916, led many fund-raising drives on behalf of China and the Chinese community, and, along with other Chinese Christian wives, took the initiative to sponsor community forums on nationalist and women's issues.[124]

Chinese women's involvement in church activities expanded their gender roles, in effect. The Won family, for example, was first exposed to Christianity when a Chinese missionary came to their house to tell them Bible stories. The five daughters in the family were encouraged to attend an embroidery class at the Methodist church, and all were baptized at the Congregational church. They then persuaded their mother, Wong Ho, to attend church as well. "We were very fortunate that mother listened to us and was willing to go to church and to some of the meetings," said one of the five daughters, Won King Yoak. "By associating with other church members, my mother became more open-minded. We were all well read and up-to-date with the latest news."[125] The women in the family later became the first Chinese American women to join Dr. Sun Yat-sen's revolutionary party and to be married in the Western tradition.

One of the earliest Christian organizations to serve Chinese American women, and certainly the longest-lasting, was the Chinese YWCA, established in 1916 and still functioning today in San Francisco Chinatown.[126] Its homogeneous membership, reflecting the segregated living patterns in existence even today, is indicative of a time when Chinese women were excluded from both white female and Chinese male organizations. Unlike YWCA branches in the South, however, the Chinese YWCA worked from the very beginning to garner the involvement and support of Chinese women and the Chinatown community in all aspects of its operations[127]—a strategy more in keeping with the national organization's goals of inclusiveness, local autonomy, and indigenous programs. It also paralleled the YWCA's efforts in China at the time, which sought to improve literacy, health care, and job and leadership skills among women who were assuming new roles because of industrialization.[128] In San Francisco, Chinese Christians, particularly educated

Chinese YWCA Board of Directors, 1920s. Emily Fong (Mrs. B. S. Fong) and Chun Fah (Mrs. Ng Poon Chew) are in the first row, second and third from left; Won King Yoak (Mrs. Daniel Wu) is in the back row, fourth from left. (Courtesy of Chinese YWCA, San Francisco)

middle-class women like Mrs. Ng Poon Chew, Mrs. Theodore Chow, the wife of a Methodist pastor, and Mrs. H. Y. Chang, the wife of the secretary of the Chinese Legation, were involved in the planning stages of the Chinese YWCA. Although the local branch was headed by white women until Rose Chew was appointed in 1932, a predominantly Chinese board of directors and bilingual staff set policies, implemented programs, and handled casework. By 1929, all but one of the board members were Chinese women—the wives of merchants and ministers as well as single women with professional backgrounds.

The YWCA was well regarded by progressive elements in the Chinese community because of the organization's promotion of Chinese nationalism. According to an editorial in *CSYP*, "The hand that rocks the cradle rules the world. . . . By helping our women develop morally, intellectually, physically, and socially . . . the YWCA is benefiting the family and the future citizens of tomorrow and, therefore, the Chinese community as well as our country."[129] The YWCA nurtured this positive image by making extensive use of the Chinese press to publicize its programs and by maintaining direct involvement in community and fundraising activities, such as Red Cross work, benefits for Chinese Hospital, famine and war relief work for China, receptions for Chinese dignitaries, and Chinese Independence Day parades. The YWCA also took the leadership role in promoting better housing, health, and child care services and countering negative images of Chinese Americans in movies and Chinatown tours. Its repeated successful drives for new members, the Community Chest, and the YWCA capital fund speak well of the relentless efforts of Chinese women who were committed to the organization and reflect the wide support the YWCA enjoyed in the community. During the first year of its operation, 1916, the organization attracted 280 members. By 1920 it had grown to 500 members, and five years later, to 699 members. But its programs and services reached beyond these numbers, serving an average of 15,000 persons a year in the 1920s. Even in the midst of the depression, women who were earning only $1.25 a day gave $1.00 to renew their annual membership, and the community came through with $25,000 to help build a new facility at the organization's present site on Clay Street.

During its first fifteen years, and before the emergence of the second generation, the Chinese YWCA focused on serving immigrant women with home visits, English classes, advice on household sanitation and baby care, interpreting services, and help with employment, immigration, and domestic problems. Similar to the YWCA's program in China, the purpose of these services was less to convert souls than to Americanize the foreign-born and improve their working and living conditions. At a time when social workers were not yet on the scene, the YWCA, along with the Mission Homes, was an important resource for women in need. As the following case shows, Chinese staff were sensitive to the needs of their clients and effective in helping them resolve their problems. During the time that Florence Chinn Kwan was associate secretary of the Chinese YWCA, from 1921 to 1923, she encountered a young woman who had been forced into an arranged marriage. The husband had died of tuberculosis early on in the marriage, and the mother-in-law was intolerable. The widow asked Florence to help her escape to the Presby-

Participants in Well Baby Contest sponsored by Chinese YWCA and Department of Public Health, 1928. (Courtesy of Chinese YWCA, San Francisco)

terian Mission Home. "So, little by little, when she came to the YWCA for English class, she'd bring her jewelry to me and I would keep it for her. Then one day I took her to the home. She taught Chinese there, became a Christian, and never remarried."[130] Immigrant women also came to the YWCA for help when they needed an interpreter or when they felt unfairly treated at work.

Americanization efforts on the part of the YWCA were directed much more strongly at second-generation daughters than at immigrant mothers. Yet one area where the American way was pushed was child care, as exemplified by the Well Baby Contest that the YWCA co-sponsored with the city's Public Health Department in 1928. Part of a national campaign promoted by the National Council of Mothers to lower infant mortality by educating mothers about infant hygiene, the contest was distinctly American.[131] Even so, Chinese women responded enthusiastically because of the pride they took in their children's well-being as well as the community effort that went into the event. Over sixty mothers entered 176 babies ranging in age from six months to five years in the contest. Three babies were chosen as the healthiest by physicians of

Chinese Hospital and awarded prizes. Follow-up workshops were held at the YWCA on baby care, and the book used by the winning baby's mother, *Baby Diet,* was translated into Chinese for the benefit of other immigrant mothers. Through such cooperative programs and the day-to-day services it offered immigrant women, the Chinese YWCA succeeded in helping them with their personal problems, changing their attitudes toward Western institutions, and drawing some out of their homes into the public arena for self-improvement and social interaction.

Christian organizations such as the YWCA were not the only force having an impact on Chinese women's lives during this time; the intense nationalistic spirit that took hold in the early twentieth century also affected Chinese women in far-reaching ways. Not only did the call for modernization include the need to improve conditions for Chinese women, but reformers also solicited women's active participation in national salvation work. Fund-raising for disaster relief and the revolution in China opened up opportunities for women to become involved in the community, develop leadership abilities, and move into the male-dominated public sphere. In 1907, for example, *CSYP* printed an article about flood and famine in the lower Yangtze River area, appealing specifically to Chinese women in the United States to follow the example of American women in other cities who had already donated over $430,000. The article encouraged the growing numbers of literate Chinese women to take heed and help spread the word among women everywhere.[132] When the same area was hard hit by another natural disaster in the early part of 1911, women participated in a program of songs and drama sponsored by the Presbyterian Church and, later, by the Chinese Six Companies to raise money.[133] These efforts on the part of Chinese women established a pattern of community involvement that would repeat itself each time a nationalist or community cause demanded their help, thus furthering women's participation in public affairs.

Chinese American women first entered the political arena in support of the 1911 Revolution. The Tongmenghui, the revolutionary party founded by Dr. Sun Yat-sen to overthrow the Qing dynasty and establish a republic in China, was the earliest organization to accept them into its ranks. Several dozen women—primarily relatives of Tongmenghui men—are known to have joined the San Francisco branch in 1910, making it the first sexually integrated organization in San Francisco Chinatown.[134] Among them were Wong Ho and her five daughters, who had harbored Sun in their home during one of his secret visits to San Francisco. Wong Ho's son, Won Hongfei, was one of the founding members of the San Francisco branch of the Tongmenghui, and he later served as Dr. Sun's personal secretary in China. It was he who encouraged his mother to allow all the girls to attend church, become educated, and contribute to the revolutionary effort. Despite the objections of relatives who believed that women should not be seen in public, Wong Ho later allowed her daughters to sit on a decorated float during the 1912 celebration of the founding of the Chinese Republic. Soon after, Lilly King Gee Won, one of the daughters, followed the revolution to China, where she spent the next sixty-eight years of her life helping to build a new China.[135]

In support of the revolution, women in China participated in benefit performances, enlisted in the army, and engaged in dangerous undercover work. Although far from the war front, Chinese women in San Francisco, gripped by the same patriotic fervor, moved into the public arena to do their share. They made "speeches of fire and patriotism" that called for the destruction of the Manchu dynasty and for woman's suffrage in China; they donated money and jewelry for the cause; and they helped with Red Cross work—doing fund-raising, preparing bandages and medicines, and sewing garments for the war effort—sometimes under the auspices of Protestant churches, other times under the banner of the Women's Young China Society.[136] A core group of women, including the Won sisters, attended political rallies, helped roll bandages at the Congregational church, and made handcrafted items to sell at fund-raising events.

The national crisis encouraged changes in gender roles for women in China and America, inspiring them to become "new women" like Qiu Jin. Born into the gentry class, Qiu Jin was an accomplished poet, horseback rider, and fencer. In response to the failure of the 1898 reforms and the Allied sacking of Beijing during the Boxer Rebellion, she resolved to help save China and to fight for women's rights. When her arranged marriage proved a failure, she left her conservative husband and went to study in Japan. There she became involved in radical politics and the Tongmenghui.[137] Like Sieh King King, she was both a nationalist and a feminist, as evidenced in her actions and her writings. For example:

Women's Rights

We want our emancipation!
For our liberty we'll drink a cup,
Men and women are born equal,

Why should we let men hold sway?
We will rise and save ourselves,
Ridding the nation of all her shame.
In the steps of Joan of Arc,
With our own hands will we regain our land.[138]

While organizing for the revolution in Zhejiang, Qiu Jin was arrested and put to death; she was only thirty-two. Newspapers in both China and the United States expressed outrage over her execution; she was equally mourned by revolutionaries on both sides of the Pacific Ocean.[139] Dr. Sun, in his many talks to overseas Chinese, often pointed to Qiu Jin as a role model for Chinese women—a far cry from the traditional model of passivity and subservience. His words did not go unheeded. A few women in San Francisco followed her example and cut their hair as a revolutionary gesture; others redoubled their commitment to the revolutionary cause.[140]

Although the success of the revolution and the establishment of a republic in China failed to bring peace and prosperity to the country, it did have a lasting impact on the lives of Chinese American women. Jane Kwong Lee later commented, "After the establishment of the Republic of China, Chinese women in this country picked up the forward-looking trend for equality with men. They could go to school, speak in public places, have their feet freed from binding, and go out to work in stores and small factories if they needed to work."[141]

Indeed, the ultimate symbol of subjugation—the crippling practice of footbinding—was brought to an end. The new republican government, linking the elimination of footbinding with women's emancipation, halted the practice by issuing prohibition orders against it and by promoting women's education. Following the example of women in China, Chinese women in America also began to unbind their feet (a process that was often just as painful as having the feet bound) and to stop binding their daughters' feet. By the 1920s, the only trace of footbinding that remained was the unnaturally small feet of older women encased in specially made leather shoes.[142]

Women also began to leave the confines of the home for wage work, community activities, and political involvement. The following story of how the 1911 Revolution changed one woman's life in Butte, Montana, is applicable to Chinese women's experience in San Francisco:

When I came to America as a bride, I never knew I would be coming to a prison. Until the Revolution, I was allowed out of the house but once a year. That was during New Year's when families exchanged New Year calls and feasts. We would dress in our long, plaited, brocaded, hand-embroidered skirts. These were a part of our wedding dowry brought from China. Over these we wore long-sleeved, short satin or damask jackets. We wore all of our jewelry, and we put jeweled ornaments in our hair.

The father of my children hired a closed carriage to take me and the children calling. Of course, he did not go with us, as this was against the custom practiced in China. The carriage would take us even if we went around the corner, for no family women walked. The carriage waited until we were ready to leave, which would be hours later, for the women saw each other so seldom that we talked and reviewed all that went on since we saw each other.

The women were always glad to see each other; we exchanged news of our families and friends in China. We admired each other's clothes and jewels. As we ate separately from the men, we talked about things that concerned women. When the New Year festivals were over, we would put away our clothes and take them out when another feast was held. Sometimes, we went to a feast when a baby born into a family association was a month old. Otherwise, we seldom visited each other; it was considered immodest to be seen too many times during the year.

After the Revolution in China, I heard that women there were free to go out. When the father of my children cut his queue he adopted new habits; I discarded my Chinese clothes and began to wear American clothes. By that time my children were going to American schools, could speak English, and they helped me buy what I needed. Gradually the other women followed my example. We began to go out more frequently and since then I go out all the time.[143]

Meanwhile in San Francisco, Mrs. Owyang and Mrs. Chu Chin Shung, wives of the outgoing and incoming Chinese consuls, respectively, caused quite a stir when they attended a Chinese banquet with their husbands. "The fact that women were present was taken as an indication of the democracy of the new China," the reporter covering the event wrote.[144] A year later, the same newspaper found it newsworthy to report that Chinese women had not only marched in a parade through Chinatown for the first time, but at a banquet hosted by the Chinese Nationalist League of America "they made speeches just as the men did."[145] Because of the changes wrought by the Revolution, Chinese women in San Francisco were beginning to flex their political muscles.

In keeping with this new image of women, the Chinese Women's Jeleab [Self-Reliance] Association was established in 1913. As indicated by its name, this organization was unique in that it was started by Chinese American women unaffiliated with a church or nationalist cause. Its origin, purpose, and membership were a combination of San Francisco and Oakland, of Chinese nationalism and Western progressivism, of immigrant mothers and American-born daughters. According to a full-page story that appeared in the *San Francisco Chronicle*—complete with a photograph of the group's members holding the American flag and their club banner inscribed with its Chinese name—the Jeleab Association was inspired by the Chinese revolution and American progressivism. In the words of its "thoroughly Americanized" president, Mrs. C. G. Lee (Clara Lee):

> How did it start? It's hard to say exactly. It's one of those things that grow out of a need. For two years the women of the Chinese quarters of San Francisco and Oakland have watched the progress of the men and encouraged them all they could. They were interested in what the men were doing and were yearning to do something themselves, but so few of them had any education at all. Why some couldn't even read and write their own language. Many were too poor to afford an education; and others couldn't be spared from family duties. It didn't look very bright at first.[146]

The organization, she continued, was patterned after the Chinese Native Sons of the Golden State, which excluded female membership;[147] and was also broadened to include foreign-born women:

> The idea first started with the Chinese Native Sons' parlor. If a Native Sons' parlor, why not a Native Daughters'? But we soon found that that wouldn't do [since many of the members were not native-born], so we concluded to have simply a woman's club for the purpose that had brought us together. Then we had to have an American name, for we intended to incorporate and have a charter. It was impossible, however, to find an English word that would combine all the reasons for which the club was formed. . . . The name would have to stand for independence, educational and progressive. We finally decided to take a Chinese word [*jeleab*], and, by using it, Anglicize it.[148]

Led by educated, middle-class women like Clara Lee, the Jeleab Association chose to follow the example of other American clubs and file incorporation papers in Sacramento, stating its purpose as "social intercourse, benevolent work, educational advantages, and mutual assistance and benefit, and not for pecuniary profit."[149] But a more elaborate purpose was given in a statement by member Liu Yilan published in the *Sai*

Clara Lee, founder and president of the Chinese Women's Jeleab [Self-Reliance] Association, 1913. (Courtesy of Dr. Lester Lee)

Gai Yat Po or *Chinese World* on August 22, 1913. Liu Yilan pressed the point that Chinese women's subordination was due to their lack of education and self-reliance. That could change for Chinese women in America, "where education flourishes and women's rights are allowed to develop," she said. "Women who are born and raised here have the chance to enter school when young and receive the same education as men. Even the older women who came from China have been inspired, after being continuously exposed to talk of freedom and equality, and after seeing for themselves the elevated status enjoyed by women here as opposed to the inferior position of women back home." The key, she concluded, was for women to band together and learn from each other:

> It is important that we broaden our contacts by making new friends and not keep to ourselves and become limited to our own little world. If we women are to become independent, we must form a big group so we can cull and share ideas and benefit from each other. Therefore, those of us who are of like mind have decided to form this group and to call it Lumei Zhongguo Nüjie Zili Hui [Chinese Women's Jeleab Association]. Our goal is to cultivate self-reliance in each of us and, further, to promote and propagate this concept in China, so as to strip away the black curtain that has blocked our [women's] view of the sky for thousands of years. This, then, is the purpose of our group.[150]

Herein was a new ideology concerning Chinese women's emancipation, one that combined Chinese nationalist thoughts on women's right to education with American ideals of freedom and equality. Equally important, it advocated self-improvement through social interaction in line with the progressive views of women's clubs in America. Indeed, the self-initiated Jeleab Association represented a new awakening in the social consciousness of Chinese immigrant women, a recognition of a higher status of womanhood to which they could aspire in America.

According to the newspaper article, in 1913 the Jeleab Association boasted a membership of two hundred Chinese women from San Francisco and Oakland, all immigrant mothers and American-born daughters, who met regularly in the parlor of the Chinese Native Sons of the Golden State in Oakland. As the immediate need was to educate the illiterate, an evening class was established for the study of Chinese under the direction of Mrs. T. L. Lee, a Baptist minister's wife, with plans to tackle English next. Seventy-five years later, Clara Lee noted in an interview that the Jeleab Association, despite its auspicious beginnings, disbanded a few years later. "It didn't last very long," she said. "Some lived [too far away] in San Francisco, and some moved away later."[151]

The other successful program, she recalled, was a class that met every Monday afternoon for instruction in using American sewing patterns. But even without the organization, progressive women like Clara Lee continued to practice self-reliance while influencing others to become "new women." Aside from being the first Chinese woman to register to vote in 1911 and the founder of the Jeleab Association, Clara was also an active member of the YWCA, the International Institute, and Fidelis Coterie, and she devoted much of her life to volunteer work on behalf of immigrant women and the Chinese community.[152]

Immigration to the United States proved to be a double-edged sword for Chinese women in the early twentieth century. Saddled by cultural restrictions, racial and sex discrimination, and labor exploitation, many suffered undue hardships and led strenuous lives. Yet socioeconomic conditions and historical forces at the time afforded women like Wong Ah So, Law Shee Low, and Jane Kwong Lee opportunities to unbind their lives and reshape gender roles—in essence, to change their circumstances for the better. Their daughters, second-generation women born and raised in the United States, would benefit by their experiences. Without bound feet and bound lives but still fettered by race, gender, and class oppression, their challenge would be to break the double binds of cultural conflict at home and discrimination in the larger society, and take the first steps toward realizing their full potential as Chinese American women.

CHAPTER 3

First Steps

The Second Generation, 1920s

The second-generation Chinese girl . . . is a thing apart from her sister of the older generation who was bound by the traditions of many centuries. Freed from old restraints, yet hampered by many new problems which she meets in her daily living, she is still an uncertain quantity. Consciously and unconsciously she reflects the conflict within her caused by her Chinese heritage and American environment. She has broken her link with the East. She has not as yet found one with the West.

Janie Chu
"The Oriental Girl in the Occident," 1926

Although Chinese immigration to America largely began in the mid–nineteenth century, the second generation of Chinese Americans did not come to maturity until the 1920s. By keeping Chinese laborers, and by extension their wives and families, out of the country, the Chinese Exclusion Act of 1882 had effectively delayed the natural growth of the second generation. However, as increasing numbers of wives immigrated by way of the exempt classes, women and children began to make their presence felt in San Francisco Chinatown. Between 1900 and 1940, the foreign-born Chinese population was reduced by half, while native-born Chinese population quadrupled. A large part of the increase in the native-born can be attributed to the one major exempt class of the Exclusion Act—"paper sons," boys who were born in China but who claimed derivative citizenship in order to immigrate to the United States. The increase in the female population was even more pronounced: the number of foreign-born Chinese females more than doubled, while native-born Chinese females increased sixfold owing to the arrival of "paper daughters" and a high childbirth rate among Chi-

nese immigrant women. Nationwide, native-born Chinese females outnumbered foreign-born as early as 1900. In contrast, native-born Chinese males still represented a minority (45 percent) of the Chinese male
population in 1940. That same year, the native-born made up a high 72
percent of the Chinese female population (see appendix tables 8 and 9).

Coming of age in the 1920s, second-generation women, unlike their
mothers, were not fettered by bound feet; nor were they as constrained
by Chinese traditions. Born and raised in the United States, they had
political rights as native Americans; they could speak English and were
educated and acculturated through the public schools, church, and popular culture. While the first generation had been almost totally concerned
with economic survival, this generation yearned for the realization of a
different American dream. As U.S. citizens, they wanted and expected
to fulfill their potential in all aspects of their lives—in education and work,
in social and political activities; but they were prevented from doing so
by sexism at home and racism in the larger society. Many young Chinese women found themselves caught in a cultural dilemma. In exercising their desires and rights as individuals, they often had to go against
the traditional gender role expectations of their parents. Although there
was a marked difference in their educational and social background vis-
à-vis the first generation, they still found themselves limited to living in
Chinatown, working at low-paying jobs, and excluded from participation in mainstream society.

The sociologist Robert E. Park of the University of Chicago was the
first to study the assimilation patterns of "Orientals" on the Pacific Coast.
Under his directorship, the Survey of Race Relations project interviewed
over two hundred Chinese Americans in the 1920s about their life histories and encounters with racism. Park was convinced that all groups,
regardless of race or ethnicity, would eventually become integrated into
mainstream American life, according to his postulated race relations cycle of contact, competition, accommodation, and assimilation.[1] Although Park's research materials remain important, the weight of schol-
arly opinion has long since turned against him. Beginning with Milton
E. Gordon in 1964 and continuing through Michael Omi and Howard
Winant today, sociologists have shown that assimilation is a two-way
process. A group can acculturate (change values, customs, and cultural
forms) but not assimilate (change primary and institutional relationships)
unless it is accepted and allowed to do so by the majority group.[2] The
experiences of second-generation Chinese Americans during this period
support this point of view. Although they found that they could accul-

turate into American life in terms of values, customs, and cultural forms, because of racial barriers they could not totally assimilate or become integrated into American society. Ching Chao Wu, who studied Chinatown life under Park, came to this conclusion in 1928:

> To sum up, it may be said that on the road of assimilation, the native-born Chinese have gone much farther than the Chinese of early days. They have been Americanized to such an extent that their relatives in China may find little in common with them. But the native-born Chinese are not completely assimilated, for they still have race-consciousness.[3]

Despite the insurmountable barriers, some Chinese Americans continued to push in that direction, while others became resigned to their second-class status. Most, however, moved toward accommodation—making the best of the situation until social conditions changed.

In their efforts to take the first steps toward breaking the double binds of sexism at home and racism on the outside, to define their own ethnic and gender identity, second-generation women were greatly influenced by Chinese nationalism, Christianity, and acculturation to American life. As their stories demonstrate, the ideals of women's emancipation that were embedded in the Chinese nationalist movement encouraged parents to educate their daughters, allow them to work outside the home, engage in free marriage (as opposed to arranged marriage), and become politically active for the sake of a stronger and more modern China. Christianity reinforced many of these same values. By emphasizing female identity, independence, education, and spiritual equality, Protestant institutions such as the YWCA drew Chinese girls and women into the public sphere, familiarized them with Western customs and beliefs, and encouraged them to participate more actively in civic affairs. Public schools and the mass media further instilled in them the values of individuality, equality, and freedom as well as the desire for the good life, characterized by fashionable clothes, romantic affairs, sports, jazz, moving pictures, partying, and the like. However, as second-generation women tried to become Americanized, their newly adopted lifestyle often clashed with their cultural upbringing at home.

Cultural Upbringing at Home

As children, most Chinatown girls led sheltered lives following Chinese traditions. Their mothers usually taught them to follow the "three obediences and four virtues" and groomed them to become virtuous wives and mothers. Daughters growing up in the early 1900s were expected to give unquestioning obedience to their parents and remain close to home, where they helped their mothers with income-generating work, shopping, and housework. Nurtured in Chinese culture, they spoke Chinese, ate Chinese food, and celebrated Chinese holidays. Although sons were still favored over daughters, girls were often more valued in America than in China because of their scarcity and the increased opportunities available to them. Moreover, Christian doctrine and Chinese nationalist ideology both advocated women's rights and, together, influenced social attitudes toward the value and upbringing of girls, especially among middle-class families. A comparative look at the early years of Alice Sue Fun and Florence Chinn Kwan, both of whom grew up in San Francisco Chinatown in the 1900s, shows how these factors affected the cultural upbringing of Chinese American girls.

Given the working-class background of most Chinese families in San Francisco at this time, Alice's story is the more representative of the two.[4] She was only seven years old when she lost her father because of the 1906 earthquake and fire. Forced to evacuate their home in Chinatown, the family moved across the bay to Oakland, where they lived in a makeshift tent. "My father dug clams and got sick eating them," Alice recalled. "Contaminated water, you know. So he died soon after of typhoid fever. That was in September. My sister was born four days after my father died." Alice's mother decided to move her six children back to San Francisco Chinatown. A year later, she remarried.

While her stepfather worked as a cook, her mother supplemented the family income by sewing at home. When she was eight, Alice began attending the Oriental Public School from 9:00 to 2:30 and True Sunshine Chinese School from 2:30 to 5:00. Then she would come home and help with the housework and take care of her younger brothers and sisters. "I was the one who sewed their clothes, using those old foot-treadle machines. Everything was used. I would take an old shirt apart and repiece it together for Little Brother's trousers." Because her mother followed tradition and rarely left the house, it also fell on Alice to do the shopping. Both of her parents were very strict. When she misbehaved, her mother would punish her with a *ling gok* (a knuckle-rap on the head) or, worse, with a switch, hitting her "until flower patterns [black and blue marks] broke out." Alice particularly resented the lack of freedom of movement:

> It wasn't easy. Mother watched us like a hawk. We couldn't move without telling her. When we were growing up, we were never allowed to go out unless accompanied by an older brother, sister, or somebody else. . . .

Alice Sue Fun (*center*) with (*from left to right*) Uncle holding Harris, Elsie, and Mother during Chinese New Year, 1904. (Arnold Genthe photo; courtesy of Library of Congress)

If you wanted to go shopping, you might as well forget it because, one thing, you didn't have any money. Secondly, you knew your mother wouldn't let you go, so what's the use of asking, right?

There was little time for play, but Alice had fond memories of Chinese celebrations, the Chinese opera, embroidery classes at the Congregational church on Saturdays, and the 1915 Panama-Pacific International Exposition. Although Alice attended church on Sundays, her mother preferred to worship her Chinese gods at home. She also brewed Chinese herbs whenever anyone became sick, cooked all the special dishes during the Chinese holidays, related legendary stories associated with the holidays as well as scary ghost stories, and took the children with her whenever she went to the Chinese opera.

> In the old days, there were two operas a day. It cost a little over a dollar for the grand admission ticket, but after nine o'clock the admission would be lowered to twenty-five cents. Free for children if accompanied by an adult. Everyone ate and talked during the opera. It was quite festive. That's how I learned to love the opera.

In this way, Alice grew to appreciate her Chinese cultural heritage. The highlight of her childhood was the 1915 International Exposition held in San Francisco to celebrate the opening of the Panama Canal and the rebirth of the city following the earthquake. "It was once in a lifetime and we saved to go see the fair. For about twenty cents a day you could spend the whole day there. There were so many things to see, but I was always partial to the Chinese exhibits," she said.

When Alice turned fifteen, her mother decided that was enough education for a girl and that Alice should help the family out.[5] Alice found a sales job at the Canton Bazaar and gave half her earnings—$25 a month in gold pieces—to her mother. Experiencing a degree of freedom and economic independence, she decided to strike out on her own. Against her mother's wishes, she married her Chinese teacher, whom she described as "poorer than a church mouse," and moved to New York. When her marriage failed, she left her husband and traveled around the world as maid and companion to the actress Lola Fisher. "She treated me very well," said Alice. "Working those few years with Miss Fisher educated me, broadened my outlook, and made a different person out of me." As she had deeply resented her sheltered and strict upbringing, she especially appreciated the opportunity the job gave her to travel, to go beyond her mother's limited world. Years later, she compared her life with that of her mother in this way:

Alice Sue Fun at the Canton Bazaar, where she worked as a salesgirl in 1915. (Courtesy of Alice Sue Fun)

My mother lived a very sheltered life. Even up to her old age, she never trusted herself to go out alone. She was afraid that she'll get lost. And then she didn't like to exercise a lot, or walk a lot. . . . I would go out anytime I want and anywhere I want. Even in foreign countries, I wasn't afraid to go out alone. In Hong Kong, I went exploring all over on the bus. . . . I like to be independent. I don't like to always be accompanied by people. I guess I had enough of that when I was a young girl.

Whereas Alice was raised according to Chinese tradition, Florence Chinn Kwan faced fewer restrictions growing up in San Francisco Chinatown because of the liberal middle-class background of her parents. Her father was a missionary teacher who had come to the United States when he was twelve years old. He later returned to China to marry and was able to bring his wife back to America. Both parents were highly

Pauline Fong Woo (*left*) and
Florence Chinn Kwan (*right*) as
flower girls in 1908. (Courtesy
of Florence Chinn Kwan)

nationalistic toward their homeland and modern in their chosen lifestyle.
After the 1911 Revolution, her father was among the first to cut his
queue; her mother, to unbind her feet; and both, to allow their daughter to appear as a princess in the parade that celebrated the founding of
the new republic. Whereas Alice always dressed in Chinese-style clothes,
Florence wore Western dresses. "My father didn't want me to wear Chinese clothes. He said he didn't want people staring at me and saying
you're Chinese, you're not American," she explained.[6] Although she,
too, was not allowed to go out alone, her parents were not as strict as
Alice's. Her father took her along on his daily walks to the park, and often downtown or to Chinatown to shop. Also unlike Alice, she was rarely
physically punished. The only time it happened was when she slid down
a bannister and broke her front teeth.

While Alice described her parents as uneducated, hard-working,
strict, and distant to their children, Florence remembered her father as
gentle, honest, and devout. "He would hold me on his lap while reading in his study. He was quite artistic and used to draw pictures for me
when I was a child." Her mother was patient, alert, and humble, with a

great capacity for learning. Like Alice's mother, she sewed at home to supplement her husband's income. But as Florence recalled, she was also quite active outside the home. Aside from starting the Women's Missionary Society at the Chinese Congregational church, "she was always helping the sick and the needy by going to their homes, cooking for them and caring for them all without compensation."[7]

Florence's leisurely life was a marked contrast to Alice's burdensome one. She had few responsibilities at home, aside from occasionally helping with the dishes. She recalled playing tennis on Saturdays with her brothers in the Italian section of town, where Chinese were not welcomed. "We would go early and climb the fence," she said.[8] To do her share for the church, Florence taught English to Chinese immigrants at home five days a week, contributing her monthly earnings of $5 to the Women's Missionary Society.

Whereas Alice's parents did not believe that girls needed more than an elementary education (nor could they afford it), Florence's father treated her like his sons and encouraged her to pursue college—at a time when it was still considered unusual for Chinese girls to finish high school. As a young girl, Florence was also one of the few Chinese Americans to attend school outside Chinatown. Her parents enrolled her at Denman Girls' School until the board of education insisted that all Chinese students be restricted to the Oriental Public School. After elementary school, Florence went on to graduate from Girls' High School in 1915. Throughout her public school years, her parents also had her attend the Chinese school they had started at the Chinese Congregational church. Although her mother wanted her to marry and settle down to a domestic life upon graduation from high school, her father told her to continue on to college, earn a Ph.D., and then go serve China:

> He said that people are coming over here and the United States was building things over there and they wanted better relations between [the two countries]. My father was teaching English to men here, and if I went back to teach, then when they came they would get better jobs over here. . . . And also, my mother had that missionary goal of bringing Christianity to China.[9]

In this way, the Christian and nationalist idea of serving China and her people were instilled in Florence at an early age. After attaining a bachelor's degree in sociology at the all-women's Mills College (she was the first Chinese woman to graduate from there, in 1919) and a master's degree in sociology at the University of Chicago, Florence decided to try and serve the needs of Chinese women in San Francisco. For two years she worked as the associate secretary of the Chinese YWCA, and she also helped to start the Girls' Club at the Chinese Congregational church. Then she decided to marry a medical student from China whom she had met at the University of Chicago. She gave up her job at the YWCA to accompany him to China, where he worked as a physician and she as an English teacher for the next twenty-six years, thereby fulfilling her parents' wishes of serving China.

Although both Alice and Florence ended up leaving the sheltered environment of Chinatown to go abroad, major differences in their upbringing led each of them to make that decision for their own reasons. Coming from a working-class background and raised according to traditional values, Alice was not given the same educational and social opportunities as Florence. But having to leave home to work made her a more independent woman, allowing her to marry the man of her choice against her parents' wishes and then take a job in which she could travel around the world. In contrast, because Florence's parents were middle-class and guided by Christian and Chinese nationalist values, she received a more progressive upbringing than Alice. Not only did Florence enjoy a more intimate relationship with her parents, but she was also encouraged to pursue higher education with the goal of serving China. Whereas Alice had to defy her parents, both of Florence's parents supported her choice of marriage partner and the decision to make her life with him in China. Indeed, it was her mother's "pin money" from taking in sewing for many years that paid for the young couple's passage to China in 1923.

Cultural Conflicts at Home

As young daughters, Chinese American girls had little choice but to give unquestioning obedience to their parents. However, as they became older and more exposed to a Western lifestyle and ideas of individuality and equality through public school, church, and popular culture, some began to resist the traditional beliefs and practices of their immigrant parents, even to the extent of ridiculing their "old-fashioned" ways. Like most second-generation children, Chinese Americans experienced cultural conflicts and identity dilemmas when they tried to reconcile the different value system of their home culture with that of mainstream American society.[10] Many disagreed with their parents over the degree of individuality and freedom allowable, the proper relationship between sexes, and choice of leisure activities, education, occupation, and marriage. For young Chinese American women, the cultural clash was often compounded by stricter adherence to traditional gender roles and by the parental favoritism bestowed on the boys in the family. Depending on the family's economic circumstances, daughters were usually expected to forgo higher education in deference to their brothers. They were also expected to stay close to home and do all the housework, while their brothers were allowed greater freedom of movement and had fewer responsibilities at home. Parents frowned on their sons taking up sports and partying instead of studying, but disapproved of their daughters going out at all, dancing, or even mixing, with the opposite sex. Adhering to the double moral standards in the community, they were more concerned about regulating their daughters' sexuality than their sons', of protecting their daughters' virginity and the family's upright standing in the community.[11]

It is evident from written accounts that second-generation women of middle-class background were preoccupied with generational and cultural conflicts, especially those that revolved around gender. The same cannot be said of working-class women, in the absence of comparable evidence. Most likely, working-class daughters also experienced such conflicts, but they were probably more concerned with making a living than with challenging traditional gender roles. As the following stories of Jade Snow Wong, Esther Wong, and Flora Belle Jan (all of middle-class background) reveal, there were at least three patterns of response to the conflict over gender roles: acquiescence, resistance, or accommodation—creating a new gender identity by combining different aspects of two cultures. Borrowing from Karl Mannheim's concept of the sociology of generations, we find that accommodation—as exemplified in the story of Jade Snow Wong's life—was the dominant response of the second generation under study.[12]

As she states in her first autobiography, *Fifth Chinese Daughter*, Jade Snow Wong was the fifth daughter in a family of seven children.[13] Her father owned and ran a Chinatown garment factory and was an ordained Protestant minister on the side. Her mother was the faithful wife and benevolent mother, constantly hard at work at the sewing machine. The family was among the first in Chinatown to have a bathroom equipped with running water in their home. Although her father was progressive in many ways, he still believed in a Confucian upbringing for his children. From an early age, Jade Snow was taught her proper place as a daughter in a traditional Chinese family and insulated community:

A little girl never questioned the commands of Mother and Father, unless prepared to receive painful consequences. She never addressed an older person by name. . . . Even in handing them something, she must use both hands to signify that she paid them undivided attention. Respect and order—these were the key words of life. It did not matter what were the thoughts of a little girl; she did not voice them.[14]

So ingrained was this deference in her that even as an adult she chose to write her autobiography in the third person singular, signifying her understanding of her proper place in the Confucian hierarchal order:

Although a "first person singular" book, this story is written in the third person from Chinese habit. The submergence of the individual is literally practiced. In written Chinese, prose or poetry, the word "I" almost never appears, but is understood. In corresponding with an older person like my father, I would write in words half the size of the regular ideographs, "small daughter Jade Snow," when referring to myself; to one of contemporary age, I would put in small characters, "younger sister"— but never "I." Should my father, who owes me no respect, write to me, he would still refer to himself in the third person, "Father." Even written in English, an "I" book by a Chinese would seem outrageously immodest to anyone raised in the spirit of Chinese propriety.[15]

As was true for most of her peers, Jade Snow's parents did not spare the rod. "Teaching and whipping were almost synonymous," Jade Snow wrote. "No one ever troubled to explain. Only through punishment did she learn that what was proper was right and what was improper was wrong."[16] It was expected that she excel in both American and Chinese schools, that she learn to cook and sew, that she look after her baby brother, work in her father's sewing factory, and help her mother with the household chores, and that she never go out unless escorted and with her parents' permission.

In the area of education, Jade Snow's father was more progressive than most other Chinese parents. As a Christian and a nationalist reformer, he believed in education for his daughters as well as his sons, at least through high school. Expressing the sentiments of a Chinese nationalist, he explained to Jade Snow:

Many Chinese were very short-sighted. They felt that since their daughters would marry into a family of another name, they would not belong permanently in their own family clan. Therefore, they argued that it was not worth while to invest in their daughters' book education. But my answer was that since sons and their education are of primary importance, we must have intelligent mothers. If nobody educates his daughters, how can we have intelligent mothers for our sons? If we do not have good family training, how can China be a strong nation?[17]

For the sake of a strong China, it was equally important that his children be educated in the Chinese language and have an appreciation of Chinese culture. Even before Jade Snow started kindergarten, her father began tutoring her in Chinese at home. By the time she was ready for Chinese school, she knew enough Chinese to be placed in the third grade. Jade Snow, in essence, had a bilingual and bicultural education, which would later help shape her ethnic and gender identity.

Once Jade Snow left the sheltered environment of home for public school, she began to notice subtle but significant differences between Western and Chinese ways. Creativity that had been stifled in the regimentation and rote memorization of Chinese school was given free rein in public school activities such as making butter, painting, and sports. Children were encouraged to speak their minds and expected to strike back in self-defense when hit. Whereas her parents believed in maintaining a distance and encouraging their children through negative reinforcement, her public school teachers practiced the opposite. When Jade Snow was hurt by a flying baseball bat, her teacher Miss Mullohand comforted her by embracing her. Unaccustomed to such intimacy, Jade Snow broke away in confusion and embarrassment.

Christian organizations such as the Chinese YWCA and library books also broadened her outlook on life. When she went to the Chinese YWCA for piano lessons, she experienced "American dishes of strange and deliciously different flavors" cooked by her older sister who worked there, and she found that to see other faces than those of her friends at school and at the factory, and "to play without care for an hour or two were real joys."[18] Through reading, she discovered how different life was outside Chinatown: "Temporarily she forgot who she was, or the constant requirements of Chinese life, while she delighted in the adventures of the *Oz* books, the *Little Colonel, Yankee Girl,* and Western cowboys, for in these books there was absolutely nothing resembling her own life."[19] Later, as a live-in housekeeper with the Kaisers, a European American family composed of husband and wife, two young children, and a large dog, she was able to observe first-hand the different lifestyle of a rich family:

> It was a home where children were heard as well as seen; where parents considered who was right or wrong, rather than who should be respected; where birthday parties were a tradition, complete with lighted birthday

cakes, where the husband kissed his wife and the parents kissed their children; where the Christmas holidays meant fruit cake, cookies, presents, and gay parties; where the family was actually concerned with having fun together and going out to play together; where the problems and difficulties of domestic life and children's discipline were untangled, perhaps after tears, but also after explanations; where the husband turned over his pay check to his wife to pay the bills; and where, above all, each member, even down to and including the dog, appeared to have the inalienable right to assert his individuality—in fact, where that was expected—in an atmosphere of natural affection.[20]

Through these influences, Jade Snow unwittingly became acculturated into mainstream American life despite her parents' attempts to raise her according to Chinese tradition. Cultural conflict, not surprisingly, was the result. Her emerging desire for recognition as an individual erupted when her father denied her request for a college education because of limited family resources and because her brother—as the son who would bear the Wong name and make pilgrimages to the ancestral burial grounds—deserved it more. She bitterly questioned her father's judgment:

> How can Daddy know what an American advanced education can mean to me? Why should Older Brother be alone in enjoying the major benefits of Daddy's toil? There are no ancestral pilgrimages to be made in the United States! I can't help being born a girl. Perhaps, even being a girl, I don't want to marry, *just* to raise sons! Perhaps I have a right to want more than sons! I am a person, besides being a female! Don't the Chinese admit that women also have feelings and minds?[21]

On another occasion, she dared to argue with her parents over her right to go out on a date. She was sixteen and had found a way to attend junior college by working as a housekeeper. Inspired by a sociology professor who advocated that young people had rights as individuals, Jade Snow decided not to ask her parents for permission to go out. When her father asked where she was going and with whom, she refused to tell him. "Very well," he said sharply. "If you will not tell me, I forbid you to go! You are now too old to whip." Rising to the occasion, "in a manner that would have done credit to her sociology instructor addressing his freshman class," she delivered her declaration of independence:

> That is something you should think more about. Yes, I am too old to whip. I am too old to be treated as a child. I can now think for myself,

and you and Mama should not demand unquestioning obedience from me. You should understand me. There was a time in America when parents raised children to make them work, but now the foreigners [Westerners] regard them as individuals with rights of their own. I have worked too, but now I am an individual besides being your fifth daughter.[22]

Her defiance shocked and hurt her parents, but Jade Snow had made up her mind to find her own lifestyle, to satisfy her own quest for individual freedom and accomplishment, even if it meant going against her parents' wishes. It was in the pursuit of these liberating ideas that placed the person's needs over the group's that she became an emancipated woman in the Western sense. From then on, she came and went as she pleased.

A number of fortuitous circumstances helped her along the way. She found work as a live-in housekeeper to support her college education. After completing junior college with honors (she won an award as the most outstanding student in California and was chosen to give the commencement speech), she was introduced by the family that employed her to the president of Mills College. With the president's encouragement, Jade Snow went on to attend Mills, living with the college dean and supporting herself with scholarships and domestic work. She graduated with Phi Beta Kappa honors in economics and sociology. When opportunities opened up for Chinese Americans during World War II, she landed a job as a secretary in a shipyard and wrote an award-winning essay on absenteeism that earned her the honor of launching a ship. This time she made the front pages of the Chinatown newspapers. Despite the skepticism and disapproval of the Chinese community, she also decided to start a hand-thrown pottery business in Chinatown, which proved so successful that by the third month she was driving the first postwar automobile in Chinatown.

By the end of her autobiography, Jade Snow had come to terms with her cultural conflicts by selectively integrating elements of both cultures into her life and work as a ceramicist. Not only did she come to appreciate Western thought and culture through her education and social life at Mills College, but she also returned to her community to rediscover the rich cultural heritage to be found in Chinese foods, medicine, opera, and the established artisans she came to know. Her pottery, which combined classic Chinese and Western utilitarian motifs, reflected this newfound bicultural identity. She was indeed at home in both cultures, having achieved personal autonomy and self-definition as a second-generation Chinese American woman. More important, Jade Snow had proven her worth as a daughter to her parents through her many accomplishments, which had brought honor to them and earned her their respect. Her father paid her the highest compliment when he acknowledged that her example had helped to wash away the former "shameful and degraded position into which the Chinese culture has pushed its women." Jade Snow ended her autobiography with the comforting thought that she had at last claimed her niche in life: "She had found herself and struck her speed. And when she came home now, it was to see Mama and Daddy look up from their work, and smile at her, and say, 'It is good to have you home again.'"[23]

While most of Jade Snow's peers took the same middle road of accommodation through bicultural fusion, there were others who either acquiesced or rebelled against traditional gender roles. Jade Snow's own older half-sister Esther Wong (Jade Swallow) initially chose the acquiescing route. According to a Survey of Race Relations interview conducted in 1924, Esther was born in China and immigrated to America with her mother and younger sister, Ruth Wong (Jade Lotus), when she was five years old.[24] As with Jade Snow, Esther's childhood was one of strict discipline and hard work. Her day started with Chinese lessons with her father at 6 A.M., followed by public school and then work at her father's overall factory from 3 to 9 P.M. every weekday, all day on Saturday. When only twelve years old, she was put in charge of supervising twenty-five male workers. She also had to help with the housework, and later, when her mother fell ill for a year, she had to nurse her at home. Esther did not resent the heavy responsibilities or her lack of leisure time, but what she found unfair was her father's lack of understanding and the preferential treatment accorded her brother.

> When I was 13 my brother was born and then he [her father] lost interest in us girls, did not care to bother teaching girls, and seemed to forget what we were like. When we were small he used to work at a machine next to ours, and when we were all busy he would tell us stories as we worked; but later he became very stern and cold and did not try to understand us at all. My brother has a great deal of spending money and a bank account of his own and can do just about as he likes. We girls were expected to do everything and to pay for our room and board, which we thought was hard, as that is not the Chinese way, usually that is given to children.[25]

Considering herself an "old-fashioned girl," Esther was always careful about conducting herself properly in public.[26]

> I was brought up in the very strictest Chinese way. I have never been to a dance, never had a caller that I received, although some have come, never had what is called "fun" in my life. Father did not believe in it. He

was one of the prominent leaders of the Chinese National League of America, and acted as Treasurer, handling large sums of money. I used to be all alone in the office, receiving large sums, but was perfectly safe, no one ever spoke to me except when necessary, because I had the right Chinese manner, very cold and proper, which the Chinese look for in women, and so I was not ever spoken to, except in a business way. These League Teams always end in a feast, but though I was on many different teams at different times I never went to a feast, and so I could not be criticized. Perhaps you could not find a family that would better illustrate the conflict between the old and the new. We were brought up more strictly than most girls, even according to Chinese ideas, and my sister and I have kept these habits, never going to dances, or having company, always working.[27]

What led Esther to challenge her parents' traditional expectations of her were their efforts to arrange a marriage for her to suitors she found unacceptable. The havoc that the controversy created in Esther's life led her finally to stand up for herself. "I was 17 years old, and I hated them both [the suitors], and I stood out against them all. I finally said that I would pack my suitcase and go, if they did not stop this torture."[28] Esther did indeed move out, found a job that supported her through Mills College, and then went to China to teach, where she remained until war broke out between China and Japan in 1937.

At the other extreme of responses to cultural conflicts was the rebel who totally rejected traditional gender roles. Like the "flappers" of the 1920s jazz age, she was someone who defied social control and conventions, who was modern, sophisticated, and frank in speech, dress, morals, and lifestyle.[29] The best-known Chinese flapper was Anna May Wong, who broke convention by becoming a Hollywood actress. She made more than one hundred films in her thirty-seven-year career, most of which typecast her in the limited role of "Oriental villainess." The image she projected in the movie magazines, however, was that of a beautiful and fashionable modern woman, who lived in her own apartment, dressed in the most up-to-date fashion, and spoke the latest slang.[30] As for her counterpart in San Francisco Chinatown, according to Rev. Ng Poon Chew, the Chinese flapper in her "bobbed-haired, ear-muffed, lipsticked, powder-puffed loveliness" was but an "Oriental echo of the American manifestation of youth. . . . Today she not only wants to select her own husband, but she wants the freedom of the chop-suey restaurants, the jazz cabarets, the moving pictures and long evenings with her beau, minus the chaperone, a 1,000 year old concomitant of Chinese civilization."[31]

Flora Belle Jan can be considered such a Chinese flapper. The third child in a family of seven children, she was born in 1906 in Fresno, California. She later moved to San Francisco to attend college in 1925. Like Jade Snow and Esther Wong's parents, Flora Belle's parents were immigrants from Guangdong Province; but unlike the Wongs, they were not influenced by Christianity or Chinese nationalism in deciding how to raise their children. Although relatively well off—they owned and operated the Yet Far Low Restaurant in Fresno Chinatown—they did not encourage any of their sons or daughters to pursue higher education. They were quite strict with Flora Belle, wanting to maintain control over her comings and goings, to mold her into a "proper" Chinese woman, though they evidently failed.

Influenced more by her teachers, peers, and mainstream culture than by her tradition-bound parents, Flora Belle became a rebel at an early age. As she described herself in a Survey of Race Relations interview conducted in 1924, she was not one to hold back her true feelings:

> When I was a little girl, I grew to dislike the conventionality and rules of Chinese life. The superstitions and customs seemed ridiculous to me. My parents have wanted me to grow up a good Chinese girl, but I am an American and I can't accept all the old Chinese ways and ideas. A few years ago when my Mother took me to worship at the shrine of my ancestor and offer a plate of food, I decided it was time to stop this foolish custom. So I got up and slammed down the rice in front of the idol and said, "So long Old Top, I don't believe in you anyway." My mother didn't like it a little bit.[32]

To expose the hypocrisy that she saw in both Chinese and mainstream American society, Flora Belle wrote scathing articles, poems, stories, and skits, some of which were published in the *Fresno Bee, San Francisco Examiner*, and *Chinese Students' Monthly*. One article, "Chinatown Sheiks Are Modest Lot; Eschew Slang, Love-Moaning Blues," used the latest slang to poke fun at her male contemporaries, while another sketch, "Old Mother Grundy and Her Brood of Unbaptized Nuns," ridiculed the American flapper.[33]

Letters that Flora Belle wrote to her best friend, Ludmelia Holstein, from 1918 to 1949 reveal a young woman struggling with generational and cultural conflicts at home.[34] Her parents obviously did not approve of Flora Belle's writings, her plans to go away to college, or her active social life. When they scolded her for leaving home for two weeks without permission, Flora Belle responded in anger by writing Ludmelia: "I *hate* my parents, *both*, now, and I want to show them that I can do something in spite of their dog-gone skepticism, old-fashionism, and unpardonable unparentliness."[35]

Like many other American girls, Flora Belle was interested in the latest fashions, romance, and having a good time—values promoted by the mass media during a period of postwar prosperity and consumerism. She wrote Ludmelia about accepting automobile rides with boys, of lying to her parents in order "to keep pace with Dame Fashion," of how she would "rather be a vamp and have a Theda Bar-ist time in S.F." than spend $20 to attend a religious convention at Asilomar.[36] She also had aspirations to be a famous writer. Both Flora Belle and Ludmelia evidently wrote poems, stories, and songs, which they submitted to newspapers and magazines for publication. She took her ambition to write seriously, for when admonished by Ludmelia for taking too much interest in boys, she wrote back:

> Oh, dear me! Please, dear chum, *don't* say such an awful, awful thing. You are going to discourage me, utterly dishearten me, and take away all my ambition. *Don't* say that I will be married before you finish college. It will be impossible to adapt myself to a settled-down condition. Oh, how can I bear it, to be a mother and take care of children and live an uneventful life, and die, "unwept, unhonored, and unsung," by the world of Fame; only by friends and relatives! No, Luddy dear, I can not, simply will not do it. You must encourage me, and tell me constantly that I must achieve fame and fortune before I consider my task is done.[37]

Although her parents did not instill Chinese nationalism in her, she was exposed to it during her visits to the San Francisco Bay Area. In another letter to Ludmelia, she wrote about wanting to work in China: "When I went to 'B' [Berkeley] I got loaded with patriotism, and now my ambition is to graduate from U. of C. [University of California] and go back and teach. Lucy told me that (she's been back there) teachers were in terrible demand in China now."[38] After graduating from Fresno Junior College in 1925, Flora Belle did attend the University of California, Berkeley, but only for six months. To support her college education, she worked first in an ice cream parlor and later as a check girl at the Mandarin Cafe while writing feature stories for the *San Francisco Examiner*—jobs that were not considered respectable by Chinatown standards. According to her last letter from San Francisco, too much partying, riding in automobiles, and "scandalous" columns in the *San Francisco Examiner* had earned her a bad reputation in the close-knit, conservative Chinese community of San Francisco. With the help of Robert E. Park, who had met her in the process of conducting his Survey of Race Relations on the Pacific Coast, Flora Belle left San Francisco to study journalism at the University of Chicago. There she met and fell in love with a graduate student from China. Upon graduation in 1926 she married him and, a year later, they had their first child. In 1932 she accompanied him to China, where they made their home for the next sixteen years.

The life stories of Jade Snow Wong, Esther Wong, and Flora Belle Jan demonstrate the extent of sexism and cultural conflicts faced at home by second-generation women of middle-class background. Their stories also show the different responses that women brought to bear on intergenerational conflicts over gender roles. While some, like Esther, acquiesced and accepted the traditional role for Chinese women, a few, like Flora Belle, openly rebelled and tried to become liberated women. Most, however, took the accommodation route, as Jade Snow Wong did. Caught in the webs of two cultures and the double binds of sexism and racism, they sought to define their own ethnic and gender identity, to find their own cultural niche by selectively adopting a bicultural lifestyle that allowed them to enjoy what they felt was the best of two worlds.

Racial Discrimination at School

The second generation could become Americanized regardless of their parents' wishes, but they could not break down racial barriers and become accepted as equals in mainstream society. No matter how acculturated, their physical features set them apart, subjecting them to racial discrimination. Before World War II, Chinese Americans were denied equal education, employment, housing, and excluded from mainstream society. Sexism both within and outside of Chinatown compounded difficulties for Chinese American women. As a result, Chinese Americans were forced to lead a de facto segregated existence in all aspects of their lives. Nevertheless, Chinese American women took advantage of whatever opportunities were opened to them in an effort to shape new gender roles for themselves. Education was one such accessible avenue of opportunity.

The high esteem that Chinese accorded education proved a boon in America. Because Chinese parents firmly believed that education led to upward mobility, many willingly sacrificed for their children's education, putting them through public school, Chinese school, and college if at all possible. An American education would, they believed, prepare their sons and daughters for gainful employment in America or in China, while a Chinese education would develop their character, instill in them a sense of nationalist and cultural pride, and also prepare them for employment in China should appropriate opportunities in America prove impossible.

With the new emphasis in China on educating women and the free, public education available to girls in America, many Chinese parents were encouraged to educate their daughters as well as their sons. However, few working-class parents could afford to support their daughters beyond elementary school, especially when economic circumstances required them to work or help out at home, as in the case of Alice Sue Fun. Not until after World War I, when compulsory education became instituted, did Chinese girls graduate from high school in equal numbers to boys.

Up to that time, Chinese American children were categorically denied an equal education. Until 1884, provisions for the schooling of Chinese were not even included in the California school codes. Of the approximately 1,700 Chinese school-age children in San Francisco in the 1870s, only 20 percent received an education, and that was only thanks to missionary and private efforts. Petitions by clergymen and Chinese merchants to the San Francisco Board of Education went unanswered until the school district was sued by Mary and Joseph Tape in the case of *Tape v. Hurley* (1884). As a result of that suit, the segregated Chinese Primary School [a.k.a. Oriental Public School] was established as an alternative to admitting Chinese students to white schools.[39] In its first year of operation, there were only three girls among the thirty-eight enrolled students. By 1904 this number had increased to twenty, and after the 1911 Revolution, to fifty-eight.[40]

Some parents chose to send their daughters to classes or schools established for their benefit by Protestant missionaries concerned about the high illiteracy rate among Chinese women and aware of the strict Chinese practice of sex segregation. Indeed, Christian institutions were the first to address the issue of education for Chinese girls and women. As early as 1903, the Baptist mission started a girls' school in Chinatown to teach them Chinese, English, and the fine arts. *Chung Sai Yat Po* announced that tuition would be free and transportation to and from home provided.[41] Also according to *CSYP*, another girls' school was established in 1913 by Chinese Christians on Clay Street for the purpose of educating them so that they could "achieve gender equality and become better mothers of China's future citizens."[42] By 1920, 250, or 65 percent of the population of Chinese girls in San Francisco, were enrolled in the Oriental Public School (grades K–8), and illiteracy among native-born Chinese women had dropped from a high 77 percent in 1900 to a low 13 percent in 1920 (see appendix table 5).[43]

According to a 1921 study by Mary Bo-Tze Lee, the quality of education at the Oriental Public School was not equal to that of other city schools. Graduates of the Oriental Public School experienced difficulties in both academic standards and social interactions when they moved on to an integrated high school. Lee recommended that the Oriental Public School be given an increased budget, more conscientious teachers, and special courses to help the foreign-born learn English.[44] Some parents, aware of the inferior educational standards, tried to send their sons and daughters to other schools in the city. They succeeded only so long as there were openings and white parents did not object. When objections were raised, Chinese parents took the case to court but inevitably lost. In contrast, when Japanese students were ordered to attend the Oriental Public School in 1905, the Japanese government interceded on their behalf and President Theodore Roosevelt himself pleaded with the school district to allow Japanese students to attend the white public schools. Having just defeated Russia in the Russo-Japanese War, Japan, unlike China at the time, was an international power to be respected and feared. In exchange for allowing Japanese students to continue attending white schools, the Japanese government signed the Gentlemen's Agreement in 1907, restricting the further immigration of Japanese laborers. Finally, in 1926, as increased numbers of Chinese students graduated from the Oriental Public School and the school became overcrowded, Chinese students were allowed to attend Francisco Junior High School, but only after another major battle was waged by Chinese community leaders against Italian parents who wanted to keep the Chinese out.[45] The victory paved the way for Chinese Americans to attend public schools outside of Chinatown. In 1928, 11 Chinese girls graduated from Francisco Junior High School along with 15 boys. Ten years later, Chinese Americans made up more than half of the graduating class: there were 37 Chinese girls and 61 Chinese boys, among a total of 172 graduates.[46]

Although Chinese American students were finally allowed to sit in the same classroom with white students, they were not always readily accepted by their white classmates or white teachers. A 1937 study of Chinese high school students in San Francisco by Shih Hsien-ju indicated that Chinese students were participating in social activities as much as their white counterparts, but their activities were more limited in variety and tended to be segregated. While Chinese boys gravitated toward Chinese school clubs and the Chinese YMCA, Chinese girls joined club activities at the Chinese YWCA.[47] The situation did not improve in college. Often treated as foreign students, Chinese Americans were not permitted to join fraternities and sororities. Chinese students at Stanford University, expelled from the dormitory by white students, had to establish their own residential Chinese Club House. In the face of social exclusion, most participated in segregated organizations on campus, such as the nationwide Chinese Students' Alliance and the Sigma Omicron Pi Chinese Sorority, which was founded by Chinese women at San Francisco State Teachers' College in 1930.

Their segregated social life stemmed from deep-seated racial prejudice. As Eva Lowe, who attended Francisco Junior High and Girls' High School in the 1920s, recalled:

> We used to have streetcars on Stockton Street. After school, some kids would ride streetcars home, instead of walking home. And those Italian boys pulled them down from the streetcars. Chinese and Italian boys always had fights. Then when we had lunch period, even in high school, if we sit in the dining room at a certain table, next day the Caucasian girls won't sit there. They see a Chinese sitting there, they moved.[48]

Jade Snow Wong had similar experiences when she began attending a white public school at the age of eleven. She was never invited to any of the homes or parties of the other students. "Being shy anyway, she quietly adjusted to this new state of affairs; it did not occur to her to be bothered by it," she wrote in her autobiography. But one day she was delayed after school, and Richard, a white boy, took advantage of the situation. "I've been waiting for a chance like this," he said. With malice he taunted her, "Chinky, Chinky, Chinaman." Jade Snow was astonished but decided to ignore him. As she attempted to leave, he threw a blackboard eraser at her, which left a white chalk mark on her back. Although the act hurt her sense of pride and dignity, she chose to overlook it, reasoning, as her parents had taught her, that Richard lacked proper home training. "She looked neither to the right nor left, but proceeded sedately down the stairs and out the front door." Richard followed and danced around her, chortling: "Look at the eraser mark on the yellow Chinaman. Chinky, Chinky, no tickee, no washee, no shirtee!" But still Jade Snow ignored him, and he finally went away, puzzled by her lack of response. "When she arrived home, she took off her coat and brushed off the chalk mark," as if to erase it from her mind.[49] Her passivity was a defense stance of accommodation that the second generation had been taught to assume when confronted by racial conflict.

Access to quality education for Chinese Americans was further marred by insensitive teachers and vocational tracking into undesirable jobs. Until 1926, when Alice Fong Yu was hired by the San Francisco public schools, all of the teachers were white. Many Chinese American women recalled teachers who took an interest in them and regarded them stereotypically as model students—quiet, diligent, attentive, and obedient. Daisy Wong Chinn, who attended the Oriental Public School in the early 1920s, has fond memories of one of her teachers. "My eighth-grade teacher was a wonderful woman named Agnes O'Neill," she said. "She really drilled English, spelling, and grammar into us, and she always sat me in the front of the first row." One of the highlights in Daisy's life occurred when Miss O'Neill selected her essay for a citywide Community Chest contest. Daisy placed first, and her photograph and essay appeared on the front page of the *San Francisco Call*.[50]

Some women, however, also remembered teachers who were condescending in their attitudes or who were blatantly racist. Esther Wong, for instance, will never forget how she was mistreated by her French language teacher:

> All my teachers had been good to me, kind and helpful, but this one was an Englishwoman, and she did not like Orientals, and none of them could stand her, they always got out of her class, all but one Japanese girl and me, and I stood her the longest, for 15 months, then I had to get out of her class, although I lost credits by doing so. . . . Towards the last I had to do some sight-reading for her, and I was very much frightened. She was a very stern teacher, with very strict rules about everything. You had to stand just so far from your desk, hold your back just so, and everything. Well, I read for her, and there were no mistakes. She just looked me over, from head to foot, for a minute, and I did not know what was coming, but was frightened. Then she said very slowly, "Well, you read all right, but I don't like you. You belong to a dirty race that spits at missionaries."[51]

Such incidents, in combination with vocational tracking, inflicted irreparable damage on Chinese American students' sense of ethnic pride and self-esteem.

According to Shih Hsien-ju's study, Chinese boys in high school showed less vocational ambition than their white counterparts; none expressed interest in becoming lawyers, army officers, public officers, or policemen. Chinese girls displayed even less ambition than either white girls or Chinese boys. Although Chinese and white girls were interested in teaching, sales, and clerical work, the similarities ended there. Twice as many white girls as Chinese mentioned professional work, and only Chinese girls selected design, housework, and dressmaking as occupational choices. Chinese females were also more accepting of the idea of marriage over career. Interviews conducted with the students revealed that they were less ambitious because of their families' limited economic resources. More important, they were well aware of racial prejudice and their limited options in the labor market. A good number had even thought about going to China to find work. Shih concluded her study by recommending that the public school system join efforts with the Chinese community to provide vocational guidance and scholarships to Chinese students in need.[52]

By the time they graduated from high school, many Chinese American women, well aware of racial prejudice in the outside world, were discouraged from pursuing a college education. Moreover, few Chinese families had the financial resources to send their children to college. As second-generation Janie Chu pointed out, "Higher education is dearly loved by the Chinese, but what urge is there for the average girl to go on in school if economic conditions at home force her to employment and she feels that her prospects are not any better after years spent in higher education?"[53] The University of California, Berkeley, which enrolled the highest number of American-born Chinese in the country, had few Chinese women among its graduates in the 1920s, according to a study by Beulah Kwoh in 1947. Their numbers began to increase only in the 1930s (appendix table 10). Most of the students surveyed by Kwoh came from middle-class, educated families, and their choice of majors was usually an attempt to accommodate racial prejudice in the work world. Aware of their limited options, most planned either to be self-employed in a profession or to fill job needs in China. Thus, men tended to major in engineering, chemistry, and the biological sciences, while women were concentrated in the social sciences and medical fields.[54]

In light of the fact that few Chinese American women pursued college in the pre–World War II period, the following stories of Florence Chinn Kwan, Alice Fong Yu, and Bessie Jeong are exceptional. Nevertheless, they bear repeating, not only because they provide a personal dimension to Kwoh's statistics and analysis, but also because they offer insights into how Christianity and Chinese nationalism influenced "the cream" to pursue higher education and professional careers.[55] All three women were supported by progressive parents or Christian benefactors who believed in the importance of education for girls. As Florence pointed out, it was usually the Christian families in Chinatown who enrolled their daughters in school and who supported them through college:

> The Christian families usually did send their girls to school, but not the non-Christians. They were kept at home taking care of their brothers and sisters, learning how to sew, how to cook. Although I was the only girl in the family, my father was a missionary teacher, so I went to grammar school and Girls' High School. . . . All the girls then were marrying at around sixteen, seventeen, eighteen, and I was eighteen after high school when my mother chose someone for me. He was a very nice bachelor from church. But my father said, "No, go to college and get your Ph.D. and then go back to China to teach English."[56]

Alice Fong Yu credited her father, who was well educated and a Chinese nationalist with a progressive outlook, for encouraging all the children in the family to seek higher education. All six daughters in the family eventually graduated from college and pursued professions. As far back as Alice could remember, she was encouraged by her parents to become a teacher. The director of the local Red Cross, impressed by Alice's ability to fund-raise in the YWCA Girls Reserve, personally introduced her to the president of San Francisco State Teachers' College. The president tried to dissuade her by saying no school would ever hire a Chinese. Alice retorted, "But I'm not going to stay here. I just want the education to be a teacher. I'm going to China to teach my people."[57] She was accepted into Teacher's College but never did teach in China. Upon graduation in 1926, she found a job awaiting her at Commodore Stockton Elementary School (formerly, Oriental Public School), where a new principal recognized the need for a Chinese-speaking teacher. Alice, the first Chinese American to be hired by the San Francisco public schools, taught there for thirty-one years. With similar support from their parents, her sisters did equally well as first in the country to enter certain professional fields: Mickey Fong became the first Chinese American public health nurse; Marian Fong, the first Chinese American dental hygienist; and Martha Fong, the first Chinese American nursery school teacher.

Bessie Jeong, one of the earliest Chinese American physicians, did not have such supportive parents. On the contrary, her family did not believe education was important for girls. But she was fortunate to have the generous assistance of Christian benefactors. When her father tried to take her to China at the age of fifteen, Bessie ran away to the Pres-

The Fong family in 1930. *Front row, left to right:* Mother Lonnie Tom, Lorraine, Father Poy Mun Fong (a.k.a. Fong Chow); *back row, left to right:* Leslie, Marian, Alice, Taft, Albert, Helen, Mickey, and Martha. (Courtesy of H. Kim and Gordon H. Chang)

byterian Mission Home, believing that he only wanted to marry her off in China. With encouragement and financial support from Donaldina Cameron and other Christian sponsors, Bessie enrolled in Lux Normal School, a semiprivate high school for girls. She was among the first at Lux to say, "Hey, we're not going to be homemakers, we're going to be career girls. We're not having babies, we're going out in the world and contribute." Because of her Christian upbringing and sense of mission, she planned to become a medical missionary:

> I realized very young that China was overpopulated and that I didn't need to go to China and have children. For some reason, I seemed to know that China needed someone to help the people. And I didn't like the idea of just preaching. I wanted to do something constructive, and we [her sister and she] thought a medical missionary would be good.[58]

With the help of missionary women, a series of part-time jobs as a domestic worker, strong determination, and hard work, Bessie became the
first Chinese American woman to graduate from Stanford University in
1927, and she went on to earn a medical degree from the Women's Medical College of Pennsylvania.

Other exceptional Chinese American women who graduated from college and entered professions at this time almost all did so with the support of Christian parents or benefactors. Aside from Bessie Jeong, Faith
So Leung, the first Chinese woman dentist in America in 1905, was also
nurtured and supported by Protestant missionaries. Born in Canton in
1880, Faith was brought to the United States when she was thirteen by
Mrs. F. A. Nickerson, a missionary who later adopted her and provided
her with an education. It was Nickerson, who, seeing that Faith was "very
dexterous with her hands and evinced decided mechanical talent," encouraged her to pursue dentistry.[59] The only Chinese and female graduate among forty students, Faith received an ovation from her classmates
at the graduation ceremonies. She then established her practice in Chinatown and became the only female member of the Chinese Dental Club
in San Francisco.[60]

In the case of Soo Hoo Nam Art's family, all five sons and six daughters were encouraged to pursue a college education. Soo Hoo was an
ordained minister and, according to one of his daughters, Lily Sung,
was "*much* criticized for allowing a *daughter* to go to college."[61] Upon
graduation from college, all the sons became engineers, while the daughters became teachers; six of the children established careers in China.

Most Chinese American women, in the face of racism and sexism and
lacking economic means, were not able to pursue higher education or
professional careers in the 1920s. Although they were better educated
than the first generation, because of discrimination in the labor market
this advantage did not necessarily lead them to better-paying jobs.

Limited Work Opportunities

Like their mothers before them, second-generation women
generally had to work because of the denial of a family wage to most
Chinese men. Indeed, as Evelyn Nakano Glenn points out in her study
of Chinese American families, the small-producer family in which all
family members, including children, worked without wages in a family

business—usually a laundry, restaurant, grocery store, or garment shop
—predominated from the 1920s to the 1960s.[62] For those families in
San Francisco that did not own a small business, a family economy in
which individual family members worked at various jobs to help make
ends meet still prevailed. It was not uncommon for daughters to work
part-time throughout their public school years and quit school in their
teens to work full-time to help out their families. May Kew Fung, for
example, began working at the early age of seven to help her widowed
mother support a family of seven children. "I never had a childhood like
other kids," May told her grandson Jeffrey Ow many years later. "I had
nothing as a child. No toys, no place to go."[63] She started out peeling
shrimp, shelling clams, and stringing stringbeans, then moved on to
sewing in her uncle's garment shop. At fifteen, although she enjoyed
school and wanted to become a stenographer, May put the family's interest first. She quit school to work full-time sewing blue jeans during
the day, and at night she worked as an usher in a Chinese opera house
for an extra dollar.

Second-generation daughters, less encumbered by traditional gender roles that dictated women remain within the home, were considered "liberated" in being able to work outside the home in the labor
market.[64] But once there, they found themselves at a disadvantage
because of race and gender discrimination. Despite their English profi-
ciency, educational background, and Western orientation, most experienced underemployment and found themselves locked into low-paying,
dead-end jobs. One second-generation Chinese summed it up this way
in the *Chinese Times:*

> So far as the occupational opportunities are concerned, the American-
> born Chinese is a most unfortunate group of human beings. . . . The
> Americans will not accept us as citizens. . . . We cannot get occupational
> status in the American community, not because we are not worthy, but
> because we have yellow skin over our faces. If we turn back to the Chi-
> nese community there are not many places which can employ us. . . .
> There is a barrier between us and the old Chinese who are hosts of the
> Chinese community. We cannot get occupational status there either. The
> Americans discriminate against us, and we cannot get along in the Chi-
> nese community very well; what opportunities do we have in the coun-
> try?[65]

Still, second-generation women, though forced to endure discrimination in the workplace, took advantage of whatever opportunities arose,
tried to find meaning and purpose in their jobs, and worked doubly
hard to prove themselves. Here again, because examples of educated,

middle-class women are more abundant, their stories form the core of this section on the work lives of the second generation. The degree of economic independence that these women thus gained allowed some to shape new gender roles as well as elevate their social status at home and in the community.

Initially, second-generation women's occupations were not very different from those of their immigrant mothers. The 1900 and 1910 manuscript censuses indicate that Chinese women in San Francisco, whether immigrant or native-born, worked as either prostitutes or seamstresses. By 1920, however, as increased numbers of the second generation became better educated and more Americanized, their work pattern was taking a path distinctly different from that of their mothers. They began to branch into clerical and sales jobs (see appendix table 6). As Rose Chew, a social worker and second-generation woman herself, observed in 1930, whereas immigrant mothers worked primarily in garment and shrimp factories, did hemstitching and embroidery work, and served as domestic day workers, daughters were working outside the community as waitresses, stock girls, and elevator operators. Within the community, a few were now employed as public school teachers, doctors, dentists, bank managers and tellers, nurses, and beauty parlor owners.[66]

Although their work lives were an improvement relative to the drudgery and low wages of their parents, many of the second generation were disappointed by America's false promises of equal opportunity. They had studied hard in school, but despite their qualifications they were not given the same consideration in the job market as white Americans. College placement officers at both the University of California, Berkeley, and Stanford University, for example, found it almost impossible to place the few Chinese or Japanese American graduates there were in any positions, whether in engineering, manufacturing, or business. According to the personnel officer at Stanford,

> Many firms have general regulations against employing them; others object to them on the ground that the other men employed by the firms do not care to work with them. Just recently, a Chinese graduate of Stanford University, who was brought up on the Stanford campus with the children of the professors, who speaks English perfectly, and who is thoroughly Americanized, was refused consideration by a prominent California corporation because they do not employ Orientals in their offices.[67]

Occupational opportunities for American-born Chinese women were further circumscribed by gender. Economic pressures at home often forced girls to curtail their education and enter the labor force, where they worked at the same menial, low-wage jobs as their immigrant mothers. Domestic work was one such option. Protestant missionaries particularly encouraged Chinese girls to pursue this line of work because it prepared them for their future role as homemakers. They also regarded domestic work as "honest toil," unlike service in tearooms, restaurants, and clubs that "leads to many serious dangers for young and attractive Oriental girls."[68] Here again, missionary women were imposing their Victorian moral values on Chinese women. Although great care was taken to place Chinese women in "respectable" Christian homes, many were unhappy in these positions, complaining about the low pay, heavy workload, intrusive supervision, and rude condescension they experienced on the job. Unlike Japanese women, few Chinese women wanted to make a career out of domestic work.[69]

Compared to second-generation European American women, who were finding upward mobility in office and factory work, Chinese American women were not doing as well. When they tried to compete for office jobs outside Chinatown, they were generally told, "We do not hire Orientals," or "Our white employees will object to working with you." In many cases white establishments that hired them did so only to exploit their "picturesque" appearance or their bilingual skills in Chinatown branch offices. According to the sociologist William Carlson Smith,

> Chinese or Japanese girls on the Coast have been employed in certain positions as "figure-heads," as they themselves termed it, where they were required to wear oriental costumes as "atmosphere.". . . A merchant on Market Street in San Francisco said of the Chinese girls: "They dress in native costumes, they attract attention, and they can meet the public. That is why many of them are working as elevator girls and salesladies in big department stores, some as secretaries and others in clerical positions. One girl is a secretary in a radio station and she, too, wears Chinese dress."[70]

Gladys Ng Gin and Rose Yuen Ow are examples of Chinese American women who were willing to work in teahouses, restaurants, stores, and nightclubs as "figure-heads." Their stories shed light on how second-generation women were able to use the stereotyped images of Chinese women in mainstream culture to their advantage. Although they recognized that they were being used as "exotic showpieces," young women like Gladys and Rose took the jobs because there were few positions open to them that paid as well. In most cases they were temporary jobs, because once the novelty wore off the women were usually let go.

Although American-born, Gladys was practically illiterate in English as well as Chinese, her education having been interrupted when she was taken to China as a young girl. She therefore considered herself "lucky" when she found work as an usher at a downtown theater upon her return from China in 1918. She was only fifteen and did not know how to speak English. It didn't matter, she said, because all they wanted her to do was read numbers and take people to their seats. The one requirement was that she wear Chinese dress. For six months she was quite happy, because despite the trouble of constantly having to wash and starch the white Chinese dress she had to wear, she was making good money. But gradually, she and the twelve other girls were laid off one after another. In 1926, after Gladys learned English, she got a job running an elevator at a department store downtown. Again she was required to wear Chinese dress, but the hours and wages were equally good, so she was willing to tolerate the inconvenience. "Worked nine to six, six days a week," she said. "Seventy-five dollars a month was very good then. I was considered lucky to have found such a *see mun* [genteel] job." This time she stayed on the job for over ten years.[71]

Rose Yuen Ow, whose parents were quite open-minded (in spite of strong objections from relatives, her mother dressed her in Western clothes, refused to bind her feet, and allowed her to attend public school until she reached the eighth grade), was among the first in her generation to work outside the home in 1909. She recalled facing more discrimination in the Chinese community than in the outside labor market. "The first place I worked at in Chinatown was a movie house," she said. "I sat there and sold tickets. The cousins immediately told my father to get me home." She was about fourteen or fifteen years old then, and her father paid no attention to this meddling. In 1913, when she went to work at Tait's Cafe, a cabaret outside Chinatown, handing out biscuits and candy before and after dinner, "everyone talked about me and said I worked and roamed the streets." Men would even follow her to work from Chinatown to see where she was going. But despite what people in the community said about her, her father permitted her to continue working at the cabaret. Like Gladys, she was required to wear Chinese dress to provide atmosphere; otherwise, it was an easy job. And she was earning good money for the time—$50 a week.[72]

Rosie later moved up the wage ladder by capitalizing on mainstream America's interest in Chinese novelty acts. Chinese performers who sang American ballads and danced the foxtrot or black bottom were popular nightclub acts in the 1920s and 1930s. Billed as "Chung and Rosie Moy,"

Rose and her husband, Joe, performed in the Ziegfield Follies and in big theaters across the country with stars such as Jack Benny, Will Rogers, and the Marx Brothers. While the interest lasted, Rose earned as much as $200 to $300 a week. She would never earn that much money again. With the exception of Anna May Wong, few Chinese American entertainers ever made it big in show business. Despite their many talents, racism prevented them from making a profitable career out of it.

The double bind of sexism within the Chinese community and racism in the larger society also made it difficult for women who tried to enter and succeed in the business and professional fields. When white firms did hire Chinese American women, it was usually for the purpose of attracting Chinese business to their branch offices in Chinatown. Such was the situation for Dolly Gee, who had to fight both race and sex discrimination in order to establish a career in banking. At a time when there were few business opportunities for women in Chinatown, Dolly was regarded by her contemporaries as an exceptionally successful career woman. With the help of her father, Charles Gee, a prominent banker, she got her first experience working at the French American Bank in 1914 at the young age of fifteen. As she told the story, her father was initially hesitant to recommend her for the job because she was female:

> Early in 1914 I heard him say that another bank, the French American, desired to expand its savings activities and that there was a need for such a service in Chinatown. He said it was a fine opportunity for a young man, and regretted he had no son ready to take it up and follow in his footsteps as a banker. I immediately pointed out that although he had no son old enough, he had an energetic and ambitious daughter. I could see no reason why I could not take on the job and bring credit to my house, and he could advance no reason against it that I would listen to.[73]

When Dolly was introduced to the head of the bank, he raised objections to both her age and her gender. "I am surprised that you would consider allowing your daughter to go to work, like a common laborer," the bank manager said. "In two or three years she should be married, according to your custom." "It's true she is only fifteen years old," replied her father. "But you'd better take her on. I'll never hear the last of it if you don't. If she fails, it will be out of her head and no harm will be done." That challenge drove Dolly to prove herself. She canvassed Chinese households and refused to budge until she got an account or two from each family. She later recalled:

> Naturally I met opposition because of my sex and my youth. This was before the [Second] World War, remember, before even American girls

had invaded the business world to any significant extent. But I did get accounts, even among horrified elders who shook their heads at me while shelling out. Second-generation Chinese, born in this country, were more amenable.[74]

In 1923, when the French American Bank opened a branch in Chinatown, Dolly became the manager. And in 1929, when the bank merged with the Bank of America and the branch office moved to a new location, she was retained as manager. She hired an all-female staff of bank tellers to work under her and operated on the principles of trust and personal service to the Chinese community. As the first woman bank manager in the nation, Dolly Gee built "a brilliant record for herself in banking," according to one corporate publication.[75] Despite her abilities to draw deposit accounts and run an efficient branch, however, she was never promoted to a higher position outside Chinatown.

Unable to find jobs except in Chinatown, many Chinese American women who were high school graduates and bilingual worked as clerks and salespersons in local gift shops and businesses. Although these jobs were better-paying and more prestigious than domestic work, they seldom compensated women for their education and skills or led to higher positions of responsibility. Women who worked at the Chinatown Telephone Exchange, for example, had to know not only English but also five Chinese dialects and subdialects, memorize 2,200 phone numbers, and handle an average of 13,000 calls a day.[76] Until the 1906 earthquake led to the rebuilding of Chinatown, only male operators had been employed at the Chinatown Exchange. Because of the low pay and customer complaints about the men's gruff voices and curt manner, however, they were replaced by women, who had more pleasant voices and accommodating ways—and who, when dressed in Chinese clothing, also proved to be tourist attractions. In the 1920s, telephone operators, working eight hours a day, seven days a week, earned only $40 a month, compared to $50 a month earned by housekeepers and $60 a month by clerks and stock girls. Yet the limited number of jobs open to them and the family atmosphere of their work environment both still made employment as a telephone operator desirable for second-generation women.[77] Indeed, Chinese telephone operators were grateful for their jobs and seldom complained about the dress code or the working conditions, which other female operators deemed unsatisfactory.[78]

The few college graduates who had professional degrees also found themselves underemployed and confined to Chinatown because of racism in the larger labor market. Many an engineer and scientist ended

Operator working the switchboard at the Chinatown Telephone Exchange, 1920s. (Courtesy of the Telephone Pioneer Communications Museum)

up working in Chinese restaurants and laundries. As was true for black professionals, white employers would not hire them, and white clients would not use their services.[79] When Jade Snow Wong went to the college placement office for help, she was bluntly told, "If you are smart, you will look for a job only among your Chinese firms. You cannot expect to get anywhere in American business houses. After all, I am sure you are conscious that racial prejudice on the Pacific Coast will be a great handicap to you."[80] Later, frustrated by the limited role of a secretary, she sought advice from her boss about a career change and discovered that Chinese American women like her also had to contend with sexism. Her boss said,

> Don't you know by now that as long as you are a woman, you can't compete for an equal salary in a man's world? If I were running a business, of course, I would favor a man over a woman for most jobs. You're always taking a chance that a woman might marry or have a baby. That's just a biological fact of life. But you know that all things being equal, a

man will stay with you, and you won't lose your investment in his train-ing. Moreover, he's the one who has to support a wife and family, and you have to make allowance for that in the larger salary you give him. It's not a question of whether he's smarter than a woman or whether a woman is smarter than he. It's just plain economics![81]

Aware of both racial and sex discrimination in the job market, Jade Snow took the accommodating route by pursuing writing and ceramics, two fields in which she thought she would not have to compete with men or be judged by her race. These creative channels also allowed her to meld unique styles of expression that utilized both her Chinese and West-ern sensibilities. Her books, *Fifth Chinese Daughter* and *No Chinese Stranger*, addressed her experiences as a Chinese American woman; her pottery combined Chinese classic lines with Western functional forms. She also chose to set up shop in Chinatown, where she could attract the tourist trade. By making the best of her circumstances, she found an eco-nomic niche and became both a recognized writer and ceramicist.

Their experiences paralleling those of black professional women, Chi-nese American women who were the first to enter professions had trou-ble establishing careers for themselves, even in female-dominated occu-pations like teaching and nursing. When Alice Fong Yu appeared before the examination board of the San Francisco School District, they asked her pointed questions not usually asked of white candidates, such as "How [in what language] do you dream?"[82] Although she was hired as a schoolteacher, she was deliberately kept out of the classroom and as-signed the tasks of an assistant principal, but without due recognition or compensation. In addition, she was overworked and asked to perform duties beyond her classification. As the only Chinese-speaking teacher, Alice was called upon to counsel, translate, and act in the capacity of clerk, nurse, and social worker to the 100 percent Chinese student pop-ulation at Commodore Stockton Elementary School.

Her sister Mickey Fong also faced difficulties in entering and ad-vancing in the nursing profession. First, her application to the Stanford School of Nursing was rejected because at the time Asians were not per-mitted to enroll. Next, upon graduation from the San Francisco Hos-pital School of Nursing, she was discouraged from taking the public health nurses' examination: "they said I was Chinese and how would I get along with the white community." Then, a minimum height re-quirement of 5 feet 2 inches stopped Chinese women like her who were short from taking the examination for field nursing. Only after protests by both European and Chinese American doctors, the Chinese Six Companies, and Chinese American Citizens Alliance was the requirement waived for her and then stricken from all examinations. Finally, when it came time for Mickey to take the supervisor's examination, she had an equally hard time with the Civil Service Commission. "The Commission people were quite prejudiced," she recalled. "They didn't seem very friendly or encouraging. One of them said, 'How do you think that you could supervise American nurses!' in that tone of voice." With a great deal of pluck, Mickey retorted, "Well, if I'm qualified, and if I pass the examination, I don't see why not." Mickey did pass the examination, but chose to continue working as a public health nurse in Chinatown until she moved to Washington, D.C., with her husband in 1945.[83]

Racial and gender barriers also made it difficult for the first Chinese American women who chose medicine as their profession. Considered "men's work," being a doctor was popular among Chinese Americans for status reasons and also because they could work as doctors in their own communities should their services not be welcome in the larger society. The few Chinese women who held medical degrees inevitably had to establish their practices in Chinatown, though even there they were not always accorded the same respect as male doctors. Dr. Bessie Jeong, for example, had to omit her first name in public listings in order to attract patients who might be prejudiced against female doctors. "If they see 'Bessie,' they hesitate, even women sometimes, to go to a woman doctor," she said. "So I put 'B. Jeong' and before they know it—it's kind of embarrassing to turn and run, you know—they sit down and I try to make them feel at home with me."[84] Dr. Margaret Chung initially moved to San Francisco to escape discrimination in Los Angeles against single women, although she also wanted to serve the Chinese community. Being young, female, and non-Chinese-speaking, however, she found it difficult to gain the trust of Chinese patients there. Not until she proved her surgical skills and commitment to community service did Chinese patients begin coming to her.[85] Dr. Rose Goong, an obstetrician/gynecologist, had less trouble finding Chinese clients, largely because Chinese women were still reluctant to see male physicians. But she was also popular because she was known for being available around-the-clock to her patients and for providing free postnatal care to mothers and their babies.[86]

An alternative to unemployment or underemployment in America for the second generation was to seek work in China. Many middle-class parents, fired by nationalist sentiment and aware of discrimination in America and of China's need for professional and skilled personnel, encouraged their children in this direction. Jade Snow Wong's father tutored all his children in Chinese studies because he believed that "a Chinese could realize his optimum achievement only in China."[87] Although Jade Snow never fulfilled his plan, her older half-sister Esther spent a number of years teaching in China. Similarly, Alice Fong Yu was encouraged by her parents to pursue college with China in mind. "We were all told to get an education and go back to help the people in China. They knew we weren't wanted here," she said.[88] Alice did not go to China either, but a handful like Florence Chinn Kwan, Lilly King Gee Won, Rose Hum Lee, and Flora Belle Jan did. Florence found work teaching English and also served on the board of the YWCA; Lilly was professor of English at the Shanghai Foreign Language Institute for sixteen years until she retired in 1974; Rose worked for government bureaus and American corporations in Canton until the escalating war with Japan forced her to return to America; and Flora Belle found work as a journalist with a number of English-language publications.

Only Flora Belle, the most Americanized of the four women, had difficulties adapting to life in China. Although her husband's salary as a professor provided her and their three children a comfortable lifestyle, Flora was never happy there. Her elder daughter explained:

> The years in Peking were good ones for my father but not particularly for my mother. Mainly because she was an American and she did not like China. She could neither read or write the language. . . . She thought it [China] was filthy. She boiled everything. She was always interfering in the kitchen because she thought the servants were too dirty for her standards.[89]

Flora insisted on speaking English at home, dressing the children in Western clothes and taking them to see American movies, cooking and eating American food, and inviting only English-speaking diplomats, business people, and students to parties that she hosted.

Compounding her problems was the discrimination she faced as a Chinese American and woman in journalism. Because of her language limitations, she could only seek work with English-language publications. Her letters to Ludmelia were filled with complaints about white male supervisors who treated her unfairly in terms of work assignments, wages, and promotional opportunities. While at the Office of War Information, she wrote:

> My education and previous experience were not considered when I came here. I was given a stenographic test like any China born and I was paid

like them. Although after one month of work as a permanent staff member, I was given a $24 raise U.S. because I had shown efficiency. I am still getting a smaller salary than four other girls, two of whom have never been out of China. All around me are staff members who are no older than I, and, who are no better educated, who hold executive positions with four times my salary, good living quarters, and a living allowance. You wonder I am dissatisfied? It is hard to be born a woman but hopeless to be born a Chinese. There is nothing to hold me here. I shall go at an instance's notice.[90]

Her life in China proved to her that she was too Americanized ever to fit in. As hardships during the war years took their toll on her and she watched others less worthy reap benefits and rewards because they were white men or because they were women who knew how to flatter the boss, she became more cynical and determined to return home:

I have become philosophic about life and somewhat of a social recluse. I don't have the acute enthusiasm of my youth, nor the abysmal disappointments. I have learned to control my temper and am generally calm and collected. Often I wonder about what pays off in this mortal world and what price, talent and ability and conscientious effort? Our values are all wrong. What usually counts most is hidden and unrecognized. What pays off is vulgar, shallow, and cheap. . . . Somewhere, Ludy, there are green hills, calm blue skies, a musical running brook, a cow grazing contentedly on the pasture, and a clean white cottage where peace and goodness dwell. I shall not give up until I find this place on this awesome, other earth. I cannot say when I am coming back to America, but I shall come if it is just to die.[91]

In 1949, she finally came home with her two daughters and high hopes of fulfilling her literary aspirations. After a brief visit in Fresno, they went to live with Ludmelia in Yuma, Arizona, where Flora Belle found work as a secretary and spent all her spare time composing at the typewriter. But her health never recovered from the hardships she had suffered in China. A year later, at the age of forty-three, Flora Belle Jan died of high blood pressure and kidney failure. Her children had inscribed on her gravestone: "A journalist and feminist before her time. A talent and beauty extinguished in her prime. Our beloved mother."

Chinese Americans who could speak Chinese and who were more acculturated in the Chinese lifestyle had an easier time in that country. Rose Hum Lee, for example, felt she had found her niche in China, and she would have stayed except for the war. She had less trouble finding work and adjusting to life in China because her mother had insisted on

Flora Belle Jan in the 1930s.
(Courtesy of Flora Belle Jan's
daughters)

educating all her daughters and instilling in them a love for China and
a deep appreciation for Chinese culture. Like Flora Belle, Rose grew up
outside San Francisco—in Butte, Montana. But unlike Flora Belle, Rose
was well versed in Chinese language and art. Writing as a sociologist years
later, she expressed an understanding of the second generation's mission in China that Flora Belle lacked. China's need for manpower and
the discriminatory practices of the dominant American society, she
pointed out, had motivated many of the second generation to seek economic improvement and political expression in China. And for the most
part, China did not disappoint them.

> The men could effect more rapid social and occupational mobility in
> China as teachers, professors, foreign firm representatives, minor consular
> officials, junior executives of foreign branch offices, engineers, doctors,
> dentists, salesmen, business men, manufacturers, chemists, physicists, etc.
> The girls could find work in foreign and Chinese firms, government of-
> fices, educational institutions, and churches. They lived in better resi-
> dential areas, often peopled entirely by American-born Chinese and so-

journers, and could maintain a lifestyle and a standard of living far above that of the local population.[92]

Such opportunities were unavailable to them in America. In addition, they were able to enjoy a high social status and sense of belonging in China. When the war against Japan escalated, Rose did her part by organizing emergency social services for refugees and war orphans in Canton and serving as a radio receptor and interpreter of Tokyo broadcasts.

Upon return to the United States and a booming war economy, second-generation Chinese Americans like her were able to put their experiences in China to good use, achieving occupational mobility and social acceptance. Rose herself continued to help in the war effort, lecturing across the country through the United China Relief Speakers Bureau and participating actively in the American Women's Volunteer Services. With the support of her mother, she went on to college and became the first Chinese American woman to earn a Ph.D. in sociology (from the University of Chicago) and to head a department at an American university (the sociology department at Roosevelt University). At the time of her death in 1959, Rose had earned a national reputation for her pioneering work on urban development and the assimilation experience of Chinese Americans and had just received the Woman of Achievement Award of B'nai B'rith for her contributions to ecumenical cooperation.[93]

The work lives of second-generation women attest to the extent of racial and sex discrimination they faced in the labor market and the ways in which they were able to cope. Most accommodated by making the most of their limited circumstances; some went to China for better economic opportunities. Even though discrimination in the work world often stopped them from fulfilling their potential in their chosen occupational fields, Chinese American women managed to earn enough to support themselves and, more often than not, help out their families. At the same time, their work experiences drew them away from the influences of their cultural upbringing at home and further into the public arena, broadening their outlook in life and encouraging them in the direction of American consumerism and modern living.

A Segregated Social Life

Second-generation Chinese Americans came of age during a decade of revolutionary change in the country's manners and morals caused by the convergence of postwar prosperity and rebellious youth. The 1920s, known as the modern era of flappers, jazz, and gin, was marked by consumerism promoted by corporate capitalism and social permissiveness, as manifested in the new codes of collegiate dress, leisure activities, and sexual mores. It was considered fashionable for young men to dress in baggy tweeds, knickers, and raccoon coats, while women wore knee-length dresses, flesh-colored stockings, yellow rain slickers, and multicolored bandannas. Commercial advertising and Hollywood films projected a carefree life of fun and pleasure to be found in smoking, drinking, dancing, parties, movies, sports, automobile rides, and free love; necking and petting were condoned. To be a "new woman" in the 1920s was to hold high the banners of individuality, independence, and self-fulfillment and to find emotional satisfaction and intimacy through relationships with men.[94] In contrast to the women's suffrage period, feminism was downplayed.

Despite the apparent laxity, there were racial and class limitations as to who could partake of this carefree lifestyle. Most Chinese Americans could not. Nevertheless, they, like other American adolescents who were influenced by what they saw on the silver screen or read about in the magazines, yearned for the same freedom and excitement in their lives. Chingwah Lee, a second-generation Chinese American, had this to say about his peers:

> They study Chinese and speak English, admire Confucius or adore Jesus, like Chinese literature, art and festivals, but dance to American music, and motor, hike and attend theaters as do the Americans. Never before had they experienced a change in their racial history more dramatic, more drastic, and more significant.[95]

Chinese American women, too, wanted to be part of this new social landscape. Janie Chu, also second generation, observed that the Chinese American woman

> gets her knowledge of social America from the "movies," from the street, from what she hears from the girls at service in homes. She wants to be American and she has always a struggle in her mind as to what is right and what is not right in respect to Occidental thinking. She teems with the life that urges on this new generation of Americans. She wants excitement and thrills. She wants to live.[96]

At the same time that economic constraints stopped many Chinese American women from responding to the mass media's lure of consumerism, traditional concepts of gender roles and racism also made it difficult for them to partake of this life.[97] Although they had rejected the social life and institutions of their parents' generation, they still could not integrate into mainstream society. Traditional ideas about sex segregation further limited their social activities in Chinatown. Like their mothers, they were not allowed to join the male-dominated family and district associations. Political and social organizations started by their male peers, such as the Chinese American Citizens Alliance, Chinese YMCA, and Yoke Choy Club, were also off-limits to them. (The bylaws of the Chinese American Citizens Alliance were not changed to admit women members until 1973.) Although the Chinese YMCA Board of Directors was willing to allow girls from the YWCA to attend monthly socials and Sunday vesper services at the YMCA, they refused their request for use of the gymnasium because board members felt "there would be community criticism having girls use a boys' building on specified nights."[98] The Chinese students' clubs in the high schools and colleges were among the few groups to allow coeducational membership. Nor could Chinese women freely integrate into the larger society. Like other Americans, they went to the movies and theaters, attended parties and dances, participated in sports, went hiking and on picnics, but almost all of these activities occurred in a segregated setting. Nevertheless, their social life moved them in the direction of defining a gender role and relationship different from that of their mothers—a definition that was shaped by the influence of assimilation within the limitations imposed by racism and sexism.

One early sign of their break with tradition—one that even met with community approval—was the staging of Chinatown's first beauty contest in 1915. Initiated by the Chinese Six Companies, the competition for the title of Chinatown queen emulated the American cultural practice of crowning festival queens. The winner—whoever sold the greatest number of raffle tickets—was to preside over Chinatown celebrations in connection with the Panama-Pacific Exposition. "It wasn't a matter of intelligence or beauty, just popularity," recalled Rose Yuen Ow, one of the contestants. As it turned out, wealthy customers at Tait's Cafe, where she was working, surprised her by sending a $5,000 check to the Chinese Six Companies in her name. Bedlam broke out. "So they said it wasn't right. So everyone fought about it," said Rose. Her father threatened to call out the tongs to settle the matter, but Rose decided to concede the title of Chinatown queen to Rose Lew. A lavish coronation ball attended by over four hundred Chinese and Western guests was held at the Fairmont Hotel. According to newspaper accounts, the affair was bicultural. The queen and her court dressed in Chinese clothing, while the guests dressed in Western clothing. There was lion dancing as well as dancing to Western music. But so afraid was the queen of further trouble that she did not show up to lead the parade through Chinatown that evening.[99]

Despite the mishaps, the event was considered successful, and thereafter it became a tradition in Chinatown to sponsor beauty contests whenever fund-raising needs arose. Although such occasions helped to boost the self-esteem of Chinese American women by offering them a rare opportunity to take center stage in the public arena, beauty contests were clearly a form of sexual exploitation. Totally run by male community leaders, they did little to empower women; rather, Chinese women were simply used as attractive vehicles to draw tourists and money into the community.[100] Be that as it may, the fact that Chinese women were encouraged to enter beauty contests indicated a change in attitude toward their public roles in Chinatown.

Perhaps the most extreme challenge to the status quo came from flappers like Flora Belle Jan, who, living on her own and without parental supervision, didn't think twice about indulging her desires for fashionable clothes and romantic affairs, writing scandalous newspaper columns, and leading an active social life. But even for liberated women like her, racial discrimination limited the social expression of "flapperism." While attending the University of California, Flora Belle was never really part of the flapper movement; she could not join a sorority or date white boys. So she became active in the Chinese Students' Alliance, went to Chinese fraternity parties, competed for the title of Chinatown queen, and dated "Chinatown sheiks," who she said knew how to "shimmy 'Chicago' and tango . . . buy candy for the Shebas, take them to the theater, sing them all kinds of 'I've got the blues' songs, and do everything else that American sheiks indulge in."[101] However, her unconventional writings and behavior were too extreme for Chinatown; social ostracism forced her to consider transferring to the University of Chicago. She wrote to her friend Ludmelia:

> And, Ludie, listen to this—I have been out with so many people for the past few years that I can't help but be known and notorious, and those that I meet now, whom I really care to associate with, feel that I am a friend to too many people, and I cannot be limited to them, so better friendships are impossible. I put this mildly. My reputation, while not at stake, is winked at by many people. I didn't use to care—but I can't help it now. Of course I can *never* be so wicked as they regard me—but what is the use of virtue when it isn't recognized? Anyway, I am tired of everybody here—and I want to go away to Chicago, where the distractions of

the multitude will not hurt me. There I can perhaps write, and become a worthwhile personage. Here—mediocrity and the lowering influence of the masses are harmful. There is no incentive to rise, one has to be like the others or be criticized.[102]

Because Flora Belle had grown up in Fresno, where she had been exposed to a broad range of people and experiences, she was more adept at interethnic mixing than her peers in San Francisco. However, a few other young women in San Francisco Chinatown had grown up as Americanized and independent as Flora Belle. Florence Lee Loo, for example, initially led a sheltered life, attending Oriental Public School and Chinese language school. "Not only did I go to Chinese school," she said, "but my mother even had a Chinese tutor come and tutor us three sisters in the Chinese classics. Oh, yes, my identification in Chinese is very strong. We were always taught to be terribly proud of our heritage . . . that we are so much more superior than *sai yun* [Westerners]." Her parents were relatively well off (her father owned a small cigar factory that employed four workers), liberal minded, and willing to indulge some of her fancies. Her mother trusted Florence to always do the right thing. "Because if she forbid me, she knows I will do it anyway," she added. For instance, she and her sister were allowed to go horseback riding, a rather expensive sport. As she told the story:

> Chinese girls at that time never go horseback riding, but Daisy and I, we went horseback riding because one summer, we all had the flu, and the doctor said, go to the country to recuperate. So we went to Fairfax. At that time, it was not developed at all. And then we got a cabin and it was very inexpensive. Nearby was a stable for the cowboys and they taught us how to ride. So when we came back to San Francisco, my, I really splurged [claps her hands gleefully]. I went to Magnin's and bought myself a hauberk and boots. That time it was very expensive. But I said, I don't care. I put every cent into my britches and we went riding in Golden Gate Park.

Not only were the Lee sisters the only Chinese Americans to go horseback riding, but they were also probably among a handful who could afford to vacation in Fairfax and shop at Magnin's department store downtown. While in high school Florence was also allowed to go hiking, swim, and play tennis, and she went out dancing until two or three o'clock in the morning. Aside from having liberal, middle-class parents, Florence also attributed her active social life to having worked outside Chinatown. "I went to work at this tearoom after school," she said. "All the cus-

tomers were very, very sweet to me. And I'm an outgoing person anyway, so I got along with lots of them. And they would invite me home
for lunch and tea and things like that. And so, I had a glimpse of another part of society besides my own."[103]

Christianity also played an important role in acculturating Chinese
girls to American life and middle-class values. Compared to that of Flora
Belle Jan and Florence Lee Loo, the social life of most Chinatown daughters was quite circumscribed. Adherence to traditional gender roles was
constantly enforced by protective parents and reinforced by the watchful eyes of an insular community. Most of their time and energy was
taken up by school and work, with little left for play. As proper young
women, they were not allowed out unescorted, nor could they socialize
with boys; dating was out of the question. Participation in Christian activities, however, was considered wholesome and safe and was permitted even by non-Christian parents. Indeed, the churches were the first
institutions to provide services to the second generation, including Sunday school, Chinese school, shelters for the homeless, boarding homes
for working girls, and organized recreational activities.[104]

During the early 1900s, attending church was often the only acceptable outside activity allowed girls by immigrant parents. In 1920,
almost all of the Chinese children (close to one thousand) attended Sunday school in Chinatown. In addition, many young people participated
in choirs and church-sponsored debates and athletic events. By 1930
there were ten churches in Chinatown competing against each other to
attract the second generation into their folds: the Chinese Presbyterian,
Methodist Episcopal, Chinese Congregational, Chinese First Baptist, Salvation Army, Chinese Cumberland, Protestant Episcopal, Chinese Independent Baptist, St. Mary's Catholic, and Seventh Day Adventist. Having failed to convert many of the first generation to Christianity—less
than 2 percent of the Chinese population was Christian in 1892—missionaries attempted to attract their offspring. Catering to the interests
of the young people, the various churches offered a range of activities,
including Bible classes, club activities, Saturday night socials, discussion
groups, and summer recreational programs. In 1930, the largest mission was the St. Mary's Catholic Chinese Center. Aside from being a
parochial school through the eighth grade for children during the day,
it was a Chinese school in the late afternoons and a social center for young
adults in the evenings. Chinese girls met there on Friday nights to cook,
paint, play the piano, sew, or participate in drama or basketball. The center also sponsored a science club for both boys and girls and provided

young members with vocational guidance, which was sorely lacking in the public schools.[105]

By reaching out to the second generation in this way, Chinatown churches hoped to fulfill their mission of simultaneously Christianizing and acculturating this growing group of Chinese Americans. Most Chinese girls participated in church more for social than for religious reasons. Alice Sue Fun, for example, considered attending embroidery classes at the Chinese Congregational church a social highlight of her childhood, while many others, like Jade Snow Wong, became Americanized through their participation in Christian organizations such as the Chinese YWCA. But even as they adopted Western ways and middle-class values, they did not totally forsake the Chinese values and customs fostered by their families and community. Most continued to maintain traditional values of respect for the elderly, family harmony and unity, discipline and excellence in education and work, as well as an appreciation for Chinese opera and art, food, and celebrations. In this way, they were pragmatic like their mothers, taking what was useful to them from Western religion and seeing no contradiction in practicing both cultures at the same time.

In the 1920s, second-generation girls were particularly drawn to the Chinese YWCA because its wide range of services met many of their needs. It provided them with a quiet place to study; a library collection for leisure reading; kitchen and bath facilities, which were appreciated by those from crowded homes; a piano and sewing machine; access to the swimming pool at the Central YWCA; classes in gymnastics, American cooking, dressmaking, and music; employment and housing assistance; and social interaction in recreational clubs that were organized and run democratically by the girls themselves.[106]

The YWCA also groomed its members for civic duty. Its oratorical contests, cosponsored with the YMCA, helped women develop public speaking skills, self-confidence, and political consciousness. One competition, for example, focused on "Our Duty to Serve Chinatown."[107] Emma Lum, who won first prize, later became the first Chinese woman to practice law in California in 1953. The YWCA constantly reminded Chinese American women to exercise their right to vote, and it also nurtured their participation in fund-raising efforts and major events in the community. Moreover, the Girl Reserves was often the only avenue by which some Chinese girls socially interacted with other races outside Chinatown. In these ways, the YWCA helped them broaden their social life, develop their leadership skills, and become more active in group functions and community affairs.

Christianity, along with Chinese nationalism, also inspired the founding of the Square and Circle Club, the earliest and most enduring service organization of second-generation Chinese women. It all began on a Sunday afternoon in 1924 when seven young women—Alice Fong, Daisy L. Wong, Ann Lee, Ivy Lee, Bessie Wong, Daisy K. Wong, and Jennie Lee—got together as usual after Sunday service at the Chinese Congregational church to chat, read the Sunday papers, and do the crossword puzzle. That day, an article about flood and famine in the Guangdong area of China caught their attention. This distressful news stirred them to action. Organized as the Square and Circle Club—in keeping with the shape of the Chinese coin and a Chinese motto, "In deeds be square, in knowledge be all-around"—the young women embarked on their first fund-raising event, a jazz dance benefit to be held outside Chinatown.[108] The nationalist cause that had spurred their social activism was no different than that which had first propelled their mothers into the public arena; but the modern, bicultural style of their first event clearly reflected their unique identity as American-born Chinese women with middle-class values.

The local newspaper called attention to this unconventional event, which marked the debut of a new generation of Chinatown daughters:

"Shake Wicked Hoof in Yankee Hop" Chinese Jazz Dance Tonight: Square and Circle Club to Give Real American "Hop"

A new blend of the oriental and the occidental in San Francisco! Sixteen little Chinese co-eds are sponsoring an American jazz dance.

To those who know the customs of old China, this undertaking of the flappers of Chinatown is a remarkable event in the annals of convention smashing. . . .

The dance combines the characteristics of both peoples—American jazz by Chinese orchestra, and American dancing by Chinese girls in American party frocks and high heels.

As observed by the reporter, second-generation women were breaking out of their traditional gender mold in assuming the responsibility for organizing a major fund-raising event in the same way that other American girls did:

The members of the Square and Circle Club—American-born Chinese girls—have startled Chinatown with their occidental managing of a dance to be given tonight in Native Sons' Hall at Geary and Mason streets for the benefit of the Chinese Flood and Famine Relief.

"Usually the Chinese Chamber of Commerce or the Six Companies are in charge of these charitable and public affairs," Alice Fong, presi-

Charter members of the Square and Circle Club, founded in 1924.
Clockwise from top: Alice Fong (Yu), Daisy K. Wong, Ann Lee (Leong),
Jennie Lee, Bessie Wong (Shum), Ivy Lee (Mah), and Daisy L. Wong
(Chinn). (Judy Yung collection)

dent of the girls' club, said today. "But we wanted to help, too. American girls can do these things. Why shouldn't we?"[109]

In the years that followed, the club's membership roll continued to grow, stabilizing at about eighty members and attracting second-generation women looking for a social niche to express their bicultural identity and civic pride. As was true of other American women's clubs at this time, members tended to be middle-class women who were well educated and employed in white-collar or professional work. Likewise, almost all of the club's activities focused on charity projects that were extensions of women's domestic role as caregivers.[110] Proceeds from American-style fund-raisers—hope chest raffles, variety shows, musical

performances, and fashion shows—were used primarily to support orphans at the Chung Mei Home, Ming Quong Home, and Mei Lun Yuen;
Chinese patients at the Laguna Honda Home and Chinese Hospital; and
youth programs at the Chinese YWCA and YMCA. Like the earlier Chinese Women's Jeleab Association, the Square and Circle Club followed
the American practice of democracy by establishing bylaws that stipulated equal and active participation from its members. Both clubs also
shared the goal of providing mutual aid to their exclusively female members. During the early years, the Square and Circle Club established a
Friendship Fund, whereby grants and loans could be made to young
women for educational, health, and emergency use. Other activities included helping women find jobs, working with the Chinese YWCA to
establish and operate its dormitory, and entering the only women's float
in the Chinese New Year parade in the late 1920s.[111]

Although none of the Chinese women's organizations addressed feminist issues at this time, the Square and Circle Club did take a number
of strong stands on racial, social, and political issues that affected the
welfare of the community. Club minutes indicate that letters were written to government officials asking for longer hours and better lighting
at Chinese Playground, a dental and health clinic for Chinatown, re-
tention of Chinatown's only Chinese-speaking public health nurse, public housing, and passage of immigration legislation favorable to the Chinese. The club also worked with other community organizations to
register voters, clean up Chinatown, protest racist legislation such as the
Dickstein Nationality Bill and the Texas Anti-Alien Land Bill,[112] and support the anti-Japanese war effort in China.

To this day, although its influence has waned, the Square and Circle
Club continues to function as a women's service organization in San
Francisco. To its credit, countless numbers have benefited from its generosity and from being members in the organization. At a time when
few social channels were open to American-born Chinese women, the
Square and Circle Club provided them with an opportunity to belong,
to socialize with peers, and to exercise their civic duty. In the process,
the women developed self-confidence, leadership skills, a newfound spirit
of teamwork, and took pride in their bicultural heritage and community service. As Ruth Chinn, an active member since 1948, commented
in her 1987 senior thesis on the Square and Circle Club:

> The Hope Chest Raffle brought the members together. A night was set
> aside for knitting, embroidering, and crocheting to fill the Hope Chest.
> The shows and musical extravaganzas were projects that brought to the

forefront the many talents of the individual members. They were super-
stars, whether playing the lead or bit part in a show, singing in the choral
group, dancing in the chorus line, sewing costumes, set designing, making the props, writing the script, or being the "director"—we did it all! . . .
Together, not only did we have fun (although frustration, anger, and anx-
iety went along with it all) producing the shows, we also raised impressive funds to fill our coffers to support our many community service com-
mitments.[113]

Like the Chinese YWCA, the Square and Circle Club was established
under the auspices of a Protestant institution, but as the group developed the church ceased to be a binding force among its members. Although acculturation into American life remained a goal, it was not to
be realized at the cost of losing their Chinese heritage. What kept both
organizations viable was the growing population of Chinese American
women, their continued exclusion from mainstream society as well as
the Chinatown establishment, and the organizations' effectiveness in
serving the social needs of women. At the same time that the services
of the Chinese YWCA and Square and Circle Club benefited the Chinatown community, the leadership training that members received encouraged them to participate more actively in the political arena.

A Dual Political Identity

Compared to their mothers, second-generation women
played a relatively active political role. Their birthright, higher educational attainment, and Western orientation all served to heighten their
political consciousness and desire for civic participation. Whereas their
immigrant mothers had only been encouraged to contribute to Chinese
nationalist causes, American-born daughters became involved in both
Chinese and U.S. politics. Even as they sought ways to express their loyalty to America, they did not shirk their responsibilities to their parents'
homeland.

This dual political identity was planted in the psyches of the second
generation at an early age. Their family upbringing, Chinese school training, and community involvement emphasized their duty to China, while
their public school education and social activities instilled in them a strong
desire to be exemplary American citizens. However, their efforts to exercise their birthright were constantly thwarted by racial discrimination.

Even their citizenship status had to be protected by constant vigilance. In 1913 and again in 1923, California legislators introduced bills in Congress intended to disfranchise citizens of Chinese ancestry. The Cable Act of 1922 stipulated that a female citizen who married an "alien ineligible to citizenship" would lose her U.S. citizenship. In all three instances, the Chinese American Citizens Alliance fought successfully to protect the rights of the second generation.[114] Nevertheless, citizenship status often did not guarantee Chinese Americans equal treatment. The discrimination they experienced in school, the workplace, in public areas, housing, and marriage made them feel all too keenly their real status as second-class citizens. The following sentiments of two second-generation Chinese Americans were all too common:

> I speak fluent English, and have the American mind. I feel that I am more American than Chinese. I am an American citizen by birth, having the title for all rights, but they treat me as if I were a foreigner. They have so many restrictions against us. I cannot help it that I was born a Chinese.

> I thought I was American, but America would not have me. In many respects she would not recognize me as American. Moreover, I find racial prejudice against us everywhere. We are American citizens in name but not in fact.[115]

Unlike Mexican Americans and Japanese Americans, who, experiencing the same discriminatory treatment, refused to stake their futures in their parents' homelands, many Chinese Americans approaching adulthood in the 1920s turned to China as a possible solution to American racism.[116] Well aware of their limited opportunities for gainful employment and meaningful integration into American society, they were equally cognizant of China's need for their skilled labor. The question that nagged their consciences was "Does my future lie in China or America?" When the Ging Hawk Club of New York sponsored an essay contest on this theme, a respondent chord was struck in the hearts and minds of second-generation Chinese Americans throughout the country.[117] The range and complexity of their answers illustrate the depth of their dilemma in the face of racial discrimination, cultural conflict, and the issue of national identity. One point of view was expressed by the first-place winner, Robert Dunn, a student at Harvard University:

> Ever since I can remember, I have been taught by my parents, by my Chinese friends, and by my teacher in Chinese school, that I must be patri-

otic to China. They have said: "You should be proud of China's four thousand years of glorious and continuous history, of her four hundred million population, and of her superior culture and civilization. You must be thankful for the traditions and customs you have inherited as a member of the yellow race. What is more, you would not be living if it were not for your ancestors and parents who are Chinese. Most certainly, then, you are obliged to render service to China, especially in these days of need and stress and humiliation. Don't you realize that the Chinese are mocked at, trodden upon, disrespected, and even spit upon? Haven't you yourself been called degrading names? Have you no face, no sense of shame, no honor? How can you possibly think of staying in America to serve it?"

But as much as Robert felt an obligation to China, he also felt an obligation to America:

Somehow, however, I feel there is another side to the picture. I owe much pride and gratitude to America for the principles of liberty and equality which it upholds, for the protection its government has given me, and for its schools and institutions in which I have participated. Without them, I certainly would not be what I am now. . . . I am certainly as much indebted to America as I am to China. If this is true, then I should serve both equally; but is this possible if I choose a future that lies here in America?

After considering that employment opportunities were scarce in both China and the United States and that he, as a Chinese American, would have difficulties adjusting to life in China, Robert concluded that he could do his part just as well in America by promoting goodwill and understanding between the Chinese and American peoples and by contributing financial support to enterprises in China. He could, he believed, have it both ways.

With the conclusions, then, that I owe America as much allegiance as I do China; that it is possible to serve China while living in America; that remunerative employment, though scarce, is not impossible for me to obtain in either China or America; and that I would avoid the unhappiness and social estrangement due to conflicting cultures by staying in America: I think no one could justly accuse me of being unwise if I chose a course of life whose future lies here in America.[118]

Others, like Kaye Hong, a student at the University of Washington who won second place in the essay contest, took a different line. Their future lay in China because China needed their help and because employment opportunities were better there than in America. He wrote:

My patriotism is of a different hue and texture. It was built on the mound of shame. The ridicule heaped upon the Chinese race has long fermented within my soul. I have concluded that we, the younger generation, have nothing to be proud of except the time-worn accomplishments of our ancient ancestors, that we have been living in the shadow of glories, hoping that these arts and literature of the past will justify our present. Sad but true, they do not. To live under such illusions is to lead the life of a parasite.

In his view, it would be more meaningful for Chinese Americans to do their part in building a new nation in China. Thus, "it is for me— 'Go Further West, Young Man'. Yes, across the Pacific and to China."[119]

In response, Jane Kwong Lee wrote that both Robert Dunn and Kaye Hong had "half-cooked ideas about China" as a result of the older generation's failure to educate them properly. As long as this continued, she predicted, Robert's opinions would continue to represent the majority view, and only a small percentage of Chinese Americans would go to China in search of a future. Although she titled her essay, "The Future of Second Generation Chinese Lies in China and America," she advocated that "since China is weak and not a comfortable place to live, all Chinese, including American-born Chinese, should try to make her strong and rich."[120] A year later she amended this view, saying that it was important for college graduates seeking employment in China to know the Chinese written language and customs.[121]

Ironically, neither Robert Dunn, Kaye Hong, nor Jane Kwong Lee acted on the opinions they expressed. Despite what he said in his essay about remaining in the United States, Robert, after graduating from Harvard University in international law, went to China in 1941, where he became the secretary of one of China's top delegates to the United Nations Conference. After the 1949 revolution he returned to the United States, working as senior reference librarian at the Library of Congress until he retired. Kaye, who had advocated going "west to China," ended up staying in the United States, where he made his fortune in business. As for Jane Kwong Lee, by the time she graduated from college, her mother had passed away and, rather than returning to China, she settled down to married life and active political involvement in San Francisco. These three students' contrary actions to their earlier beliefs show how Chinese Americans had to stand ready and accommodate changing circumstances in their lives.

When polled, 75 percent of Chinese Americans who attended the Chinese Young People's Summer Conference at Lake Tahoe, California, in 1935 were in favor of serving China. During a discussion on the issue, many of them expressed the belief that the second generation not only *should* go back to China, but they *must* go back to China.[122] Similar sentiments were expressed in *CSYP*, whose line was "Once a Chinese, always a Chinese." The newspaper encouraged Chinese Americans to learn Chinese but also to take advantage of the American educational system—to acquire knowledge of mechanics and applied sciences so that they could take this knowledge back to benefit China. "Indeed," the newspaper stated, "your future lies with China, not with the United States."[123] At the same time, though, *CSYP* encouraged those entitled to vote to do so. "The thought of eventually going back to China should not keep the Chinese from voting," the newspaper pointed out. "Exercising the right to vote is one way to ensure protection for the individual and the community."[124]

Some Chinese American women, whose political identities were shaped by their parents' loyalty to their homeland and speeches by Chinese nationalists in the community, also felt strongly that their future lay in China. These thoughts, expressed by Jade Snow Wong in her commencement address at graduation from San Francisco City College, were shared by her peers:

> The Junior College has developed our initiative, fair play, and self-expression, and has given us tools for thinking and analyzing. But it seems to me that the most effective application that American-Chinese can make of their education would be in China, which needs all the Chinese talent she can muster.[125]

While second-generation women such as Florence Chinn Kwan, Lilly King Gee Won, and Rose Hum Lee did indeed put their education and talents to good use in China, most Chinese American women remained in the United States and made the most of the situation.[126] Some, particularly the daughters of educated, middle-class parents, were inspired by their dual political identity to take the first steps toward political activism.

Out of a strong sense of Chinese nationalism, many daughters first joined their mothers in raising funds for Dr. Sun Yat-sen's revolutionary cause and for war and famine relief in the years following the 1911 Revolution. When America entered World War I, they were encouraged to express their American patriotism by volunteering for Red Cross work on the home front while the men stood in long lines to enlist. Organized by the Chinese YWCA and local churches, women helped solicit donations, contributed handcrafted items to fund-raisers, wrapped bandages, sewed garments for war refugees, and knitted socks and scarves for soldiers at the war front. Chinatown newspapers also reported that young Chinese women were organizing American dances and musical events in the community to raise monies for the war effort.[127]

When the war ended and China was humiliated by the Versailles Treaty, which awarded German concessions in Shandong Province to Japan, women did not hesitate to join in the community's boycott and burning of Japanese products from Chinatown stores. According to newspaper accounts, Chinese merchants were united on boycotting the sale of Japanese art goods, rice, and seafood as long as Japan occupied Shandong. To launch the boycott, a public burning of Japanese-made goods was held in which Chinatown merchants contributed thousands of dollars of whatever Japanese merchandise they had left in their stores.[128]

Eva Lowe, who was ten years old at the time, remembered the community's outrage over the treaty.[129] "We realized that China was again being carved up like a melon," she said. "In response, we protested by burning Japanese curios in the Chinatown streets." Her early political awareness and involvement stemmed from encounters she had personally had with racism and from her exposure to nationalist sentiment in the Chinese community.

As a child growing up in Fort Bragg, California, Eva had been called "Ching Chong Chinaman" and had had horse manure and rocks thrown at her. She also recalled seeing derogatory cartoons in the American newspapers that depicted Chinese with long queues. "I felt deep inside that the Chinese were inferior and I was not proud to be a Chinese," she said. After moving to live with her sister in San Francisco, Eva became inspired by ideas of Chinese nationalism and learned to detest Japanese imperialism. On the way home from making deliveries for her sister at a local garment factory, she would pass Japanese businesses along Dupont Street. She couldn't resist shouting, "Hell, hell, hell, Japanese go to hell!" She continued doing this until "one time she [a Japanese proprietor] had a broom ready for me. And that was the end of it." Soon after, Eva left for China with her sister and brother-in-law. Her four years of education there further politicized her about Chinese nationalism and women's rights and made her a "fighter for the underdog" upon her return to the United States.

The aviators Ouyang Ying (Mrs. Frances Lee) and Katherine Cheung are further examples of the kind of educated, middle-class Chinese

American women who moved into the political arena—and in their cases, into a male-dominated field—because of Chinese nationalism. Ouyang Ying was one of the first Chinese Americans to answer the Chinese government's call for trained aviators to help China build up its air defenses. Born in 1895 in Courtland, California, she was a "modern woman," according to her grandson Li Yauguang. "She enjoyed motoring and horseback riding, and was quite aware of anti-Chinese discrimination, which worked to instill in her a strong sense of Chinese nationalism at an early age."[130] Ying, who studied under instructor Frank Bryant, was considered "one of the most apt pupils they have had."[131] Unfortunately, she died in a flying accident in 1920 at the young age of twenty-five, before her goal of going to China to serve could be realized.[132]

Katherine Cheung of Los Angeles gave up studying music in favor of flying for similar reasons. She was the first Chinese woman in America to earn a pilot's license (in 1931) and the first Chinese member of the 99 Club, the nationwide organization of women flyers. Katherine frequently made the San Francisco newspaper headlines because of her daring feats in navigational flying, aerobatics, and cross-country racing. When she heard that China excluded women from its aviation schools, she responded, "I don't see any valid reason why a Chinese woman can't be as good a pilot as anyone else. They drive automobiles—why not fly airplanes?"[133] She had every intention of opening an aviation school for women in China, but after the trainer plane given to her by the Chinese community in San Francisco crashed, her ailing father made her promise not to fly again. Because of strong sexism in China, even if Ouyang Ying and Katherine Cheung had succeeded in going there, it is doubtful that the Chinese government would have allowed them to serve as aviators. When aviators Hazel Ying Lee and Virginia Wong of Portland, Oregon, went to China in 1933 with eleven male Chinese American aviators, neither was allowed to serve; the Chinese Air Force simply refused to admit women.[134]

Voting was another avenue of political participation for Chinese American women. As soon as California granted women suffrage in 1911, a number of second-generation women exercised their right to vote. According to newspaper accounts, Clara Lee and Emma Tom Leong of Oakland and Tye Leung of San Francisco were among the first Chinese American women to vote. All three were featured in the local newspapers as "progressive" women when they appeared to register or cast their vote. One reporter promoted Clara and Emma as "the first Chinese of their sex to become accredited members of the American electorate"; according to the article, the two women chose to exercise their rights "because they believe that mothers as well as fathers should have a voice in making the laws which are going to govern the lives of their children."[135] Tye Leung was accorded the distinction of being "the first Chinese woman in the history of the world to exercise the electoral franchise."[136] Capitalizing on her renown, the newspaper showed her seated behind the wheel of a Studebaker-Flanders 20, a preference that she supposedly shared with Dr. Sun Yat-sen—though she in fact never owned a car in her life. "Miss Tie believes in the automobile and regards it in its various functions as a mark of progress—her own watchword." The newspaper reporter found Tye Leung a "progressive" match to the automobile: "Not only can she read and write the English language better than a great many of her adult brethren, but speaks it fluently, and is altogether familiar with the political issues involved in the Presidential primary election."[137]

In 1930, the native-born group constituted 47 percent of the total Chinese population; 19 percent of them were of voting age (2,336 males and 784 females). Yet only 40 percent of those eligible were registered to vote, and only 25 percent actually voted.[138] Local Chinese American organizations such as the Chinese American Citizens Alliance, Square and Circle Club, and Chinese YWCA constantly reminded them to exercise their right to vote: "The most important thing is to register and vote," emphasized the Chinese American Citizens Alliance. "It is the ballot that will win the political rights—and economic opportunities—for the future of American citizens of Chinese ancestry in the United States."[139] Special outreach to women included messages such as "Women's suffrage in America was only won in 1920 after many years of struggle. . . . We encourage Chinese women who qualify to vote to take advantage of this right and come to the YWCA to register."[140] As their political consciousness became aroused, a few second-generation women began to participate in partisan politics. The Community Chest 1930 Survey reported that Chinese American women were active members of a political organization to elect Al Smith president in 1928.[141] In 1931, the *San Francisco Chronicle* announced that the first Chinese women voters' club had been formed to support Angelo Rossi for mayor.[142] These were but small steps toward political activism, though. It would take the changing circumstances of World War II to motivate the second generation to participate more fully in American politics.

Clara Lee registering to vote in 1911 with (*from left to right*) Emma Leung, Tom Leung, Dr. Charles Lee, and deputy county clerk W. B. Reith. (Courtesy of Dr. Lester Lee)

A Bicultural Marriage and Family Life

Sexism at home and racism outside also affected the marriages and family life of second-generation women. The two forces influenced not only these women's choice of partners but also the quality of their married and family life, which proved to be markedly different from that of their parents. It was at this stage of their lives that Chinese American women's efforts to shape a new ethnic and gender identity for themselves really struck home.

The marriage pattern of Chinese American women differed from that of European American women. In 1920, only 14 percent of foreign-born women in America over age fifteen were single, but 37 percent of the second generation remained unmarried. According to Doris Weatherford, the general pattern in the United States had been that immigrant women often married young; third-generation women had the second highest marriage rate after the first generation; and those who were most likely to be unmarried were second-generation women (those born in America of foreign parents). She attributed the second generation's reluctance to marry to the harsh married lives of their mothers or the need for daughters to delay marriage in order to help out their families, as in the case of Irish women.[143] This was not the same for second-generation Chinese women in the insulated community of San Francisco Chinatown in the 1920s, who still considered marriage and motherhood as their destiny. Just when and how they married, however, depended upon their class background, degree of acculturation, and the historical circumstances at the time.

Prior to the 1911 Revolution, it was not unusual for poor, working-class parents to marry off their daughters early in order to better provide for the rest of the family. The marriage was arranged through a matchmaker, and according to Chinese custom, the bride had no say in the choice of her partner. She was not even allowed to see him until the wedding day, when, dressed in red silk and beaded headdress, she was carried from a carriage into her husband's home. Because of the skewed Chinese sex ratio in America, the husband was usually older, China-born, and conservative. Life for most of these young brides proved to be as harsh and socially restrictive as it had been for their immigrant mothers. The case of Rose Jeong serves as an example of such a traditional marriage. Her sister Bessie Jeong described how it all happened:[144]

> In a way, she had two men to choose from, but as she had never seen either of them, only their photographs, she took her parents' advice. One was young, about twenty, and her parents put it this way: "This man is young, he has his way to make, and he has a large family of brothers and sisters. You would be a sort of slave to all of them. This other man is fifty years old, but he can give you everything, he has no family. Better to be an old man's darling than a young man's slave," or words to that effect. They told her, too, that a young man would not be constant, he would be running around with other women, it was far safer to take an older man, who would settle down. Of course she was married in the Chinese way, that is, the man handed over to her parents a sum of money. Naturally that would be far larger with an older and richer man, but the parents did not speak of that.

Having already endured a hard life as the eldest daughter responsible for housework and the care of her younger siblings, sixteen-year-old Rose dutifully agreed with her parents' choice, even though the man was thirty-four years her senior. After the wedding she followed him to the lumber camp of Weed, California, where he worked as a cook. He was a "hard taskmaster," according to Bessie, who also went to live with them in their poorly insulated log cabin. "He had a horrible disposition, suspicious and jealous, and my sister's life was one long tragedy with him." Rose worked alongside her husband in his many business ventures. He first ran a boardinghouse, then a laundry, and at another time, five different dining places in town. When his businesses later failed, he sold all of Rose's wedding jewelry. In 1918, Rose died during the flu epidemic at the young age of twenty-six.

Learning from her sister's example, Bessie was determined not to suffer the same fate. When her father, who had returned to China with the rest of the family after the 1906 earthquake, came back to fetch Bessie and, as she believed, marry her off in China, she refused to go with him. "I knew that my father was determined to take me back that time. He was going to realize money out of it or he was fulfilling his duty as a father. But I still would be on the auction block. Prized Jersey—the name 'Bessie' always made me think of some nice fat cow!" At the suggestion of her sister Rose, Bessie ran away to Donaldina Cameron and the Presbyterian Mission Home. "I had been away from my father for so long that I was not much afraid of him. . . . I was resolved not to marry, to have an education instead." With a bit of legal maneuvering, Cameron was made her legal guardian, and Bessie was able to stay at the Mission Home and pursue an education, becoming a physician. She later married a man of her choice, Dr. Ying Wing Chan, the Chinese consul in San Francisco, and was in private practice in the San Francisco Bay Area for nearly forty years.

After the 1911 Revolution, the second generation—particularly those of middle-class background—began to take a different course from that of their mothers with regard to courtship and married life. Inspired by the example of the "new woman" in China, many resisted arranged marriages and chose to follow Western courtship and marriage customs.[145] Initially, their attempts were cause for social ostracism. "Remember when young men and women were never seen together on the streets of Chinatown?" wrote Chingwah Lee in 1936. "Even as late as 1910, when the bold experiment of 'spooning' along Dupont Street (generally immediately after school, and always in droves) [happened], business would be momentarily at a standstill, and there would be a lot of [rubber]necking—on the part of the giggling spectators."[146] In 1908, when Rose Fong accepted a carriage ride through Golden Gate Park with her suitor Tsoa Min, a Chinese schoolteacher, Chinatown was scandalized, and the Chinese Six Companies tried unsuccessfully to get the young teacher removed from his post.[147] By the 1920s, however, the second generation had successfully adopted the Western practices of courtship and free marriage and formulated their own style of a Chinese American wedding. Said Caroline Chew, a daughter of Rev. Ng Poon Chew:

> In these days, the young people in America no longer wait for a go-between to arrange matters and to draw up the betrothal contract for them, but, in independent American fashion, if they have an inclination for one another's company, they take matters into their own hands and arrange things to suit themselves. They go out together whenever and wherever they please. They see all they want to of each other. There are even occasional love letters when it is deemed necessary to have their spirits buoyed up a bit. Thus betrothal is no longer a matter left for parents and "go-betweens" to take care of, except in cases where the whole family was born and brought up in China and then transplanted over here.[148]

King Yoak Won Wu, whose family was strongly influenced by Chinese nationalism and Christianity, claimed to be among the first Chinese women to have a Western wedding, in 1913. She met her husband, Rev. Daniel Wu, in church, where she worked as a volunteer rolling bandages for Dr. Sun Yat-sen's army. "He came by often when we were rolling bandages, telling us how patriotic we were. I guess he was impressed with our dedication. At other times, I would attend his lectures in church." After three years of meeting in church and at the park across from the church, they decided to get married at Grace Cathedral outside Chinatown. "My family had switched to the 'new way of thinking' for a long time. . . . We did not need a matchmaker or any of the other Chinese rituals. There was no loud crying or colorful layers of clothes. We just decided to have a Christian wedding and I even made my own wedding dress and veil."[149] According to a newspaper account of the wedding, the ceremony was conducted in Chinese and English, and the large gathering consisted of both Chinese and European American friends.[150]

Daisy Wong Chinn also met her husband, Thomas W. Chinn, at church. A founding member of the Square and Circle Club, she recalled that she and her girlfriends seldom went on individual dates. Instead they went on group outings with boys, riding the ferry to Muir Woods, hiking to the top of Mt. Tamalpais, taking a hayride down the peninsula to the new Moffitt Naval Air Hangar, and attending athletic events, musical programs, and dances. She and Thomas did not go out alone on a date until they had known each other four years. Soon after, they became engaged, and a year later, in 1930, they decided to marry. Typical of other young Chinese American couples then, they opted for a wedding that was a combination of Chinese and Western traditions. The wedding ceremony, including an altar, upright piano, minister, flower girl, and wedding party, was held at a Chinese restaurant and followed by a Chinese banquet. Limousines were hired to pick up the guests, who were greeted upon arrival by a Chinese musical trio consisting of a trumpet, cymbals, and an *erh-hu*.[151]

Most large weddings in the 1920s took place in either a church, a hotel, or a public hall. Caroline Chew wrote in 1926, "The bride and groom and all the attendants appear in conventional Western garb and the famous Wagnerian and Mendelsohnian strains are played in true Western fashion." After the ceremony, coffee and cake were served, and the bride was driven to her new home in a limousine decorated with red paper and silk. The day after the wedding, the parents usually hosted an elaborate wedding feast in Chinatown, consisting of fifteen to twenty courses. Most important, the bride did not live with her husband's family after her marriage but established her own home, "where she reigns supreme from the very outset."[152]

Although more second-generation women were allowed to choose a groom after 1911 than before, they found their decisions encumbered by discriminatory laws that discouraged their marriage to foreign-born Chinese and prevented marriage to white Americans. The Cable Act of 1922 reversed the Expatriation Act of 1907, which had required women to assume their husband's nationality upon marriage. The 1922 act provided that a female citizen would no longer lose her citizenship by marrying an alien and, conversely, that an alien woman would no longer gain U.S. citizenship by marrying a citizen. However, section 3 of the Cable Act stipulated that "any woman citizen who marries an alien ineligible to citizenship shall cease to be a citizen of the United States." Although section 4 allowed that "a woman who, before the passage of this Act, has lost her United States citizenship by reason of her marriage to an alien eligible for citizenship, may be naturalized," section 5 stated that "no woman whose husband is not eligible to citizenship shall be naturalized during the continuance of the marital status."[153] The Cable Act, in effect, stripped any American-born Chinese woman of her citizenship status should she choose to marry a foreign-born Chinese with no hope of naturalization, since she herself, by virtue of her race, thereby became an "alien ineligible to citizenship." Moreover, once a woman lost her citizenship, she could no longer confer derivative citizenship to any of her children who might be born outside the United States. She also lost her rights to own property, vote, and travel abroad freely.[154] Until these stipulations were repealed by the Cable Amendment of 1931, Chinese American women like Florence Chinn Kwan and Flora Belle Jan who chose to marry Chinese foreign students fell victims to the Cable Act.

Florence met her husband while studying at the University of Chicago. Upon their marriage in 1923, they decided to go live in China. Five years later, when they returned to the United States, he, as a student, was permitted to land immediately, but she and her two children were detained on the boat. "The immigration officer said, 'It's because you're married to an alien and lost your citizenship.' And that was the first time that I knew that I had lost my citizenship when I married," she recalled. Only after a friend who worked for the Immigration Service vouched for her identity was she allowed to land. "[On her word] I got off without paying the $2,000 bond for me and $2,000 for the children. After that, I said, I'm not coming back here any more."[155] But her husband's work as a physician necessitated trips to the United States every five years, so finally, in 1936, she applied for naturalization and regained her U.S. citizenship.

Flora Belle also met her foreign-born husband while a student at the University of Chicago. They married in 1926, and she decided to return to China with him in 1932. According to a letter she wrote her friend Ludmelia before departing, she was aware of the impact the Cable Act had on her and zealously tried to adjust her status through naturalization before leaving for China.

> Here's the problem. I must have my birth certificate. After that, I must apply for citizenship since I lost it by marrying an alien according to a recent law. I am permitted to apply for it by paying a $10 fee and passing an examination, providing that I have my birth certificate. I must go through this before I ever dare leave America because once I am out of the country, as an alien, I'll have a devil of a time trying to get back. And I know that I will always want to come back because it is my home.[156]

Unfortunately, no doctor had presided at Flora's birth; therefore, no birth certificate was on file in Fresno County, where she was born. But a U.S. District Court judge in Chicago evidently believed her and allowed her to "repatriate" as a U.S. citizen before she left for China.[157] Her foresight in this matter allowed her to escape war conditions in China and return to the United States in 1949 as a U.S. citizen along with her two daughters who had been born in China.

Aside from the Cable Act, anti-miscegenation attitudes and laws that

prevented interracial marriage between Chinese and whites discriminated against Chinese women as well. Compounding the problem was
ostracism in the Chinese community with respect to intermarriages. Tye
Leung, who had run away to the Presbyterian Mission Home to avoid
an arranged marriage, found herself the target of such shunning. While
employed as an assistant to the matrons at Angel Island, she met and
fell in love with an immigration inspector, Charles Schulze. They had to
travel to Vancouver, Washington, to become legally married. "His
mother and my folks disapprove very much, but when two people are
in love, they don't think of the future or what [might] happen," she
wrote later in an autobiographical essay.[158] After their marriage both had
to resign from their civil service jobs because of social ostracism. Charles
went on to work for many years for the Southern Pacific Company as a
mechanic, and Tye found a job as a telephone operator at the Chinatown Exchange. Although they were "the talk of Chinatown," according to one of her contemporaries, the Schulzes chose to live close to
Chinatown, and Tye remained active in the Chinese Presbyterian church.
Their children, Fred and Louise, recalled that they were one of the few
interracial families in Chinatown, and although they as children were
sometimes called *fan gwai jai* (literally, foreign devil child), they were
accepted in the community, most likely because their mother spent many
hours volunteering in the community.[159] Her son Fred said, "She was
very kind and always willing to help other people go see the doctor, interpret, go to immigration, and things like that. Very often she would
take the streetcar and go out to Children's Hospital to interpret on a
volunteer basis."[160]

Discriminatory laws such as the Cable Act and the Anti-Miscegenation Act went hand-in-hand with other anti-Chinese measures and practices that sought to stop Chinese immigration and the integration of Chinese into mainstream America. Such laws were often both racist and sexist
in character and created hardships for Chinese American women already
hampered by cultural conflict at home. They were painful reminders of
the vulnerable existence of the second generation, who, in spite of their
rights as U.S. citizens, could easily become disenfranchised on the basis
of race alone.

Other American laws, however, such as divorce laws, gave Chinese
American women leverage and latitude in changing their marital circumstances. Although few cases of divorce among Chinese Americans
were reported in the local newspapers, Caroline Chew wrote in 1926
that "divorce among Chinese in America has become comparatively com-

Charles and Tye Leung Schulze. (Courtesy of Louise Schulze Lee)

mon, and although it is still looked upon with a little distaste, if it is quite justifiable, no one has anything disparaging to say." She added that, unlike in China, wives in America had just as much right as husbands to sue for divorce.[161] According to local newspapers, one major source of information on divorce patterns in the Chinese American community, important causes of divorce among second-generation women included wife abuse and polygamy. In 1923, for example, Emma Soohoo sued her American-born husband, Henry, for divorce on grounds that he "cruelly beat her and then deserted her," and she requested sole custody of their twenty-month-old baby.[162] As another example, in 1928 Amy Quan Tong, the owner of a manicuring parlor in Chinatown, filed for divorce from her American-born husband, Quan Tong, because, as she told the judge, he had put her to work at low wages in his Hong Kong candy store and taken a second wife.[163]

Like second-generation European American women, Chinese American women who married men of their own choice often embarked on a life quite different from that of their immigrant mothers. To start, they were not as confined to the domestic sphere, as Caroline Chew points out:

> She is perfectly free to come and go as she pleases and has free access to the streets. She goes out and does her own marketing; goes calling on her friends when she so desires; dines at restaurants occasionally; and even ventures to go beyond the precincts of "Chinatown" quite frequently— all of which have hitherto never been done by a Chinese woman. Fifteen or twenty years ago such conduct would have been considered most outrageous and would have caused a woman to be all but ostracized.[164]

There was also more equality, mutual affection, and companionship in second-generation marriages. Not only did couples go out together, but they were not afraid to express their affection in public. Because both worked and contributed to the family income, they tended to discuss matters and make joint decisions regarding the family's welfare. Second-generation husbands were also less resistant to helping with the housework and sharing their outside concerns with their wives. Daisy Wong Chinn found her marriage of fifty-two years fulfilling as well as happy because she and her husband, Thomas W. Chinn, communicated well and worked together on many community projects. Thomas was always forward-looking, she noted. He opened the first sporting goods store in Chinatown in 1929 and founded the *Chinese Digest* in 1935. "Whatever projects he has," she said, "he always says, 'Well, what do you think of this?' And I'm his best critic because I always tell him what I really think; and then he can decide for himself whether my thoughts are better." In most cases, she said, he took her suggestions.[165]

Jade Snow Wong shared a similarly close and equal relationship with her husband, Woody Ong, about whom she wrote in *No Chinese Stranger*, the sequel to *Fifth Chinese Daughter*. Old family friends, the two became reacquainted after they had both established their businesses in Chinatown and were thrown together by a family emergency. As Jade Snow put it, "Each grew in awareness of the other, and devotion flowered." Their married life was wedded to their work life, as they lived and worked together on the same premises.

> In this first year of marriage, they often walked the three blocks to Chinatown for a restaurant lunch, after which they would purchase groceries for that night's late Chinese dinner at home. The division of their studio work was natural. Financial records and bank deposits, mechanical

problems, chemical formulas, checking kiln action, packing, pickup, and deliveries naturally fell into Woody's hands while Jade Snow stayed close to home, working on designs, supervising staff schedules, and keeping house. True to tradition, once Woody had locked the studio door and come upstairs, he was home as a Chinese husband, expecting their house to be immaculate and to be waited upon and indulged. They could consult with each other on just about every subject without disagreement. Kindness, devotion, protection with strength new to her, and extravagant gifts were privileges that gladdened Jade Snow's heart, while her husband's physical comfort and mental relaxation were her responsibility.[166]

Although their marriage revealed a traditional gender division of labor, neither partner dominated the other. As their family grew to four children and they added an active travel business to their ceramics work, Woody proved a supportive partner, helping with the children and household chores, encouraging Jade Snow's career in ceramics and writing, nursing her back to health when she became ill, and sharing responsibilities with her on the many tours to Asia that they cosponsored.

Similarly, Tye Leung's marriage to Charles Schulze, despite being handicapped by the taboo against interracial marriage, was successful because it was both egalitarian and interdependent. According to their son, Fred, "We had good family relations. I never heard arguments, fights, or anything." Both parents were kind and mild-tempered, and both worked to provide for the family. Tye did most of the cooking and housework, but in the evenings, when she was working at the telephone exchange, Charles would take care of the children and of Tye's mother, who lived with them. Fred fondly recalled: "Before we went to bed each night, my father would always bring us a cup of cocoa. Then after he gave us our cocoa, he would take the dishes out to the kitchen, wash them, and put them away."[167]

Both parents loved music and led an active social life. Tye played the piano and Chinese butterfly harp and attended the Chinese Presbyterian church regularly; Charles played the French horn with a military band and was active at Grace Cathedral. Tye would often go to the Chinese opera, weddings, and birthday parties in Chinatown accompanied by her children, while Charles played with various musical bands in the city and attended regular meetings of the Odd Fellows Lodge. Although they led different social lives, they were a close family. They always ate and played together at home on Sundays, Fred recalled. Not only was the marriage a happy one, but the children benefited from the cultural strengths of both parents and the warm family life they provided.

Jade Snow Wong and her
husband, Woodrow Ong,
packing her ceramics, which
accompanied them on her
speaking tour in Asia for the
U.S. State Department, 1953.
(Associated Press photo;
courtesy of Jade Snow Wong)

Further factors that distinguished between traditional and modern
marriages among Chinese Americans included the size of the family and
the quality of home life. Unlike their mothers, second-generation
women knew about and had access to birth control, which became more
available to American women in the 1920s. "My friends were very good
to me and told me what to do," said Gladys Ng Gin. "When it was time
to have my first baby, a good friend of mine said, 'Gladys, you have to
go to the hospital,' and she introduced a woman doctor to me."[168] Most
of her contemporaries—both European and Chinese American—limited their families to two or three children and had them in the hospital. However, some "modern" husbands proved uncooperative. Flora
Belle Jan's health was ruined after five abortions because her husband
refused to practice birth control. She confided to Ludmelia:

> I have been thinking that I have given the six best years of my life to a
> man who is not worth it. . . . When I first met him, I was idealistic and
> enthusiastic and ambitious. I had a body that was sound and healthy.
> Now I am completely disillusioned, entirely lacking any enthusiasm, and
> utterly devoid of ambition. . . . I had my first abortion in September,
> 1928, at a time when I was pathetically struggling with some editorial

work for which I was never paid. The next abortion came the following spring. Then in September, 1929, I was fortunate enough to get a job at the Methodist Book Concern, the salary from which helped [my husband] to go back to school. In January, 1930, I had my third abortion. My memory is a bit hazy but I think the fourth came in December of 1931. I struggled with contraceptives, begged [my husband] to use condoms for added precaution but he stubbornly refused. Then I had a fifth abortion in January, 1932. For these abortions, I have pawned my mother's jewelry, modelled in art schools, slaved at office routine, stood the boresome company of a Chinese newspaper editor whom I taught English, neglected [my son] to go out to work, gone without the decencies of life and the clothes I long for with all the fever of youth. Why have I had to undergo this torture? Because of a man who prides himself on his intelligence [but] is hopelessly lacking in understanding.[169]

Despite her husband's shortcomings, Flora remained married to him and bore him three children, two of whom were born in China. The last pregnancy almost cost her her life. That was when she finally insisted on having a tubal ligation.

Although they faced discrimination in the labor market and in their search for decent housing, second-generation Chinese were still able to take advantage of their education and achieve a degree of upward mobility. The combined income of this generation of middle-class Chinese American couples afforded them modern apartments outside of Chinatown, albeit on the fringes. Chew Fong Low, frustrated by housing discrimination in San Francisco, spent a quarter of a million dollars constructing the Low Apartments on the outskirts of Chinatown in order to give her family and "her people an opportunity to live in true American style in a building constructed by American workmen from American plans."[170] The apartment building was made of steel frame and concrete and contained twenty-five apartments, all featuring modern kitchens, tiled bathrooms, separate shower cabinets, French doors and windows, built-in mirrors, hot water heaters, and outlets for radio and private telephone lines. Other Chinese American couples, like the Schulzes, were able to rent accommodations, complete with running water and a private bathroom, above Powell Street in the 1920s. They were also among the first in Chinatown to have modern appliances such as a radio, toaster, iron, and refrigerator.[171]

Although they preferred to live in modern apartments, young Chinese American couples generally tried to combine Chinese and Western customs in their home life. The Schulzes, for example, had Western food for breakfast and lunch but Chinese food for dinner. They celebrated

Thanksgiving and Christmas but also Chinese New Year and the Moon Festival. They spoke both Chinese and English at home with the children. They went to church, but every year at Ching Ming, Tye took the children to the Chinese cemetery to pay proper respect to her parents. Nor did Tye physically punish her children, as was the practice among Chinese parents then. Fred and Louise Schulze could not remember ever being spanked. "She was always very gentle. She never raised her voice," said Fred.[172]

Although Jade Snow Wong had spent her college years away from home and Chinatown, after her marriage she chose to live close to Chinatown so that her children might learn from their grandparents and come to appreciate their bicultural heritage. The children attended Chinese school and were introduced to Chinese foods, holidays, and the arts, but they were also raised on Christmas parties, Easter egg hunts, trips to museums and libraries, and vacations in Hawaii and Canada. Ultimately, Jade Snow instilled the same traditional values of honor, courage, honesty, personal conviction, and service to fellow humans in all her children that she had been taught by her parents. Representative of her generation, she had come full circle in her search for a new ethnic and gender identity conditioned by the discrimination she had experienced as a dutiful daughter at home and a young woman growing up in a prejudiced society. As she wrote in *No Chinese Stranger*, a work that compares socialist life in China with democratic life in America:

> Each Chinese-American like me has the opportunity to assess his talents, define his individual stature, and choose his personal balance of old and new, Chinese and Western ways, hopefully including the best of both. Father Wong's prize, more meaningful than gold, has also been the legacy he gave his children and grandchildren: he, and others like him, first gave us our cultural identity and then, by remaining in this country, permitted us the American freedom to attain individual self-images which ought to be constructive for the state but not subordinate to it. My own children may be potential revolutionaries who will throw their javelins earnestly and strongly; and I hope their targets will be the alleviation of mankind's miseries. When they drink water, as the old Chinese saying goes, I hope that they will think of its source, so that when they reach out to drop *their* aerial roots, their growth will bear the fruit of the banyan tree—wisdom.

She concluded her second autobiography on an optimistic note:

> My future is in this land where Daddy and his progeny have sunk their roots around the rocks of prejudice, rather than closer to the shelter of

the mother trunk. As I encourage my children's roots, I take heart from that "Foolish Old Man" in Ming Choy's lesson. With strong belief in our purpose, it may not be folly for the determined, with the hearts of children, to attack the high mountain of prejudice in our own way. When we die, our children and grandchildren will keep on working until, some day, the mountain will diminish. Then there will be no Chinese stranger.[173]

By the time of the Great Depression, second-generation women under the influence of Chinese nationalism, Christianity, and acculturation had indeed taken the first steps toward challenging traditional gender roles and racial discrimination in the larger society. Compared to their mothers, they were better educated, more economically mobile, socially active, politically aware, and equal partners in marriage. Although they still had a difficult time assimilating into mainstream society, they had learned to accommodate racism and establish a new bicultural identity and lifestyle for themselves. As the Great Depression loomed before them, they would draw strength from the wellspring of their bicultural heritage to weather the storm ahead.

CHAPTER 4

Long Strides

The Great Depression, 1930s

Women in this community are keeping pace with the quick changes of the modern world. The shy Chinese maidens in bound feet are forever gone, making place for active and intelligent young women.

Jane Kwong Lee
Chinese Digest, June 1938

We will fight our fight to the end, and hope to raise the living conditions not only for ourselves but for the other workers in Chinatown as well. . . . "The ILGWU is behind us. We shall not be moved."

Chinese Ladies' Garment Workers' Union
letter to the ILGWU membership, April 1938

The prosperous years of the Roaring Twenties in America came to an abrupt halt on Black Thursday, October 24, 1929, when the stock market crashed. By the end of that year, stock prices had dropped 50 percent. Investment funds dried up, factories closed, and workers lost their jobs. In the next three years, 40 percent of the nation's farms were mortgaged, industrial production was cut in half, thirteen million Americans—one-quarter of the work force—became unemployed, and over five thousand banks went out of business. With little savings and no government relief, many Americans across the country found themselves homeless, without any means of support. In Seattle, it was reported, families unable to pay for electricity spent their evenings by candlelight or in the dark. One couple in New York City lived in a cave in Central Park for half a year. Many others lived on the outskirts of towns in shacks made of tar paper, cardboard boxes, orange crates, or rusted car bodies—in settlements that became sardonically known as

Hoovervilles. Starving families subsisted on stale bread, potatoes, and even dandelions. Farmers who lost their homes and crops in the dust storms packed their families into dilapidated cars and drove west, hoping to find work in the orange groves and lettuce fields of California. In desperation, one old man who found himself unemployed came home and turned on the gas. His widow sat alone for three days and then did the same.[1]

The devastating impact of the Great Depression on the American population has been well documented in books, photographs, and films.[2] More recent studies have explored its negative effects on the lives of the women and minority groups hardest hit by the economic crisis.[3] What is missing from this larger picture is a sense of how the depression affected Chinese American men and women in different parts of the country. Pertinent to the present investigation is a narrower question: What impact did race, class, gender, and nativity have on the economic survival of Chinese women in San Francisco, and how did their experiences differ from the experiences of other groups of Americans during this period?

Although little has been written about how Chinese Americans weathered the depression, oral history interviews indicate that many faced the same hardships as the rest of America's population. By the time the depression was in full swing, the Chinese American work force had long since been driven out of the better-paying jobs in the Western states and was concentrated in either domestic and personal services or retail trade in urban areas of the country. Many Chinese families, eking out a living in small laundry, restaurant, and grocery businesses, were hard hit by the depression. Wong Wee Ying, the only Chinese woman in the steel-mill town of Midland, Pennsylvania, recalled seeing people sleeping out in the streets and standing in line for government permits to sell apples or shoelaces. "If you can see no smoke from the factory chimneys, you know things are bad for everyone," she said.[4] The bad economy affected her family laundry business: "We just had a few collars to wash. There was no work, so how can people afford to send out their laundry to wash?"[5] Like many other resourceful American women, Wee Ying made clothes out of old rice sacks for her six children, reinforced their shoes with tin cans to make them last longer, and made a lot of thin soup out of rice or oatmeal and vegetables from their family garden.

Helen Hong Wong, who in 1928 had just arrived in Fort Wayne, Indiana, as a young bride, also saw her husband's restaurant business decline because of the depression. "The restaurant used to make over two hundred dollars a day with the lunch meal alone," she said. "During the depression we were lucky to make two or three dollars a day. People had no jobs and of course no money. The department stores were all empty. You couldn't find a single person in there." When they couldn't pay the rent anymore, the Wongs closed their restaurant and moved to Chicago. Too intimidated to stand in the food lines, her husband finally went to the Chinatown gaming tables to borrow "lucky money" from the winners. The winter months were the hardest because the family couldn't afford heat. "A bushel of coal would have to last us a whole week. I would wrap my two daughters in blankets and heavy coats all the time and only burn the coals at night. But even at that, it was still down to forty degrees at night."[6]

Americans across the country were hard hit by the Great Depression. The Chinese community in San Francisco, however, was not only spared some of the worst hardships, but in some ways, Chinese women came out ahead. Ironically, the segregated economy and community resources of Chinatown—developed as an outcome of Chinese exclusion and exploitation in America—protected residents from the worst effects of the economic downturn. And for the first time in their history, Chinese Americans, who had always been marginalized, became beneficiaries of federal relief programs and were welcomed into the rank and file of the growing labor movement. Although hundreds of Chinese men lost their jobs as cooks, seasonal laborers, and laundrymen, most Chinese women continued to find employment in the female-dominated areas of sewing, domestic service, and sales and clerical work. Less affected by unemployment than their men and encouraged by the political conditions of the depression era, Chinese American women were able to improve their circumstances as well as to assume a larger share of responsibility for their families and community. Thus, the depression both required and allowed them to make long strides during a time of setbacks for most other Americans.

Ironies of the Depression: San Francisco Chinatown

The silver lining in the Great Depression for the Chinese in San Francisco should be viewed in its proper perspective; that is, given their low socioeconomic status, Chinese Americans had less to lose by the economic catastrophe and more to gain by government assistance than the average American. In a strange way, it might be said that the Chinese benefited from past discrimination. Even during the worst years of the Great Depression, before President Franklin Delano Roosevelt's New Deal went into effect, there were no breadlines or traces of Hoovervilles in Chinatown; nor were Chinese violently scapegoated by white workers as happened in the depression of the 1870s. Overall, because their ethnic economy afforded them some protection against unemployment, the Chinese in San Francisco did not suffer as severely as Chinese, black, and Mexican Americans in other parts of the country. Almost all the Chinese in the city lived in Chinatown, which provided them with essential foods and services as well as jobs that relied primarily on trade with China. They were not in competition with white workers for work, nor were they greatly affected by plummeting agricultural prices or the closure of industrial plants. In contrast, blacks in San Francisco suffered the highest rate of unemployment among all groups throughout the depression because they were concentrated in those occupational areas—unskilled labor and the service sector—most vulnerable to unemployment.[7] Likewise, because few Chinese invested in stocks and bonds, were able to own property, or had accumulated much savings in banks, they were less affected by the stock market crash, property foreclosures, and bank runs than the rest of the country. Chinatown was also blessed with its own backup support of local district and family associations. In combination with churches and other charitable organizations, the kin network provided a stopgap resource for most Chinese in need.[8] The unemployed could always count on their family or district associations to *hoi fan*—provide dinner for a nickel—while families relied on the tradition of *wan fan*—the taking of leftovers from the dining tables of Chinatown businesses that provided meals to their workers. It was not unusual for six to eight single men to share one room and to chip in for food. Fong, a laborer, described how this worked in the documentary study *Longtime Californ'*:

> Now during the Depression I was so broke, quite often I was with no money in my pocket. . . . You wonder how I lived? . . . . We got a room, there's five or six of us and sometimes we pay rent, sometimes we don't. We got a sack of rice for a coupla dollars and we all cook every day and we eat there. Sometimes one night you see forty or fifty guys come in and out, the old guys go to each's place, sit down, talk all night long before they go to sleep the next day. . . . So we got our food one way or the other, lots of vegetables real cheap at the time, and that's how I passed by.[9]

As the depression deepened and the Chinese kin associations and community charities found themselves no longer able to handle the situation, the Chinese discovered a new source of relief in the local, state, and federal governments.

Accustomed to solving the community's problems in their own autocratic and patriarchal way, the merchant elites that ruled Chinatown did not seek outside assistance. But as conditions for the Chinese working class deteriorated, the unemployed found a new political voice in the Huaren Shiyi Hui (Chinese Unemployed Alliance), a group formed by the Chinese Marxist left in January 1931 to organize the working class and aid the unemployed. Reflecting the rise in radical politics throughout the country, the Shiyi Hui joined with the Unemployed Council of the U.S.A. (organized by the U.S. Communist Party) to call for racial and class unity on unemployment issues and to demonstrate for relief aid from the U.S. government. In March 1931, the Shiyi Hui reported that there were 3,000 to 3,500 unemployed Chinese in the city, 12 percent of whom were women and more than 1,000 of whom were heads of households with an average of three dependents. Those below the poverty level amounted to 20 percent of the unemployed.[10] The alliance then organized several hundred unemployed Chinese workers to march on the Chinese Six Companies and demand immediate relief, thereby challenging the ruling merchant class. At the end of the march, a mass meeting was held, at which Eva Lowe, the only female member of the Shiyi Hui, presented the organization's demands for (1) shelter and food for the unemployed, (2) free hospital services for the unemployed, (3) free education for unemployed women, and (4) an employment office, to be administered by a board selected by the Shiyi Hui. Later, many participants also joined a massive demonstration of the unemployed in San Francisco's financial district, marking one of the earliest instances of Chinese involvement in a political event outside Chinatown.[11]

Response—albeit slow—came first from the city government. According to one analyst, compared to other cities San Francisco took better care of its unemployed citizens during the first two and a half years of the depression because of its sturdier economy, strong banks and credit rating, skillful budget balancing, effective relief programs, and generous citizens who not only gave to charities but also repeatedly voted for relief bonds.[12] In November 1930, the city and county of San Francisco made its first appropriation for relief in the amount of $200,000. Three months later, it passed a bond issue of $2.5 million for work relief (primarily to construct the Golden Gate and Bay Bridges). In the four years from 1929 to 1932, the public portion of contributions to Associated Charities, a humanitarian organization that provided for the poor, rose from 8.5 percent to 84 percent, and the city government distributed $3.8 million worth of aid in work or direct relief.

It was not until mid-1932, however, that any attention was paid to the needs of the Chinese community. After the city passed another bond issue, funds were finally made available to open a Chinese-staffed office for family relief in Chinatown, enabling needy Chinese families to go on relief for the first time. It took another year before the city established a Chinese Single Men Registry in the building of the Chinese Six Companies so that Chinese bachelors, who were the hardest hit by unemployment, could also begin applying for relief. That same year, the Chinese Six Companies, working with the city government, opened a shelter with forty beds and a reading room for unemployed Chinese men. Free showers were provided at the Chinese YMCA, where Chinese cooks were hired to cook two free meals a day for two hundred needy persons, and Chinese Hospital began providing free medical care to the unemployed.[13]

Just as the city's relief funds dried up, Congress passed the Federal Emergency Relief Act (FERA), allocating $500 million for the unemployed. Word began to spread in Chinatown about the benevolence of *wong ga* (literally, "imperial family"; that is, the U.S. government), and the Chinese learned to swallow their pride and accept the concept of public assistance as an individual's right in America—at least for the duration of the depression. By 1935, approximately 2,300, or 18 percent, of the Chinese population in San Francisco (as compared to 22 percent of the total U.S. population) were on government assistance. This number included approximately 350 families, 25 unmarried women, and 500 unmarried men. The relief initially took the form of groceries that were delivered by a local Chinese grocery store to the families. Then, beginning in 1934, the government issued a weekly check to each family for food, rent, utilities, and clothing, supplemented by free medical care at a local clinic.[14] Lim P. Lee, who served as postmaster of San Francisco from 1966 to 1980, was a social worker during the depression; he recalled: "Where the Chinese Recreation Center is today used to be the Washington Grammar School. They had a backyard there, and on payday, when they came to get their relief checks, we had lines of four to six deep."[15]

Both Lim P. Lee and Ethel Lum, also a social worker, emphasized that there was no discrimination in the distribution of unemployment relief to the Chinese in San Francisco. "Because of language difficulties and differences in habits and customs, the Chinese on relief have always received special consideration, and have been treated fairly and justly," wrote Ethel Lum in 1935. "They receive identically the same allowances for food as do the white families; whereas in several counties in California, Chinese and other racial groups, Filipino, Mexican, etc., are accorded a lower food budget, a difference of from 10 to 20 per cent, on the belief that these racial groups have less expensive diets."[16] This egalitarian treatment may have been due to accusations that had circulated in the community a year before charging the authorities with providing Chinese families less relief because of their lower standard of living. In response, FERA officials had assigned a bilingual social worker to investigate and correct the matter.[17] As it was, "the unemployment relief checks were hardly enough for bare existence for the single men," said Lim P. Lee. "The families had more allowance, but there were more mouths to feed."[18] Monthly relief for the Chinese in San Francisco was averaging $16.43 per single person and $69.79 per family, far below the $30 a month needed to support one Chinese person or the $120 required to sustain an average-sized Chinese family of eight for a month.[19]

Then in October 1935, when the Works Progress Administration (WPA) went into action, 331 single men and 164 families were transferred from the relief rolls to the federal work program. The idea was to shift the unemployed from direct relief to work relief before family relations eroded any further and men became too dependent on public assistance.[20] WPA jobs required U.S. citizenship and benefited both blue-collar and white-collar workers. Because most unemployed Chinese men fell into the former class, they were employed by WPA mainly as unskilled labor on public projects—constructing public buildings, parks, roads, bridges, and airports. Fong was one of the "lucky" ones hired under the WPA program. As he put it,

Then Roosevelt come out and he created the word NRA [National Recovery Administration], gave work to people, a lotta guys, but later on it got so sour. Like they got jobs, for instance I went in on one of them, a railroad job inside Elko. They paid seventy-two dollars, I think, and they give you jobs like that so you can make a living, and I worked there a few months. It was awfully hot, hot like everything! In fact you could see the blaze movin' around hotly. And people come back workin' in the railroad, they come back for dinner they practically stink because their clothing been in that sunlight so damn long. And that's the way it is, I lived out there. You don't go nowhere, it's right out in the middle of the desert, see, that's the way it is. There's quite a few jobs similar like that that Roosevelt put out later on.[21]

But not everybody who needed a job qualified for relief work. Because U.S. citizenship was required, many Mexicans, Chinese, Japanese, and Filipinos could not apply, which explains their low percentages on the WPA employment rolls as compared to blacks. In 1940, for instance, only 7 percent of unemployed Japanese in California, 12 percent of Chinese, and 14 percent of Filipinos were employed by WPA, as compared to 60 percent of all unemployed blacks in the state.[22] The monthly wage of $60 for a minimum of 120 hours of work was four times the sum granted in direct relief for single men, but there was no supplementary assistance in cash, medical services, surplus clothing, or food. Since each family could have only one WPA worker, for large families of six to eleven persons WPA employment resulted in less money per month than direct relief; thus wives were forced to look for work in order to make ends meet.[23] Over 70 percent of racial minorities on relief projects did hard work as semiskilled and unskilled labor.[24] Whether one was considered "lucky" in landing a WPA job was therefore debatable, according to Fong:

> They're always trying to push you down to these jobs, no matter how much or how good you are. Like that NRA was like all the other things, at first you don't realize, but nevertheless, in due time and in the long run, you find out it will never have any advantage toward the Chinese. The thing is that they do it in such a close way, undercover way, that you barely notice it. So, as I said, that NRA, "Never Rebuffed American," pretty soon the thing went sour all around and people began to sneer at it.[25]

However, over 20 percent of racial minorities employed by WPA were in the white-collar sector.[26] Chinese American men like Lim P. Lee and women like Ethel Lum were hired as social workers, recreation aides, teachers, and clerks at prevailing professional rates to dispense financial aid to the needy, extend services to individuals and families, and help improve living conditions in the community. Aside from earning this group of white-collar workers a salary, their services assisted individuals through the depression and were instrumental in procuring a public health clinic, nursery schools, improved housing and street lighting, and English and job training classes for the Chinatown community. Overseeing a staff of twenty-five, Lim P. Lee headed the Real Property Sur-

vey in 1939, which resulted in the construction of low-cost public housing in Chinatown after World War II.

Chinese Americans also had the option of returning to China to escape the depression. As Jade Snow Wong wrote in her second autobiography, many Chinese did just that, which explains the uncongested
streets and vacancy signs on Chinatown apartment buildings she recalled
seeing as an eleven-year-old.[27] China was at the time also in the thick of
fighting the Japanese on its soil and in need of any help that overseas
Chinese could give. One editorial in *CSYP* recommended that Chinese
with technical skills consider returning to China to work and that those
with capital use it to develop industries in China.[28] Another article provided instructions on how Chinese Americans could reclaim their assets
in their ancestral villages.[29] This was also the time when the *Chinese Digest* published the winning essays on "Does My Future Lie in China or
America?" From 1930 to 1934, 7,000 Chinese departed from the port
of San Francisco, while only 2,500 entered.[30] Most had sufficient personal resources to return with their families, but at least twenty-five older
men took advantage of the U.S. government's offer of a one-way ticket
to go home alone in 1936.[31] According to the *Chinese Digest*, most of
these men were hard-working laborers in their senior years and now on
relief. The periodical interviewed four of the repatriates, "all [of whom]
had wives, children, and grandchildren in China and were glad to be
sent back to their families to spend their remaining years."[32]

In contrast, large numbers of unemployed Mexicans and Filipinos
were pressured to return home. Between 1929 and 1939, approximately
half a million Mexicans, or close to one-third of the Mexican population in the country, were either deported or repatriated, even though
many had been born in the United States.[33] In 1935, in response to the
demands of exclusionists on the West Coast, Congress passed the Repatriation Act, which offered Filipinos on the mainland free transportation back to the Philippines on the condition that they not return to the
United States. Only 2,190, or approximately 7 percent of the Filipino
population, took up the offer and repatriated.[34]

Chinese workers actually came out ahead after Congress passed the
National Labor Relations Act (a.k.a. the Wagner Act) in 1935, which
granted organized labor the right to collective bargaining. Between 1936
and 1941, as a result, the strength of the labor movement doubled in
numbers. Communist Party organizers and the Congress of Industrial
Organizations were particularly instrumental in promoting industrial
unionism and recruiting minority and women workers into unions.

Strikes became commonplace across the country as workers successfully fought for improved hours and wages in the needle trades, coalfields, steel and rubber industries, and agriculture. Chinese and black workers in San Francisco, who had historically been excluded from the labor movement, joined white workers in picket lines during the maritime strike of 1934 and the hotel strike of 1937, after which they became welcomed members in major labor unions such as the International Longshoremen and Warehousemen's Union, Culinary and Miscellaneous Workers' Union, and Apartment and Hotel Union.[35] Chinese and black workers were also involved in picketing the Alaskan Packers' Association, which resulted in the abolition of the contract system and the establishment of the Chinese Workers Mutual Aid Association.[36] Given the overall liberal temper and China's alliance with the United States at the time, local unions openly solicited Chinese members and worked with them to protest fascism abroad.[37]

Because of the foresight of the younger generation of Chinese American businessmen, who were quick to take advantage of the repeal of prohibition laws and promote tourism, recovery for San Francisco Chinatown came earlier than for the rest of the country. Chinese import trade, which had declined precipitously since 1931, recovered to about a fourth of the 1929 level by 1935.[38] To encourage tourism, entrepreneurs renovated stores, invested in modern bars, restaurants, and coffee shops, and created an atmosphere of "Old Chinatown" to attract out-of-towners attending conventions and the 1939 International Exposition at Treasure Island. As Fong observed:

> Then around the middle of the Depression the change come along and everything goes zoom! The whole place begins to look different because they start building it up. . . . Before that, not that there wasn't any bars in Chinatown, but they weren't noticeable nowhere. They were just down, beatup places, the bars for low-down people and drunks and all that. But during the Depression a bar changed names to some kind of a club, and then all those fancy names comes. Then the same thing happens with the restaurants. . . . In fact, maybe Chinatown is the place that start everything rumbling during the Depression. Such as like these dance halls, the bars, and all that.[39]

Taking note of the brisk business these newly established enterprises were enjoying, the *Chinese Digest* concluded in 1936 that Chinatown had "passed its winter" and was "now greeting the loveliest of all seasons, the season of gentle awakening and of growth."[40] As the New Deal continued to provide jobs for the unemployed and as business improved in

Chinatown, the number of unemployed Chinese dropped from 2,300 in 1935 to 700 in 1937.[41] For the rest of the country, however, recovery was delayed by a recession in 1937–38 and was not fully achieved until the United States entered World War II in 1941.

Ironies of the Depression: Immigrant Women

Compared to their men and the rest of the country, Chinese women in San Francisco were relatively unaffected by unemployment. Following the national pattern—in which the unemployment rate for men, who were concentrated in hard-hit production jobs, was almost twice as high as for women, who tended to work in protected clerical and service occupations—Chinese immigrant men who had been chiefly employed as seasonal workers, laundrymen, and cooks were the first to lose their jobs. Immigrant women, however, who worked primarily in the garment industry, continued to find employment. This situation made some immigrant wives the breadwinners, albeit marginal ones, during a time when their husbands were unemployed and relief funds were either unavailable or inadequate to support their families. While a significant number of urban black and white working-class families experienced discord and disintegration during this time, Chinese women were able to keep their families together by providing them with emotional support, stretching family means, and tapping resources in the community. And while the reversal of gender roles proved controversial in many parts of the nation,[42] the social status of Chinese women in San Francisco was elevated as a result of their indispensable contributions.

Statistics from the 1930 U.S. census indicate that many more men than women became unemployed at the beginning of the depression. Nationally, the unemployment rate was 7.1 percent for men and 4.7 percent for women; in San Francisco, 8.3 percent for men and 4.3 percent for women.[43] As a number of studies have pointed out, women experienced a lower unemployment rate owing to the rigid sex segregation in the labor force. Clerical, trade, and service occupations, in which women dominated, contracted less than the male manufacturing occupations.[44] The same held true in San Francisco, where men employed in the manufacturing and mechanical industries suffered the highest rate of unemployment.[45] Because the Chinese were concentrated in ethnic enterprises instead of in large-scale industrial occupations, they were less affected by these citywide contractions than other groups. The majority of the unemployed Chinese, in fact, had worked outside the Chinatown economy, as reported in a 1935 study of the occupational history of Chinese men on relief. Single men who became unemployed came from the ranks of farm and seasonal workers (25.5 percent), laundrymen (21.3 percent), family and hotel cooks (15.2 percent), and restaurant workers (14.1 percent). Among the family men, the hardest hit were family and hotel cooks (20.4 percent), clerks and salesmen (17.1 percent), and semiskilled workers (16.8 percent).[46]

An industrial survey of women workers, by contrast, reveals that in 1935 approximately 564 Chinese women (a 54 percent *increase* over 1930) were employed in sixty-five factories (forty-nine of which were garment factories), though 19 percent of their husbands were unemployed at the time.[47] The majority of these women were foreign-born and married with young children. A second survey of living conditions in Chinatown in 1935 shows that among families on relief, unemployed men outnumbered unemployed women. Of 163 families, 29 percent (48 families) were found to be on some form of relief; 37 of these families had an unemployed male head of the household. Of the 22 families without fathers, only half of the mothers were on relief; the remaining half were reportedly supporting their families with their earnings as garment workers.[48] It should be noted that the larger number of unemployed males relative to females among families on relief was due in part to the preferential treatment accorded male-headed households by relief programs. As Linda Gordon points out in her study on the welfare state, most welfare programs have been designed to shore up male-breadwinner families and keep women subordinate in the male-dominated family wage system.[49]

The stories of Law Shee Low and Wong Shee Chan (my maternal grandaunt) illustrate how the depression affected Chinese immigrant women with large families, as well as the strategies some women employed to cope with the hard economic times. Law recalled, "Those were very poor and tough years for us. When my uncle who became penniless died and we were all asked to help with the funeral expenses, we could only afford to give a few dimes. We were so poor, we wanted to die." Her husband, who had been working twelve hours a day at a Chinatown restaurant for $60 a month, lost his job. For a brief period, he lived and worked in the city of Vallejo. "Just made $40 at a restaurant. He gave me $20 and kept $20 for himself. I sewed and made another $30 or $40. So we struggled on."[50] When he was laid off again, she became the chief wage earner. There was still sewing to keep them going, and her husband helped her sew at home and did the shopping. But when even sewing became scarce for a spell, they had to dip into their small savings and seek outside help. "Joe Shoong [the owner of a large garment factory and Law's clansman] was giving out rice, so my husband went and carried back a fifty-pound sack. Food was cheap then. A dime or two would buy you some *sung* [vegetable or meat dishes to go with the rice]."[51] With an unemployed man and four dependents in the house, the family qualified for free milk and food rations from the federal government. And when FERA established a much-needed nursery school in Chinatown, two of their children were among the first to enroll.

Wong Shee Chan recalled similar hard times. Betrothed when ten years old and married at seventeen to my great-grandfather Chin Lung's eldest son, Chin Wing, she was admitted to the United States in 1920 as a U.S. citizen's wife. They initially farmed land that Great-Grandfather had purchased in Oregon but, soon after, returned to San Francisco and worked at Chin Lung's trunk factory on Stockton Street. In 1932, Great-Grandfather decided to retire to China to avoid the depression, leaving what business assets he had left to his sons. Chin Wing tried to maintain the trunk factory, but to no avail. The family had to pawn Grandaunt's jewelry in order to make ends meet. "Those were the worst years for us," recalled Grandaunt, who by then had six children to support. "Life was very hard. I just went from day to day." They considered themselves lucky when they could borrow a dime or a quarter. "A quarter was enough for dinner," she said. "With that I bought two pieces of fish to steam, three bunches of vegetables (two to stir-fry and the third to put in the soup), and some pork for the soup."[52] For a brief period, while her husband was unemployed, the family qualified for federal aid; but after he went to work as a seaman, Grandaunt was left alone to care for the children. She had to find work to help support the family. Encouraged by friends, she went to beauty school to learn how to be a hairdresser. At that time, there were sixteen beauty parlors in Chinatown—the only businesses in the community to be run by Chinese women.[53] After she passed the licensing examination, which she was able to take in the Chinese language, Grandaunt opened a beauty parlor and bathhouse in Chinatown, working from 7 A.M. to 11 P.M. seven days a week. She kept the children with her at the shop and had the older ones help her with the work. Thus she was able to keep the family together and make it through the depression.

Women across the country likewise found ways to "make do." When

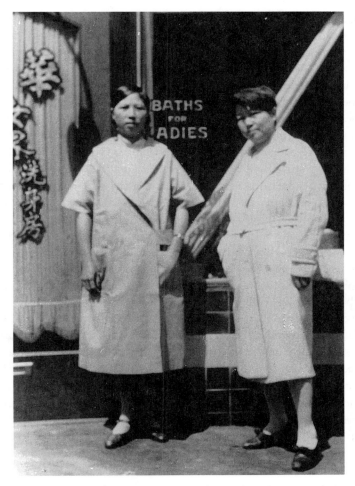

Grandaunt Wong Shee Chan (*left*) in front of her beauty parlor and bathhouse in the 1930s. (Judy Yung collection)

their husbands and sons became unemployed, many white women entered the labor market for the first time, finding work in female-dominated occupations—clerical work, trade, and services. In the decade between 1930 and 1940, the number of married women in the labor force increased nearly 50 percent despite mounting public pressure that they not compete with men for jobs. Often, in fact, it was not men who were edged out of jobs by white women, but black women—particularly domestic workers—who were already at the bottom of the labor ladder.

Concentrated in the marginal occupations of sharecropping, household service, and unskilled factory work, black women suffered the highest unemployment rate among all groups of women.[54] Most other working-class women were able to keep a tenuous hold on their jobs in the industrial and service sectors even as their husbands became unemployed. Women's marginal wages thus often kept whole families alive. Women also learned to cut back on family expenditures, substituting store-bought items with homemade products. They planted gardens, canned fruits and vegetables, remade old clothing, baked bread, raised livestock, rented out sleeping space, and did odd jobs. Pooling resources with relatives and neighbors provided mutual assistance in terms of shared household duties and child care. As a last resort, some women turned to prostitution. And among those who qualified, many went on relief.[55]

It has generally been assumed that women also managed to provide sufficient emotional support to keep the family together during these troubled times. In 1987, however, Lois Rita Helmbold threw that assumption into question. After examining 1,340 interviews with white and black working-class women in the urban North and Midwest that were conducted by the Women's Bureau in the 1930s, Helmbold concluded that a significant number of families were in fact torn apart by the financial and emotional strains of the depression. The expectations and actualities of female self-sacrifice resulted in unresolvable conflicts between parents and children, husbands and wives; relatives, it is clear, did not always come to the aid of unattached women. Family and marital breakups became widespread.[56] Moreover, as Jacqueline Jones points out in her study on black women and the depression, federal aid to mothers with dependent children (started in 1935) may have inadvertently contributed to the disintegration of black families, for by "deserting" their families, unemployed fathers enabled them to qualify for relief. Jones's argument is supported by statistics: in the mid-1930s, approximately 40 percent of all husband-absent black families received public assistance; and by 1940, 31 percent of all black households had a female head.[57]

In contrast, Chinese families held together. Whereas the nation experienced an increase in the divorce rate from the mid-1930s on, the rate remained low among Chinese Americans. Chinese newspapers reported only nine cases of divorce in the 1930s, most of which were filed by women on grounds of wife abuse, although three women also cited lack of child support as a reason.[58] No doubt, Chinese women experienced their share of emotional stress during the depression, but because of cultural taboos against divorce they found other ways to cope. My grandaunt Wong Shee Chan recalled a number of occasions when her unemployed husband took his frustrations out on her. "I remember buying two sand dabs to steam for dinner," she said. "Because he didn't like the fish, he flipped the plate over and ruined the dinner for the entire family. Even the children could not eat it then. See what a mean heart he had?"[59] Having promised her father that she would never disgrace the Wong family's name by disobeying or divorcing her husband, she gritted her teeth and carried on. But when the situation at home became unbearable, Grandaunt would go to the Presbyterian Mission Home for help. "She went there a couple of times, and each time it got ironed out and she came home," recalled her eldest daughter, Penny.[60] Jane Kwong Lee, who was coordinator of the Chinese YWCA in the 1930s, noted the added emotional stress that many women unaccustomed to accepting public assistance felt:

> There is a family with a father, mother, and five small children. The father was unemployed for several years before he obtained work relief. The family is expressively grateful, for they are no longer afraid of starvation. Outwardly, the mother appears happy. Yet, when I talk with her further, I can sense the struggle within her. She cannot bear the thought of being on the relief roll. Her people in China think she is enjoying life here in the "Golden Mountain." She dares not inform them about the family's sufferings and hardships. If she does, she would "lose face." Although the relief money is enough to feed and clothe the family, it is not sufficient to allow for better living quarters than the two rooms they now occupy, without a private kitchen or a private bath. She can afford no heat in the rooms even when the children are ill in bed. This family is on the bare existence line. As in many other cases, at first she felt humiliated about her surroundings. Later on, she got used to it. Now she regards relief as a matter-of-fact.[61]

This pragmatic approach to life, kindled by personal initiative and a strong sense of obligatory self-sacrifice in the interest of the family, helped many Chinese immigrant women through the hardships that they faced in America, including the depression.

The adverse impact of the depression was also blunted by the benefit that Chinese immigrant women and their families drew from federal legislation and programs. Many of the New Deal programs discriminated against women and racial minorities in terms of direct relief, jobs, and wages. One-fourth of the NRA codes, for example, established lower wage rates for women, ranging from 14 to 30 percent below men's rates.

Relief jobs went overwhelmingly to male breadwinners, and significant numbers of female workers in the areas of domestic service, farming, and cannery work were not covered by the Fair Labor Standards Act or Social Security Act. Black, Mexican, and Asian women who were concentrated in these job sectors were thus denied equal protection from labor exploitation and access to insurance benefits. Moreover, under federal guidelines, Mexican and Asian aliens could not qualify for WPA jobs and were in constant fear of deportation.[62] Nevertheless, considering their prior situation, Chinese women had more to gain than lose by the New Deal. For the first time, they were entitled to public assistance. At least 350 families were spared starvation and provided with clothing, housing, and medical care to tide them over the depression. In addition, more than fifty single mothers qualified for either Widow Pension Aid or Aid to Dependent Children.[63] The garment industry—which employed most of the Chinese immigrant women—was covered by the NRA. At the urging of the International Ladies' Garment Workers' Union (ILGWU), sweeps through Chinatown were periodically made to ensure the enforcement of the new minimum-wage levels, work hours, banned child labor law, and safety standards.[64] NRA codes, however, were insufficient to change sweatshop conditions in Chinatown, as employers circumvented or nullified the imposed labor standards through speed-ups and tampered records. Only when workers took matters into their own hands, as in the case of the 1938 National Dollar Stores strike, were employers forced to comply with federal labor laws.

The New Deal did have a positive impact on the living environment of Chinese families. A 1935 study of Chinatown's social needs and problems sponsored by the California State Emergency Relief Administration (CSERA) indicated that housing was woefully substandard, playground space and hours of operation inadequate, and health and day child care sorely lacking.[65] Federal programs, staffed by Chinese American social workers in cooperation with churches and community organizations, were instituted to deal with these specific problems. Families were moved out of tenement houses to apartments and flats close by. Playground hours were extended and street lighting improved. Immigrant mothers learned about American standards of sanitation and nutrition, particularly the importance of milk in their diet, and had access to birth control and health care at the newly established public clinic in the community. They were also entitled to attend English and job-training classes and, as in the case of Law Shee Low, enroll their children in nursery school. As a result, not only did some immigrant women receive direct relief, but their overall quality of life was somewhat improved by the New Deal.

Although in many quarters of the nation the issue of working wives was controversial, it was not a problem in San Francisco Chinatown, where wives and mothers had always had to work to help support their families. On the contrary, as their economic and social roles expanded and their families grew increasingly dependent on them during the depression, the community's attitude toward working women took a turn for the better. According to the 1935 survey conducted by CSERA, women's place in the work world outside the home was no longer questioned:

> The Chinese women of today are much more fortunate and certainly more independent than they were ten or twenty years ago. They are now permitted by their husbands to work outside their homes and the fear of mockery by their neighbors has ceased since it has become the vogue to work, whether to help out the family finances or to have a little pin money. Generally speaking, to help the family finances, since most of them are hard pressed.[66]

Gender relations also improved in their favor, as reflected in newspaper reports. In 1933, for instance, the Chinese Six Companies sided with a widow whose relatives were trying to rob her of her inheritance and force her to marry a man of their choice.[67] *CSYP* published articles appealing to husbands to treat their wives better: "Don't be a tyrannical lord over her, but respect her opinions, speak to her gently, and involve her in all your affairs."[68] In another editorial, after praising Jane Addams's exemplary work with the poor and her involvement with the women's and peace movements, the newspaper encouraged the modern Chinese woman to be aware of her rights, become physically fit, satisfy her domestic duties, attend to the children, and serve the community.[69]

Jane Kwong Lee was one of the few Chinese women who fulfilled this role of the modern woman in the 1930s. After becoming the mother of two and upon graduation from Mills College, she decided to go back to work, even though her husband still had his meat market in Oakland. "To stay home and take care of my children was, of course, my primary concern," she wrote in her autobiography, "but in the midst of the depression period, it was necessary for me to seek employment."[70] Unable to find work in white establishments because of racism, Jane finally secured a part-time job at the Chinese YWCA, at a time when bilingual community workers were sorely needed. It was her responsibility to make home visits and to provide assistance to immigrant women regarding immigration, health and birth control, housing, domestic problems, and applications for government relief. Until she was offered a full-time job as coordinator two years later, she also taught at a Chinese school in the evenings. How did she manage it all?

> In these two years of my life, I actually divided my attention in three different directions—my family, the YWCA, and the Chinese Language School. Aside from providing the necessary care for my children, I did not have any other worries for my family as they were healthy; my husband left for work in the East Bay every morning without asking me to prepare breakfast and came home after work to look after the children. I considered myself lucky to have his cooperation in raising two normal children and maintaining a normal family life.

With her husband's support and cooperation, Jane was able to raise a family and devote herself to her work at the YWCA, which she called "my JOB, in capital letters."[71] Because of her leadership skills and hard work, the YWCA soon broadened its services, grew in membership, moved into a new building, and garnered the respect and support of the community.

To meet the diverse needs of Chinese women who crossed generational and class lines, Jane organized clubs, classes, and programs with specific groups of women in mind. To dispel the mistrust of the older generation and to attract immigrant women to the YWCA, she utilized the Chinese newspapers and personally distributed Chinese leaflets to publicize events that catered to their interests: lectures and plays in Chinese on history, politics, culture, and the status of women; workshops on nutrition (including how to cook with relief food distributed by the government) and health issues; and field trips to take women out of the community to visit local bread and milk factories. Her newspaper articles helped to promote the YWCA's services while at the same time advocating women's liberation. In one front-page editorial titled "Why Chinese Americans Should Support the YWCA" she wrote:

> The degree of success of the YWCA is a reflection of the development of our society. Why do I make such a statement? It is because women constitute half of the human race. If women, who make up half of the human race, do not unite and improve themselves in the areas of character, intellectual, physical, and social development, then no matter how high-minded and knowledgeable the men—the other half of the human race—are, the entire society will not advance. In old China, men were held to be better than women. Men had ambitions to be educated so that they might roam the world and bring glory to their family. Women,

on the other hand, were not educated, so that they might remain virtuous. They were slighted and confined to their bedchambers, ignorant of the world and its affairs. That is why the Chinese people have become weak and it is so difficult to help them. Yet those with foresight have long realized that liberating women so that they may develop and improve themselves is something that should not be delayed.[72]

Aware that many immigrant women were illiterate, Jane devised a strategy of going door-to-door to personally publicize the YWCA's services. In this way she gained firsthand knowledge of family conditions and women's needs that later proved useful in her plans for programs and services. The personal contact also made her a familiar figure and the YWCA an accepted institution in the community. On behalf of the Chinese YWCA she ventured out of the local community as well, giving talks on Chinese American culture and attending national conventions in Colorado Springs and Atlantic City. These occasions allowed her not only to visit such places as the Grand Canyon and see snow for the first time, but also to meet with a diverse range of women of common interests and, more important, to promote goodwill and understanding on behalf of Chinese Americans.

Reflecting on her important role as a community activist, a role that often took her away from her family, Jane wrote years later:

> In turning my attention to the position of Community Worker, I had a varied spectrum—a link between persons, between individuals and groups, between groups and groups, and between country to country, even. For instance, when I interpreted for a Mrs. So and So, this was a connection between her and her physician; when I asked a girl to be a member of a club, I acted as a link between this girl and the YWCA; when I went out on a financial campaign for a school house, I acted as a link between the school house and the community in which the school house was to be erected; and when I volunteered to get help from America for flood victims in China, I acted as a link between China and America. Thus, I considered my job as a very important and beneficial one, and I was doing it with deep dedication and zeal. Later on, I might be accused of being too career-minded, but I could not help in shaping my professional attitude of devoting my best to what was to be done. I might have to apologize to my children that I should have given them more of my time and care, but I have to admit that my love for them has never diminished an iota, no matter how deeply involved I was in community affairs.[73]

Jane's dedication and effectiveness as a community leader did not go unnoticed. Whereas the community had once disapproved of women in the public arena, she found that her role as a female activist was respected by the Chinatown establishment. Once her bilingual speaking abilities and organizational skills became known, she was courted by Chinatown churches and invited to speak before the Chinese Six Companies and other Chinatown organizations on behalf of the Chinese YWCA and for various nationalist causes. She considered these requests "a good omen for me to take part in the Chinese community life of San Francisco."[74] Even as she was proving useful to the community, she was paving the way for other bilingual social workers, who were sought after by agencies with federal funding to expand their services. Already a prominent figure in the community, Jane was asked to serve on the civil service examination board that helped hire the first Chinese-speaking social workers for the city.

Ironies of the Depression: Second-Generation Women

Even more so than immigrant women, second-generation women—who made up 69 percent of the Chinese female population in San Francisco in 1930—had more to gain than lose from the depression. Their occupational niches were relatively safe from the threat of unemployment. Moreover, many were able to take advantage of new opportunities and favorable federal policies and make strides in terms of their work, family, and political lives. This is not to say that second-generation women were all spared hardships during the depression. They, more than the first generation, tended to bank their money, and some even invested in stocks and bonds. Among those who lost their life savings in the stock market crash were Alice Sue Fun and Chew Fong Low. After returning from her trip around the world with the actress Lola Fisher, Alice had remarried and was operating a corner grocery store with her husband in Oakland. With their savings, they had purchased a house, a car, and some $3,000 worth of stocks. "That was a lot of money in stocks," she recalled. "But I didn't have to jump off the building, because I had paid for them in full and wasn't in debt. It's when you owe money and don't know where to raise it that you'd be in trouble."[75] They recovered, and after her husband died she continued to speculate in real estate and invest her money in "safe stocks," the proceeds of which allowed her to retire comfortably and maintain an independent lifestyle until she died at the age of ninety. Chew Fong Low, who had built the luxurious Low apartment building for Chinese Americans in 1927, did not fare as well. Having invested a fortune in stocks and bonds, she lost heavily. The shock was too much for her frail health, and she passed away in 1936 at the age of sixty-seven.[76]

Some second-generation women, like Kathy Ng Pon, had to go on relief. Her sister Gladys Ng Gin recalled that although she and her mother remained employed, Kathy, who had seven children and a husband with heart trouble, qualified for public assistance. "Instead of money, she was given fifty, a hundred pounds of potatoes, a sack of flour, butter, and things like that. Every six months, she would go buy shoes from Bally's shoestore," said Gladys. Because their dwelling was considered substandard and unsanitary, they were also assisted in moving to a three-bedroom apartment close by. After her husband passed away, Kathy worked at home so she could take care of her young children. "She would make bean paste and take it to the vegetable market to sell; crochet purses for $4 that I would take to work and sell for $20. Sold like hotcakes. So that's how she raised the seven children," said Gladys.[77]

Such cases among the second generation appear to be in the minority. For the most part, the race- and sex-segregated labor force protected Chinese American women from unemployment, while the New Deal and the entertainment and tourist industries offered them new opportunities. Although discrimination in the labor market continued to bar them from white-collar jobs outside Chinatown, their concentration in the operative, service, and clerical sectors of the economy meant continued employment. Jobs such as housekeeping, picking and sorting fruits at closeby ranches or canneries, sewing in Chinatown garment shops, waitressing in downtown restaurants and teahouses, running elevators in department stores, and professional, sales, and clerical work in Chinatown were available to them throughout the depression years. In the middle of the depression, too, federal civil service jobs opened up to Chinese Americans for the first time. Mary Tong, for instance, became the first Chinese American woman to be hired by the U.S. Post Office.[78] As Chinese Americans became more acculturated and recognized as potential consumers, department stores downtown also began to hire Chinese American women as salespersons.[79]

Thanks to the New Deal, those who had lost their jobs could seek help at the employment offices set up at the Chinese YWCA and the Chinese Catholic Center, although most of the job referrals were for household employment at exploitive wages. According to case worker Ethel Lum in 1936, "Private families, realizing that Chinese girls can usually be employed at a wage scale lower, but an efficiency level higher, than the average white girl, show a preference for engaging Oriental help."[80] At that time, according to advertisements in the Chinese news-papers, a live-in nanny earned only $15 a month; a housekeeper who worked eight hours a day, $25 a month; and a live-in housekeeper, $12 a month.[81] Although these wages were far better than those paid to black domestic workers in the North and South—10 to 15 cents an hour[82]—they were not considered desirable jobs by Chinese American women who had better options. Part of the problem was that the occupational category of domestic service was exempt from the NRA codes because it was not an interstate commerce industry. The YWCA tried to work around this loophole by lobbying the federal government to implement a code specifying a ten-hour day, six-day week, $9 minimum for live-in servants, and hourly and overtime rates for day help, but to no avail.[83] The Chinese YWCA also tried to ensure a minimum work rate for Chinese women in domestic service. Together with the Emanu-El Sister-hood, which looked after the interests of Jewish working girls, it estab-lished the Institute of Practical Arts to train women in household employment. Graduates of the course were guaranteed a job at mini-mum wages.[84] However, no followup reports were issued to suggest how successful the program actually was.

Although WPA jobs went mainly to unemployed men over women, women fortunate enough to be placed in relief jobs often experienced a degree of upward mobility as a result. Of the 4,215 women (as op-posed to 10,272 men) in San Francisco who held "emergency" jobs in 1937, the majority were in the professional, clerical, skilled, and semi-skilled sectors of the labor market. Whereas black women workers thereby gained access to semiskilled jobs that had been previously closed to them,[85] Chinese American women now entered the profession of so-cial work for the first time. As bilingual social workers, they made home visits, dispensed financial aid, and helped Chinese clients adjust to the economic situation. In 1936, Lily K. Jean passed the civil service exam-ination to become San Francisco's first Chinese American social worker. An editorial in the *Chinese Digest* hailed her appointment as "a forward step in public social service on behalf of the large Chinese population in this city and county."[86] A number of Chinese American women were also hired by the WPA to work in the community as teachers, recreation aides, and assistants in conducting community surveys, which led to im-provements in social services and living conditions in the community.

Because the entertainment industry continued to thrive, thanks in part to the depression—movies and radio shows were inexpensive diversions for the American public—Chinese American women found some work, albeit in limited and often stereotypical roles, in show business. In 1934, *CSYP* announced that a local theater was auditioning Chinese American talent and that at least ten girls had come to demonstrate their singing and acting abilities.[87] A year later, Hollywood's Metro-Goldwyn-Mayer ran announcements in the same newspaper, looking for Chinese American extras, women in particular, for the filming of Pearl Buck's *The Good Earth*.[88] Although the movie was about peasant life in China, all of the major Chinese roles went to white actors. Even Anna May Wong, who was at the pinnacle of her acting career, was turned down for the lead role of O-lan, which went instead to Luise Rainer. Some Chinese Americans, discouraged by racism in the film industry, began to star in and produce their own films. In 1936, Cathay Pictures announced the release of *Heartaches*, a film about an aviation student in America who falls in love with an opera star. Except for the well-known Chinese actress Wei Kim Fong, all the other players in the production were said to be "American-Chinese."[89]

That same year, soon after prohibition was lifted, Chinatown's first two cocktail bars opened—Chinese Village and Twin Dragon; they provided Chinese American women with a new, better-paying, but controversial line of work as cocktail waitresses and nightclub entertainers. Gladys Ng Gin was among the first to try out for these jobs. She was making $75 a month running an elevator when a friend encouraged her to become a waitress at the Chinese Village. As she recalled, "I didn't know the difference between gin to rum, scotch or bourbon, but it was good money. Ten dollars a week but great tips." Being illiterate in both Chinese and English, she found it difficult to take orders. "I had to memorize over one hundred kinds of alcohol because I couldn't write," she said. "You ordered and I told the bartender. Then the bartender made the drink and I served it. But you have to remember what each customer is drinking. And sometimes you go for another order and then come back for the first drink."[90] After two years at the Chinese Village, Gladys followed the owner, Charlie Low, to Forbidden City, one of Chinatown's first nightclubs. Although her mother did not object to her working in a bar, many other people in the conservative community considered such work immoral. As it turned out, most Chinatown women were so inhibited by their social upbringing that the nightclubs had to recruit the large part of their talent from outside.

When he first opened Forbidden City on the outskirts of Chinatown,

Charlie Low recalled, he was determined to present a modern version of the Chinese American woman, "not the old fashioned way, all bundled up with four or five pairs of trousers," he said. "We can't be backwards all the time; we've got to show the world that we're on an equal basis. Why, Chinese have limbs just as pretty as anyone else!"[91] Purported noble intentions aside, Charlie Low, the son of Chew Fong Low, was known to be a shrewd businessman. Capitalizing on the end of prohibition and the beginning of the nightclub era, he invested in Forbidden City, an oriental nightclub with an American beat. What gave Forbidden City instant fame was Charlie Low's publicity skills and his ability to showcase Chinese Americans in cabaret-style entertainment—doing Cole Porter and Sophie Tucker, dancing tap, ballroom, and soft-shoe, parodying Western musicals in cowboy outfits, and kicking it up in chorus lines. Besides challenging Hollywood's misconceptions of Chinese American talent, the novelty acts broke popular stereotypes of Chinese Americans as necessarily exotic and foreign. Most important, Forbidden City provided Chinese American women employment and a rare opportunity to show off their talents. "It was a beginning," said Mary Mammon, a member of the original chorus line. "There was just no way you could go to Hollywood [which] had a low regard for Chinese American talents. We [supposedly] had bad legs, spoke pidgin English, and had no rhythm."[92] Bertha Hing, who needed a job to support herself through college, was one of the few local Chinatown women to join the chorus line. "Chinatown mothers wouldn't let their daughters do anything like that. But what they didn't realize was that we all just loved to dance. And we didn't particularly care for drinking or smoking or anything like that. It was just another way of earning a living," she said.[93]

From the beginning, the Chinese community felt that no respectable parents would want their daughter to be seen in such an establishment. As dancer Jadin Wong recalled, "Chinese people in San Francisco were ready to spit in our faces because we were nightclub performers. They wouldn't talk with us because they thought we were whores. We used to get mail at Forbidden City—'Why don't you get a decent job and stop disgracing the Chinese? You should be ashamed of yourself, walking around and showing your legs!'"[94] After Charlie Low added nude acts to boost business, however, his sexploitation tactics became clear, and the nightclub's reputation plummeted to a new low. Although many of the female performers would have preferred not to bare their bodies, most went along with it to keep their jobs.[95] Years later, when asked in an oral history interview if she had ever felt exploited while working at the Forbidden City, Bertha Hing replied:

Chorus line of the Gay Ninety Revue, Forbidden City, 1942. *From left to right:* Lily Pon, Ginger Lee, Connie Parks, Diane Shinn, Dottie Sun, and Mei Tai Sing. (John Grau collection)

I tell you, those of us who started in together really loved to dance and we liked what we were doing. I never felt like I was exploited, because I felt that I had a choice of whether I danced or go into something else. It was my choice and the other girls felt the same way. But I think that we were exploited this way: We were underpaid. The waitresses were getting a lot of money from tips and what-not, than we did in dancing. But then, we loved dancing and how are you going to dance when there are no opportunities to, except that.[96]

Despite the Chinese community's condemnation and the compromises they had to make, Chinese American women continued to work at the Forbidden City and other nightclubs through the 1930s and 1940s. During its best years, the Forbidden City attracted one hundred thousand customers a year, including senators, governors, and Hollywood stars like Ronald Reagan. By the time the World War II economy set in, more than a hundred Chinese American women were employed in Chinatown's dozen nightclubs, and the composition of the audience had changed from all white to half Chinese, indicating the attraction that nightclub entertainment now held for middle-class Chinese Americans.[97]

In 1938, tourism in Chinatown was bringing in $5 million annually and keeping many Chinese American women employed.[98] The traffic from the 1939 Golden Gate International Exposition added to the Chinatown coffers and provided additional jobs for Chinese Americans. Merchants invested $1.25 million to build a replica of a Chinese village at the Treasure Island fairgrounds and organized parades and festivals in Chinatown to attract tourists into the community. Two hundred positions opened up at the fairgrounds and another fifty in Chinatown. Young women were particularly sought after to provide "atmosphere" during the fair, serving as hostesses, secretaries, "cigarette girls," and waitresses.[99] Even after the exposition ended in 1940, there was no decline in the tourist trade in Chinatown. Moreover, the booming war economy that followed not only ended the depression but also provided unprecedented job opportunities for Chinese American women outside the local economy.

The depressed economy and government relief ultimately led to improved conditions for second-generation Chinese American women in a number of other ways. Because of deflation, those who remained employed were able to stretch their salaries during the depression. "For a dollar, my husband, myself, and my two children could enjoy a full dinner at the Far East Cafe," said Jane Kwong Lee.[100] Modern and affordable housing on the fringes of Chinatown was also more available to the growing numbers of second-generation families. According to the CSERA,

> Since the economic depression of 1929, many of the houses of the Nob Hill District were left vacant. The Chinese were willing to pay more than the previous rent for houses in this district. As a result many a landlord was willing to set aside prejudice for economic gain. Consequently, a large number of residents are moving rapidly towards Nob Hill district. Forty-eight per cent of the properties occupied by Chinese west of Stockton Street are owned by them.[101]

This is not to say housing discrimination vanished during the depression years. Eva Lowe, for one, was rebuffed a number of times when she tried to rent an apartment with her white girlfriend during the early

1930s. They would say yes to her girlfriend, but when they saw that Eva was the roommate in question, they would renege, saying, "We don't rent to Orientals." They finally found a place on Russian Hill—but only after Eva claimed to be her friend's maid.[102]

Less affected by unemployment, a certain segment of the second generation continued their quest of the good life. As one Stanford student told a news reporter in 1936, "Certainly we want to live American lives; we eat American foods, play bridge, go to the movies and thrill over Clark Gable and Myrna Loy; we have penthouse parties, play football, tennis and golf; attend your churches and your schools."[103] The social, fashion, and sports pages of the *Chinese Digest* in the 1930s give the impression that the depression was not an issue for the growing middle class of young Chinese Americans. As the rest of the country recovered from the hard times, certain young Chinese women in San Francisco were competing in tennis, basketball, bowling, and track, learning the latest dance, the Lambert Walk, going to the beauty parlor, and worrying about what to wear to the next formal dance. Investigating the social life of San Francisco Chinatown as a WPA worker, Pardee Lowe—a second-generation Chinese American himself—remarked on the good life he saw in Chinatown, reflected in the "sleek-looking automobiles" that crowded Chinatown's streets and the "flivvers operated by its collegiate sons and daughters."[104]

While local newspapers expressed concern about the second generation's fast pace of acculturation and self-indulgent ways, the need for gender roles to keep up with modern times was also recognized. As Jane Kwong Lee wrote in the *Chinese Digest*,

> In spite of their frivolities in many ways, they [American-born Chinese] show keen interest and thought in weighty questions of their age. Girls no longer take marriage as the end of their career; they want to be financially independent just as much as all other American women. They prepare themselves to meet all future emergencies. They study Chinese in addition to English so that in case they go to China some day they will be able to use the language. . . . Women in this community are keeping pace with the quick changes of the modern world. The shy Chinese maidens in bound feet are forever gone, making place for active and intelligent young women.[105]

To guide them in making the necessary family and social adjustments, Jane reoriented the YWCA program to serve their specific needs, just as she had done for immigrant women. Adolescents were able to enjoy sports, crafts, drama, dancing, and parties and take advantage of vocational guidance and job training classes. Business and professional women as well as young wives participated in Chinese language classes, social dinners, recreational sports, and group discussions on topics such as race prejudice, Chinese culture, current events, marital ethics, and child rearing. Through these kinds of activities, the YWCA fulfilled its goal of helping second-generation women develop socially, physically, morally, and intellectually. The YWCA also encouraged them to expand their public roles by helping to raise funds for the Community Chest and participate in the Rice Bowl parades and opening celebrations of the Golden Gate and Bay Bridges.

Spurred by economic and political conditions in the 1930s, the second generation did indeed assume a larger leadership role in the Chinese community, paralleling that of second-generation Mexican Americans in Los Angeles during this same period.[106] The *Chinese Digest*, founded in 1935 by Thomas W. Chinn and Chingwah Lee as the voice of this new generation, served as the clarion for social action. During its five years of existence, the *Chinese Digest* unified Chinese Americans across the country, encouraging them to act on the many social problems their community faced: poverty, health care, housing, employment, child care, recreation, education, and political and workers' rights. For its time, the *Chinese Digest* held a progressive perspective, advocating tourism as a viable economic base for Chinatown and the ballot as the political means by which to fight racial discrimination and improve living conditions. It also supported the war effort in China.

In contrast to *CSYP*, the *Chinese Digest* included many more news and feature stories of interest to second-generation women. Clara Chan had a regular column on women's fashion; Ethel Lum wrote on sociological topics, including women's issues; and P'ing (Alice Fong) Yu's "Jade Box" featured women's fashions, recipes, and social as well as political news. Taken as a whole, the articles reflected the effects of acculturation on the social consciousness of second-generation women, some of whom became political activists during the depression years. Tracing the development of two such women, Eva Lowe and Alice Fong Yu, sheds light on how some Chinese American women, inspired by the political temper of the 1930s, became more active in community reform, electoral politics, and Chinese nationalism.

Eva Lowe, who had followed her brother-in-law and sister to China in 1919 at the age of ten, returned to San Francisco a changed person four years later. "In China," she said, "I went to Chinese school and I learned about Chinese history, from the Tang dynasty through the end of the Qing dynasty and how the imperialist countries took over China. Like Dr. Sun Yat-sen said, China was cut up like a watermelon and each European imperialist country had a piece of it. I remember thinking, you know, China used to be so strong, and now this; and I cried in class."[107] Other incidents—the mistreatment of her mother by her grandmother because she did not bear sons, the banning of her step-mother from the village because a man was seen entering her room, and a chance meeting with a female scholar who first introduced her to feminism and socialism—alerted her to the unfair treatment of Chinese women and the need to fight back by becoming politically active.

Upon her return to San Francisco she attended high school and became involved with the Chinese Students Association, which claimed a membership of three thousand.[108] What appealed to her was the group's anti-imperialist stance and concern for China's future. She did not hesitate to join in making "soap box" speeches in Chinatown condemning Japanese aggression in China. "People still recall the slogan I coined, 'If you have money, give money. If you have muscles, give muscles. I have neither money or muscles, but I can give my voice [to the cause],'" she said.[109] Wanting to do her part to help the disadvantaged, Eva assisted families in applying for relief during the depression and joined the Huaren Shiyi Hui in demanding action from the Chinese Six Companies on behalf of the unemployed. She also supported the longshoremen's strike and participated in the hunger march in San Francisco, shouting, "We want work! We want work!" with the masses of people pouring down Market Street to City Hall. Because these groups were ostracized by the community as Communist, her friends dropped out one by one owing to parental pressure, but Eva remained active in leftist politics until she married and left for Hong Kong with her husband and son in 1937. "I always believed in fighting for the underdog," she reflected years later.[110]

While Chinese nationalism was what motivated Eva Lowe to engage in politics, Alice Fong Yu, the first Chinese American schoolteacher in the San Francisco public schools, was influenced to contribute to the community by her family upbringing as well as Christianity.[111] "*Ho ga gow* [good family training]— that's what my parents gave me," said Alice. Growing up in Washington (Nevada County), California, she became aware early on of racial discrimination:

> It is surprising, isn't it, that [in] just a small one-room school and [among] just a handful of children, they still thought we were queer. They would sing "Ching Chong Chinaman" and all those things to make fun of us

and make you feel like nobody, and then when we would play games, they wouldn't hold our hands, as if they would be contaminated by our hands, and so they wouldn't accept us.

The Fong children, disappointed and hurt, sought comfort from their parents, who told them, "You shouldn't let those things bother you, because they are just barbarians; that's why they treat you like that. You have culture. Our people have a long history. Wait until you get your education and go back to China, where they will look up to you. But these people are barbarians; don't let them worry you."

Although their white classmates shunned them and the teachers made them feel inferior, the church welcomed them into its fold, sending a Sunday school teacher to Vallejo Chinatown, where the family had moved in 1923, to teach the children the Bible and take them to Christian retreats. "The Christians were the ones who accepted us in the early days," Alice said, and "gave us a chance to intermingle with other races." Encouraged both by her parents and by her involvement in the YWCA Girls Reserve, Alice became a community activist after she moved to San Francisco. During the 1930s, Alice was involved with many Chinatown organizations, including the Square and Circle Club, YWCA, Chinese Needlework Guild, and Tahoe Christian Conference. A founding member of the Square and Circle Club, Alice helped raise funds for Chinese orphans, the elderly, and needy families. She also worked with other community organizations to register American-born Chinese to vote, campaign for the reelection of Congresswoman Florence Kahn, and lobby for improved housing and recreational facilities in Chinatown. Alice became particularly well known in the community for planning and coordinating Square and Circle fashion shows as fund-raisers and leading the boycott against the wearing of silk stockings during the War of Resistance Against Japan (1937–45). In her capacity as a teacher at Commodore Stockton Elementary School, she also helped found the Chinese chapter of the Needlework Guild, which provided clothing and shoes to needy children in Chinatown.[112] "The mothers couldn't speak English well enough to join the P.T.A., so we started our own group," she explained. "We got together to sew and talk about things. Whenever we found out about an impoverished family, we would help them get on welfare."[113]

In 1933, Alice joined with Ira Lee and Edwar Lee to organize the first Lake Tahoe Chinese Young People's Christian Conference, in which second-generation Chinese from all over California came together to discuss common problems and concerns. According to Ira, he, Alice, and Edwar hoped to duplicate the social gospel spirit and fellowship that so moved them at YMCA conferences. They also wanted to provide a place for young Chinese Americans from different church denominations to meet outside of Chinatown. What started as an experimental retreat at the Presbyterian conference grounds at Zephyr Point, Lake Tahoe, continued as an annual conference until the 1960s. At the beginning, topics of discussion focused on Christianity and the situation in China. Then in the later 1930s, as the group grew to more than one hundred participants, including some non-Christians, interest turned to discrimination, marriage and family life, political involvement, community problems, and the question of serving China. Resolutions were passed calling for increased social integration, vocational guidance, involvement in American politics, adoption of Western-style marriages and family life, and recreational interests beyond mah-jongg and dancing. Although the discussions lacked structure or follow-through, the retreats provided the second generation with an opportunity to socialize, share views, and vent frustrations. The benefits accrued were less to the church or the community as to the individual participants, who learned new organizational skills and carried the ideas for and commitment to social change back to their respective communities. One offshoot of the Tahoe Conference was the Chinese Young People's Forum, an interdenominational group started by Alice that met weekly at Cameron House to continue discussing ways to solve the community's problems.[114]

Thus, although the depression was a time of economic strife for most of America, for a significant number of Chinese women in San Francisco it was a time of stable employment, social growth, and political activism. This positive side became even more evident when Chinese women went on strike for the first time against the National Dollar Stores, the largest garment factory in Chinatown.

Joining the Labor Movement: The 1938 Garment Workers' Strike

Chinese women's hard-won victory in their strike against National Dollar Stores was due as much to their determination for social change in the workplace as to the economic and political circumstances of the depression that nurtured their union activism. Their ability to sustain a strike for 105 days, supported by a white labor union as well as left organizations in Chinatown, proved that Chinese women could stand up for themselves and work across generational, racial, gender, and political lines to gain better working conditions in Chinatown. Although little was gained in terms of higher wages and job security (the factory closed a year after the strike), the experience moved women well beyond the domestic sphere into the political arena: it raised their political consciousness and organizing skills, allowed them to become part of the labor movement and to find jobs outside Chinatown, and, most important, marked their first stand against labor exploitation in the garment industry. The strike also provides insights into the class and gender dynamics of ethnic enterprises and the possibilities of organizing Chinese women workers in the garment industry.

In 1938, when the strike against National Dollar Stores was launched, the garment industry was the largest employer in Chinatown. More than one thousand women worked in sixty-nine garment factories in Chinatown. Most of these factories were small, with fewer than fifty employees toiling under sweatshop conditions: poor lighting and ventilation, long hours, low wages. All were nonunion and operating on a piece-rate basis, earning wages ranging from $4 to $16 a week—as compared to union workers who received from $19 to $30 a week for a shorter workweek.[115] Ben Fee, a labor organizer and Communist Party member, stated in *CSYP* that Chinatown's garment industry had reached a crisis situation in part because of the depression, but more so because small contractors with inadequate capital and unsound management practices persisted in underbidding each other and cutting workers' salaries in order to compete in the highly seasonal industry. As a result, he pointed out, there was a high turnover and shortage of skilled labor, the stiff market competition allowed jobbers to keep contract prices low, and factories proved unable to meet NRA labor standards. He advocated that Chinese contractors unite to eliminate competition among themselves and that workers organize to improve their own lives. He also had the foresight to call for ethnic unity across class lines: "Overseas Chinese, be they factory owners or workers, are all living under the economic repression of another race, so we should work together to come up with a long-term plan that will enable us to co-exist with each other."[116] Needless to say, he was not heeded.

Unlike other Chinatown garment shops, National Dollar Stores, which employed 125 Chinese workers, mostly women, was vertically integrated; that is, it controlled all aspects of production, from manufacturing to contracting out to retailing. Owned by Joe Shoong, one of the

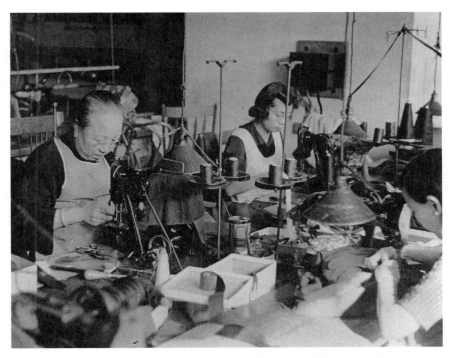

Garment workers in San Francisco Chinatown. (Courtesy of Labor Archives and Research Center, San Francisco State University)

wealthiest Chinese businessmen in the country, the National Dollar Stores factory specialized in women's light apparel for exclusive distribution to National Dollar Stores' thirty-seven retail outlets on the West Coast. In 1937, gross sales for the chain amounted to $7 million, and profits to about $170,000. Joe Shoong's salary that year was $141,000, with dividends earning him another $40,000. Known as a generous philanthropist in the Chinatown community, he lived in a large stucco house in Oakland, had five cars, and was a Shriner as well as a thirty-second-degree Mason.[117]

In all of Chinatown, Joe Shoong's factory was the cleanest and most modern, and it offered the best wages—supposedly $13.33 for a forty-eight-hour week, the minimum rate in California. The strike came about only after many frustrating attempts by workers to negotiate steady employment and increased wages. "Wages was the main issue," recalled Sue Ko Lee, who was a buttonhole machine operator at National Dollar

Stores before the strike. "That time the [minimum] wage law was already in, but we weren't getting that. We didn't keep the hours according to law. And there was already a homework rule but they were sending work out to homeworkers."[118] According to Jennie Matyas, labor organizer for the ILGWU at the time, the workers first approached the union for help in 1937.

> Japan and China were at war. Most of the Chinese here had relatives back home. They all felt very loyal to their home relatives and wanted to support them. [Yet] the workers in the National Dollar factory found themselves underbid by other workers in Chinatown. They found that the work went to other Chinese contractors who did the work cheaper than they did. . . . They decided to supplicate the owner to remember that they needed money to send home to China and wouldn't he provide them with more work.[119]

Unable to get a positive response from the factory owner, garment workers decided to organize themselves. This was the moment the ILGWU had been waiting for, because up to that point they had been unsuccessful in organizing the Chinese.

In San Francisco, where Chinese dominated the garment industry and often underbid union shops on contracts with downtown manufacturers, the strategy the ILGWU adopted was to organize and control the Chinese or drive them out of business. "The situation is getting more desperate," Matyas told the *Chinese Digest*, "and if the Chinese contractors and dressmakers do not heed the writing on the wall and organize, it is possible that the American garment workers, backed by the ILGWU, may declare war on the Chinese garment industry." The *Digest*, recognizing the veiled threat behind the labor union's determination to organize Chinatown workers, stressed that the community could no longer afford to remain outside the labor movement:

> With the tide of the labor movement as it is in the United States today, Chinese who work in any big scale industry cannot remain aloof from the trend of unionization. . . . As the situation stands now, failure on the part of the Chinese to organize will mean that they will only continue to work for low wages and long hours. Eventually, as we have already hinted, it may mean that the American garment workers' unions may take drastic measures to combat the competition of the Chinese in this industry. In such an event the Chinese, in all probability, will be the losers.[120]

Historically, however, Chinese workers had been regarded by white workers as unfair competition, scapegoated and attacked during hard economic times, relegated to unskilled, low-wage, and dead-end jobs, and actively excluded from the larger labor movement; it was therefore not surprising that they resisted the ILGWU's attempts to unionize them. If Chinatown garment shops were to have any work at all, they had little choice but to bid low on contracts and cut into their workers' wages to make up the difference. Chinese workers who did not speak English, had few marketable skills, and faced racial discrimination in the labor market had little choice but to accept the poor working conditions in Chinatown. To compound matters, they were usually also beholden to their employers, who in most cases were kin.

Chinese workers at the National Dollar Stores factory were aware of the union's motives. "They wanted to organize us," said Sue Ko Lee, who became involved in the 1938 strike. "They tried and tried, but they couldn't break the barrier. The white shops were already organized and they were clamoring that the contractors were sending work out to the Chinese workers, and that was a thorn in their sides. So they had to organize the Chinese."[121] This was indeed the situation in 1934, when Rose Pesotta, a committed labor organizer for the ILGWU, blew the whistle on the deplorable working conditions in the Chinese "subterranean sweatshops" in an attempt to bring Chinatown into the union's fold.[122] NRA code enforcers were called in, and a number of Chinese garment shops were cited or shut down for code violations.[123] But try as she did, Pesotta was not successful in unionizing Chinatown shops. She simply could not convince Chinese employers or employees that the ILGWU could protect them from racial discrimination in the open market. Nor could she get other trade unions to support her on the issue.[124]

Next Ben Fee was hired by ILGWU to organize garment workers in Chinatown. The son of an American-born Chinese interpreter, he arrived in the United States in 1922 when he was thirteen years old. He was one of the first Chinese to be recruited into the U.S. Communist Party and was active in such leftist organizations as the Chinese Students Association, the Alaska Cannery Workers Union, and the Chinese Workers Mutual Aid Association. Neither the Chinatown establishment nor the ILGWU appreciated his radical views. Shortly after his appointment, he was forced out of the ILGWU because of his Communist background. In 1938, Ben Fee left San Francisco for New York because of marital problems that had destroyed his credibility in the Chinese community.[125]

Jennie Matyas, who next took on the challenge, had more success. A dedicated Socialist and union organizer, she was able to gain the trust of the Chinese workers because of her gender, strong personality, and cultural sensitivity. According to Sue Ko Lee, "She's not Chinese, but she's a woman. She's dedicated and she's honest. Now you read about the corruption in the unions. I don't think you could corrupt her. She really wanted to help us. . . . Everyone trusted her within the group."[126] Jennie Matyas, moreover, arrived on the scene when the legal protections accorded by the Wagner Act were bolstering the greatest organizing drive in the history of the American labor movement. Whereas in 1933 only 6 percent of American workers were unionized, by 1939 a full 17 percent were; female membership in unions grew from 200,000 in 1924 to 800,000 in 1938. Women strikers were now highly visible in the pecan fields of Texas, the garment plants of Michigan, and retail stores throughout Ohio.[127] In 1933 alone, the ILGWU, which had been on the wane since the 1920s, increased its nationwide membership 400 percent (from 40,000 to 200,000 strong) after mounting a massive organizing drive in sixty cities. Operating on the principle of racial equality, it welcomed large numbers of black and Mexican American women into its rank and file.[128] But organizing Chinese workers proved more difficult—until frustrated workers at the National Dollar Stores factory decided enough was enough.

With Matyas's assistance, eighty workers at the National Dollar Stores signed certification cards favoring a union shop, and in November 1937 Local 341 of the Chinese Ladies' Garment Workers' Union (LGWU) was chartered under the ILGWU. In response, the factory fired four of the active union members and demoted Willie Go, the chief organizer. (Later, however, under pressure from the ILGWU, which threatened to call a strike during the Christmas season with support from the Retail Department Store Employees' Union, which had jurisdiction over employees at Shoong's retail stores, National Dollar Stores reinstated the men.)[129]

National Dollar Stores then insisted that a vote be taken to prove that the workers wanted the ILGWU as their collective bargaining agent. The bilingual-ballot election, supervised by the regional National Labor Relations Board on January 24, 1938, endorsed the ILGWU, and an agreement was reached the next day between factory and union representatives. Wage increases, to be agreed upon at a later date, would be paid retroactively to January 24, 1938, and the factory would become a closed shop (all employees had to join the union), with all hiring to be done through the union. Two weeks later, National Dollar Stores announced that it had sold the Chinatown factory to Golden Gate Manufacturing, though it was keeping the retailing sector. The garment workers saw this move as a subterfuge to freeze them out and break up the union. Now having to negotiate with the new owners, G. N. Wong and Hoo Joe Sun—the former foreman and manager of the National Dollar Stores, respectively—the ILGWU demanded that National Dollar Stores buy all its manufactured goods from Golden Gate and that Golden Gate guarantee work for a minimum of eleven months of the year and ensure this minimum with a $10,000 bond. These demands were in addition to recognition of a union shop and $20 wages for a thirty-five-hour workweek. National Dollar Stores and Golden Gate Company refused to comply with any of these demands, and on February 26, 1938, at 8 A.M., the Chinese LGWU officially called a strike and began picketing the factory and three National Dollar retail stores in San Francisco.[130]

According to the Chinese LGWU's official releases and flyers directed at the public, the unscrupulous practices of the National Dollar Stores were the catalyst that caused 108 workers to go on strike:

> We are on strike for increased wages to support our livelihood. . . . We have tried repeatedly to negotiate in good faith with our employer, but he has consistently used the oppressive tactics of the capitalist to delay us. He forced us to have an election supervised by the National Labor Relations Board which resulted in recognition of our union. His legal representatives signed an agreement with ours, but he continued to use all kinds of unscrupulous tactics to try and break up our collective effort, even to the point of changing the ownership of the factory. His goal is to break our ricebowl strategy. We have no choice but to strike for fair treatment.[131]

National Dollar Stores, also seeking support from the community, responded that since the factory had been sold, the workers were illegally picketing the retail stores; the factory had in the past always complied with the law; and the Chinese community needed to unite in the face of hard times.[132] To this, the Chinese LGWU replied:

> If National Dollar Stores is really interested in the national welfare, they should negotiate with the workers in good faith and allow workers to make a decent living so that they can afford to buy war bonds to support the war effort in China. How can we survive on $13.30 a week and still contribute to the war effort? The worker's welfare is the nation's welfare.[133]

When the Golden Gate Company pointed out that even white factories did not guarantee work or ensure it with a bond deposit,[134] the Chinese LGWU replied that its demands were not unreasonable. During the negotiations with Golden Gate, the local union explained, the employer had reduced work to one or two days a week, thus applying economic pressure to control the workers. The union had no choice but to demand steady work for its members. The stipulation of eleven months of guaranteed work in a year was based on the average amount of work at National Dollar Stores in its past sixteen-plus years of existence. The $10,000 bond request was based on Golden Gate's purchase of the factory from National Dollar Stores on a $5,000 deposit and agreement to make monthly payments of $5,000. Workers needed the assurance that the new owners would be able to cover salaries for more than one hundred employees, or $13,000 a month, which is why the bond was set at $10,000. Furthermore, the Chinese LGWU said, contrary to a previous story of the benevolent treatment accorded workers at the National Dollar Stores—that they got an annual bonus at the end of the year as well as presents of new clothes—such favors were given out only in 1935 and 1936, and then only to men who had worked at least one full year. "Women who had worked over ten years did not get a dime or half a dollar extra, and they make up 80 percent of the workforce in the factory," the union stated.[135] The workers, angered by these injustices, vowed "to fight our fight to the end, and hope to raise the living conditions not only for ourselves but for the other workers in Chinatown as well."[136]

At the time, most of the women workers were foreign-born and spoke no English. Although they were in the majority at the rank-and-file level, they elected men to be the key officers to speak on their behalf. Much the same situation held in the ILGWU and most other unions as well.[137] Sue Ko Lee said that although Chinese women did not usually speak up at the union meetings, which were conducted in English and Chinese, they understood the issues. More important, they were quite visible in the picket lines. The old and the young, the foreign- and the American-born, all did their share. "The ones on the picket line were all together," Sue emphasized. "We never mentioned anything about why we were doing this. But what is there? Maybe they won't reopen the shop for us. There was no other recourse. There was nothing else. We were determined to close them down if necessary."[138]

Jennie Matyas recalled, "This was one strike I had in which I was able to turn almost everything over to the Chinese members themselves. They arranged their picketing schedules; they arranged who was to be on what shift. It was all very democratically done. They took turns, they lived up to it completely."[139] The first shift met at the ILGWU headquarters each

Two generations of garment workers joining efforts in the 1938 National Dollar Stores strike. (*Chinese Digest;* Judy Yung collection)

morning at six o'clock. After donuts and coffee provided by the union, workers would be on the picket line by seven. Then at the end of the day, they would return to the union hall for meetings. During the strike ILGWU gave each worker $5 a week from its strike fund. "That won't pay your rent," said Sue Ko Lee. "I don't know how we managed on that, but when you're young, you don't think about those things."[140]

Aside from an offer to mediate by the Chinese Six Companies, no help was forthcoming from any of the established Chinatown organizations, local restaurants, or stores. In fact, stores stopped extending credit to the strikers. Although sympathetic, the community was hesitant about condemning Joe Shoong, who was not only one of their own but also one of the most generous contributors to community and nationalist causes. Since Chinatown was still under the control of the merchant elite class, it didn't help matters that the strike was openly supported by such leftist organizations as the Ping Sheh (Equality Society) and Chinese Workers Mutual Aid Association.[141] Leftist influence was obvious from the political rhetoric of the union literature: the labeling of Joe Shoong as a "capitalist," the argument that "the worker's welfare is the nation's welfare," and the call for workers to "arise and dare to struggle for an equal livelihood."[142] These groups' names often appeared in the campaign literature to win public support for the strike. Not surprisingly, Sue Ko Lee noted, established Chinatown organizations "didn't do anything [against us], but they didn't show us any support because we were all called troublemakers." Although the strikers were not avowed Marxists, they were well aware of the class rift. "I remember we were on the picket line and here came Mrs. [Joe] Shoong and she said, *'Ni di sui tong yun!'* [These rotten Chinese]. So she's not Chinese, right?" Sue was indignant even years later.[143]

Workers like Sue and her husband, Jow Hing Lee, who was vice-president of the Chinese LGWU and, prior to the strike, bookkeeper for National Dollar Stores, had savings to fall back on. Others, such as Edna Lee, a presser, went hungry during the strike, but still they did not waver in their commitment to the cause. Jennie Matyas described the situation:

> It was one of the most inspiring experiences I've ever had. . . . We had one girl, her name was Edna Lee. Pretty as could be. No parents, she was an orphan, and she had younger sisters or brothers. Anyhow, she was sort of the head of the family. I was told one day that she couldn't be on picket duty because she was sick, so I went to her house to see whether I could do anything. I saw the house in which she lived. It was one room somewhere on Grant Avenue, a kitchen was shared by the other tenants on the floor. When I went in to see Edna, she was in bed. I asked her how sick she was. "Oh," she said, "I'm not sick at all." I said, "Well, why are you in bed if you're not sick at all?" "Well, you know, it's funny, but if I stay in bed I don't get hungry. And so I often stay in bed because then I don't get hungry." Now, the International helped with strike relief, but it was just relief, it wasn't wages. This girl, Edna, said, "You see, before the strike I could buy groceries on credit. Now, none of the merchants will give us credit.". . . I gave her a little more [money], but she wouldn't take it. She was very proud. She said that if that was all the others got, that's all she got.[144]

Although the Chinese LGWU and the 1938 strike were initiated and sustained by determined garment workers like Edna Lee, credit must also go to the ILGWU, and Jennie Matyas in particular, said Sue Ko Lee. "We knew the union was behind us. We all worked on it, the schedules and all, with the Chinese leadership and advice from the top because we didn't know anything . . . the legal stuff they had to do it for us."[145] The ILGWU not only took care of legal matters, conducted the negotiations, provided relief monies, and sponsored English classes for the workers, but it also sought the sanction of the San Francisco Labor Council and the cooperation of the Retail Department Store Employees' Union. Only when the white retail clerks refused to cross the picket line at the three local National Dollar Stores, thus closing down the stores for two weeks, did Joe Shoong feel compelled to deal with the situation. He filed an injunction against picketing at his stores, then sued the ILGWU and the Employees' Union for $500,000 in damages. In response, the union went to the National Labor Relations Board and charged National Dollar Stores with unfair labor practices, arguing that the sale of the garment factory had been made for the express purpose of circumventing collective bargaining. On March 19, 1938, the Superior Court of San Francisco granted National Dollar Stores a restraining order, and pickets were removed from the three retail stores but allowed to remain at the factory.[146]

The 105-day strike against National Dollar Stores was at the time the longest strike in the history of San Francisco Chinatown.[147] Thanks to the support of the ILGWU and the determination of the Chinese workers to win, an agreement was finally reached on June 8, 1938. National Dollar Stores withdrew its $500,000 damage suit, and the union dropped its charges with the National Labor Relations Board. The factory would be a closed union shop. In addition, there would be a 5 percent raise (to $14 per week minimum except for apprentices); a forty-hour workweek, with time-and-a-half for overtime; a paid holiday for Labor Day; enforcement of health, fire, and sanitary conditions; a guaranteed half-day of work whenever workers were called in; a shop steward authorized to collect dues and deal with grievances; the right to a hearing before an arbitration committee in the case of a dispute over the contract or a questionable discharge; and a price committee to step in whenever piece rates did not yield the minimum wages for 75 percent of the factory workers. The National Dollar Stores also agreed to continue contracting at least some work to the Golden Gate Company.[148]

The ILGWU felt that while not a complete victory, the settlement was fair; it therefore urged workers to accept the terms.[149] The Chinese LGWU was divided on the contract. "I had the time of my life to get the workers to accept that settlement," recalled Matyas. "Some of the

members upon whom I relied very greatly and who had become personal friends left the union because they thought the acceptance of such
a settlement was a hurt to their pride, it was so much less than they had
hoped to get."[150] The debate was intense, and the vote was close: thirty-
one for the agreement, twenty-seven against.[151] "Some of the militant
members were against it. It wasn't good enough for them," recalled Sue
Ko Lee. That's when she spoke out. "I said, 'At least that's something
to begin with.'" After all, she explained, "You had to start someplace.
There was nothing, right? At least you got something for one year. And
maybe something better would come out of it. If you take longer, people are not going to stand around. They can't afford to."[152]

Workers went back to their jobs a few days later, and although the
National Dollar Stores continued to contract work out to other shops,
there were enough orders to keep the Golden Gate factory open. When
the year was up and the contract expired, the factory conveniently went
out of business, claiming "financial losses."[153] Despite a long history of
Chinese workers not being hired at the white shops downtown, the
ILGWU was eventually able to find jobs for many of its Chinese members. With the closing of the factory and the dispersal of its workers,
membership in the Chinese LGWU dwindled from more than one hundred to less than forty. The remaining members finally voted to disband
and join the predominantly white Local 101.[154]

Patricia M. Fong has argued in her study of the 1938 National Dollar Stores strike that everyone gained from the strike except the workers: "Who received the most satisfaction from the outcome? Probably
the ILGWU, the National Dollar Stores Ltd., and the Golden Gate Manufacturing Company. The workers were (sold out by the union?) dis-
satisfied with the terms of the contract, they all lost their jobs within
two years, and the union could not really help them much after-
wards."[155] Sue Ko Lee disagreed with this opinion. In her view, the experience changed the course of history for Chinese American women
like herself.[156] For the first time in their lives, Chinese American
women—both foreign- and American-born—banded together, supported by the ILGWU and Chinese leftist organizations, to challenge
unfair labor practices in the Chinatown garment industry. Determined
to win, they were able to sustain a strike for fifteen weeks despite economic hardships to themselves and their families and with little support
from the local community. Complicating matters, they were constantly
harassed by American Federation of Labor (AFL) organizers, who were
in competition with the ILGWU to recruit Chinese workers into their

union. But as Matyas proudly wrote, the Chinese LGWU refused to desert the ILGWU. "Can these Chinese stick together? Can they build a Union?" she asked. "In the face of heartbreaking adversity they have shown that they can stick together, fight together and build together."[157]

Moreover, Sue pointed out, the ILGWU was able to help the Chinese workers break the racial barrier and find jobs in white shops downtown after the Golden Gate Company closed the factory. This was no easy task. As if the language barrier, the different sewing machines used by the Chinese workers (with horizontal instead of vertical stitching), and the reluctance of Chinese workers to venture outside Chinatown were not enough, there was also the problem of racial discrimination. Jennie Matyas had to convince white employers that Chinese workers were just as good as white workers. "They didn't want any Chinese because of the reputation that the Chinese will work for nothing and cut the wages down," Sue recalled. "Finally she got Edna [Lee] in, and she proved her worth. And after that, the door was open and employers began asking for Chinese workers. . . . And that was how the Chinese workers got out of Chinatown to work elsewhere." She concluded emphatically: "The strike was the best thing that ever happened. It changed our lives."[158]

Sue and her husband were successfully placed as machine operator and cutter, respectively, in union shops outside Chinatown. "You made more money and you had set hours," she said in comparing the working conditions in shops downtown with those in Chinatown. "It was still piecework, but the price had to come up so that you made your minimum. It's controlled that way. So the faster ones can make more but at least the slowest one made the minimum."[159] In her new job, she also had the benefits of holiday and vacation pay and, later, health benefits and a pension. When Koret Corporation took over the small shop in which she worked, Sue was promoted to quality control. A loyal union supporter, she became secretary of both Local 101 and the San Francisco ILGWU Joint Board.

While the Chinese LGWU was active, Chinese American women proved themselves stalwart members of the labor movement and significant contributors to the anti-Japanese war effort. When downtown department store employees went on strike, these activists beseeched the Chinese community not to cross the picket lines, and they contributed 2 percent of their earnings to the strike fund. They also campaigned against antilabor legislation, participated in the drive protesting the U.S. shipment of war materials to Japan, and supported the boycott of nonunion-made lisle stockings, which women wore in lieu of silk stockings.[160] The National Dollar Stores strike and its aftermath, however, did not go far enough in sustaining Chinese women's involvement in the labor movement or improving labor conditions in Chinatown. In the final analysis, the ILGWU lost its chance to organize Chinatown effectively as the labor movement dissipated with the coming of war, the end of the depression, and the repression of the left following World War II.

Ironically, Chinese women in San Francisco stood to gain more than lose by the depressed times precisely because they had been discriminated against on the basis of race, gender, and class. Their low position in the rigid race- and sex-segregated labor market kept them employed even as Chinese men lost their jobs. Experienced survivors of multiple forms of oppression, they proved resourceful, becoming the temporary breadwinners and providing the necessary support to pull their families through the depression. Nor did they hesitate to take advantage of New Deal opportunities to change working and living conditions for themselves and their families. Thus, at a time of great economic strife for most of America, Chinese women in San Francisco were able to take long strides to improve their socioeconomic status and work for the betterment of the community. World War II would afford them further chances to expand their gender roles and fall in step with the rest of the country.

CHAPTER 5

In Step

The War Years, 1931–1945

Everyone, man and woman, has a responsibility in the rise and fall of a nation.

Zuo Xueli
CSYP, August 19, 1936

The crisis of December 7 has emancipated the Chinese in the United States.

Rose Hum Lee
Survey Graphic, October 1942

World War II was a watershed for all Americans. It brought the Great Depression to an end and marked the beginning of significant socioeconomic and political change for women and racial minorities. It also encouraged Americans from all walks of life to put aside their differences and pull together in a national effort to win the fight against fascism. Chinese Americans were very much a part of this effort. Indeed, because of the War of Resistance against Japanese military aggression in China since 1931, they had even more at stake in this struggle than most other Americans. Moved by both Chinese nationalism and American patriotism, Chinese American women responded with an outpouring of highly organized activities in the areas of fund-raising, propaganda, civil defense, and Red Cross work on the home front. While some enlisted in the armed services, many others went to work in the defense factories and private sector outside Chinatown for the first time. The war years thus provided Chinese American women with unprecedented opportunities to improve their socioeconomic status, broaden their public role, and fall in step with their men and fellow Americans during a time of national crisis.

As many studies on women and World War II have shown, the women's sphere—particularly their economic roles—expanded during the war, but inequities persisted in terms of wages, upward mobility, and gender relations. American women's entry into the men's work world was always seen as a temporary arrangement that would return to "normal" after the war.[1] Indeed, most women lost their economic gains once the war ended and they were forced back into female occupations or out of the labor market altogether. Although black women achieved a degree of economic progress during the war years despite virulent racism, they too were prevented from holding on to these gains.[2] This was not the case for Chinese American women, who experienced less discrimination during and after the war because of China's allied relationship to the United States. (In stark contrast, Japanese American women—and men—suffered immense setbacks immediately after Japan's surprise attack on Pearl Harbor and continuing through their incarceration in U.S. concentration camps.)[3] Even as Chinese American women remained subordinate to men through the war years and for some decades thereafter, they continued to move forward by taking advantage of educational, employment, and political opportunities after the war to build on the socioeconomic gains they had made during the conflict. For them, their role in World War II was not just a temporary response to a national crisis, but a turning point in their lives. Once they entered the public arena, they would not only prove their mettle and win the respect of their community but also gain a new sense of self-confidence and pride as Chinese American women.

The War of Resistance: 1931

As far as the Chinese and Chinese Americans were concerned, World War II started on September 18, 1931, with the Mukden Incident. On that fateful day, the Japanese army used a mysterious explosion that destroyed a few feet of track on the South Manchurian Railway line as a pretext to attack Mukden. Generalissimo Chiang Kai-shek, too preoccupied with fighting the Communists, chose not to resist. General Ma Zhanshan and his troops, contravening Chiang's orders, took matters into their own hands and fought back heroically. But to little avail, for within a short time, the Japanese had occupied Northeastern China. The incident angered Chinese throughout the world, who had anxiously watched Japan's every move to expand into Manchuria since the Sino-Japanese War of 1894–95.

Chinese communities in the United States responded immediately to China's crisis. On September 22, only a few days after the incident, *CSYP* carried on its editorial page the declaration "Chinese Should Declare War on Japan Now." The Chinese Six Companies wired both the Nanking (Nationalist) and Canton (Communist) governments, urging them to stop their in-house warfare and work together to defeat the Japanese. The Six Companies also sent telegrams of protest to the League of Nations and President Herbert Hoover, asking them to intervene. Outraged by Japan's naked aggression, Chinese Americans put aside their political differences to work together in any way possible to help resist the Japanese and save China.[4]

Taking the initiative, the Chinese Six Companies called a meeting of all Chinatown organizations on September 24, at which time the Anti-Japanese Chinese Salvation Society was founded. The society immediately started working toward three goals: a boycott of Japanese products, a propaganda campaign to keep overseas Chinese and Americans informed of war conditions in China, and a fund-raising drive to send money to General Ma's troops. The Chinese Six Companies directed all other fund-raisers in the community to defer to the war.[5] Under banners that read, "Down with Japanese Imperialism" and "All Chinese Must Unite to Fight the Japanese," hundreds of people marched through Chinatown to protest the Japanese occupation of Manchuria. The parade was followed by a rally at the Great Star Theater on Jackson Street, where community representatives gave patriotic speeches. A manifesto was read at the mass meeting: "If the world will not help China get justice, the Chinese government is urged to adopt the necessary extreme measures to regain and protect home and country. It is the sense of the Chinese at the patriotic rally that the world must uphold the Kellogg pact and force Japan to withdraw her troops from Manchuria."[6] So incensed were Chinese Americans by Japan's aggressive act that within three months of the Mukden Incident, and despite the depression, they sent over $625,000 to support General Ma's army.[7]

Then on January 28, 1932, Japanese troops attacked Shanghai, bombing, burning, and killing soldiers and civilians alike. Against Chiang's orders, General Tsai Ting-kai's Nineteenth Route Army resisted, fighting valiantly against superior forces for thirty-four days before retreating. Sharing the popular Chinese sentiment of support for Tsai (who hailed from Guangdong Province, the same place as most Chinese immigrants in the United States), overseas Chinese communities responded with further financial aid. In the next six months, over $750,000 was raised in the United States alone, most of which went to Tsai's army and to the refugee relief effort in Shanghai.[8] Still Chiang retained his stubborn military stance: "First reunification, then resistance." Refusing to fight the Japanese, he relied instead on a powerless League of Nations to solve the problem while he continued to battle the Communists.

Frustrated but undeterred by Chiang's policy and by the rest of the world's inaction, overseas Chinese communities persevered in trying to save China, though they themselves were grappling with the depression, racial discrimination, and political dissension. At issue were blood ties and Chinese nationalism, as well as the belief that only through a stronger China could they hope to improve their status in America, where they were treated as unwanted aliens. In the words of Zuo Xueli, a woman who spoke at an anti-Japanese war rally in San Francisco,

> It is the sacred duty of the Chinese in America to resist Japan and save China. Everyone, man and woman, has a responsibility in the rise and fall of a nation. To promote our interests, we must (1) enhance the international status of the Republic of China; (2) abolish all unequal treaties and develop the industries and businesses of overseas Chinese; and (3) publicize the valiant contributions made by our forefathers to gold mining and railroad construction in the United States in order to dispel discrimination against the Chinese in America. . . . With China facing such a crisis, if we don't take immediate steps to defend and preserve our country, then I fear the future standing of the Chinese in America will be even lower than the blacks. If we can unite and resist Japan, recover our lost territory, and defeat Japanese imperialism, our allies will look at us with respect.[9]

In response to the 9-18 and 1-28 incidents (as the Japanese attacks of September 18, 1931, and January 28, 1932, came to be called by the Chinese), young and old, rich and poor, Chinese-born and American-born, men and women—all gave what they could to the war effort. They donated their hard-earned savings, boycotted Japanese products, participated in protest parades and rallies, and supported aviation clubs and schools (to train pilots for the Chinese air force). Fund-raisers for the war effort and refugee relief became the mainstay of political and social activities.[10] When General Tsai Ting-kai came through San Francisco in 1934 as part of an American tour to rally support for China, he was greeted at the train station by a crowd of four thousand and given a hero's welcome. His patriotic fans, gathered at the local playground to hear him speak, cheered themselves hoarse as the general denounced Japanese aggression and beseeched their continued support. Six Chinatown restaurants hosted a banquet reception in his honor, and that evening firecrackers crackled while all the shops in Chinatown were illuminated to show their appreciation of the general's valor.[11]

Japan, though, was intent on continental expansion and domination. On July 7, 1937, without issuing a formal declaration of war, Japan invaded China. Claiming that Japanese soldiers who had left their night posts to relieve themselves had been captured by the Chinese, Japanese army divisions took over the Lugouqiao railway station, outside Peking, and engaged Chinese troops in battle at the Marco Polo Bridge. By August, Japanese troops were in control of Peking and Tientsin. By the end of the year, they had taken Shanghai, Hankow, Canton, and Nanking, leaving a bloody trail of rape, pillage, and plunder. Chiang Kai-shek and the Nationalist Party had no choice but to declare war on Japan and form a united front with the Chinese Communist Party. It would be a protracted war against a military force far superior in technology and brutal in its policy of *sanko seisaku* ("the three alls"—kill all, burn all, destroy all). It would cost the country some $50 billion in property damage and over ten million lives. And once again, as in past national crises, overseas Chinese responded to the call to rescue their homeland.

The 7-7 incident (as the Marco Polo Bridge Incident of July 7, 1937, was called) put an immediate end to any remaining political dissension among Chinese Americans and infused the ongoing anti-Japanese war effort in the United States with a new sense of urgency. This time, in light of the united front in China and the dire circumstances at hand, all political factions put aside their differences to participate. "War fever was heightened by a fervor for solidarity and unity," the *Chinese Digest* said. "For the first time in the community's history every group, faction, clique, society, association, and lodge joined hands and fraternized with each other. It provided a spectacle never before witnessed."[12] On August 21, the Chinese Six Companies in San Francisco called a meeting of representatives from ninety-one community groups to organize a new national campaign for the war effort. In the spirit of "country and victory first," the Chinese War Relief Association (CWRA) was established to coordinate the fund-raising efforts of some three hundred communities throughout the United States, Mexico, and Central and South America. B. S. Fong, president of the Chinese Six Companies, was elected chairman to lead the campaign.[13] Most significantly, representatives from women's organizations were allowed into the inner sanctums of the Chinese Six Companies to participate in CWRA deliberations as equals for the first time.

In the eight years of war that followed, Chinese throughout America remained steadfast in their commitment to save China. Under the leadership of the CWRA in twenty major cities, a total of $20 million was raised for China through door-to-door solicitation, Rice Bowl parties, bazaars and parades, and war bond sales. Clothing, medical supplies, ambulances, airplanes, gas masks, and mosquito nets were also sent to China. In this sustained fund-raising effort, the Chinese in San Francisco were the most active of all, raising $5 million—one-fourth of the total amount.[14] Within a week after the CWRA was formed, contributions amounting to $30,000 were raised, $15,000 of which came from Joe Shoong of the National Dollar Stores. His employees set the example of pledging one month's salary to the war relief budget; other Chinatown businesses quickly followed suit. Other fund-raising efforts ranged from selling flowers and shining shoes to the mounting of large benefit performances and arranging for the donation of gate receipts from the International Exposition at Treasure Island.[15] Quotas were often set, such as a $30 minimum from each working adult during one fund-raising campaign, or $2.50 per person during a drive for winter clothing.[16] Although most people were more than willing to give, others, who either did not have the funds or who resented being coerced, refused and were punished by means of boycotts, imposed fines, and other strong-arm tactics.[17] "The CWRA," an announcement in *CSYP* warned, "can obtain the names and addresses of non-contributors and send people after them."[18] On at least two occasions, individuals who had refused to cooperate were denounced and paraded through the streets of Chinatown.[19]

In addition to fund-raising activities, Chinese Americans mounted a propaganda campaign to keep all Americans informed of war developments in China and to appeal for widespread financial and political support. While foreign-born Chinese kept the Chinese immigrant population informed and involved through Chinese newspapers, street broadcasts, parades, and rallies, the American-born made a special effort to reach out to mainstream America, as well as the English-language press and government officials in Washington, D.C., encouraging them to contribute to China's war fund and to take action against Japan. Everyone, especially labor organizations, was encouraged to boycott Japanese products. Chinatown stores that did not comply were fined $500, and individuals, $5 or more.[20] Chinese Americans in port cities such as Seattle, Portland, Los Angeles, and San Francisco organized waterfront picket lines to protest the sending of scrap iron and war supplies to Japan. Over two hundred Chinese American aviators also volunteered for service in China, several dozen of whom are known to have died in battle.[21]

Women's Role in the War of Resistance

Even more so than with past nationalist causes, immigrant and American-born women were visibly active in war relief work. They were concerned about the grave developments in China and especially outraged by reports of Japanese atrocities against women and children. News from China constantly reminded them that their motherland was under brutal attack and that the national crisis demanded the contribution of every son and daughter. Xiang Dingrong, a provincial party representative, reportedly said at an anti-Japanese rally in Hangzhou, "There is an old saying, 'Every man has a responsibility in the rise and fall of a nation.' Actually, the fate of a country should not rest only on men. I would change the saying to, 'Every woman has a responsibility in the rise and fall of a nation.'"[22] This slogan became the rallying cry for women's participation in the war effort both in China and overseas.

For the duration of the war, women were called upon to emulate the legendary woman warrior Hua Mulan and the revolutionary heroine Qiu Jin and to shoulder the same responsibilities as men if they were to prove themselves worthy of equal rights. The Chinese press in the United States played heavily on the themes of nationalism and feminism in an attempt to link Chinese American women to the fate of their sisters in China and to arouse them to action, as exemplified in the following *Chinese Times* editorial:

We must understand that the Chinese Women's Movement and the liberation of the Chinese people are inseparable. Chinese women make up half of the country's population. United they represent a great force. Women who love their country and who don't want to sell out should organize and mobilize this force, answer to the call of their leaders, and use whatever knowledge and abilities they have for the war effort. By contributing to country and humanity, women can thus prove they are as valuable as men. When women have fulfilled their responsibilities to national salvation, society will naturally give wide support to the women's movement.[23]

Echoing the revolutionary war cry of 1911, the message was for women to put nationalist concerns before feminist ones and, once again, to prove themselves worthy of equal rights. The lessons of history should have warned them that there were no sure guarantees. Chinese women did not gain suffrage or equal rights after the 1911 Revolution. Rather, they followed the pattern set by Hua Mulan, who, on returning from battle, donned feminine attire and resumed the traditional role of a woman. Now, however, fired by Chinese nationalism, women chose to ignore the past and allow themselves once again to take up the fight.

Given the national emergency, women from all walks of life were encouraged to enter the public sphere and contribute to the war effort, but only in subordinate or auxiliary roles. According to Madame Chiang Kai-shek:

> We women are citizens, just as much as are our men . . . our line of usefulness may be different but each must do what best can be done to contribute our share to rescue our nation from defeat and slavery. While during war time the men are the fighters, it is the women who bear the brunt of carrying on at the rear.[24]

She instructed women to combine the principles of the New Life Movement, which promoted the Confucian ethics of propriety, loyalty, integrity, and honor, and the Christian values of clean living, education, and charitable activity, with war work. Although hundreds of women did fight heroically at the front lines, thousands more were mobilized to serve behind the lines in China, raising funds for military spending, sewing and providing supplies for the soldiers, caring for the wounded, refugees, and war orphans, contributing to production, and doing propaganda work.[25] Back in the United States, Chinese women's activities in war work were also limited to female tasks such as fund-raising, conducting propaganda campaigns among women, and engaging in Red Cross work, all under the male-dominated leadership of the CWRA. Nevertheless, as in China, national salvation work drew Chinese American women into new public activities, giving them an opportunity to develop leadership skills, learn to work cooperatively, and gain confidence and respect as active participants in a political movement. In this sense, it brought them closer to the promise of women's emancipation in the overall process of social change.[26]

ORGANIZATION AND MOBILIZATION

Soon after the Mukden Incident, women's organizations formed across the country—in New York, San Francisco, Chicago, Seattle, and Portland—to support the war effort. One of the earliest and most outspoken groups was the Chinese Women's Association in New York. As early as October 14, 1931, it fired off letters to newspaper editors who had been advocating that the United States take a "hands-off policy" with respect to the war in China. Calling this stance "immoral" and "cowardly" in view of the intense human suffering caused by Japanese war atrocities, the women argued that the United States should uphold the pledge it had made in the Nine-Power Treaty[27] and the Kellogg-Briand pact: to help settle all international disputes by peaceful means. Then, in a letter dated February 18, 1932, the association appealed to "Chinese womanhood in the U.S.A." to boycott Japanese products, publicize China's just cause, and help raise $25,000 for the relief of war victims. Arguing that women must unite against the Japanese, the letter concluded: "With Manchuria already under the complete domination of Japan; with Shanghai and other cities being bombarded, killing thousands of civilians—mostly women and children; with China's millions still in the aftermath of a devastating flood, it is high time that the Chinese Womanhood should rise as ONE in order to put an end to these inhuman atrocities and wanton massacres."[28] Within a year, the Chinese Women's Association raised $30,000 for the war effort by sponsoring a parade and street festival, a week-long charity bazaar, and a fund-raising campaign that lasted nine days. When General Tsai Ting-kai came to New York to thank the Chinese community for their support, the Women's Association independently sponsored a testimonial dinner in his honor, which was attended by an enthusiastic crowd of two hundred members and friends.

More numerous and diverse than Chinese women in New York, Chinese women in San Francisco contributed to the war effort by participating in one or more of seven women's groups organized on the basis of nativity, class, age, and cultural and political orientation. Whereas middle-class immigrant women belonged to the Funü Ju Ri Jiuguo Hui (Women's Patriotic Club) and Funü Xinyun Hui (New Life Association), working-class immigrant women participated in the activities of the Funü Zhanqu Nanmin Chouzhen Hui (Women's War Zone Refugee Relief Committee) and Funü Xie Hui (Women's Council). The Women's Patriotic Club and Women's Council were politically left of the New Life

Association and Women's War Zone Refugee Relief Committee and tended to be more autonomous and critical of Chiang Kai-shek and his Nationalist Party. As for American-born women, the young ones were attracted to the Chinese YWCA, while business and professional women in their thirties were drawn to the Square and Circle Club. Fidelis Coteri stood apart as an organization of well-to-do matrons in their fifties. Although all these organizations performed gendered tasks dictated by the CWRA, each group's choice of activities reflected the class and cultural background of its members. Middle-class immigrant women, for example, concentrated on door-to-door solicitation and propaganda work in the Chinese language; working-class immigrant women favored sewing projects; and American-born women organized dance and fashion show benefits, volunteered for Red Cross work, and did outreach in the non-Chinese community.

The involvement of immigrant women, who understandably felt closer to China than the second generation, was particularly notable during the war years. Among the first organizations to speak up in San Francisco was the Women's Patriotic Club in the winter of 1932. Choosing to align themselves with the Communists rather than the Nationalists, group members publicly addressed a letter to Soong Ching-ling (Madame Sun Yat-sen) in which they wrote: "In the face of the destruction of our country and home, calamity and danger, how can we not give voice to our grief and anger?"[29] They were moved by General Ma's resistance in Heilongjiang, Manchuria, and angered by Chiang Kai-shek's passive stance:

> The situation threatening China is getting worse every day, and the ambition of the Japanese keeps increasing. Yet all that the authorities in charge do is keep making compromises and retreating. Even so, that has not satisfied the appetite of the Japanese. Sometime in the future, China will have to take a stand and fight.

The club members firmly believed that the rise and fall of a nation was the responsibility of women as well as men. Using examples of heroic women in Chinese history, they tried to mobilize other Chinese women to join their cause:

> Liang Hongyu beat the drums and enemy soldiers were slaughtered. Hong Xuanjiao took the bracelets off her own wrist to give to the troops. These women can serve as our models. All that we are saying is the result of long and deep reflection. Won't you sisters who share a love for China rise up and join us?[30]

Unlike the Chinese Women's Association in New York, however, the Women's Patriotic Club gained few members—only forty were on the rolls in 1942. Nonetheless, the organization was effective in raising funds through direct solicitation, drama benefits, selling handmade flowers, and collecting clothes and medical supplies to send to Shanghai and Canton.

In contrast, the New Life Association, an official branch of Madame Chiang Kai-shek's Women's Committee for the New Life Movement, had a large membership; it also reflected a conservative point of view. Thanks to the efforts of Wu Minchi, the principal of Hong Kong's Mei Fang Girls' Middle School who was sent by Madame Chiang to organize and mobilize overseas Chinese women, the New Life Association grew to become a prestigious women's organization with chapters in Los Angeles, Chicago, Sacramento, New York, Boston, Portland, and Seattle.[31] Most of the members were Chinese-born, middle-class, married to businessmen, ministers, or community leaders, and already active in charitable work. Under the leadership of Emily Lee Fong (the wife of B. S. Fong, CWRA chairman) and King Yoak Won Wu (the wife of Rev. Daniel Wu), the San Francisco chapter wrote to President Roosevelt urging him to break off trade with Japan. It also sponsored talks on the war and the New Life Movement, receptions for dignitaries from China, and classes to learn Mandarin (the official Chinese language). Fund-raisers to benefit war orphans and wounded soldiers in China included raffles, dramatic plays, and the selling of confetti on New Year's Eve.[32]

In contrast to the middle-class background of the Patriotic Club and New Life Association members, the Women's War Zone Refugee Relief Committee and the Women's Council drew support from the working mass of immigrant women. Soon after the CWRA was formed in 1937, the Refugee Relief Committee came into existence as a women's auxiliary with the primary purpose of mobilizing women to collect clothing and supplies for refugees in China and participate in the various parades and demonstrations. Donations and materials were solicited from the community through the sales of "lucky coins" (Chinese coins tied with a red-white-and-blue ribbon to be worn on lapels), patriotic scarves (made of a material other than silk, since Japanese silk was being boycotted), confetti on New Year's Eve, and raffle tickets. Group members as well as seamstresses in the community were asked to help with sewing. Employees at the National Dollar Stores factory, for example, volunteered one and a half days to sew winter clothing for refugees in China. In this way, the committee was able to send fourteen crates of supplies in 1937,

Women and children making lucky coins for the war effort in China. (Courtesy of Lorena How)

another two in 1938, and one hundred sets of cotton clothing in 1939, all for the relief of war victims in China.[33] Like the Women's Patriotic Club, the Women's Council, established in 1936, chose to align itself with the left, but it was less active and outspoken. Among the group's most publicized events was a program held at CWRA headquarters on September 26, 1938, which featured speeches by China's representatives to the Second International Youth Conference and a movie on Japanese war atrocities. According to *CSYP*, garment workers were particularly encouraged to attend.[34]

Lai Yee Guey How was a typical example of the working-class women sought after by the Refugee Relief Committee and the Women's Council. Her story also suggests the extent of sacrifices that many hardworking Chinese women were willing to make for the cause of national salvation. As her daughter Lorena How recalled, "My mother became very concerned and wanted to help when the Japanese invaded China. She knew that she would not be able to go back to China [to help] because of her family and responsibilities here [so] she tried to do her share in the war effort." At the time, Lai Yee was the sole provider for her five children. Also, Lorena had a congenital heart defect and required constant care. Although Lai Yee worked long hours at home making Chinese dresses to order while attending to her children, she still managed to volunteer time to make lucky coins at the CWRA headquarters, to be among the women who held the stretched-out Chinese flag in the anti-Japanese parades, and to join the picket line to protest the sending of scrap iron to Japan. "We ourselves were in need, but my mother still continued to donate quarters whenever she saw one of those tin cans in the stores," said Lorena.[35]

By successfully drawing mothers into the war effort, the CWRA often gained the support and contributions of their children as well. Following the examples of their patriotic mothers, boys and girls were inspired to do their share of propaganda work and fund-raising. They sold handmade flowers and polished shoes in the streets, wrote essays and made speeches in school condemning Japanese militarism, and commemorated the 9-18 and 1-28 "Humiliation Days" by marching in parades.[36] Influenced by her mother and older sister, Lorena, who was about nine years old at the time, became intensely anti-Japanese. "I remember one lady gave me a doll when I was sick in the hospital," she said. "I turned it over and saw that it was made in Japan. I gave it right back to her. I remember saying, 'I don't want this doll, it is made in Japan.'" To do their part for the war effort, she and other Chinese children tried to discourage white customers from patronizing the Japanese curio stores on Grant Avenue. "My friends and I would all run into the store and shout in our best English, 'Don't buy here, ladies, this is a Japanese store.' The Japanese ladies would chase us with a large broom back to Clay Street."[37]

Second-generation women, not to be outdone by their mothers, also made important contributions to the war effort. The Chinese YWCA became the focal point for their involvement owing to its central location, spacious quarters, large and dedicated membership, and the nationalist spirit and leadership skills of Jane Kwong Lee, who was employed there from 1933 to 1944. Wherever there was need—whether in attendance at CWRA meetings, door-to-door solicitation, Rice Bowl parades, benefits, or picket lines—the YWCA was always well represented. One of its most successful fund-raisers was a raffle for 118 pieces of jewelry donated by Chinese women in the San Francisco Bay Area: $6,723 was raised in a single month.[38]

Because of Jane Kwong Lee's bilingual skills, her strong political and feminist consciousness, and her good reputation in the Chinese community, she was the ideal person to mobilize both Chinese- and American-born women to engage in national salvation work. She recognized that the war effort presented Chinese women a rare opportunity to prove themselves and raise their social standing. As she wrote in *CSYP*:

> The status that American women enjoy today did not develop by chance. They had to prove their abilities through different stages before they earned public recognition of their rightful status and rights. If we Chinese women can do as well behind the lines as the men at the war front during this anti-Japanese war period in building up our nation and protecting our citizens, who can look down at us? Who will dare say women are not equal to men?

Aside from seizing this opportunity to prove themselves, she continued, Chinese Americans who spoke English and understood international politics should take the responsibility of getting support from mainstream America for the war against Japan. In addition, the first generation should work with the second generation to patiently instill nationalism in those young Chinese Americans who lacked the opportunity to learn Chinese language and culture. "Only by the collective effort of all Chinese Americans can we claim victory in the War of Resistance," she concluded.[39]

Representing the YWCA in the CWRA, Jane was an especially effective advocate for the war effort. She served on the propaganda committee and worked hard to host receptions for Chinese dignitaries, sponsor speakers, and produce plays at the YWCA that aroused women to action. As she later said:

> Newspapers were publishing all the war news and reporting all the cruel actions of the Japanese soldiers. We were especially touched by the news that soldiers not only killed, but also raped women and girls. Upon hearing such sad news about women and girls suffering such indignities from the enemy, we women here in a foreign land were exceedingly angry. We tried to think of some indirect action that might help. I put out a skit to show that women wanted to do what they could.[40]

The Chinese-language plays that Jane wrote and directed (and in which she sometimes acted) served both propaganda and fund-raising purposes. Tickets were sold in advance to audiences who came as much for the cause as for the entertainment. In keeping with Jane's nationalist and feminist convictions, most of the plays were about heroic actions by women involved in war work, and much of the content was based on newspaper reports of Chinese women in nontraditional gender roles. In "Boycott Silk Stockings," for instance, five Chinese American women resolve not to buy or wear silk stockings for the duration of the war. In "Blood Stains Rivers and Mountains," two college students become aviators and go to China "to sacrifice for our country." Although they both fall in love, they nobly put their country ahead of marriage. "We are people who have high ambitions! We should do something great. We should do something for society, for the country, and for the world before we marry." Both die martyrs while serving in the Guangdong Province Aviation Department. In "To the Front" and "Zong Dongyuan (The Chief Mobilization)," the lead characters make the difficult choice of disobeying their parents in order to serve China, the moral being "Country first and family next." "To the Front" and "Huan Xing Xiongsi (Awake the Heroic Lion)" depict the plight of refugees and the dangerous work of female commandos at the war front. Jane's plays served the interest of the war effort as well as of feminism. "The intent was to show the audience the voracity of the war," said Jane. "Thus, their emotions were aroused to give whatever they could afford to alleviate the human sufferings of war."[41]

Members of the Square and Circle Club, who were predominantly business and professional women, were the most active in war work among the second generation. Long involved in community service and famine relief for China, they sold bilingual greeting cards, raised money for cotton uniforms, surgical supplies, and airplanes, volunteered for Red Cross work, assisted with benefits, sponsored plays and raffle drawings, participated in parades and protests, and pressed Congress to break its neutral stance and declare an embargo against Japan.[42] The club became particularly well known for two female-gendered activities: fashion show benefits and the boycott against silk stockings.

The fashion shows—always highlights of the Rice Bowl parties (see below)—were major productions that featured scores of Chinese American women modeling elaborate clothing from the Tang dynasty to modern times, to the accompaniment of instrumental music. "They were very popular in those days," said Alice Fong Yu, who directed many such shows. "Ticket lines were so crowded that the lines formed around the block on Washington Street. After each show, we had to let the audience out the back door. As soon as we let one group out, new people were pushing in already—just one show after another." The show also went on the road in chartered buses, to small towns like San Mateo, Vallejo, and Grass Valley.[43] As *CSYP* commented, not only did the fashion shows generate support for the war effort in China, but they also promoted appreciation for Chinese culture among Westerners.[44]

Following the suggestion of *Nation* magazine and the examples of movie stars Loretta Young, Sylvia Sidney, and Frances Farmer, Square and Circle members joined the movement against wearing silk stockings as part of the nationwide boycott of Japanese goods.[45] Since 90 percent of the silk in women's hosiery came from Japan (silk, indeed, was one of Japan's chief exports), wearing cotton instead of silk stockings was one direct way women could express their opposition to Japanese aggression in China. The Square and Circle Club took the lead in Chinatown, encouraging women's organizations to endorse the "Non-Silk Movement" and individual women to refrain from wearing silk stockings.[46] Alice Fong Yu chided women who did not support the boycott in the *Chinese Digest:*

> There is an appalling lack of conscience among many Chinatown girls who continue to buy the "latest shades" in silk stockings to help extend Japan's ability to get more munitions with which to shoot down our helpless brethren across the seas. . . . Silk is the lifeline which connects Japan with credit and resources abroad and Chinese women in America can exert considerable strength toward severing this strong and important link.[47]

Wearing cotton stockings, club members appeared in publicity photos with the caption "Be in style, wear lisle," in local publications as well as *Life.*[48] The boycott was so effective that Japan's export of silk was reduced by three-fifths in 1938 relative to two years before.[49]

The most elite of the seven organizations was the Fidelis Coteri. Started by Mrs. Joe Shoong in 1932, Fidelis Coteri comprised well-to-do matrons from San Francisco and Oakland who met regularly at expensive restaurants "for the sake of friendship and to promote good family life."[50] The group was known for its annual formal dinner dances, which attracted a mix of Chinese and white Americans. By sponsoring dance benefits and soliciting donations from its wealthy members, the organization was able to send clothing and money to war victims in China. In addition, it participated in CWRA meetings, Rice Bowl parades, hosted receptions for visiting dignitaries, and helped with Red Cross work.[51]

Although the seven women's groups differed in membership and fund-raising approaches, their paths had a common goal. Working together, they were a formidable force, contributing immensely to the war effort. As the war continued, these organizations found many opportunities to collaborate in Rice Bowl parties and parades, picket lines at the waterfront, fund-raising drives, Red Cross work, and hosting receptions for war heroines. According to the *Chinese Digest:*

> Practically every sizeable Chinese organization in America is now going out individually or has teamed up with other organizations to raise war refugee relief funds in their own communities and elsewhere. For the first time the second generation has suddenly realized how much their motherland means to them now that it is in danger of being conquered, and the young men and women have gone in to raise relief money side by side with the older generation. This fact should warm the heart of every Chinese.[52]

RICE BOWL PARTIES

Held nationwide in over seven hundred cities, Rice Bowl parties and parades proved to be the most effective means of raising money and spreading propaganda for war relief in China. Initiated by CWRA chairman B. S. Fong, *San Francisco Chronicle* editor Paul C. Smith, and the physician Margaret Chung, the first Rice Bowl party was held in San Francisco Chinatown on June 17, 1938; the second occurred February 9–11, 1940; and the third took place May 2–5, 1941. To be successful, each party required months of planning and the cooperation and involvement of everyone in the community. Billed as being as festive as New Orleans's Mardi Gras, the first party started with a parade from the Civic Center to Grant Avenue and was followed by cultural entertainment that lasted into the morning hours. More than two hundred thousand people packed the confetti-filled streets and alleys of Chinatown during the first Rice Bowl party to enjoy fashion shows, indoor and outdoor dancing, Chinese and Western music, theatrical acts, a mock air raid at midnight, and dragon dancing at 1 A.M. A recreated "Old Chinatown"—complete with banners of colorful couplets, illuminated lanterns, and men and women dressed in traditional Chinese clothing—held an open house for people from outside Chinatown who came to support the cause or, as was advertised in the *San Francisco Chronicle*, "to see for the first time behind the veil of mystery with which tradition cloaks this Oriental outpost."[53] Everyone entering Chinatown had to wear a "Humanity button," which sold for fifty cents, or suffer the consequences of being tried before a "kangaroo court" of volunteer judges and fined up to hundreds of dollars. Throughout the streets of Chinatown, Chinese artists and "beggars" asked for coins in the custom of the homeland. In that one day of festivities in San Francisco, $55,000 was collected for the war effort in China, more than in any other city in the United States.[54] Of the first Rice Bowl party, the reporter William Hoy wrote in the *Chinese Digest:*

> All Chinatown has come to agree that it was the most magnificent, heart-warming and spontaneous spectacle ever given in this 90-year community. . . . Chinatownians had always known the sympathy and generosity of the American people toward the people of China. But whereas before they had only read or been told of it, on the night of June 17 they saw it—saw it in the faces of 200,000 Americans as they milled into Chinatown, as they vied on purchasing "Humanity" badges, and as they literally poured money into rice bowls placed everywhere for that purpose. The cause of this active sympathy was very pithily expressed in four Chinese characters written on a strip of rice paper pasted in front of a store which read: "America Believes in Righteousness."[55]

So great was the success of San Francisco's first Rice Bowl party that the community decided to expand the second one to three days in 1940, and the third one to four days in 1941. These parties were even more spectacular, with the addition of fireworks that reproduced historical Chinese and American scenes, floats that blended Chinese history and mythology, an auction of donated Chinese merchandise—tea, jewelry, and art goods—that lasted for hours and brought in thousands of dollars, and a new dragon, constructed by Chinese artisans from the International Exposition at Treasure Island. The second Rice Bowl party brought in $87,000, while the third reaped $93,000.[56]

The Rice Bowl parties would not have been as successful without the active participation of women in the origin, planning, and implementation of the event. Where Chinese women particularly stood out was in their role carrying the Chinese flag in the parades. Measuring seventy-five feet long and forty-five feet wide, the flag weighed over three hundred pounds and required one hundred women to hold it aloft. As the women marched through the streets, coins and bills were thrown into the outstretched flag. So heavy did the flag become that each parade had to be stopped at least three times for the flag to be emptied.[57] This scene of a hundred proud women—young and old, all wearing *cheong sam*, China's national dress—was repeated throughout the country every time there was a parade to raise funds or commemorate the Humiliation Days when Japan attacked China. Their high visibility as flag carriers in these parades could be said to symbolize the merging of nationalism with feminism: the move of Chinese American women from the domestic into the public arena on behalf of the war effort.

Women proudly carrying the Chinese flag through the streets of Chinatown to raise money for the war effort in China. (Harry Jew photo)

PICKET DUTY

The other dramatic image of Chinese women during the war years is of picketers protesting the shipping of scrap iron to Japan. Organized by the Chinese Workers Mutual Aid Association and as reported by Lim P. Lee in the *Chinese Digest,* a mass protest in San Francisco was set for 11 A.M. on December 16, 1938. By word of mouth, people began gathering for picket duty at 10:30 at the corner of Stockton and Clay Streets. By "zero hour," more than two hundred volunteers had arrived; they were transported, singing, shouting, and cheering, to Pier 45, where the *S.S. Spyros,* a ship owned by Japan's Mitsui Company, was docked. There they were joined by three hundred sympathetic Greeks, Jews, and other European Americans. As the word spread, Chinatown restaurants and grocery stores did their part by providing free drinks and food—roast pig, sandwiches, pork buns, oranges—

to the picketers and longshoremen for the duration of the demonstration.[58]

The picket line comprised many different factions, including the political right and left, Christian and secular groups, all classes and ages. One reporter described the scene thus:

> Despite the pouring rain and the muddy roads, both men and women assembled on time, the most enthusiastic participants coming from the Chinese YWCA, Chick Char Musical Club, United Protestants Association, Presbyterian Mission Home, and the Kin Kuo Chinese School. Ten Chinese women who came all the way from Stockton further aroused the spirit of the occasion. As the men and women marched in a circle in the pouring rain, the red ink on their signs ran and their faces became wet with raindrops so that it appeared as if they were splattered with blood and tears. . . . Joining the picket line was a number of elderly women, hobbling on feet once bound. Old men, hunched and bald, marched alongside the young and strong. The scene was enough to move one to tears.[59]

The picketers' cries of "Longshoremen, be with us! Longshoremen, be with us!" and their picket signs, "Stop U.S. scrap iron to Japan! Prevent murder of Chinese women and children!" succeeded in gaining the sympathy and support of the longshoremen who were responsible for loading the *S.S. Spyros* with scrap metal bound for Japan. In political solidarity, the majority of the longshoremen refused to cross the picket line upon their return from lunch break. By the fourth day of the protest, with Chinese American supporters pouring in from nearby towns, the picket line had grown to five thousand strong and now included the *S.S. Beckenham*, an English freighter docked at the same pier. A vote by the full membership of the International Longshoremen and Warehousemen's Union (ILWU) resulted in "100 percent opposed to passing the picket line," despite threats of a coastwide lockout of all longshoremen by the Waterfront Employers Association. For five days the *Spyros* lay quiet. After negotiations between the ILWU and CWRA, the protest was finally called off on December 20 with the understanding that the union would organize a coastwide conference to promote an embargo on all materials to Japan. Not wanting to hurt commercial business in San Francisco further, and considering their goal of publicizing the need for an embargo against Japan accomplished, the Chinese picketers withdrew. They marched past the longshoremen's headquarters to express their appreciation and then through downtown San Francisco and back to Chinatown, singing China's song of resistance, "Chi Lai (Arise)" or "March of the Volunteers." True to their word, organized

Lai Yee Guey How with son Art (*left*) and Nellie Tom
Quock (*right*) lead the picket line against sending scrap iron
to Japan. (Courtesy of Lorena How)

labor, in cooperation with American Friends of China, the Church Federation, and CWRA, spearheaded an embargo petition campaign and organized mass meetings in January and February to launch a national embargo movement. Chinese Americans continued to press for an embargo until 1941, when Congress finally authorized President Roosevelt to prohibit the sales of arms to Japan.[60] In this effort, women played a major role by assuming picket duty and lobbying Congress.

FUND-RAISING AND RED CROSS WORK

Two areas that were considered the domain of women in the war effort were direct solicitation of money and Red Cross work. Because men found asking for donations distasteful, they pushed the task onto women, whom they said people in the community found more difficult to refuse. The CWRA made it a point to organize women's brigades whenever it sponsored a fund-raising campaign.[61] During the CWRA's second relief campaign in 1937, for example, fifty-four women made up six of the twelve brigades responsible for canvassing the San Francisco Bay Area for contributions. By the fifth day of the campaign, *CSYP* reported that one-quarter of the $600,000 goal had been met, and one of the women's brigades was praised for bringing in the top amount of $3,800 on that day.[62] This was no mean feat, considering the depressed times and the many noteworthy causes that competed for donations in the community, including victims of natural disasters in China; schools, hospitals, and orphanages in China; the Community Chest; Chinese Hospital; Chinese schools; churches and community organizations such as the YWCA, YMCA, and Square and Circle Club; Mei Lun Yuen orphanage; and Chinese deportees from Cuba.[63]

Throughout the war years, Chinese women from various walks of life also assumed the traditional female tasks of Red Cross work. Soon after the 9-18 and 1-28 incidents, women volunteers gathered at the Chinese YWCA, Chinese Hospital, Baptist Church, and Presbyterian Mission Home to prepare bandages and medical supplies for China's battlefronts.[64] As the war intensified and the community was bombarded with reports of wounded soldiers and civilians, women increased their volunteer Red Cross activities. During the summer months of 1937, for example, garment workers in Chinatown made, on their own time, six thousand flannel jackets of double construction for civilians in the war zones. In December of that same year, they volunteered to sew ten thousand inner garments for wounded soldiers.[65] Many Chinese American women also put in regular hours preparing supplies for refugee relief at the Chinese American Citizens Alliance and at the San Francisco branch of the American Red Cross.[66]

Among the most active in Red Cross work was none other than Dr. Margaret Chung. She had volunteered for medical service at the front lines but had been dissuaded by both the Chinese and American governments. "They felt I could do more good raising funds for medical supplies here in this country," she told radio audiences. "Today women and children are suffering in China—dying without even a chance to be saved. There is a great need for the most elementary sort of medical supplies. And I have made the raising of a medical fund my work for the present."[67] A charismatic figure, Dr. Chung took it upon herself to lecture all over the country on behalf of the war effort in China and to use her social connections in show business to sponsor benefit performances in local theaters outside Chinatown. One such benefit that featured both Chinese and American stars raised enough money to send $1,700 worth of drugs, medical supplies, and vaccines to China via the National Women's Relief Association in Hong Kong.[68] With foresight she worked with the American Red Cross to establish a Disaster Relief Station in the basement of Grace Cathedral in the Nob Hill district in 1939. "Some people do not realize how efficiently and farsightedly the American Red Cross works, but when the Japanese struck on December 7, 1941, we worked feverishly and by 10:00 that night huge packing cases were loaded upon the decks of the *U.S.S. Mariposa* and were sent away out to Pearl Harbor," she wrote years later. For her "meritorious personal service performed in behalf of the nation, her Armed Services, and suffering humanity in the Second World War," Dr. Chung received a special citation from the American Red Cross.[69]

RECEPTIONS FOR WAR HEROES

Women's war work also included hosting receptions for Chinese dignitaries and war heroes when they came through San Francisco. Particularly notable were the large welcoming receptions that Chinese women hosted for female role models such as the war hero Yang Hueimei, the aviator Lee Ya Ching, Madame Chiang Kai-shek, and United Nations delegate Wu Yifang. Here were four Chinese women held in high regard by their countrymen and countrywomen for contributions that broke with traditional gender roles. Meeting and hearing them speak on the role of women in the war not only boosted nationalist fervor but also inspired feminist pride among Chinese American women.

Yang Hueimei, famous for carrying the Chinese flag and supplies across enemy lines during a decisive battle in Shanghai, was given a hero's welcome when she came to San Francisco in 1938, after attending the Second International Youth and Peace Conference in New York. *CSYP* reported that among the seventy-eight carloads of people who greeted her at the pier were representatives from five women's groups, part of CWRA's welcoming committee.[70] "She was adored by all the inhabitants of Chinatown," recalled Jane Kwong Lee. "And when she made an appearance at the Chinese YWCA auditorium, the hall was jammed."[71] Her speech was inspiring:

> I thank you for the title of "hero," but I am a mere citizen. In this time of national crisis, I am but fulfilling my duty. The loss of Canton recently

has caused overseas Chinese much pain and grief, but we must not despair. . . . The enemy's airplanes are indeed powerful, but our blood and flesh are even more powerful. We must use our blood and flesh to wash away our country's humiliation and build a new China. Your contributions as overseas Chinese are important. . . . We must unite and fight to the end, for the final victory will be ours.[72]

Many more women converged on Oakland Airport on April 26, 1939, to welcome Lee Ya Ching as she piloted her plane in from San Diego. Trained in Geneva, Switzerland, and Oakland, China's foremost female aviator had once starred in movies and worked as a copilot for Southwestern Airlines in China. Prior to returning to the United States on a national tour to solicit aid for war relief, she taught aviation in Hong Kong, piloted a government plane around China to interest young men in aviation, and organized nursing schools and refugee camps in Shanghai.[73] Like the aviator Katherine Cheung, who had in 1936 won the admiration of the Chinese community with her daring aerobatic skills and commitment to serve China through aviation, Lee Ya Ching impressed audiences with her aerial displays and stirring speeches on women's role in the War of Resistance:

> There might have been a time when it was all right for women to let their men go out and defend them and their homes. But men can't defend women and homes from bombs out of the sky. Since we risk as much by doing nothing, we prefer to become soldiers and fight for our country.[74]

As one reporter remarked, "She not only brings glory to China's Air Force but she does likewise for all Chinese women."[75]

Every Chinese woman was thrilled about Madame Chiang's visit to San Francisco in March 1943 as part of a nationwide speaking tour to foster support for China. They were proud of the intelligent and dignified manner in which she had represented China to Congress and the rest of America, and they were also inspired by her personal charisma and fearless leadership as China's first lady and foremost ambassador of goodwill. Two years before, the various women's organizations involved in war work had joined efforts to send her a scroll of appreciation for her "service to China and the Chinese people."[76] During this six-day visit in San Francisco, however, they rolled out the red carpet for her. They assisted the CWRA in arranging all the particulars, greeted her at the port when she arrived, marched in the grand parades held in her honor, and attended all her public appearances and speeches.[77] In recognition of their contributions to the war effort, Madame Chiang held a private audience with representatives of the six key women's organizations at the Palace Hotel before she left for Los Angeles, at which time she thanked them for the warm reception she had received in San Francisco and reminded them to uphold the principles of the New Life Movement in their daily lives. Only in this way, she said, would racial discrimination against the Chinese be lessened. She further stressed women's important role in teaching their children Chinese language and culture, grooming their daughters for the betterment of family and community life, and promoting goodwill among Westerners.[78]

The fact that the Chinese government chose to send Dr. Wu Yifang, principal of Ginling Women's College and the only woman among nine delegates, to represent China at the founding meeting of the United Nations was a source of pride for the Chinese American community, especially since Russia, known for its strong stance on gender equality, had sent only men.[79] The reception held in Dr. Wu's honor at the Chinese YWCA in 1945 was as much a tribute to her as a celebration of the enhanced status of Chinese women due to their contributions in war work. As Dr. Wu had said over a decade before, "Progress of a nation is relatively dependent upon the progress of its women. China is going through a transition that is not yet completed, but one that eventually will mean a new China."[80] Six women, representing each of the six key Chinese women's organizations, walked in with Dr. Wu at the beginning of the program and sat with her on stage. In her speech that day, Dr. Wu acknowledged "the immense contributions that women have made to the War of Resistance and now to the peace effort after the war." Taking note of how smoothly the program went, one reporter commented, "This well-organized event is indeed a good example of the ability of our women's groups to work together."[81]

In sum, as with previous national crises in China, the War of Resistance called for the contribution of every man and woman not only in China but also overseas. Women in China, in shouldering guns at the battlefront, administering to the wounded, devoting themselves to wartime propaganda, contributing to production, and maintaining their homes and neighborhoods, more than proved their mettle. The result, the aviator Lee Ya Ching pointed out, was that "Chinese women who wouldn't have broken from tradition for another century perhaps are thinking and acting for themselves, in the great national emergency. . . . Naturally, you can't liberate a mind and then expect it to go back behind deadening prison walls."[82] Likewise, Chinese women in the United States were moved to action, participating in many new avenues of po-

At the welcoming reception for Dr. Wu Yifang. *From left to right:* Mickey Fong Lee, Chinese YWCA; Mrs. Kwock Chang Lien, Women's Patriotic Club; Mrs. Jue Jun Yew, New Life Association; Mrs. Chan Gum, Women's Council; Nellie Tom Quock, reception chair; Dr. Wu Yifang; May Chan, Fidelis Coteri; Jessie Dong, Square and Circle Club; and Jane Kwong Lee, translator. (Courtesy of Chinese YWCA, San Francisco)

litical involvement, although still in gender-specific ways and in subordinate roles to men. In the process, they too proved their worth and elevated their status in the community. As one reporter noted on the occasion of Women's Day in 1945:

> After the War of Resistance started, because of the efforts of overseas Chinese in national salvation work, the overseas Chinese women's movement has taken off with remarkable speed. Women's organizations have formed and earned good marks for their fundraising and war relief work. In addition, women's thinking has progressed. They have joined the men in national salvation work. They understand that only by liberating the people can the women's liberation movement have a bright future.[83]

America's entry into the war after the bombing of Pearl Harbor would give Chinese women further cause to express their patriotism and find places for themselves in the public arena; only this time they would be in step with mainstream society.

The All-American War Effort: 1941

All of America was stunned on the morning of December 7, 1941, when 353 Japanese bombers and fighters swooped over Pearl Harbor, breaking the backbone of the country's Pacific Fleet during a two-hour preemptive strike. President Roosevelt declared war on Japan and the Axis powers within twenty-four hours of the attack, thus ending the debate on whether the United States should enter the war once and for all. America's entry into World War II was the turning point for both the Allies and the country's economic slump. Almost overnight, the United States turned its full attention to war production, supplying the Soviet Union and Britain with much-needed military equipment and supplies to fight the Nazis. As the Soviet army finally succeeded in driving Hitler's army out of Eastern Europe after a series of savage and bloody battles, Americans joined forces with the British, successfully pushing the German army out of Northern Africa, Sicily, Italy, and France. In May 1945, the Allies took Berlin, Hitler committed suicide, and the Nazi regime was toppled. Attention then was focused on the war in the Pacific, where the U.S. Navy had been waging an "island-hopping" offensive to prepare for a full-scale invasion of Japan. America's use of its newly developed atomic bomb on Hiroshima on August 6, 1945, and on Nagasaki three days later (before giving Japan a chance to surrender) finally brought Japan to its knees and ended World War II.

On the home front, the war accomplished what the New Deal had failed to do—bring about economic recovery. Massive government deficit spending in war production resulted in a boom economy for the country. The GNP rose from $125 billion in 1941 to $212 billion in 1945; total output of manufactured goods increased 300 percent between 1940 and 1944; and government expenditures soared from a mere $11 billion in 1939 to $117 billion in 1945. As thousands of men were sent to the battlefront, a labor shortage occurred in the expanded war economy. Wages increased 44 percent in four years, and jobs in the war industries and in the private sector opened up for both women and racial minorities. Swept up by the tide of patriotism in the face of a national crisis, Americans across the country bought war bonds, cooperated with war production and rationing, and volunteered for civil defense and Red Cross work.

Chinese Americans, although deeply immersed in a nationalist movement to resist Japanese aggression in China, were as shocked as other

Americans by Japan's bold move at Pearl Harbor. Lonnie Quan, who was living in San Francisco Chinatown at the time of the attack, recalled that "day of infamy":

> I remember December 7th so clearly. I was living at Gum Moon Residence Club on Washington Street. It was Sunday. I didn't have a radio in the room. I didn't know what was going on. And my date came to take me out, and he said, "This is it." And I didn't know what he was talking about. He said, "President Roosevelt declared war. Pearl Harbor was attacked." I was shocked. I think everybody was in a state of shock for a few weeks. I remember going to work in a restaurant, Cathay House. And everybody was just kind of glued to the radio. And for the next few weeks, it seemed like everything was at a standstill.[84]

Whereas Japanese Americans were seen as enemy aliens, stripped of their civil rights, and herded into concentration camps for the duration of the war, the mass media promoted Chinese Americans, along with Filipino, Korean, and Asian Indian Americans, as valiant allies and loyal sons and daughters of Uncle Sam.[85] Chinese Americans, fearful of being mistaken for Japanese, displayed signs in their windows announcing, "This is a Chinese Shop," wearing buttons that read "I am Chinese," or carrying identification cards signed by the Chinese consul general.[86] Social attitudes toward Chinese Americans changed overnight. Once considered immoral, unclean, and a threat to the American way of life, they were now depicted as good, honest, hardworking Americans. According to Helen Pon Onyett, who had experienced discrimination living in Waterbury, Connecticut, up to the time of the war:

> Really at that time, even being second generation, it was a little bit difficult being in the minority. You weren't really a part of things. Then when World War II happened, everyone couldn't do enough for China. And Madame Chiang Kai-shek came and provoked a lot of sympathy and everyone started feeling, we are Americans and we should support China. And I could feel the reaction toward me. We were the only Chinese family in town, and their reaction toward us was really a turnabout.[87]

The overwhelmingly positive response to Madame Chiang Kai-shek's visit in 1943 was indicative of mainstream America's new attitude regarding China and Chinese Americans. Educated at Wellesley College and an accomplished orator who spoke impeccable English, Madame Chiang addressed Congress with an eloquent but forceful speech on behalf of China's war effort. "The U.S. Senate is not in the habit of rising to its feet to applaud," wrote a reporter in *Time*. "For Madame Chiang it rose and thundered."[88] She spoke as an equal, subtly condemning the United States for its lack of support in the last five and a half years of war. However important Hitler might be, she pointed out, the United States must act now and join China's fight, or lose the possibility of creating a world democracy.[89] When she finished, one grizzled congressman was heard muttering, "Goddam it, I never saw anything like it. Madame Chiang had me on the verge of bursting into tears."[90] She made a similar impact on the thousands of Americans who came out to welcome her in New York, Boston, Chicago, San Francisco, and Los Angeles. Her dignified presence shattered the stereotyped image of China as a weak, backward nation and of Chinese women as exotic porcelain dolls. Representing China, now America's ally, she was, in the words of one Chinese American reporter, "A lady of tact and charm, as well as courage and intelligence. A lady who speaks for and is symbolic of a great people."[91] It was partly thanks to her efforts that the Chinese exclusion laws were repealed: as she indicated to several key congressmen at a dinner party on May 15, repeal would give a good boost to Chinese morale.[92]

Soon after Madame Chiang's visit, Senator Warren Magnuson introduced a bill in Congress calling for the repeal of the Exclusion acts. Widely supported by religious, civic, and even labor organizations, its passage on December 17, 1943, was based largely on wartime enthusiasm for China, commercial interests in China, and the need to challenge Japanese propaganda in Asia. As President Roosevelt put it to Congress, "I regard this legislation as important in the cause of winning the war and of establishing a secure peace. China is our ally. For many long years she stood alone in the fight against aggression. Today we fight at her side. . . . By the repeal of the Chinese exclusion laws, we can correct a historic mistake and silence the distorted Japanese propaganda."[93]

In 1944, open Chinese immigration was resumed after sixty-one years of Exclusion (though at a token allocation of 105 per year) and Chinese aliens were finally granted the right to naturalization. Because of the war emergency, other discriminatory barriers were lowered as well; Chinese Americans were now allowed to join the armed services on an equal basis, to work in white-collar jobs, skilled trades, and for the civil service, to live outside of Chinatowns, and to be included in the all-American war effort. The sociologist Rose Hum Lee went so far as to proclaim:

For them [Chinese Americans] the present crisis is another stepping stone toward complete assimilation. No longer do Americans think of the Chinese as mysterious Orientals from a little known land. Most of these Chinese living among them are fellow citizens. The rest of them, as well as their cousins in the old country, are Allies. The crisis of December 7 has emancipated the Chinese in the United States.[95]

Certainly, the impact of World War II on Chinese American women was far-reaching. As they volunteered for the armed services, took jobs in defense factories and the private sector, and redoubled their efforts in war relief work on the home front, their horizons broadened, their socioeconomic status improved, and they found themselves falling in step with the rest of America. Lonnie Quan recalled,

> All of a sudden, San Francisco started being a boom town. Everybody was getting jobs. The shipyards were open and it was very exciting [because] you didn't know when you were going to war. . . . And that's when it's romantic in a way, and sometimes, it's very sad. You see all your friends going away to war and maybe not coming back.[96]

In contrast, Japanese American men and women were pushed out of step: they lost their freedom, suffered heavy economic losses, and received permanent psychological scars from being incarcerated in concentration camps without just cause or due process of the law.[97]

IN THE ARMED FORCES

Approximately eleven million men and women were inducted into the U.S. armed forces between 1941 and 1945. With the growing demand for manpower and the steady application of political pressure by black and women's groups, racial and gender barriers were lowered. Resident aliens were permitted to enlist, with promises of U.S. citizenship down the line. Of the 59,803 Chinese adult males in the United States at the time, over 20 percent joined the U.S. Army. A smaller percentage also served in the navy, Marine Corps, and Coast Guard. Because Chinese men at the time were predominantly single, they were susceptible to the draft, but almost all went willingly out of a strong sense of both Chinese nationalism and American patriotism. Chinese Americans in New York cheered themselves hoarse when the first draft numbers included Chinese names. In Butte, Montana, all eleven Chinese men of draft age enlisted before they were drafted.[98] As Private Charles Leong wrote from Buckley Field in Denver, Colorado:

> The average Chinese GI Joe likes and swears by the army. The most obvious reason, of course, is the fact that every Chinese would like to par-

ticipate in defeating our common enemy—the Jap. Reason Number Two
is perhaps more complex, but equally important. . . . To GI Joe Wong,
in the army a "Chinaman's chance" means a fair chance, one based not
on race or creed, but on the stuff of the man who wears the uniform of
the U.S. Army.[99]

Unlike blacks and Japanese Americans, who were placed in segregated
units, Chinese Americans were generally integrated into the military.[100]
A high percentage of Chinese G.I.'s saw combat duty in Europe and in
the Pacific. Of the 12,041 Chinese draftees, 214 died in the war.[101]

As the country geared up for war, it became apparent that valuable
manpower was being wasted in duties such as office work that could be
carried out by women. Within the first fourteen months of the war, Congress passed bills to establish women's corps in the army, navy, Coast
Guard, and marines, with the stipulation that enlisted women be confined to noncombat duties. Out of patriotism and a sense of adventure,
and attracted by the economic benefits, over 350,000 women volunteered, making up 2 percent of the military. Most were white, single
women. Black women, numbering 4,000 in the Women's Army Corps
(WAC) alone, were the only sizable racial minority group. Like their male
counterparts, they were often kept segregated and bore the brunt of racial
discrimination in terms of poor work assignments, lack of promotion,
and overall treatment. Black women were outright excluded from the
WAVES (Women Accepted for Volunteer Emergency Service, the women's corps in the navy) until 1945. In contrast, the small numbers of
Puerto Rican, Chinese, Japanese, and Native American women who
served were integrated into the women's military units and suffered less
discrimination.[102] While most servicewomen experienced a sense of personal development and satisfaction in rising to the challenges of military service, they were never treated on a par with the men or allowed
to share power. Women, including officers, were generally assigned traditional female tasks of office work, communication, and health care.
Sexual harassment and male hostility were pervasive, and the inefficient
use of women's time and abilities contributed to lapses in morale.[103] As
one historian put it, "Wacs, Waves, Spars, and women Marines were war
orphans whom no one loved."[104]

The exception to this rule was nurses, who were welcomed into the
military from the beginning because of their sought-after skills as well
as the popular acceptance of nursing as noble war work for women. The
76,000 women who served in this capacity represented 31 percent of all
active professional nurses in the nation. Many risked their lives behind

the battle lines, caring for the wounded under enemy fire. In return, they were the first servicewomen to be accorded equal pay and full military rank.[105] Helen Pon Onyett was among the first Chinese American women to volunteer for the Army Nurse Corps.[106] Twenty-five years old at the time and with four years of nursing experience under her belt, she welcomed the opportunity "to do better in the military." She recalled how she reached her decision to enlist:

> I was visiting New York Chinatown with some friends of mine. On one of those side streets they had stuck on the wall an announcement that Pearl Harbor had been attacked. And all those people were milling around there, and everybody was so excited about it and up in arms. It shook everyone up. I was so irritated about it [the attack], whereas what was happening over there in Germany didn't affect me as much. That's what got me thinking about it. I ought to contribute something, so finally, after a year or so, I volunteered.

Her first hurdle was to pass "boot camp," where she learned military maneuvers and survival techniques. "I hated it," she said, "wearing fatigues and helmets, living in tents that weren't temperaturized, and learning to abandon ship on rope ladders. It was all quite strenuous."

For the duration of the war Helen nursed the wounded aboard transports off North Africa and the acutely injured at a military hospital back in the United States. "I can't swim, so I wore my Mae West [life jacket] twenty-four hours a day," she said. "It was scary, especially when some of the ships you would be traveling with would be sunk right under your nose. All I could think was, 'If you gotta go, you gotta go.'" Compared to the five hundred black nurses, who were kept in segregated units and served only black troops, Helen experienced no racial discrimination. On the contrary, she insisted, "I was treated as a nurse nurse, not an Oriental somebody." So rewarding was her military experience that Helen decided to stay on after the war, serving more than thirty years in the reserves and becoming one of the few women to be promoted to the rank of full colonel (in 1971). "When I spoke before audiences," she pointed out, "people gawked at me, saying, 'Oh, my God, she's a colonel,' not 'She's Oriental.'" When the general awarded her the Meritorious Service medal, one of eight major decorations for distinguished military service that she would receive, she added, "all the wives came over and said, 'It's about time someone recognized a woman.' See, not Oriental, but just a woman."

Jessie Lee Yip was one of the few Chinese women in San Francisco

Sergeant Jessie Lee. (Courtesy of Jessie Lee Yip)

to become a Wac.[107] She remembered first feeling the impact of World War II at her high school graduation:

> All I remember is that we were graduating. We were all in a row and you stood up to go get your diploma. I was near the front, and boys and girls wore different colored robes. This one row stood up, and it was all girls. And I heard a gasp from the audience because they were so shocked that there were no boys. The reason was, most of the boys had enlisted.

Upon graduation, Jessie got a job at Western Union as a teletypist. Inspired by a family friend, Lt. Emily Lee Shek, the first Chinese American woman to join the WAC, she considered signing up out of a strong sense of patriotism. However, most Chinatown parents opposed their daughters enlisting. "Like dancing or anything that was different, all the parents were against it," said Jessie. "I asked a couple of friends to join with me, and they said they wouldn't even think about it because their parents wouldn't let them."[108] Despite the special efforts of Madame Chiang Kai-shek and WAC recruiters to lower height and weight requirements and entice women to form an all Chinese women's air unit, few Chinese women in San Francisco volunteered for military service.[109] "I had wanted to go on a ship and be a steward," said Jessie, "but family friends said, 'Nah, you don't want to do that, because on the ship people get sick and you have to clean it up.' They thought I wouldn't be happy or able to hack it." When Western Union switched her to the graveyard shift, however, she finally decided to quit her job and enlist, with the blessings of her liberal-minded mother. "My mother's more modern," Jessie explained. "She was born in America and lived in New York. In fact, I have a hunch she wanted to go [into the service] herself. She's that kind."

The WAVES, known for being discriminatory, turned her down, so she tried the WAC. After she had passed all the required tests, "they sent a staff car out for me, and within five minutes I was a Wac." Six weeks of basic training in Fort Des Moines, Iowa, followed: "It was to get us used to military life. We had to parade. We had taps [bugle calls], shots, KP, calisthenics, and everything but the front-line stuff." Jessie was then assigned to the Third Air Force headquarters in Tampa, Florida, as a teletypist. Local people would stare at the sight of a Chinese woman in uniform, but, like Helen Pon Onyett, she did not recall experiencing discrimination while in the service. Jessie became close friends with two other Wacs who were white, and because they went everywhere together, they became known as the Three Musketeers. Being one of the few Chinese women in the WAC had its advantages. She was "queen bee" to Chinese G.I.'s on the base, who all courted her. Her only complaints were having to work the night shift, endure the heat, and do without good, Chinese home cooking. Like Helen, Jessie signed up for the reserves after the war, but she served only a brief period as a recruiter in San Francisco Chinatown before returning to school on the G.I. bill.

In contrast to Helen's and Jessie's experiences, Charlotte Sexton, an Amerasian from Hawaii who worked as a teletypist at army bases in Oregon, Virginia, and Maryland, recalled incidents of both racism and sexism. In one case, her friend Alice Chow was accosted while off duty. "Alice really looks Oriental; and this fellow came up and spun her around in the middle of the street in Baltimore, Maryland. He said, 'You damn Jap, get out of that uniform!'" Charlotte also noted that men whom she and other teletypists trained were often promoted ahead of them: "We taught the men how to do it, what to do, and kind of overseeing them. Then lo and behold, not only one of them but two or three of them would come up the ranks and pass us. Before you know it, they were over us and not knowing any more than we knew."[110]

Maggie Gee, one of two Chinese American women who volunteered with the Women's Airforce Service Pilots Program (WASP) transporting military aircraft around the country, was very aware of sexism in the service. She had dropped out of college to work at the Mare Island Naval Shipyard in north San Francisco Bay, drawing plans for the repair of destroyers and submarines. "What we were doing in the shipyard was important," she said, "but we wanted to do something more, something more exciting."[111] Inspired by Amelia Earhart and the romance of flying, she and two other friends left Mare Island to enroll in flight school. They later joined the WASP when the age requirement was lowered to eighteen. Of 25,000 women who applied, only 2,000 were accepted, and 1,074 graduated and received their wings. "Our flight training was the same as the men pilots. In primary training, we flew the open cockpit Stearman, which you might see today in airshows doing aerobatics," she explained. "In basic training, we flew the 450-horsepower canopied BT-13. And in advance training we flew the 650-horsepower AT-6, which had radio and retractable landing gear—the kind of plane used in combat in China."[112] By the fall of 1944, half of the ferrying division's fighter pilots were women, and three-fourths of all domestic deliveries were done by Wasps. They also flight-tested damaged airplanes and flew B-17s. Thirty-eight woman pilots died because of mechanical failures, including the only other Chinese American woman, Hazel Ying Lee of Portland, Oregon. Yet they were known for flying longer hours and having fewer accidents than their fellow male pilots. Despite their track record, however, the civilian group of female pilots was forced to disband a few months before the end of the war because of lobbying on the part of the male pilots.[113] "Even though our numbers were small and the war was not over, we were sent home," said Maggie. "It was difficult for men to admit that women could fly as well as or better than men."[114] To add insult to injury, Congress chose not to classify the WASP as military. While other servicewomen were granted full veteran status in 1948, Wasps did not receive the same recognition until 1977. Nor could they find jobs as test pilots with aircraft companies or airlines after the war because of sex discrimination. Still, for Maggie the experience opened up new vistas, transforming her into a more outgoing and politically aware person. "I returned to Berkeley, California, with a lot more self-confidence," she said. "My horizon had broadened by the friendships I made with active women—doers from all parts of the country."[115] Maggie, who never married, went on to become a physicist and political activist.

Overall, Chinese American women who enlisted in the military found

Maggie Gee (*second from left*) and fellow members of the Women's Airforce Service Pilots Program. (Courtesy of Maggie Gee)

the experience rewarding. Besides giving them the satisfaction of serving their country, it gave them a wider perspective, gained them new
friends, made them more independent and self-confident, allowed them
to travel, and opened up new educational and employment opportunities. "I wouldn't have done half the things I did if I hadn't been in the
service," said Helen Pon Onyett. "Not only did it give me retirement
benefits, but I had a chance to go to school on the G.I. bill and to improve my standing."[116] Jessie Lee Yip, who later became a court recorder,
also profited from the G.I. bill, which financed her education in stenog-
raphy after the war. "It also helped me to grow up, get along with people, and it allowed me to travel," she added.[117] Similarly, because of her
two years of service in the WAC, May Lew Gee of San Francisco had a
chance to attend secretarial training school after the war. Her military
experiences also spurred her to become an active member of the Cathay
Post in San Francisco and the American Legion Post in Pacifica, California, as well as to run for public office. May was on the Pacifica Planning Commission for twelve years and has been on the Water Board there
for seventeen years.[118]

Marietta Chong Eng of Hawaii, who was motivated to join the
WAVES because her brother was in the navy, found her one year of service as an occupational therapist at Mare Island more positive than negative:

> In reflection, my one year of service as a WAVES ensign was like no other
> single year of my life. Wearing the uniform made me feel different. On
> the streets of San Francisco or at the navy base, I attracted much atten-
> tion and maybe admiration. On the negative side, I was in uniform in
> New York City crossing a busy street when a young hoodlum pointed at
> me in surprise and said, "Look, a Chinaman." I guess it was startling to
> see a Chinese in uniform. All in all, though, my navy experience was a
> good one.

So proud was she of the uniform that she wore it at her wedding: "I felt
that I could not find a more distinctive wedding outfit than this one,"
she said.[119] Marietta settled in Oakland, where she raised three children
and worked for many years as an occupational therapist with the mentally ill.

Ruth Chan Jang, who left a well-paying job with the State of California to join the Women's Air Corps in 1944, said it was a turning point
in her life. Growing up in Locke, California, she had experienced racial
discrimination and been made to feel ashamed of her Chinese background. The service changed all that. As the only Chinese in her unit,

she was treated very well, Ruth emphasized. "I was accepted as one of them. They never made me feel like you have to hang back and be subservient." While in the service she was captain of the basketball team, given her first surprise birthday party, and promoted to corporal at the suggestion of the nurses under whom she worked as a secretary. After the war, Ruth also took advantage of the G.I. bill and went back to college, eventually becoming a teacher. There can be no better testament of her positive experience in the service and the patriotism it nurtured in her than her sincere wish that she and her husband, who also served in the air force during World War II, will "someday, somehow" be buried at Arlington National Cemetery.[120]

IN THE LABOR FORCE

The draft and the rapid growth of the war industry resulted in a labor shortage that in turn opened up significant job opportunities for racial minorities and women. With the men away at war and President Roosevelt's executive order against discriminatory hiring practices in place, their labor became crucial in guaranteeing the output of war materials and food. Black, Mexican, Chinese, and Native American workers migrated in large numbers to urban centers and city ports to fill jobs in the defense industries. At the same time, many women found work in the manufacturing and clerical sectors, while others were able to enter business and professional fields previously closed to them. Wartime propaganda played on the themes of patriotism and glamor to recruit married women into the labor force. Women were encouraged to emulate Rosie the Riveter—a muscular but pert, rosy-cheeked young woman, rivet gun slung across her lap and a powder puff and mirror peeking out of her coverall pocket—to take a war job and so stand behind the man with the gun. During the war years the female labor force increased by more than 50 percent overall, and by 140 percent in manufacturing and 460 percent in the major war industries. Married women exceeded single women in the work force for the first time in U.S. history, and woman workers were at last able to gain access to higher pay, union representation, and such traditionally male jobs as mechanic, engineer, lumberjack, bus driver, and police dispatcher.[121]

The employment of black women increased by more than one-third during the war years, but racism and sexism combined to hinder their wartime gains relative to those of white women and black men. On the positive side, black women were able to move from farm and domestic

Corporal Ruth Chan. (Courtesy of Ruth Chan Jang)

labor into better-paying jobs in hotels, restaurants, and defense factories. On the negative side, however, black workers of both sexes were often subjected to discrimination in hiring, training, job assignment, wages, and promotion.[122] Fanny Christina Hill, who spent forty years as an aircraft worker after getting her start during World War II, put it like this: "We always say that Lincoln took the bale off of the Negroes. I think there is a statue up there in Washington, D.C., where he's lifting something off the Negro. Well, my sister always said that Hitler was the one that got us out of the white folks' kitchen." As Fanny found out, though, it was an uphill battle:

> They fought hand, tooth, and nail to get in there. And the first five or six Negroes who went in there, they were well educated, but they started them off as janitors. After they once got their foot in the door and was there for three months—you work for three months before they say you're hired—then they had to start fighting all over again to get off of that broom and get something decent. And some of them did.[123]

Overall, despite the new employment opportunities and higher wages for women during the war years, gender inequality persisted in terms of pay differences and job mobility, not to mention household and child care responsibilities. After the war, a Women's Bureau poll showed that 74 percent of women workers wanted to remain in the labor force and 86 percent wanted to retain their current jobs; however, public opinion prevailed: women, it was generally believed, belonged in the home. As the men returned from the war front, women were laid off at a rate 75 percent higher than that for men, and the occupational structure returned to its prewar status.[124]

World War II proved to be a job boom for Chinese Americans, who for the first time found well-paying jobs in factories—building ships, aircraft, and war vehicles and producing ammunition—as well as in private industries. Nationwide, Chinese American men made substantial gains in the professional/technical and craft fields, while the women, whose labor force participation almost tripled between 1940 and 1950, made inroads in the clerical/sales, professional/technical, and proprietor/managerial classifications. The image and roles of Chinese American women on the home front changed dramatically as government propaganda declared them patriotic daughters who were doing their part for the war effort:

> Daughters of women, who, in the Chinese homeland, lived out their whole lives in the cloistered seclusion of the enclosed courtyard of the traditional Chinese home, are today not only seeking careers in their adopted country but are banded together as volunteers to help win the war. . . . In aircraft plants, training camps, and hospital wards, at filter boards and bond booths, in shipyards, canteens, and Red Cross classes, these girls . . . these Chinese daughters of Uncle Sam . . . are doing their utmost to blend their new-world education and their old-world talents to hasten the end of the war.[125]

As far as Lucy Lee of Houston, Texas, was concerned, World War II was the most important event in her lifetime in terms of job opportunities. A member of one of the first Chinese families in Houston, she recalled, "We really were a minority. We were not white; we were not black. Jobs were not open to us at all." Classmates and children in the neighborhood constantly called them names. "I couldn't tell you how many [fist]fights I got into trying to protect my brothers and sisters." Then came the war. "It changed life around. People started to look at you a little differently and you could get jobs. With no men around, we had all kinds of opportunities."[126]

Census statistics provide strong evidence that the Chinese in San Francisco not only made major economic gains during the war but also were able to hold on to those gains afterward. Between 1940 and 1950, the numbers of Chinese men in domestic service declined, while they increased in the crafts as well as in the professional, technical, and managerial categories. Chinese women fared even better, moving from their prewar predominantly operative status to jobs in the clerical and sales fields. Compared to the prewar years, although the labor market was still stratified by race and gender, Chinese Americans were able to make some inroads thanks to the war. In 1940, white men dominated the primary sector (professional, managerial, clerical, and craft occupations), followed by white women; Chinese men and women, however, were concentrated in the secondary sector (operative, service, and manual labor jobs). In 1950, although white men and women still dominated the primary sector, they were joined by a significant number of both Chinese men and women. Whereas in 1940, 36.3 percent of Chinese male workers and 30.8 percent of Chinese female workers were in the primary labor market, by 1950, those figures had climbed to 49.8 and 59 percent, respectively. In contrast, 75 percent of black male workers and 82 percent of black female workers remained in the secondary labor market after the war (see appendix tables 11 and 12).

War production revitalized the San Francisco Bay Area, which developed into the largest shipbuilding center in the world during World War II. Because of the labor shortage as well as federal guidelines against discrimination, all six major shipyards in the Bay Area were willing to hire racial minorities and women to build the cargo ships and tankers needed for America to win the war.[127] With the government sponsoring free classes in marine sheetmetal, pipefitting, electricity, shipfitting, and drafting, the shipyards carried a labor recruitment campaign to San Francisco and Oakland Chinatowns.[128] According to the *Chinese Press*, in 1942 some 1,600 Chinese Americans, out of a total population of 18,000, were in defense work, primarily the shipbuilding trades; and in 1943, Chinese workers constituted 15 percent of the shipyard work force in the San Francisco Bay Area.[129] In contrast, some 15,000 blacks worked in the Bay Area shipyards in 1943; at its peak period of production, the Kaiser shipyard alone employed 25,000 blacks.[130]

The largest shipyard in the Bay Area, the Henry J. Kaiser shipyard in Richmond, boasted that it employed 20,000 women out of a total work force of 90,000, as well as a number of efficient all-Chinese male work crews that were always ahead of schedule. "I will stack them up against any other crew in the yard," remarked one superintendent to a newspaper reporter. The point was often made that Chinese shipyard workers were motivated by more than just American patriotism. "The Chinese are intent upon building ships as quickly as they can," another reporter wrote; she then quoted a Chinese worker: "We're doing our part for the United States [and] our efforts aid China. This is the chance we've been seeking." Even Chinese women were leaving their homes to work in the shipyards, "to show their spirit since women in China are to do their share."[131] The Kaiser shipyard's in-house publication, *Fore 'n Aft*, often singled out Chinese employees as model workers doubly driven by the desire to help both China and the United States win the war. In a sexist way, the publication commented on how even "pretty" and "delicate" women like Jane Jeong and Leong Bo San were proving to be "amazing" workers:

> Pretty Jane Jeong had an ambition to fly for China, but when the United States entered the war, she decided she could better beat the Japs by building ships instead. So Jane's a burner trainee at Yard Two. Two hundred flying hours are not the fighting lady's only accomplishment, for she's been a dancer and manager of night club and vaudeville performers. Jane's husband is a merchant seaman and has not been home once in the four months of their marriage.[132]

> "Shanghai Lil" is the name they know her by, over at Assembly 11 on graveyard shift. . . . Her name is Leong Bo San. Born in Shanghai, she was the daughter of a silk merchant. She is five feet, one inch tall, and she weighs 102 pounds. . . . She has six children. One son is an Air Corps meteorologist, another is an attorney. Tiny and delicate as she looks, she works with an energy that amazes people twice her size. Says her boss, James G. Zack: "I wish I had a whole crew of people like her."[133]

Marinship in Sausalito also boasted of large numbers of women and racial minorities in its work force of 20,000 in 1943, 300 of whom were Chinese. In a special issue of its publication *Marin-er* on "The New China," Marinship expressed its pride in its Chinese American workers: "They are practical, teachable, and wonderfully gifted with common sense; they are excellent artisans, reliable workmen, and of a good faith that every one acknowledges and admires in their commercial dealings."[134] In the same issue, Jade Snow Wong, who was working as a clerk-typist at Marinship, wrote that Chinese workers came from all walks of life and worked in all areas—as janitors, cooks, burners, draftsmen, time keepers, boilermakers, and secretaries. "They are giving their all to the job because they know from their Chinese countrymen what Japanese

Shipyard worker Lonnie
Young. (Judy Yung collection)

warfare is all about," she said. "Chinese at Marinship are each in his or
her own way working out their answer to Japanese aggression: by producing ships which will mean their home land's liberation."[135]

Kenneth Bechtel, president of Marinship, said much the same thing
in a letter he wrote to Generalissimo Chiang Kai-shek, praising the Chinese workers' patriotic drive and crucial contributions to war production:

> The men and women of Marinship, together with all United Nations pa-
> triots, pay tribute to the people of China. For more than five years they
> have successfully withstood the maraudings of the evil foe, until now our
> common road to Victory lies clearly in sight. No small part of the credit
> for past accomplishment and future hope belongs to the brave and sturdy
> Chinese-Americans who work and fight in the United States. More than
> 300 such patriots, both men and women, are working every day at Marin-
> ship, building cargo ships and tankers. We have learned that these Chi-
> nese-Americans are among the finest workmen. They are skillful, reliable—
> and inspired with a double allegiance. They know that every blow they
> strike in building these ships is a blow of freedom for the land of their
> fathers as well as for the land of their homes.[136]

Indeed, when Marinship became the first shipyard to launch a liberty ship in honor of a Chinese statesman—the S.S. Sun Yat-sen—Chinese American employees voluntarily pledged one day's pay to the relief of Chinese war orphans.[137]

As Jade Snow Wong pointed out, a mixture of first- and second-generation Chinese Americans from all walks of life found work at the shipyards. Depending on their educational background, Chinese male workers were assigned jobs in all departments except administration, from assembly line to construction line to maintenance and services. As for the women, older immigrants worked in janitorial services, younger women were trained as draftswomen, burners, and flangers, while high school graduates and college students were hired as office workers. Despite the obvious absence of Chinese in the top positions, these jobs provided Chinese Americans with union wages and benefits, training and work experience outside of Chinatown, and the opportunity to contribute to the Allied war effort.

Although yard newspapers claimed that Chinese workers were well liked and well treated, there were reports of racial and sex discrimination at all the shipyards. Despite liberal hiring policies, blacks were denied membership in parent unions and disadvantaged by restrictive, union-enforced limitations on their employment and promotions. The last to be hired and the first to be laid off, they were kept in low-paying unskilled positions and rarely promoted to positions of authority.[138] Women, who in 1943 made up 20 percent of the shipyard labor force in the Bay Area, met with male resistance and were held back in almost all job categories. Black women, facing both racial and sex discrimination, were generally confined to laboring and housekeeping types of jobs and were underrepresented in the crafts.[139] According to Katherine Archibald, who worked at Moore Dry Dock in Oakland, whites and Native Americans topped the racial hierarchy in the shipyards, Okies, Jews, and Chinese were in the middle, and Portuguese and blacks were stuck at the bottom. "The Chinese," she wrote, "were accepted without resistance or dislike, though with little positive friendliness."[140] It was known that Chinese at Moore Dry Dock and Kaiser often worked in segregated crews because of the racist sentiments of fellow employees. "It's easier to adjust working conditions than try to adjust the prejudice," a San Francisco Chronicle reporter stated. A Chinese shipyard worker interviewed by this journalist complained about being called a "Chink" by his supervisor and about the lack of promotional opportunities for Chinese Americans. "I don't think a Chinese boy has a Chinaman's chance," he said. "I have been here many months. Do you think I can become a leaderman?"[141] Although shipyard workers were earning the highest wages of any industry and women were generally receiving equal pay for equal work, Chinese workers were held back in almost all job categories and locked out of certain crafts. Few were ever promoted to supervisory positions.

Nevertheless, most Chinese American women recalled their shipyard experience as only positive. Frances Jong, who accompanied her four brothers to the Mare Island yard, was hired as a shipfitter's assistant. She said, "It wasn't difficult work. I just carried these angle bars, followed this Chinese shipfitter around, and did what he told me to do. I learned a new trade and got good pay for it."[142] The only Chinese woman in her unit, she did not remember any discrimination. Similarly, Maggie Gee, who was the only Chinese American and one of only three women in the drafting department at Mare Island, experienced no discrimination, nor did her mother, An Yoke Gee, who worked as a burner. "It was a positive experience for her," said Maggie. "She made non-Chinese friends for the first time, and it broadened her outlook in life. She was satisfied with being part of a Chinese community where she lived, but this allowed her to become part of the whole."[143] Working in the shipyard also introduced Maggie to new friends, a new line of work, and a new sense of political consciousness. In 1943 she left the shipyard with two female co-workers she had befriended to join the WASP.

For May Lew Gee, who worked as a tacker at the Kaiser shipyard, "it was the patriotic thing to do, to work in some kind of war industry." It was also "great money" and a way to acquire new skills. Whereas before she had earned only 25 cents an hour waitressing, in the shipyard she earned $1.26 an hour on the graveyard shift tacking pieces of metal onto the bottoms of ship bulkheads for the welder to weld together. "Every couple of days, there's a new ship and you start all over again," she said. "They were building them faster than you can ever count." Although she did "the same thing over and over again," she did not consider the job boring, hard, or dangerous. "We heard about accidents, about people falling off the ship and drowning, but I never saw any or paid any attention. We just kept working," she said. Nor did she remember any instances of discrimination. "There was a terrific mixture [of people] and everyone got along well. They were there to do a certain job . . . build ships so they can go and fight the war." After two years as a tacker, May left to accompany a pregnant friend back to Detroit, Michigan. Unable to find transportation home, she ended up enlisting in the WAC.[144]

For someone like Rena Jung Chung, who has always enjoyed "fiddling with machines," working as a burner at the Kaiser shipyard was the chance of a lifetime. When war broke out, she was the only woman mechanic at a shop that made spray guns. Her boss closed the shop and told everyone to go work at the shipyards. Although she was a trained machinist, Rena started out as a machinist's helper in prefab, where the front and back parts of ships were built. "All I had to do was to go get the tools for the machinist and then just stand there doing nothing for the rest of the day," she recalled. "So I got restless and told the foreman I wanted to do the burning job that looked more interesting to me." Ruth learned in four hours what most others took forty hours to master and was able to change her job to burner. Except for the "Okies [who] asked you all kinds of crazy questions [because] they have never seen a Chinese [before]," she got along with everyone "because I spoke good English and I didn't let them pick on me." In addition to receiving good pay, she got to indulge her machinist passions as well as contribute to the war effort.[145]

Jade Snow Wong wrote in her autobiography that the job of clerk-typist at Marinship during the war helped her develop confidence in dealing with male co-workers. Contrary to the opinion of her college placement officer, who had told her that being Chinese would only be a handicap in the work world, she found that she was accorded nothing but respect at the shipyard. While there she won first prize in a national essay-writing contest on the topic of absenteeism. As a reward she was given the honor of launching the *S.S. William A. Jones,* which gained her recognition both at the shipyard and in the Chinese community. At the launching ceremonies, she said it was her Chinese and American education that helped her find a practical solution to absenteeism in the war industry; this same Chinese and American unity, she stated, would help bring the war to an early end.[146]

Because of the war economy and labor shortage, jobs also opened up for women in the private sector. White women moved en masse into factory and white-collar jobs, while black women increasingly left private household service to enter commercial and factory occupations. During the war, clerical wages increased by 15 to 30 percent, and factory wages grew by 47 percent, although women still earned less than men for the same type of work.[147] Chinese women also made inroads into the private sector, including the Chinatown business world. With the men away at war or taking on defense work, women were needed to fill Chinatown jobs. Restaurants broke with tradition and advertised for waitresses, and

Chinatown finally saw one of its curio shops under the management of a second-generation Chinese American woman.[148] Overall, Chinatown restaurants experienced a 300 percent increase in business between 1941 and 1943, while bars and nightclubs did a brisk trade serving soldiers and a fully employed wartime population.[149] As Gladys Ng Gin, who was working as a cocktail waitress at the Forbidden City, exclaimed, "During the Second World War, it was good money—fifty to sixty dollars a night in tips alone—wow!"[150]

Most important, the war gave second-generation women an opportunity to work outside Chinatown in better-paying jobs. For the first time, Chinese American women had their pick of positions that were commensurate with their skills. Jane Kwong Lee recalled how the entire employment picture for Chinese American women brightened as a result of the war:

> As manpower became scarce, some mothers [seeking domestic help] were desperate. Our [Chinese YWCA] office telephone was flooded with frantic calls, but our desk clerk simply took the messages and politely answered that we would do our best. After a while everybody realized that requesting for help in homes was futile; no one would take a housework job when there were high-paying positions begging to be taken. Even school girls could fill in where vacancies were left open by adults who went to work in shipyards or defense industries.[151]

According to the local Chinese press, sewing machine operators were in demand at wages ranging from $18 to $40 a week depending on experience; laundry workers could find work at 74 cents to 99 cents an hour; girls were needed to help with the harvesting of crops on nearby farms at the rate of $4 to $8 a day; and post office jobs were available paying as much as $7.10 an hour. Clerical workers were especially sought after at war factories, government agencies, and private firms.[152] According to the *Chinese Press*, the "several hundred alert young Chinese American girls who have gone into the defense industries as office workers for the duration . . . [are] the little but important cogs in America's war machinery. . . . They help run the vital 'behind-the-lines' business of the United States at war."[153]

American-born and-educated Margaret Woo, who had been doing ironing in a Chinatown garment factory, got a job as a clerk at the Relocation Center office. With that experience under her belt, she was able to move on to clerical work in the stock market after the war.[154] Lonnie Quan, who moved from San Jose to San Francisco in 1941, also got into office work because of the war. Until then she had experienced repeated rejection whenever she applied for work at white firms:

> I went to look for a job in the insurance company and they came right out and told me, "We do not hire Chinese." Well, after a few times of *that*, you just give up. You say, "The heck with it." You just don't want to go to any more interviews. It took them a long time to realize that the Chinese girls are good workers. I was very discouraged. I was very angry. And I said, "Well, I guess I won't be working in offices. I guess I'd just as soon run an elevator," which I did.

At the beginning of the war, however, she was offered a job at the Draft Board, where she worked from 1942 until 1947. "I enjoyed working there. I had a wonderful boss who helped with all the things that needed to be done. In fact, it was the best job I had ever had." From there she moved on to the Internal Revenue Service, where she was well paid and received good benefits. "Chinese people were getting better jobs during the war," she said. "Some of the girls I knew were working in offices, in mostly government jobs. And that's how most of the Chinese girls got their office training."[155] In contrast, black women with similar skills had a difficult time landing jobs in the white-collar sector. Despite President Roosevelt's efforts to eliminate employment discrimination through executive order and the establishment of the Fair Employment Practices Committee (FEPC), racial discrimination, particularly in the private sector, was still rampant. The FEPC West Coast Regional Office investigated an average of almost seventy cases per month. Approximately 80 percent were filed by blacks, 8 percent by Mexicans, and 7 percent by Jews.[156] Chinese cases were rare.

ON THE HOME FRONT

Patriotism, a spirit of cooperation, and eagerness to sacrifice for the war effort permeated Chinatown as it did the rest of the country. Even the grim conditions of war—the draft and the loss of loved ones, food and labor shortages, and the constant threat of attack—did not dampen people's spirits. Lonnie Quan recalled those days:

> We had air raid warnings and things like that. We had blackouts in the city. Nobody could go out when the blackout was on. And you can't even light a cigarette because one little match when lit, you can see from far away. I remember the blackout curtains that we had to put up. I remember all the drills, and then, after a while, everybody got used to it and they went on living the same way, going out, having fun.[157]

While their men were away fighting, women bore the brunt of responsibilities on the home front. Spearheading their efforts in San Francisco were Chinese women leaders such as Dr. Margaret Chung, who
was affiliated with the Red Cross; Jane Kwong Lee, of the Chinese
YWCA; and Emily Lee Fong and May Chan, of the Chinese chapter of
the American Women's Volunteer Services. Certainly Chinese women
from all walks of life were behind the war effort; however, these women
and the organizations they represented were the most active in linking
the Chinese effort with that of mainstream America. Although Chinese
American women basically did female-identified tasks such as Red Cross
work, entertaining soldiers on leave, selling war bonds, and making
household goods last longer, their volunteer efforts thrust them into the
public limelight and in step with the rest of America. Men, who still
held the political power in the Chinese community, continued to direct
activities; but as the war dragged on they came to recognize the abilities of their women to cope, cooperate, contribute, and lead. Moreover,
whereas black women volunteers experienced racial discrimination in war
work (for example, black women were generally excluded from volunteer activities run by whites; and one USO club in Boston prohibited
black hostesses from dancing with white servicemen),[158] Chinese women
faced no such restrictions.

Second-generation women like Dr. Margaret Chung proved to be capable leaders as well as important links between the Chinese community and mainstream society. Already active in raising American support
for the anti-Japanese war effort in China, after the Pearl Harbor attack
she redoubled her efforts in propaganda and Red Cross work. She continued making radio speeches and went on lecture tours all over the country to promote a better understanding of China and Chinese Americans. Instrumental in establishing the Red Cross station at Grace
Cathedral, she put in many volunteer hours there as well as teaching
classes in first aid and home nursing to Chinese women in San Francisco.
She was also one of the strongest advocates of price control as a solution to wartime inflation. During World War II, in addition to shortages
of coffee, beef, sugar, flour, and milk, Chinatown residents suffered
shortages of imported Chinese staples: rice, ginger, mushrooms, water
chestnuts, soy beans, and the like. As food prices rose, newspaper editorials criticized businesses that took advantage of the situation and asked
the cooperation of every Chinese American to help curb the inflation.
Dr. Chung, in cooperation with the Office of Price Administration, encouraged merchants and housewives to comply with the price regula-

tions. "Price control keeps down the cost of war and helps plan production," she said over the radio. "Likewise, it keeps down the cost of
living so that the home front can be secured."[159]

Two projects earned her particularly high marks as a Chinese American woman in the political arena. One was her successful lobbying of
Congress to establish the WAVES; the second was the formation of the
Fair-haired Bastards Club, an organization recognized by the U.S. government as the "Phi Beta Kappa of aviation." "In 1942, when there was
such a desperate need for men to fight on the front lines, I wanted to
do something actively to help in the war effort," she wrote later in her
unpublished autobiography. "I had a pair of trained hands, a medical
degree, and I felt that there were a great many other women in the United
States who wanted to do their part in the War Effort . . . but there were
no laws which permitted women to be taken into the Armed Forces."[160]
Through her political contacts in Washington, D.C., she helped to push
through the WAVES bill in record time, allowing women into the navy.

Garnering even more renown was her wartime "adoption" of 1,500
servicemen. It all began with seven aviators in the Naval Reserve who
came to her office for an examination in 1931. Discovering that they
were hungry and broke, she took them to dinner and looked after them
while they were in town. The numbers of such servicemen increased,
and when they insisted on calling her "Mom" she protested that since
she was unmarried they would be illegitimate—and so they dubbed themselves the "fair-haired bastards of Mom Chung." By 1941, the group
had grown to 780. She took a personal interest in the young men, giving each one a jade Buddha as a talisman, writing them personal letters,
sending them gifts on holidays, and welcoming them into her home
whenever they were in town. It was not uncommon for her to have 175
of them as guests for Sunday dinner. During the war she added to this
group the Golden Dolphins, which included crewmen of U.S. submarines, and the Kiwis, a women's auxiliary that included such notable
women as Amelia Earhart and Alice Roosevelt Longsworth. Because of
these connections, she was asked by the Chinese government to recruit
the first two hundred American aviators for the Flying Tigers, and for
her services in the war effort she became the first woman in the United
States to receive China's prestigious "People's Medal," in 1945.[161]

While Margaret Chung was invaluable for bringing together the Chinese American community and the larger society, Jane Kwong Lee
proved to be an important link between immigrant and American-born
Chinese women as well as between women's groups and the male-dom-

inated CWRA. As concerned about food shortages as was Dr. Chung, Jane took a course on nutrition through University of California Extension and began offering classes at the Chinese YWCA on how to cope with the problem. "No more food imports from China need not mean poor meals for Chinatown," she told Chinese housewives. "With most of us giving extra energy to the war efforts, it is important to maintain a healthful standard in diet, and the change to an American diet, or substitution of some American foods for Chinese, is inevitable."[162] Following her advice, many housewives switched to Texas-grown rice, used substitutes in their cooking, and tried to adjust their families' palates to a Western diet. One Chinese American housewife summed up the situation thus: "Well, I'm a good American—I might as well go completely Yankee and get used to pork and beans."[163]

As director of the Chinese YWCA, Jane worked hard to galvanize the involvement of Chinese women in the all-American war effort. In cooperation with other YWCA centers in the city, she organized a wartime educational and recreational program that included activities ranging from knitting for the Red Cross to air raid precaution classes, from sports to the fine arts. "In its own way, by building up the individual's life and her group life, the YWCA is doing its part in national defense," she explained in the *Chinese Press*. "A girl who is physically and socially fit, a housewife who gives her family the right nutritional food, both help the national morale. In this respect the YWCA is very alert to the present emergency."[164] Through her leadership the YWCA became the focal point for women's contributions to the war effort. They went there to attend civil defense classes, do Red Cross work, participate in citywide parades and patriotic celebrations, and go out in work teams to forage for old magazines, yarn to be used in afghans, used leather to be converted into aviatorvestees, and used fats, tin cans, and paper boxes for the manufacture of munitions and medicines. The YWCA also sent women out to help harvest crops at nearby farms, encouraged citizens to write Congress to get the Exclusion acts repealed, and called on volunteers to visit Chinese American servicemen in the hospitals and serve as hostesses at the weekly open house for American servicemen on furlough.

Popularly referred to as the "Chinatown Canteen," the weekly event held at the Chinese YWCA on Thursday evenings was orchestrated by Chinese women but drew the support of all Chinatown. It was paid for by contributions from local residents and involved scores of business and college women as well as members of the six key women's organizations.

All volunteered to take turns shopping and cooking Chinese food as well as dancing and socializing with Chinese American soldiers, sailors, and coast guardsmen on leave. Although some of the upper-class ladies would normally not have bothered to cook at home, said Jane Kwong Lee, "wartime was different. The response to serve was spontaneous."[165] Special occasions, such as Thanksgiving and Christmas, entailed more elaborate menus and gifts. During the month of December 1943, attendance averaged sixty-five servicemen each week, and beginning in March 1944 Sunday afternoons were added to the schedule.[166]

As in the rest of America, when it came to civil defense preparedness, the *Chinese Press* proclaimed, "It's a Woman's World!"[167] Most active in this area was the newly formed Chinese chapter of the American Women's Volunteer Services (AWVS), under the leadership of Emily Lee Fong and May Chan. The AWVS sponsored air raid precaution classes in which Chinese women of all ages and backgrounds learned to make blackout curtains, convert old newspapers into flashlights, and apply first aid in the event of enemy attack. "The women of Chinatown are definitely responding to the need for gearing the home to possible wartime emergencies which the next blackout may bring," said Daisy K. Wong, one of the instructors quoted in the *Chinese Press* article.[168] Aside from skills associated with the domestic realm, courses were also offered to Chinese women in motor transportation, motor mechanics, map reading, and photography; girls at the Chinese YWCA were instructed to build model airplanes for use by the army and navy. Those trained in communications and codes volunteered for the Aircraft Warning Service and the Chinese Code Corps, which aided in directing motor convoys, shore to land signaling, and other communication duties. "Every Sunday morning from 6 A.M. to noon, we would help with charting the course of all aircraft in the area," recalled Alice Fong Yu, one of the volunteers.[169] Many AWVS members also volunteered to entertain soldiers at the Chinatown Canteen, chauffeur them around town, or work as telephone operators, interpreters, and nurses' aides at the local Red Cross and twenty-four-hour first aid station.[170]

The AWVS led Chinese women in the area of fund-raising for the Allied war effort. Having already contributed over $3 million for war relief in China since 1937, San Francisco Chinatown joined with the rest of the country to fill the American war chest. Asked to raise $10,000 for the Red Cross in 1942, the Chinese raised $18,000—on top of $30,000 for defense bonds and $50,000 for the Chinese war relief fund that same year.[171] In each of the eight national war bond cam-

Martha Taam (*front row, far left*) and the Chinese chapter of the American Women's Volunteer Services selling war bonds in Chinatown. (Courtesy of Martha Taam)

paigns, too, the Chinese community consistently raised large amounts of money—$750,000 worth in the seventh campaign alone, for example.[172] Separate women's divisions brought in the largest sums in all these various drives. Money also poured in from the AWVS war bond booth in Chinatown, which, though set up at the suggestion of the Chinese Six Companies, was staffed by women volunteers. Martha Taam, one of the volunteers, recalled: "We all dressed up in our gray uniforms and took a four-hour shift selling war bonds at this booth on Washington and Grant Avenue. It was quite successful. Stores would buy bonds, and many Chinese too."[173] Each day an average of $1,000 was collected from war bond sales alone. In addition, the AWVS chapter sponsored benefits that featured Chinese American radio and nightclub stars as well as auctions and raffles; at one such benefit, $60,000 was raised.[174]

Reflecting a united front in the merging of two war efforts, Chinatown was invited to participate in the city's Pearl Harbor anniversary parade in 1942 and the "I Am an American Day" program held at the

Civic Auditorium in 1943. Then in 1944, the Chinese community changed the annual Double Seven parade (in commemoration of 7-7, the day Japan invaded China) to the Triple Seven parade, to mark the seventh year of the War of Resistance. A special open house party was held in Chinatown and at the Civic Center to express appreciation of American support for the war in China. Chinese American women were in the forefront in all of these events. It was in large part because of their efforts that close to $13,000 was raised at the Triple Seven open house in 1944, with another $52,000 being collected for Chinatown's victory celebration in 1945.[175]

On August 14, 1945, when Japan's surrender was publicly announced, overjoyed revelers filled the streets of downtown San Francisco and the adjacent financial district. Crowds carried on all night long, making bonfires of Victory Bond booths, breaking windows, and overturning cars in uncurbed jubilation.[176] Margaret Woo, who was working downtown that afternoon, noticed all the people running outside: "There were mobs of people, and the soldiers were kissing all the girls on the street," she said. "All the stores closed for the day. Everybody was so happy, screaming, 'The war's over!'"[177] Lorena How recalled the joyous occasion in this way:

> It came around 4 P.M. in the afternoon. The siren went off at the Ferry Building. Normally the siren would go off at 12 noon and again at 4:30, so we were all very surprised when it went off at 4. Then the siren was joined by the St. Mary's bells. Then all the other church bells began ringing and chiming. My mother, who always kept up with the news, knew the war was over when she heard the siren. We all ran out into the street, got into my brother's car, and started driving around. . . . We didn't know that the gas cap was off. People were throwing confetti and firecrackers, and there was paper all over the streets. It was a wonder we didn't get blown up.[178]

A few days later, Chinatown held its own celebration and began preparations for its role in the citywide victory parade. On September 9, the day of the parade, all Chinatown businesses were closed. Twenty-eight Chinese units, including veterans, dignitaries, men and women's organizations, Chinese schools, and lion dancers, took part in the four-hour-long parade that marched from the Ferry Building to City Hall.[179]

For most Americans, World War II lasted four years. For Chinese Americans, it was a protracted war of fourteen long years. Throughout that period, despite their own socioeconomic problems, they stood steadfast in their commitment to help China and then the United States defeat their common enemy. Because of the united efforts of all Americans, victory was finally achieved in 1945. In the wake of that victory, Chinese American women, who had given generously of their time, money, and energies, found themselves in step not only with the rest of their community but also with the larger society.

Epilogue

In 1941, the same year that Japan bombed Pearl Harbor, forcing the United States to enter World War II, my mother, Jew Law Ying, set sail for America on the *S.S. President Coolidge* with her four-year-old daughter, Bak Heong (meaning "forced to leave the home village").[1] The Chinese Exclusion Act was still in force, so my father, Tom Yip Jing (a.k.a. Yung Hin Sen), changed his status from laborer to merchant by declaring partnership in a Chinese art goods business. This way, my mother could come as a merchant's wife. Mother was glad to be leaving war-torn China for what she believed would be "heaven," despite her maternal grandmother's warnings. She took with her the parting words of her mother: "Be sure to send for your two younger brothers as soon as you can." Nothing was said about her three younger sisters. Although the practice of footbinding had stopped with Great-Grandmother's generation, feudal ideology concerning male preference was still very much alive in many parts of China.

Mother and Bak Heong, upon arrival in San Francisco, were detained at the immigration station temporarily located on Silver Avenue (the Angel Island station was destroyed by fire in 1940). Their experience there was not very different from the ordeal suffered by women on Angel Island. My mother recalled:

> All of the women lived in the same large room. I think there were maybe twenty of us at the time. It was quite spacious. We would chitchat and talk a lot. Some of us would sew and read. That's about it. Other times we would become depressed because our future was so uncertain. Many of us did not know how long we would be detained and if we would set foot in San Francisco or not. Some of the women burned incense to ward off the evil spirits. Some were deported back to China. Two of the women I met there became my friends for life.

My parents, Tom Yip Jing and Jew Law Ying, and my eldest sister Bak Heong reunited in San Francisco, 1941. (Judy Yung collection)

The Tom/Yung family in 1954. *Front row, left to right:* Patricia, Jew Law Ying, Warren, Tom Yip Jing/Yung Hin Sen, Judy (author); *back row, left to right:* Sandra, Sharon, and Virginia. (Judy Yung collection)

There were at least two positive changes relative to Angel Island. According to my mother, the Chinese food at the Silver Avenue station was actually pretty good. For lunch and dinner, they always had soup and at least three different dishes to go with the rice. My father also sent her roast duck a number of times, and at the snack bar she was able to buy other Chinese food such as preserved bean cakes. The women, except for those who had failed the interrogation, were also free to come and go within the building—unlike at Angel Island, where they were locked inside their sleeping quarters.

Mother had memorized all the information concerning Dad's "paper son" side of the family with great trepidation, but for her the interrogation proved easier than expected. "They were more interested in the fact that my mother was an American citizen," she recalled. "They asked me more questions about my maternal side of the family. The entire interrogation took only half an hour. It was very simple. Everything was said through an interpreter."[2] Mom considered herself one of the lucky ones. "When I left, many of the women there were sad because they had been there so much longer than I, spending many days crying and feeling miserable."

Little did my mother know that her miserable days were just about to begin. She spent the first few years in Menlo Park, California, in a run-down house on the private estate of the Cowell family, for whom Dad worked as a gardener. "We had only a wood-burning stove and we slept in an old broken bed," she said. "Times were very hard then. I could hardly adjust. I remember crying so much because I was used to a more comfortable life [living with my grandparents] in Macao. We had servants to do everything [in Macao]. I never had to cook or chop wood before. Here there was no hot water and I had to wash all the clothes by hand." From sunrise to sunset, my mother picked suckers off flowers at one of our kinsmen's nurseries close by, making 25 cents an hour. "I would be paid at the end of the season, if the season was good," she said. "If it was a bad year, they would just owe me the money until the next year." When she was about to give birth to their second child, my father could not get her to the hospital in time because of the war curfew. An old midwife with trembling hands was called in, and Father assisted in the difficult birth. My second sister, Sandra—named See Heong ("thinking of the home village")—was thus born in circumstances far removed from the sterile hospital in Macao where Bak Heong (later named Sharon) came into the world.

By the time my mother was pregnant with their third child, the United States was deeply immersed in World War II. The family moved to San Francisco Chinatown to be closer to a modern hospital and so that my father could take advantage of the well-paying jobs in the shipyards. Mother began working in a Chinatown sweatshop, often bringing sewing home to do at night. My parents rented two rooms in a tenement. Although there was no kitchen, private bathroom, or running hot water, it was still an improvement over Menlo Park. Mother now had the comforts of an ethnic community and a network of relatives and friends close by. Virginia was born at the beginning of 1943, and Patricia at the end of that same year. I followed in 1946 and proved to be the lucky fifth daughter because I preceded the son my parents had so longed for. When my brother, Warren Tom Yung (note the middle name that honors my father's real surname), was a month old, my parents splurged and threw a Red Egg and Ginger banquet to announce his birth. And they stopped having children. (I have always been painfully aware of my possible nonexistence had my brother been born first.)

Ironically and tragically, Warren suffered an accident when he was nine years old and has since been institutionalized, confined to a wheelchair. When it became clear that he would never be able to sire children and continue the Tom family line, my mother sought solace in the Chinese Independent Baptist church. My father, however, could find no outlet for his despair. He never returned to China to pay homage to his ancestors as a filial son should. Instead it was we daughters who carried on the duties of the sons. We all worked through high school and afterward to help support the family. We took care of our parents in their old age. We represented the family at clan functions. We returned to China to worship the ancestors and sent money home to build a schoolhouse and to have our grandparents properly reburied. As the fifth daughter, I brought honor to the family name by being the first from our ancestral village to earn a doctorate. Since my father's death in 1987, we daughters have gone regularly to tend his grave at the local cemetery. We keep the lineage and stories alive, passing them on to the next generation. And those of us with children have broken tradition by celebrating every birth, regardless of gender. When my mother reflects on her bittersweet past, she recalls how our relatives used to ridicule her for bearing only girls. Now she proudly points out that her daughters have been as valuable as sons. "Just look at how good my daughters have been to me," she says. "My heart is totally satisfied."

As she had promised her mother, Mother worked hard as a seamstress to save enough to send for her two younger brothers. Although the Chinese Exclusion Act was finally repealed in 1943, the new law allowed only 105 immigrants a year from China. Many more Chinese, especially women, were able to come as non-quota immigrants under the War Brides Act of 1945, the Displaced Persons Act of 1948, and the Refugee Act of 1953. The easiest way for my mother, who was not yet a U.S. citizen, to get my Uncle Lurt to America was to buy papers for him to come as a son of a U.S. citizen. When that failed, she studied hard for six months and succeeded in becoming a naturalized citizen in 1964. The next year, Congress passed a new Immigration and Naturalization Act, which ended the restrictive quota system and placed China on an equal footing with other countries. Now that 20,000 persons per year were allowed to immigrate from China, my mother could begin the process of chain migration by bringing Uncle Lurt and his wife over from Hong Kong. Uncle Lurt, in turn, sent for his wife's parents, brother, and sister after he became a U.S. citizen. Then when China and the United States resumed full diplomatic relations in 1979, Uncle Lurt was able to help his brother, Haw, and his family immigrate directly from China. Thus, my mother fulfilled her promise. She wanted her three sisters to come too, but by the time they could emigrate after 1979, they declined to do so, saying they were too old to start over in America. So Mother has continued to send remittances home to help them. And in the last decade she has made repeated trips back to visit them in the village. Her only regret is that she was unable to provide for her parents in China. Upon her arrival in San Francisco in 1941, she immediately sent them the large sum of $100. Because of the war with Japan, however, she was unable to get any more money through to them. Both died of starvation before the war was over.

My mother's immigration to and life in America follow a pattern similar to that of Chinese women who preceded her, but with some different contours owing to the socioeconomic and historical circumstances of her time. Because of the Chinese Exclusion Act, she could only come as one of the exempt classes, and she had to endure detention and interrogation to prove her right to immigrate as a merchant's wife. It was not until the early 1950s, after political pressure was applied by the American Civil Liberties Union and Chinese American organizations because of reports of suicide by a number of despondent immigrant women, that the U.S. Immigration Service ceased the practice of detainment and began settling an immigrant's right to enter the country at the point of departure instead of the point of entry.

Although the World War II economy meant a good job for my father as a shipfitter, it was only a temporary situation. After the war he returned to being a laborer, or what he called "a mule's life." With no education or fluency in English, and handicapped by racism, the best he could do was land a job at the Mark Hopkins Hotel as a janitor; this enabled him to join the Service Employees Union and enjoy the benefits of union protection until he retired in 1968. It proved to be the best job he ever had—decent wages, regular hours, two-week vacations annually, health insurance, and a good pension plan.

My mother, however, with six children to support and a husband who was addicted to gambling for a period, had little choice but to work in a Chinatown sweatshop. The job allowed her flexible work hours, but it also exploited her by paying low piecework wages. Finding employment at a union shop in later years made no difference in terms of her wages, although it did mean set hours, medical coverage, and vacation and retirement benefits.[3] Like many other immigrant women, Mother sewed day and night while raising us children, trapped in Chinatown in a dead-end job because she never had a chance to learn English or acculturate into American society. One difference that set her life apart from the lives of her Chinese immigrant predecessors was that there was less of a gendered separation between the private and public spheres in the postwar years. Mother and her peers felt no qualms about appearing in public. They freely walked the streets of Chinatown and even went shopping downtown whenever they felt like it—usually with one of us in tow to serve as translator. On the whole, though, Mother was so busy working and taking care of us that she had little leisure time to socialize or engage in community activities. Her few pleasures were to attend the Chinese opera or movies and, later, to go to church on Sundays.

My mother's economic role had a direct impact on family gender relations. Although my father made twice as much money as she did, he always acknowledged her ability to contribute to the family income and her acumen in business affairs. (Against Father's wishes, she wisely invested in two flats in North Beach, the neighborhood adjacent to Chinatown, in the early 1960s.) Their marriage was an interdependent partnership, with priority always going to the well-being of the family. They shared decisions about our welfare, and Father was never ashamed to don an apron and help with the cooking, washing, and ironing. Mother ruled at home, controlling the pursestrings, disciplining us, and signing our report cards, but Father was always the head of the household in public, the spokesperson for the family in clan matters. Although the separation of public and private spheres had weakened over time, it remained in effect to a consistent degree: Mother always stayed home at night with us while Father went out to his tong to smoke the bamboo water pipe and socialize with his fraternal brothers.

With resumed immigration from China, Chinatown teemed with women and young children, and the community's restaurants and sweatshops benefited from the new supply of immigrant workers who, like my mother, lacked English-language and job skills to work or live anywhere but in Chinatown. In contrast, young war brides married to husbands who were somewhat educated and acculturated to American life did much better. The recipients of veteran's benefits, their husbands were able to provide for them, find housing outside Chinatown, and guide them in adjusting to life in the United States. Chinese students and professionals who had opted to remain in or come to America under the Displaced Persons or Refugee acts bypassed Chinatown altogether. Arriving at a time when attitudes and conditions were more favorable toward Chinese Americans than ever before and when their scientific and technical skills were in demand, they found work in academic and professional fields and housing in suburban communities away from Chinatown. This is not to say that racial discrimination against the Chinese ended. Although employment and housing discrimination was now illegal, Chinese Americans still experienced difficulties finding jobs commensurate with their abilities and assimilating into mainstream society. They were not always welcome as new homeowners in all-white neighborhoods or as members in certain elite social clubs.

By the 1950s, the public role of Chinese women was no longer questioned. But although they were very much a part of the labor force and public scene outside the home, they were still excluded from Chinatown's power structure. Women were yet to be made full-fledged members of the family, district, or fraternal organizations. No woman sat on the board of the Chinese Six Companies, Chinese Hospital, or Chinese American Citizens Alliance. As before, however, immigrant women of the educated, middle class continued to be active leaders in such gender-segregated organizations as the Chinese YWCA and Chinese Hospital Auxiliary. Although Protestant churches and associated organizations continued to work with Chinese women, offering them social activities and services in addition to salvation, they were not as effective as the Protestant missions of the Progressive era. Chinese nationalism, which had been the other influential force in women's emancipation, was also on the wane now that Chinese exclusion had come to an end and China had become Communist. The break in diplomatic relations between the United States and China, and the subsequent anti-Communist hysteria, forced many Chinese Americans to sever ties with their homeland and to desist in leftist political activities. Conservatism pervaded the community. Many people responded to the red-baiting tactics of this period by assuming a passive stance, coping through evasion rather than confrontation. Others sought to prove their loyalty to American democracy by supporting the Guomindang regime or engaging actively in partisan and electoral politics.

As in Jade Snow Wong's time, life as a second-generation Chinese American in San Francisco Chinatown during the Cold War era had its pluses and minuses. While we had the comforts of a safe, nurturing environment, we were often overprotected from the realities of racism and prevented from assimilating into mainstream society. Growing up in Chinatown meant attending a segregated public school with a Eurocentric curriculum taught by white teachers, and a Chinese language school where authoritarian teachers reinforced the values of unquestioned obedience, respect for the Confucian classics, and allegiance to Chiang Kai-shek's Republic of China. Among the benefits from such a dual education were bilingualism and biculturalism, and some of us developed a strong appreciation for our ethnic heritage. Yet there were costs as well: we were fit into a "model minority" mold, expected to work hard, become educated, and, by all means, not "rock the boat" or make the family, community, or the Chinese race "lose face."

Moreover, Chinese girls like myself were made consciously aware of our inferior status as females and our proper gender role as self-effacing homemakers. At home and in our limited social circles, boys were still favored over girls. My brother, Warren, always got the best servings of food at the dinner table. He had his own tricycle, while we five sisters shared a single pair of roller skates. My parents had big plans for his future, expecting him to finish college and become a doctor. As for us girls, it was considered enough that we finish high school and marry well, preferably with Chinese American men who could provide for us.

Our socialization in self-effacement was reinforced both at school and in the popular media. Women's history and contributions to society were not included in the public or Chinese school curriculums; nor was Chinese American history or the history of any minority group in the United States. In Chinese school, our role models were all male—patriotic heroes like Sun Yat-sen and Yue Fei; in public school, they were all white—George Washington, Abraham Lincoln, Florence Nightingale. Positive images of minorities and women were equally absent in the popular mass media. Hollywood moved from the China Doll and Dragon Lady roles portrayed by Anna May Wong to that of the sexy, subservient prostitute played by Nancy Kwan in *The World of Suzie Wong*. With billboards and magazines projecting the American standard of beauty as blonde, blue eyed, and big breasted, Chinese American women received a message of inferiority as strong as that conveyed at home. In spite of all of this, many of my peers strove to be all-American, participating in integrated high school club activities and competing to be cheerleaders, student body officers, and prom queens. Others of us chose to become socially active in the Chinese YWCA, Cameron House, Protestant churches, or Chinese language schools. But like the second generation of pre–World War II days, even as we sought to become assimilated into mainstream society, our physical features and our home and social life were constant reminders of our cultural differences, of our perceived racial and gender inferiority.

The combined forces of race, class, and gender oppression hit us in the face as soon as we left the safe environment of Chinatown. Our parents had drilled education and hard work into us, but, as our predecessors also discovered, the promised rewards did not always materialize. In high school, non-Chinese classmates sometimes made fun of our food and customs, called us names like "Chink" or "Suzie Wong," and didn't hesitate to beat us up if they felt like it. Although discrimination had lessened after the war and educational and employment opportunities were better than ever for the second generation (a larger proportion of Chinese American women, as compared to white women, were graduating from college, and increasing numbers of Chinese American women were moving up into the technical, sales, and professional fields), many of us still carried the double burden of being a minority within a minority in the labor market. Our predecessors had paved the way for us during the war by their proven efficiency as clerical workers in private firms outside Chinatown. But now, stereotyped as obedient "office wives," Chinese American women found themselves stuck at the clerical level, unable to move up the ladder into management. Women who entered new fields of work, such as art, science, business, law, and literature, found they had to work twice as hard in order to be considered equal. Statistics also showed that the earning power of Chinese American women was not commensurate with their level of education. In fact, the better educated we became, the further our incomes fell behind relative to white men, white women, and Chinese American men with the same educational background. Moreover, Chinese American women were noticeably underrepresented in jobs that required public contact and decision-making skills. There were more Chinese female accountants, nurses, and health technicians than lawyers, business executives, and physicians.[4]

Considering these limitations, it is not surprising that two of my sisters, Sharon and Patricia, got married right after finishing high school, while Virginia and I took the traditional female routes of becoming a schoolteacher and a librarian, respectively. Only Sandra followed a different drumbeat, choosing to pursue a master's degree in recreation and become a playground director. Much to my parents' relief, all of us married Chinese Americans with secure jobs (interracial dating and marriage were still taboo in the Chinatown community in the 1960s) and made our homes in the San Francisco Bay Area. In contrast to my mother's arranged marriage, however, all of us followed Western courtship and Chinese American wedding customs. None of us married wealthy men; as a result, we took on dual roles as wage earners and homemakers. Nevertheless, compared to the previous generation, we led lives that were much better balanced in terms of work, family, and social responsibilities; and our gender relations were much more companionate and equitable. As far as my parents were concerned, we had realized the American dream. We were part of the middle class, financially secure in our jobs, and living in two-car-garage homes outside Chinatown.

Yet our complacency was about to be shaken. The civil rights movement of the 1960s changed the course of history for all racial minorities, with reverberations felt by women, homosexuals, and the disabled further down the road. Dr. Martin Luther King Jr., preaching nonviolent civil disobedience, inspired black Americans and supporters all over the country to demand civil rights and social justice. Their peaceful demonstrations, as well as the riots that soon engulfed our cities, pressured Congress to pass legislation that prohibited discrimination in public accommodations, employment, and electoral politics. In an attempt to remedy past discriminatory practices, affirmative action programs were instituted to encourage increased representation of minorities in both the private and public sectors. Under President Lyndon B. Johnson's Great Society program, federal funds were allocated to provide social services to poverty-stricken minority communities. The black power movement further shook up the country, instilling in racial minorities a new sense of ethnic pride.

Among the inspired and the empowered were Chinese Americans. Those of us attending college at the time reached a new awareness of racial and class oppression in our own lives and of its links to other Third World communities within and countries outside the United States. Moved to act on our political consciousness, we banded together with blacks, Chicanos, Native Americans, and other Asian Americans to demand racial justice, an end to the Vietnam War, and the establishment of ethnic studies at San Francisco State College and the University of California, Berkeley. Many of us returned to Chinatown as community activists to organize and agitate for improvements in the working and living conditions there.[5] One piece of liberal legislation to come out of the civil rights period was the Immigration and Naturalization Act of 1965. As a direct result of that act, the Chinese American population doubled between 1960 and 1970, and again in the next decade, and the sex ratio finally approached parity (see appendix table 1). With priority going to family reunification, many of the new immigrants from the Guangdong area chose to settle in Chinatown, compounding already existing ghetto conditions. The mass media and the Chinatown establishment could no longer mask the fact that the community was undergoing tremendous social transformation as a result of increased immigration and that social problems of juvenile delinquency, labor exploitation, poor housing, and mental illness were threatening to break the calm face of the gilded ghetto, San Francisco's most prized tourist attraction.

Unlike earlier immigrants, the large numbers of women and families who came after the 1965 act benefited from the antipoverty programs that were established under the Johnson administration. Newly created federally funded agencies such as the Economic Opportunity Council, Chinese Newcomers Service Center, and Self-Help for the Elderly helped the newcomers learn English, acquire job skills, and adapt to life in America. In addition, a number of grass-roots organizations such as the Chinese Progressive Association and Asian Community Center took up the task of addressing political and labor issues in the community. In contrast to the male-dominated, conservative Chinatown establishment, these new organizations were often headed by bilingual Chinese Americans—many of them women—who knew how to utilize protest tactics and government funding to achieve social gains. Indeed, the 1970s saw a resurgence of the political left in Chinatown, which openly challenged the Guomindang-controlled status quo. Demonstrations became a common occurrence as immigrant and American-born men and women worked together to demand a fair share of public funding for needed social services or to protest poor working conditions in Chinatown restaurants and garment shops. The 1974 strike against the Great Chinese American (Jung Sai) Company, owned by Esprit de Corps, lasted longer than even the 1938 strike against National Dollar Stores. More than one hundred garment workers and their supporters picketed the factory for six months to protest unsanitary working conditions and interference with union activities. Like National Dollar Stores, Esprit responded by shutting the plant down. This time, with the help of the ILGWU, the women workers persisted in fighting their employer in the courts; they finally won a favorable settlement nine years later in 1983.

Although quite aware of the women's liberation movement, which followed on the heels of the civil rights movement, few Chinese American women joined in, primarily because the movement generally ignored the concerns of minority and working-class women. Nevertheless, many Chinese American women benefited from the feminists' campaign for equal pay, the widening of career choices, and the improved image gained for women as a group. Considered "double minorities," we were often sought after by universities and employers to fill affirmative action quotas in fields such as broadcast journalism, academia, construction, and law enforcement. Combined with our keen awareness of the revolutionary role of women in Communist China, who reputedly held up "half of heaven," the image of the liberated American woman moved us to take pride in our identity as Chinese American women and to link up with other Asian American and Third World women to address common issues of concern. Others of us were motivated to break our silence, reclaim our history, come out of the closet, and express ourselves in creative ways, whether it be in writing, film, dance, art, or music.

Thanks in part to the valuable training ground of minority and women's political movements and in part to improved U.S.-Chinese relations, the 1970s also saw a boost in the status of Chinese American women and their increased participation in community and mainstream politics. Events in China continued to influence our status, political ideals, and self-esteem. The normalization of relations between China and the United States meant not only a reconnection to the homeland, but also a more positive attitude toward Chinese culture and Chinese Americans on the part of the American public. During the 1970s, many community activists urged that we emulate China's progressive policies regarding the status of women and the working class. Thus encouraged, Chinese American women became increasingly active in mainstream politics as contributors, campaigners, and political candidates. California secretary of state March Fong Eu led the way when she became the first Chinese American woman to hold a state office in 1974. She was followed by Lillian Sing, who was appointed California Municipal Court judge in 1981; Julie Tang, who was elected to the San Francisco Community College Board in 1981; Mabel Teng, who was elected to the San Francisco Board of Supervisors in 1994; and Angie Fa, the first Chinese American lesbian to join the San Francisco School Board in 1992.

All of these changes have certainly made a difference for women like my mother, who today basks in her retirement, comfortable in her paid-off North Beach flat and surrounded by pictures of her grandchildren who have finished college and have families of their own. As a senior citizen, she takes advantage of the discounted bus fares and senior meals. She has also become an avid television fan because of the many Cantonese programs now available to immigrants like herself. With more time to pursue her own interests and contribute to her community, she is an active elder in the Chinese Independent Baptist church, in charge of making home visits to members in need. On her own, she has also joined tour groups and traveled to Europe, Mexico, Canada, Japan, and the Holy Land. When I asked her if she was glad she had come to America, she first echoed Great-Grandmother's sentiments: "To me, life was a lot easier in Macao. Life was so hectic here with so many children born close together and no help. America was not the heaven I expected it to be." But on further reflection, she said: "I have since traveled around a bit, and to me, America is the best country to live in. Why? Because we have our freedom here, the weather's better than in China, and food is cheap and plentiful. No matter where I go, there is no place like San Francisco."

The groundwork laid by our foremothers for a better life at home, in the workplace, and in the larger society has not been lost on today's generation of Chinese American women. Despite media reports of our success as a model minority group, we are painfully aware that racism and sexism must still be combatted, that not all of us have attained the American dream of equality and socioeconomic success. Consciously aware of how race, class, and gender intersect in our lives, we follow in our mothers' footsteps, doing what we can to improve the overall quality of life for ourselves, for our children, and for all.

Appendix

Table 1 *Chinese Population in the United States by Sex, 1860–1990*

	Total Number	Male	Female	Males per 100 Females
1860	34,933	33,149	1,784	1,858.1
1870	63,199	58,633	4,566	1,284.1
1880	105,465	100,686	4,779	2,106.8
1890	107,488	103,620	3,868	2,678.9
1900	89,863	85,341	4,522	1,887.2
1910	71,531	66,856	4,675	1,430.1
1920	61,639	53,891	7,748	695.5
1930	74,954	59,802	15,152	394.7
1940	77,504	57,389	20,115	285.3
1950	117,629	77,008	40,621	189.6
1960	237,292	135,549	101,743	133.2
1970	431,583	226,733	204,850	110.7
1980	806,040	407,544	398,496	102.3
1990	1,648,696	821,542	827,154	99.3

SOURCE: U.S. Census Bureau publications.

Table 2 *Chinese Immigrants Admitted, by Sex, 1853–1975*

	Total Number	Males		Females	
		Number	*Percent*	*Number*	*Percent*
1853	42	42	100.0	0	0.0
1854	13,100	12,427	94.9	673	5.1
1855	3,526	3,524	99.9	2	0.1
1856	4,733	4,717	99.7	16	0.3
1857	5,944	5,492	92.4	452	7.6
1858	5,128	4,808	93.8	320	6.2
1859	3,457	2,990	86.5	467	13.5
1860	5,467	5,438	99.5	29	0.5
1861	7,518	7,003	93.1	515	6.9
1862	3,633	2,983	82.1	650	17.9
1863	7,214	7,213	99.9	1	0.1
1864	2,975	2,811	94.5	164	5.5
1865	2,942	2,932	99.7	10	0.3
1866	2,385	2,380	99.8	5	0.2
1867	3,863	3,859	99.9	4	0.1
1868	5,157	5,111	99.1	46	0.9
1869	12,874	11,900	92.4	974	7.6
1870	15,740	14,624	92.9	1,116	7.1
1871	7,135	6,786	95.1	349	4.9
1872	7,788	7,605	97.7	183	2.3
1873	20,292	19,403	95.6	889	4.4
1874	13,776	13,533	98.2	243	1.8
1875	16,437	16,055	97.7	382	2.3
1876	22,781	22,521	98.9	260	1.1
1877	10,594	10,518	99.3	76	0.7
1878	8,992	8,641	96.1	351	3.9
1879	9,604	9,264	96.5	340	3.5
1880	5,802	5,732	98.8	70	1.2
1881	11,890	11,815	99.4	75	0.6
1882	39,579	39,463	99.7	116	0.3
1883	8,031	7,987	99.5	44	0.5
1884	279	241	86.4	38	13.6
1885	22	12	54.5	10	45.5
1886	40	25	62.5	15	37.5
1887	10	8	80.0	2	20.0
1888	26	21	80.8	5	19.2
1889	118	90	76.3	28	23.7
1890	1,716	1,401	81.6	315	18.4
1891	2,836	2,608	92.0	228	8.0
1892–95[a]	N/A	N/A	N/A	N/A	N/A
1896	1,441	1,382	95.9	59	4.1
1897	3,363	3,334	99.1	29	0.9
1898	2,071	2,061	99.5	10	0.5
1899	1,638	1,627	99.3	11	0.7
1900	1,250	1,241	99.3	9	0.7
1901	2,452	2,413	98.4	39	1.6

Table 2 *(continued)*

	Total Number	Males		Females	
		Number	*Percent*	*Number*	*Percent*
1902	1,631	1,587	97.3	44	2.7
1903	2,192	2,152	98.2	40	1.8
1904	4,327	4,209	97.3	118	2.7
1905	1,971	1,883	95.5	88	4.5
1906	1,485	1,397	94.1	88	5.9
1907	770	706	91.7	64	8.3
1908	1,263	1,177	93.2	86	6.8
1909	1,841	1,706	92.7	135	7.3
1910	1,770	1,598	90.3	172	9.7
1911	1,307	1,124	86.0	183	14.0
1912	1,608	1,367	85.0	241	15.0
1913	2,022	1,692	83.7	330	16.3
1914	2,354	2,052	87.2	302	12.8
1915	2,469	2,182	88.4	287	11.6
1916	2,239	1,962	87.6	277	12.4
1917	1,843	1,563	84.8	280	15.2
1918	1,576	1,276	81.0	300	19.0
1919	1,697	1,425	84.0	272	16.0
1920	2,148	1,719	80.0	429	20.0
1921	4,017	3,304	82.3	713	17.7
1922	4,465	3,622	81.1	843	18.9
1923	4,074	3,239	79.5	835	20.5
1924	4,670	3,732	79.9	938	20.1
1925	1,721	1,526	88.7	195	11.3
1926	1,375	1,182	86.0	193	14.0
1927	1,051	830	79.0	221	21.0
1928	931	668	71.8	263	28.2
1929	1,071	800	74.7	271	25.3
1930	970	721	74.3	249	25.7
1931	748	523	69.9	225	30.1
1932	534	317	58.2	228	41.8
1933–47[a]	N/A	N/A	N/A	N/A	N/A
1948	3,574	257	7.2	3,317	92.8
1949	2,490	242	9.7	2,248	90.3
1950	1,289	110	8.5	1,179	91.5
1951	1,083	126	11.6	957	88.4
1952	1,152	118	10.2	1,034	89.8
1953	1,093	203	18.6	890	81.4
1954	2,747	1,511	55.0	1,236	45.0
1955	2,628	1,261	48.0	1,367	52.0
1956	4,450	2,007	46.0	2,443	54.0
1957	5,123	2,487	48.5	2,636	51.5
1958	3,195	1,396	44.0	1,799	56.0
1959	6,031	2,846	47.2	3,185	52.8
1960	3,672	1,873	51.0	1,799	49.0
1961	3,517	1,418	40.3	2,099	59.7

Table 2 *(continued)*

	Total Number	Males		Females	
		Number	*Percent*	*Number*	*Percent*
1962	4,669	1,916	41.0	2,753	59.0
1963	5,370	2,297	42.8	3,073	57.2
1964	5,648	2,597	46.0	3,051	54.0
1965	4,769	2,242	47.0	2,527	53.0
1966	17,608	8,613	48.9	8,995	51.1
1967	25,096	12,811	51.0	12,285	49.0
1968	16,434	7,862	47.8	8,572	52.2
1969	20,893	10,001	47.9	10,892	52.1
1970	17,956	8,586	47.8	9,370	52.2
1971	17,622	8,287	47.0	9,335	53.0
1972	21,730	10,437	48.0	11,293	52.0
1973	21,656	9,937	45.9	11,719	54.1
1974	22,685	10,724	47.3	11,961	52.7
1975	23,427	11,179	47.7	12,248	52.3

SOURCE: Fu-ju Liu, "A Comparative Demographic Study of Native-born and Foreign-born Chinese Populations in the United States" (Ph.D. diss., School of Graduate Studies of Michigan, 1953), p. 223; and Helen Chen, "Chinese Immigration into the United States: An Analysis of Changes in Immigration Policies" (Ph.D. diss., Brandeis University, 1980), p. 201.

[a] Numbers in 1892–95 and 1933–47 not reported for Chinese.

Table 3   *Chinese Population in San Francisco by Sex, 1900–1950*

	Total Number	Male	Female	Males per 100 Females
1900	13,954	11,818	2,136	553.3
1910	10,582	9,235	1,347	685.6
1920	7,744	6,020	1,724	349.2
1930	16,303	12,033	4,270	281.8
1940	17,782	12,264	5,518	222.2
1950	24,813	15,595	9,218	169.2

SOURCE: U.S. Census Bureau publications.

Table 4 *Marital Status of Chinese Females (15 years of age and over) in San Francisco by Nativity, 1900–1920*

Nativity and Census Year	Total Number	Single		Married		Widowed		Divorced		Unknown	
		Number	*Percent*	*Number*	*Percent*	*Number*	*Percent*	*Number*	*Percent*	*Number*	*Percent*
All classes											
1900	1,511	424	28.0	941	62.3	146	9.7	0	0.0	0	0.0
1910	916	208	22.7	619	67.6	85	9.3	1	0.1	3	0.3
1920	952	224	23.5	596	62.6	127	13.4	0	0.0	5	0.5
Native-born											
1900	614	273	44.4	324	52.8	17	2.8	0	0.0	0	0.0
1910	475	160	33.7	287	60.4	26	5.5	0	0.0	2	0.4
1920	467	181	38.7	231	49.5	50	10.7	0	0.0	5	1.1
Foreign-born											
1900	897	151	16.8	617	68.8	129	14.4	0	0.0	0	0.0
1910	438	47	10.7	330	75.4	59	13.5	1	0.2	1	0.2
1920	485	43	8.9	365	75.2	77	15.9	0	0.0	0	0.0

SOURCE: My tally from U.S. National Archives, Record Group 29, "Census of U.S. Population" (manuscript), 1900, 1910, 1920.

Table 5 *Illiteracy of Chinese Females (10 years of age and over) in San Francisco by Nativity, 1900–1920*

	1900			1910			1920		
	Total Number	*Illiterate*		*Total Number*	*Illiterate*		*Total Number*	*Illiterate*	
		Number	Percent		Number	Percent		Number	Percent
Native-born	790	606	76.7	574	201	35.0	595	80	13.4
Foreign-born	904	791	87.9	460	218	47.4	511	235	46.0
TOTAL	1,694	1,397	82.5	1,038	419	40.4	1,106	315	28.5

SOURCE: My tally from U.S. National Archives, Record Group 29, "Census of U.S. Population" (manuscript), 1900, 1910, 1920.

NOTE: "Illiteracy" refers to the inability to write in any language.

Table 6 *Occupations of Chinese Women (10 years of age and over) in San Francisco by Nativity, 1900–1920*

	1900		1910		1920	
	Number	*Percent*	*Number*	*Percent*	*Number*	*Percent*
FOREIGN-BORN WOMEN						
Professional service	*6*	*1.7*	*1*	*.9*	*4*	*3.9*
Teacher	0		1		2	
Nurse/midwife	6		0		0	
Other	0		0		2	
Business	*4*	*1.2*	*1*	*.9*	*14*	*13.7*
Merchant	3		1		2	
Manager	1		0		2	
Clerk	0		0		3	
Saleswoman	0		0		2	
Other	0		0		5	
Manufacturing	*145*	*42.2*	*40*	*37.4*	*37*	*36.3*
Seamstress	143		40		36	
Other	2		0		1	
Domestic and personal service	*41*	*11.9*	*13*	*12.1*	*47*	*46.1*
Cook	12		2		3	
Servant	22		6		6	
Shrimp peeler	0		1		1	
Hairdresser	3		1		0	
Laborer	2		1		7	
Housekeeper[a]	1		2		29	
Other	1		0		1	
Prostitution	*148*	*43.0*	*52*	*48.6*	*0*	*0.0*
Prostitute (listed)	115		0		0	
Prostitute (probable)[b]	33		52		0	
TOTAL	344	100.0	107	99.9	102	100.0
NATIVE-BORN WOMEN						
Professional service	*2*	*.6*	*3*	*2.4*	*5*	*4.4*
Teacher	0		1		0	
Nurse	2		2		3	
Other	0		0		2	
Business	*0*	*.0*	*6*	*4.8*	*29*	*25.7*
Merchant	0		1		2	
Clerk	0		0		8	
Saleswoman	0		0		11	
Telephone operator	0		4		5	
Other	0		1		3	

Table 6 *(continued)*

	1900		1910		1920	
	Number	*Percent*	*Number*	*Percent*	*Number*	*Percent*
NATIVE-BORN WOMEN						
Manufacturing	98	31.6	53	42.1	41	36.3
Seamstress	98		53		37	
Other	0		0		4	
Domestic and personal service	19	6.1	24	19.0	38	33.6
Cook	2		1		5	
Servant	12		5		4	
Waitress	0		0		7	
Hairdresser	4		9		0	
Shrimp peeler	0		5		1	
Laborer	1		0		5	
Housekeeper[a]	0		1		14	
Other	0		3		2	
Prostitution	191	61.6	40	31.7	0	.0
Prostitute (listed)	159		7		0	
Prostitute (probable)[b]	32		33		0	
TOTAL	310	99.9	126	100.0	113	100.0

SOURCE: My tally from U.S. National Archives, Record Group 29, "Census of U.S. Population" (manuscript), 1900, 1910, 1920.

[a] These were housekeepers who worked in their own homes.

[b] Probable prostitutes are women I suspect to be prostitutes based on their living arrangements—three or more single, young women living in all-female households and with no stated occupations.

Table 7 *Occupations of Chinese Male Heads (with a female present in the household) in San Francisco, 1900–1920*

	1900		1910		1920	
	Number	*Percent*	*Number*	*Percent*	*Number*	*Percent*
Professional service	*64*	*7.5*	*31*	*5.5*	*39*	*8.6*
Actor	5		0		0	
Dentist	5		3		7	
Interpreter	7		6		6	
Journalist	3		6		4	
Physician, druggist	31		8		6	
Other	13		8		16	
Trade, clerical	*412*	*48.1*	*307*	*54.9*	*264*	*58.1*
Agent	11		6		4	
Banker	16		2		3	
Boarding housekeeper	9		5		0	
Bookkeeper	8		12		11	
Brothel keeper	37		9		0	
Clerk	5		5		19	
Labor contractor	5		3		0	
Laundryman	17		9		7	
Manager	14		78		77	
Merchant, grocer	229		104		98	
Peddler	7		1		1	
Restaurateur	12		5		1	
Salesman	11		55		37	
Teamster	11		3		2	
Other	20		10		4	
Artisan, manufacturer	*150*	*17.5*	*57*	*10.2*	*26*	*5.7*
Cigarmaker	27		3		1	
Garment manufacturer	45		14		7	
Jeweler	8		4		5	
Machinist	1		6		0	
Shoemaker	18		1		0	
Tailor	31		24		9	
Other	20		5		4	
Agriculture	*42*	*4.9*	*12*	*2.1*	*8*	*1.8*
Cannery worker	17		2		1	
Farmer	10		6		6	
Fisherman	7		2		0	
Other	8		2		1	
Domestic and personal service	*174*	*20.3*	*128*	*22.9*	*117*	*25.8*
Cook	93		54		51	
Janitor	7		1		5	
Laborer	51		55		38	

Table 7 *(continued)*

	1900		1910		1920	
	Number	*Percent*	*Number*	*Percent*	*Number*	*Percent*
Porter	3		7		5	
Servant	6		0		0	
Seaman	9		3		2	
Waiter	2		6		13	
Other	3		2		3	
TOTAL	856	99.9	559	99.9	454	100.0

SOURCE: My tally from U.S. National Archives, Record Group 29, "Census of U.S. Population" (manuscript), 1900, 1910, 1920.

Table 8 *Nativity Status of Chinese Americans in the United States by Sex, 1900–1950*

Year	Both Sexes			Male			Female		
	Total	Native-born	Foreign-born	Total	Native-born	Foreign-born	Total	Native-born	Foreign-born
1900	89,863	9,010 (10.0%)	80,853 (90.0%)	85,341	6,657 (7.8%)	78,684 (92.2%)	4,522	2,353 (52.0%)	2,169 (48.0%)
1910	71,531	14,935 (20.9%)	56,596 (79.1%)	66,856	11,921 (17.8%)	54,935 (82.2%)	4,675	3,014 (64.5%)	1,661 (35.5%)
1920	61,639	18,532 (30.1%)	43,107 (69.9%)	53,891	13,318 (24.7%)	40,573 (75.3%)	7,748	5,214 (67.3%)	2,534 (32.7%)
1930	74,954	30,868 (41.2%)	44,086 (58.8%)	59,802	20,693 (34.0%)	39,109 (66.0%)	15,152	10,175 (67.2%)	4,977 (32.8%)
1940	77,504	40,262 (51.9%)	37,242 (48.1%)	57,389	25,702 (44.8%)	31,687 (55.2%)	20,115	14,560 (72.4%)	5,555 (27.6%)
1950	117,629	45,790 (38.9%)	71,839 (61.1%)	77,008	25,219 (32.7%)	51,789 (67.3%)	40,621	20,571 (50.6%)	20,050 (49.4%)

SOURCE: U.S. Dept. of Commerce, Bureau of the Census, *Sixteenth Census of the United States. Population: 1940*, vol. 2, pt. 1, table 4, p. 19; idem, *Seventeenth Census of the United States. Census of the Population: 1950*, vol. 4, pt. 3, chap. B, table 29, p. 3B–87.

NOTE: The percentage of native-born Chinese Americans in San Francisco was approximately the same as for the country as a whole.

Table 9 *Nativity Status of Chinese Females in San Francisco, 1900–1940*

	1900		1910		1920		1930		1940	
	Number	*Percent*	*Number*	*Percent*	*Number*	*Percent*	*Number*	*Percent*	*Number*	*Percent*
Native-born	1,207	56.8	856	63.9	1,110	67.6	2,930	68.6	4,141	75.0
Foreign-born	914	43.0	478	35.7	532	32.4	1,340	31.4	1,377	25.0
Unknown	4	.2	5	.4	0	.0	0	.0	0	.0
TOTAL	2,125	100.0	1,339	100.0	1,642	100.0	4,270	100.0	5,518	100.0

SOURCE: 1900, 1910, 1920 figures are based on my tally from U.S. National Archives, Record Group 29, "Census of U.S. Population" (manuscript), 1900, 1910, 1920. U.S. Census Bureau publications recorded 2,136, 1,347, and 1,724 Chinese females in San Francisco in 1900, 1910, and 1920, respectively. 1930, 1940 figures are from U.S. Dept. of Commerce, Bureau of the Census, *Sixteenth Census of the United States. Population: 1940*, vol. 2, pt. 1, table F-36, p. 658.

Table 10 *Distribution of American-born Chinese College Graduates by Sex and by Date of Graduation, University of California, Berkeley, 1920–1942*

Date of Graduation	Male Graduates		Female Graduates		Ratio of Males to Females
	Number	Percent	Number	Percent	
1920–24	22	9.0	8	8.6	2.7
1925–29	30	12.3	10	10.8	3.0
1930–34	34	13.9	18	19.4	1.9
1935–39	79	32.4	30	32.2	2.6
1940–42	79	32.4	27	29.0	2.9
TOTAL	244	100.0	93	100.0	2.6

SOURCE: Beulah Ong Kwoh, "Occupational Status of the American-born Chinese Graduates" (Master's thesis, University of Chicago, 1947), p. 13.

Table 11 *Occupations by Race and Sex, San Francisco, 1940*

	White Males		White Females		Chinese Males		Chinese Females		Black Males		Black Females	
	Number	*Percent*	*Number*	*Percent*	*Number*	*Percent*	*Number*	*Percent*	*Number*	*Percent*	*Number*	*Percent*
Professional, Semiprofessional	13,519	7.5	11,302	14.4	217	3.7	68	7.4	32	2.8	20	2.8
Manager, Proprietor	24,109	13.5	4,956	6.3	744	12.5	32	3.5	33	2.9	11	1.6
Clerical, Sales	41,991	23.4	35,719	45.4	1,024	17.2	179	19.5	79	7.0	12	1.7
Crafts	28,470	15.9	897	1.1	175	2.9	4	0.4	53	4.7	3	0.4
Operative	27,909	15.6	9,631	12.2	999	16.8	384	41.8	112	9.9	18	2.5
Domestic service	331	0.2	5,793	7.4	780	13.1	84	9.1	37	3.3	453	63.8
Other service	26,859	15.0	9,396	11.9	1,800	30.2	155	16.9	601	53.0	178	25.1
Laborer	14,698	8.2	353	0.4	186	3.1	6	0.7	174	15.3	5	0.7
Unreported	1,208	0.7	700	0.9	28	0.5	6	0.7	12	1.1	10	1.4
TOTAL	179,094	100.0	78,747	100.0	5,953	100.0	918	100.0	1,133	100.0	710	100.0

SOURCE: U.S. Dept. of Commerce, Bureau of the Census, *Sixteenth Census of the United States. Population: 1940*, vol. 3, pt. 2, table 13, pp. 268–69, 272; vol. 2, pt. 1, table 32, p. 97.

Table 12 *Occupations by Race and Sex, San Francisco–Oakland, 1950*

	White Males		White Females		Chinese Males		Chinese Females		Black Males		Black Females	
	Number	*Percent*	*Number*	*Percent*	*Number*	*Percent*	*Number*	*Percent*	*Number*	*Percent*	*Number*	*Percent*
Professional, Technical	61,703	11.4	37,264	15.1	640	6.3	243	7.7	671	2.1	616	3.4
Manager, Proprietor	84,793	15.6	15,335	6.2	1,935	19.1	174	5.5	862	2.7	331	1.9
Clerical, Sales	99,685	18.4	124,781	50.5	1,827	18.0	1,421	45.3	2,498	7.7	1,907	10.7
Crafts	123,049	22.7	3,779	1.5	622	6.2	15	0.5	3,644	11.3	152	0.8
Operative	83,385	15.4	24,874	10.1	1,430	14.1	851	27.1	6,120	19.0	2,497	14.0
Domestic service	688	0.1	9,261	3.8	404	4.0	88	2.8	286	0.9	6,561	36.7
Other service	41,298	7.6	27,013	10.9	2,851	28.2	291	9.3	5,974	18.6	4,988	27.9
Laborer	42,720	7.9	1,693	0.7	316	3.1	23	0.7	11,733	36.5	611	3.4
Unreported	5,003	0.9	3,029	1.2	104	1.0	34	1.1	388	1.2	221	1.2
TOTAL	542,324	100.0	247,029	100.0	10,129	100.0	3,140	100.0	32,176	100.0	17,884	100.0

SOURCE: U.S. Dept. of Commerce, Bureau of the Census, *Seventeenth Census of the United States. Census of the Population: 1950*, vol. 2, pt. 5, table 77, pp. 5-356–58; vol. 4, pt. 3, chap. B, table 23, p. 3B-80.

Notes

Introduction

1. Sucheng Chan, "Chinese American Entrepreneur: The California Career of Chin Lung," *Chinese America: History and Perspectives 1987* (San Francisco, Chinese Historical Society of America), pp. 73–86; Ruthanne Lum McCunn, *Chinese American Portraits: Personal Histories, 1828–1988* (San Francisco: Chronicle Books, 1988), pp. 88–97; Jew Law Ying, interview with author, September 7, 1982, and January 14, 1987; Chin Lung, folder 12017/38498, and Leong Shee, folder 12017/37232, Chinese Departure Case Files, San Francisco District Office, Immigration and Naturalization Service, Record Group 85, National Archives, San Bruno, Calif. (hereafter cited as CDCF-SFDO).

2. Law Ying Yung, interview with author, August 15, 1992; Chin Mee Ngon, folder 19380/8-6, CDCF-SFDO.

3. Tom Yip Jing, interview with author, April 17, 1977, and November 20, 1986; Yung Hin Sen, folder 12017/51188, CDCF-SFDO. A "paper son" was a person posing as the son of a merchant or U.S. citizen, two of the exempt classes permitted entry to the United States during the Exclusion period (1882–1943).

4. Jew Law Ying, interview with author, January 14, 1987.

5. Important race theories that ignore gender include Robert E. Park's race relations cycle (see *Race and Culture* [New York: Free Press, 1950]); Robert Blauner's internal colonialism model (see *Racial Oppression in America* [New York: Harper & Row, 1972]); and Michael Omi and Howard Winant's theory of racial formation (see *Racial Formation in the United States from the 1960s to the 1980s* [New York: Routledge & Kegan Paul, 1986]). Important feminist theories that ignore race include Michelle Rosaldo's theory of private/public asymmetry (see "Woman, Culture, and Society: A Theoretical Overview," in *Woman, Culture, and Society,* ed. Michelle Zimbalist Rosaldo and Louise Lamphere [Stanford: Stanford University Press, 1974], pp. 17–42); and Heidi Hartmann's Marxist feminist model (see "Capitalism, Patriarchy, and Job Segregation by Sex," *Signs: Journal of Women in Culture and Society* 1, no. 3 [spring 1976]: 137–70).

6. See Angela Davis, *Women, Race, and Class* (New York: Random House,

1981); bell hooks, *Feminist Theory: From Margin to Center* (Boston: South End Press, 1984); and Bettina Aptheker, *Woman's Legacy: Essays on Race, Sex, and Class in American History* (Amherst: University of Massachusetts Press, 1982).

7. See Evelyn Nakano Glenn, "Racial Ethnic Women's Labor: The Intersection of Race, Gender, and Class Oppression," *Review of Radical Political Economics* 17, no. 3 (1985): 86–108.

8. See Evelyn Brooks Higginbotham, "African-American Women's History and the Metalanguage of Race," *Signs: Journal of Women in Culture and Society* 17, no. 2 (1992): 251–73; Chandra Talpade Mohanty, Ann Russo, and Lourdes Torres, eds., *Third World Women and the Politics of Feminism* (Bloomington: Indiana University Press, 1991); Maxine Baca Zinn and Bonnie Thornton Dill, eds., *Women of Color in U.S. Society* (Philadelphia: Temple University Press, 1994); Vicki L. Ruiz and Ellen Carol DuBois, *Unequal Sisters: A Multicultural Reader in U.S. Women's History* (New York: Routledge, 1994); Gloria Anzaldua, ed., *Making Face, Making Soul, Haciendo Caras: Creative and Critical Perspectives by Women of Color* (San Francisco: Aunt Lute Foundation, 1990); and Maria Jaschok and Suzanne Miers, eds., *Women and Chinese Patriarchy: Submission, Servitude, and Escape* (Hong Kong: Hong Kong University Press, 1994).

9. See Howard S. Levy, *Chinese Footbinding: The History of a Curious Erotic Custom* (New York: Walton Rawls, 1966).

10. In choosing to use the theme of footbinding to frame my study, I do not mean to lend support to the Orientalist obsession with the "victim script" of bound feet, which, as China scholars like Dorothy Ko and Susan Mann rightfully point out, have for too long dominated research on gender relations in Chinese history. Recent research on Chinese women writers and women's work in the household economy before the modern era show all too well that a significant number of women, far from being oppressed victims, did not allow their bound feet to silence their voices or hinder their productive labor. See Dorothy Ko, *Teachers of the Inner Chambers: Women and Culture in Seventeenth-Century China* (Stanford: Stanford University Press, 1994); Susan Mann, "Learned Women in the Eighteenth Century," in *Engendering China: Women, Culture, and the State*, ed. Gail Hershatter, Lisa Rofel, and Christina Gilmartin (Cambridge, Mass.: Harvard University Press, 1994), pp. 27–46; and Li Yu-ning, "Historical Roots of Changes in Women's Status in Modern China," in *Chinese Women Through Chinese Eyes*, ed. Li Yu-ning (Armonk, N.Y.: M. E. Sharpe, 1992), pp. 102–22.

11. For examples of immigration studies that refute the modernization theory that premodern immigrants to America eventually all abandon Old World traditions for new ways, see John Bodnar, *The Transplanted: A History of Immigration in Urban America* (Bloomington: Indiana University Press, 1985); and Miriam Cohen, *Workshop to Office: Two Generations of Italian Women in New York City, 1900–1950* (Ithaca: Cornell University Press, 1992).

12. Jade Snow Wong, *Fifth Chinese Daughter* (New York: Harper & Bros., 1950).

1. Bound Feet

1. Leong Shee, folder 12017/37233, CDCF-SFDO. According to the immigration file, Leong Shee claimed that she had married Chong Sung in 1885, yet she was seeking admission as the wife of Chin Lung. Immigration officials most likely did not question the discrepancy in her testimony because of her apparent upper-class background: she had bound feet.

2. Jew Law Ying, interview with author, January 14, 1987.

3. For a discussion of Chinese immigration in the context of modern world capitalism, see June Mei, "Socioeconomic Origins of Emigration: Guangdong to California, 1850 to 1882," in *Labor Migration Under Capitalism: Asian Workers in the United States Before World War II*, ed. Lucie Cheng Hirata and Edna Bonacich (Berkeley and Los Angeles: University of California Press, 1984), pp. 219–47; Sucheng Chan, *This Bittersweet Soil: The Chinese in California, 1860–1910* (Berkeley and Los Angeles: University of California Press, 1986), chap. 1 ("The Chinese Diaspora"); and idem, "European and Asian Immigration into the United States in Comparative Perspective, 1820s to 1920s," in *Immigration Reconsidered: History, Sociology, and Politics*, ed. Virginia Yans-McLaughlin (New York: Oxford University Press, 1990), pp. 37–75.

4. Sing-wu Wang, *The Organization of Chinese Emigration, 1848–1888* (San Francisco: Chinese Materials Center, 1978), pp. 8–9.

5. See Chan, *This Bittersweet Soil*, pp. 7–31. For a further discussion of the conditions in the Guangdong Province that led to emigration overseas, see Zo Kil Young, "Chinese Emigration into the United States, 1850–1880" (Ph.D. diss., Columbia University, 1971); and Frederic Wakeman, Jr., *Strangers at the Gate: Social Disorder in South China, 1839–1861* (Berkeley and Los Angeles: University of California Press, 1966).

6. The tendency in the past has been for immigration historians to view Chinese as "sojourners" and Europeans as "immigrants," the implication being that the Chinese, unlike Europeans, did not intend to stay but remained unassimilated and apart from mainstream American society; hence it was justifiable to bar their further immigration and exclude them from American social and political life. Recent scholarship, however, using return migration rates and written sentiments of immigrants, has demonstrated that many Europeans—such as Greeks, Italians, Poles, Danes, Germans, and Slovaks—shared this sojourner attitude. See Franklin Ng, "The Sojourner, Return Migration, and Immigration History," *Chinese America: History and Perspectives 1987*, pp. 53–71; and Chan, "European and Asian Immigration," pp. 38–39.

7. Charles Caldwell Dobie, *San Francisco's Chinatown* (New York: D. Appleton–Century Company, 1936), p. 41.

8. My calculations are based on statistics given in Mary Roberts Coolidge, *Chinese Immigration* (New York: Henry Holt, 1909), pp. 502, 498.

9. Lai Chun-chuen, *Remarks of the Chinese Merchants of San Francisco upon Governor John Bigler's Message and Some Common Objectives, with Some Explanations of the Character of the Chinese Companies and the Laboring Class in California* (San Francisco: Office of the Oriental, Whitton, Town & Co., 1855), p. 3.

10. New scholarship on women's prescribed roles in traditional China has

thrown into question whether these precepts do not more readily reflect the idealized social order rather than the reality of women's lives. Daughters of the gentry class were often educated by private tutors and some were thus able to distinguish themselves in the literary world. As Dorothy Ko's study of women writers in the late imperial period shows, for this group of literate women talent and virtue were compatible and, in fact, mutually reinforcing. It was precisely because women's literary talents gave them visibility and a powerful new voice that maxims such as "absence of talent in a woman is a virtue" gained popularity. See Ko, "Pursuing Talent and Virtue: Education and Women's Culture in Seventeenth- and Eighteenth-Century China," *Late Imperial China* 13, no. 1 (June 1992): 9–39; and Li Yu-ning, "Historical Roots of Changes."

11. See Kay Ann Johnson, *Women, the Family, and Peasant Revolution in China* (Chicago: University of Chicago Press, 1983), chap. 1; and Elizabeth Croll, *Familism and Socialism in China* (New York: Schocken Books, 1980), chap. 2.

12. Croll, *Feminism and Socialism in China*, p. 17; Arthur Smith, *Village Life in China: A Study in Sociology* (New York: Fleming H. Revell, 1899), pp. 275–76; Daniel Harrison Kulp, *Country Life in South China: The Sociology of Familism* (New York: Columbia University Press, 1925), pp. 89–90, 252; Holmes Beckwith, "The Chinese Family, with Special Relation to Industry" (Master's thesis, University of California, Berkeley, 1909), pp. 103–5; and Rubie S. Watson, "Girls' Houses and Working Women: Expressive Culture in the Pearl River Delta, 1900–1941," in Jaschok and Miers, eds., *Women and Chinese Patriarchy*, pp. 25–29.

13. See Marjorie Topley, "Marriage Resistance in Rural Kwangtung," in *Women in Chinese Society*, ed. Margery Wolf and Roxane Witke (Stanford: Stanford University Press, 1975), pp. 67–88; Andrea Patrice Sankar, "The Evolution of the Sisterhood in Traditional Chinese Society: From Village Girls' Houses to Chai T'angs in Hong Kong" (Ph.D. diss., University of Michigan, 1978); Janice Stockard, *Daughters of the Canton Delta: Marriage Patterns and Economic Strategies in South China, 1860–1930* (Stanford: Stanford University Press, 1989); and Kenneth Gaw, *Superior Servants: The Legendary Cantonese Amahs of the Far East* (Oxford: Oxford University Press, 1988).

14. See Ludwig J. Young, "The Emancipation of Women in China Before 1920, with Special Reference to Kwangtung" (Master's thesis, Columbia University, 1965).

15. Maxine Hong Kingston, *The Woman Warrior: Memoirs of a Girlhood Among Ghosts* (New York: Alfred A. Knopf, 1976), pp. 1–16.

16. Marlon K. Hom, *Songs of Gold Mountain: Cantonese Rhymes from San Francisco Chinatown* (Berkeley and Los Angeles: University of California Press, 1987), p. 46.

17. I am grateful to Zhao Shaoping of Xinhui District, Guangdong Province, for sharing this folk song with me.

18. Compared to Chinese and Italian women, Jewish, Polish, and Irish women were less inhibited about leaving home and emigrating to a new country. See Elizabeth Ewen, *Immigrant Women in the Land of Dollars: Life and Culture on the Lower East Side, 1890–1925* (New York: Monthly Review Press, 1985);

Virginia Yans-McLaughlin, *Family and Community: Italian Immigrants in Buffalo, 1880–1930* (Ithaca: Cornell University Press, 1971); Dino Cinel, *From Italy to San Francisco: The Immigrant Experience* (Stanford: Stanford University Press, 1982); Susan Glenn, *Daughters of the Shtetl: Life and Labor in the Immigrant Generation* (Ithaca: Cornell University Press, 1990); Hasia R. Diner, *Erin's Daughters in America: Irish Immigrant Women in the Nineteenth Century* (Baltimore: Johns Hopkins University Press, 1983); and Doris Weatherford, *Foreign and Female: Immigrant Women in America, 1840–1930* (New York: Schocken Books, 1986).

19. For an analysis of why more Chinese women immigrated to Hawaii than to California and why more Japanese women emigrated than Chinese women, see Ronald Takaki, "They Also Came: The Migration of Chinese and Japanese Women to Hawaii and the Continental United States," *Chinese America: History and Perspectives 1990*, pp. 3–19.

20. During the 1850s Chinese residents and businesses were located in different parts of the city, with a small settlement around Sacramento Street. By the 1870s Chinatown had become a segregated ethnic enclave, six blocks long (between California and Broadway Streets) by two blocks wide (between Stockton and Kearny Streets). See Thomas W. Chinn, ed., *A History of the Chinese in California: A Syllabus* (San Francisco: Chinese Historical Society of America, 1969), pp. 10–11; and Otis Gibson, *The Chinese in America* (Cincinnati: Hitchcock & Walden, 1877), pp. 63–94. For a fuller discussion of institutional racism and Chinese resistance, see Sucheng Chan, *Asian Americans: An Interpretive History* (Boston: Twayne, 1991), chap. 3; and Charles J. McClain, *In Search of Equality: The Chinese Struggle Against Discrimination in Nineteenth-Century America* (Berkeley and Los Angeles: University of California Press, 1994).

21. See Chan, *Asian Americans*, chap. 3; and Alexander Saxton, *The Indispensable Enemy: Labor and the Anti-Chinese Movement in California* (Berkeley and Los Angeles: University of California Press, 1971), chap. 10.

22. For a discussion of how immigration laws and policies in the United States shaped Chinese American family life and community development, see Bill Ong Hing, *Making and Remaking Asian America Through Immigration Policy, 1850–1990* (Stanford: Stanford University Press, 1993).

23. My calculations are based on statistics provided in S. W. Kung, *Chinese in American Life: Some Aspects of Their History, Status, Problems, and Contributions* (Westport, Conn.: Greenwood Press, 1973), pp. 33, 92–93; Coolidge, *Chinese Immigration*, p. 98; and Helen Chen, "Chinese Immigration into the United States: An Analysis of Changes in Immigration Policies" (Ph.D. diss., Brandeis University, 1980), pp. 176–91.

24. *In re Ah Quan*, 21 Federal Reporter 182 (1884); and *Case of the Chinese Wife*, 21 Federal Reporter 785 (1884). For a discussion of these and other significant cases relating to the exclusion of Chinese women, see Sucheng Chan, "The Exclusion of Chinese Women, 1870–1943," in *Entry Denied: Exclusion and the Chinese Community in America, 1882–1943*, ed. Sucheng Chan (Philadelphia: Temple University Press, 1991), pp. 94–146.

25. *In re Chung Toy Ho and Wong Choy Sin*, 42 Federal Reporter 398 (1890). See also *United States v. Gue Lim*, 88 Federal Reporter 136 (1897).

26. I am indebted to Waverly Lowell, director of the San Francisco District Office, Immigration and Naturalization Service, for this quote from the CDCF-SFDO files. The *San Francisco Call* made a similar observation on November 23, 1895, in a story about Customs detaining seven Chinese women at the Presbyterian Mission Home on suspicion of fraudulent entry: "The size of the foot is an important factor in determining the character of the women of China, and none of the ladies in Miss Houseworth's charge have the diminutive feet which are said to distinguish the ladies of the higher class" (p. 7).

27. See Weatherford, *Foreign and Female;* and Maxine Schwartz Seller, *Immigrant Women* (Philadelphia: Temple University Press, 1981).

28. See Ewen, *Immigrant Women in the Land of Dollars.*

29. See Maxine Schwartz Seller, *To Seek America: A History of Ethnic Life in the United States* (Englewood, N.J.: J. S. Ozer, 1977), pp. 127–30; S. Glenn, *Daughters of the Shtetl;* and Diner, *Erin's Daughters in America.*

30. See Paul Ong, "Chinese Labor in Early San Francisco: Racial Segmentation and Industrial Expansion," *Amerasia Journal* 8, no. 1 (spring/summer 1981): 69–92.

31. See Jacqueline Baker Barnhart, *The Fair but Frail: Prostitution in San Francisco, 1849–1900* (Reno: University of Nevada Press, 1986), chap. 5; and R. A. Burchell, *The San Francisco Irish, 1848–1880* (Manchester: Manchester University Press, 1979), pp. 17–18. According to Mary Lou Locke in "Out of the Shadows and into the Western Sun: Working Women of the Late Nineteenth-Century Urban Far West," *Journal of Urban History* 16, no. 2 (February 1990): 178, only 6 percent of the young female workers in San Francisco worked in factories in 1880.

32. "Condition of the Chinese Quarter," *San Francisco Municipal Reports for the Fiscal Year 1884–85, Ending June 30, 1885* (San Francisco: Board of Supervisors, 1885), p. 216.

33. Lucie Cheng Hirata, "Chinese Immigrant Women in Nineteenth-Century California," in *Women of America: A History,* ed. C. R. Berkin and M. B. Norton (Boston: Houghton-Mifflin, 1979), pp. 236, 239–40; and Ruth Hall Whitfield, "Public Opinion and the Chinese Question in San Francisco, 1900–1947" (Master's thesis, University of California, Berkeley, 1947), p. 7. Moreover, as pointed out in William Issel and Robert Cherny, *San Francisco, 1865–1932: Politics, Power, and Urban Development* (Berkeley and Los Angeles: University of California Press, 1986), pp. 70–73, manufacturers often paid Chinese workers less than white workers for doing the same tasks.

34. Herbert Ashbury, *The Barbary Coast: An Informal History of the San Francisco Underground* (New York: Alfred A. Knopf, 1933), pp. 32–35. Ashbury noted that within a few years of the gold rush, "San Francisco possessed a red-light district that was larger than those of many cities several times its size," and "there was no country in the world that was not represented in San Francisco by at least one prostitute" (p. 34). Like many other journalistic accounts of the heyday of prostitution in San Francisco, Ashbury's book is suspect and needs to be used judiciously in the absence of writings by Chinese prostitutes themselves.

35. Albert Benard de Russailh, *Last Adventure, San Francisco in 1851* (San Francisco: Westgate, 1931), pp. 29, 11.

36. Barnhart, *Fair but Frail*, p. 60. For other studies on prostitution in the West, see Anne Butler, *Daughters of Joy, Sisters of Misery: Prostitution in the American West, 1865–90* (Urbana: University of Illinois Press, 1985); Ruth Rosen, *The Lost Sisterhood: Prostitution in America, 1900–1918* (Baltimore: Johns Hopkins University Press, 1982); and Brenda Elaine Pillors, "The Criminalization of Prostitution in the United States: The Case of San Francisco, 1854–1919" (Ph.D. diss., University of California, Berkeley, 1982).

37. Lucie Cheng Hirata, "Free, Indentured, Enslaved: Chinese Prostitutes in Nineteenth-Century America," *Signs: Journal of Women in Culture and Society* 5, no. 1 (autumn 1979): 12. According to Ashbury, *Barbary Coast*, pp. 180–81, "The prices paid for prostitutes in the San Francisco market varied with the years and with the quality of the merchandise and was naturally dependent to a great extent upon supply and demand. Before the passage of the exclusion acts the prettiest Chinese girls could be purchased for a few hundred dollars each, but after about 1888, when it became necessary to smuggle them into this country, prices rose enormously. During the early eighteen-nineties they ranged from about $100 for a one-year-old girl to a maximum of $1,200 for a girl of fourteen, which was considered the best age for prostitution. Children of six to ten brought from $200 to $800. About 1897 girls of twelve to fifteen sometimes sold for as high as $2,500 each."

38. M. G. C. Edholm, "A Stain on the Flag," *Californian Illustrated Magazine* 1 (February 1892): 162.

39. *Chinese Immigration: The Social, Moral, and Political Effect of Chinese Immigration. Testimony Taken Before a Committee of the Senate of the State of California, Appointed April 3d, 1876* (Sacramento: State Printing Office, 1876), p. 63. Evidence that, like this contract, allegedly pointed to immoral and criminal behavior on the part of the Chinese was often used by exclusionists to justify anti-Chinese legislation.

40. On the subject of indentured servants in the United States, see Richard B. Morris, *Government and Labor in Early America* (New York: Columbia University Press, 1946); and Sharon V. Salinger, *"To Serve Well and Faithfully": Labor and Indentured Servants in Pennsylvania, 1682–1800* (Cambridge: Cambridge University Press, 1987).

41. Ashbury, *Barbary Coast*, p. 180; and Mildred Crowl Martin, *Chinatown's Angry Angel: The Story of Donaldina Cameron* (Palo Alto: Pacific Books, 1977), p. 80.

42. Hirata, "Free, Indentured, Enslaved," p. 15.

43. Ibid., p. 13; *San Francisco Chronicle*, December 5, 1869, p. 3.

44. Ashbury, *Barbary Coast*, pp. 174–76; and *Nell Kimball: The Life as an American Madam by Herself*, ed. Stephen Longstreet (New York: Macmillan, 1970), pp. 226–27. Both Ashbury and Kimball wrote about Selina, a Chinese prostitute who knew how to capitalize on the Oriental fantasies of white men. Kimball described her thus: "I myself knew Selina, a Chinese tart, the best looker I ever saw among them—what was called 'a stunner.' She had a marvelous body, thin and yet just right in hips and breasts, not skimped as with most Chinese. She could chatter the artistic comeon to a john—about scrolls, screens, and give off a sense of culture, which a man likes sometimes when he's buying a woman's time and he's budgeting his vitality. She had a place, a three room kip in Bartlett

Alley, and it was: *For Whites Only*. . . . Customers had to book her three days in ahead, she was that much in demand she claimed. And she got a whole buck, not the usual seventy-five cent price. She was a *looksee* seller, taking off her clothes for fifty cents so the trick could check for himself—as Lai [her laundry woman] told me—that in her sex parts she ran north-to-south like the white girls, and not east-to-west. It's amazing the idea you can sell a man about fornication—he'll pay and even if fooled, feel at least he's gotten some knowledge or experience" (p. 227).

45. *San Francisco Chronicle*, April 17, 1892, p. 1.

46. *San Francisco Call*, December 6, 1908, p. 3.

47. Alexander McLeod, *Pigtails and Gold Dust* (Caldwell, Idaho: Caxton Printers, 1948), p. 183.

48. Ashbury, *Barbary Coast*, pp. 176–77; Hirata, "Free, Indentured, Enslaved," pp. 13–14; and *Nell Kimball*, pp. 221–23.

49. *Chinese Immigration*, pp. 47, 80. The following sensationalized description of the "hospital" to which diseased prostitutes were brought to die appeared in the *San Francisco Chronicle* on December 5, 1869: "Led by night to this hold of a 'hospital,' she is forced within the door and made to lie down upon the shelf. A cup of water, another of boiled rice, and a little metal oil lamp are placed by her side. . . . Those who have immediate charge of the establishment know how long the oil should last, and when the limit is reached they return to the 'hospital,' unbar the door and enter. . . . Generally the woman is dead, either by starvation or from her own hand; but sometimes life is not extinct; the spark yet remains when the 'doctors' enter; yet this makes but little difference to them. They come for a corpse, and they never go away without it" (p. 3).

50. My calculations are based on statistics given in Hirata, "Free, Indentured, Enslaved," pp. 23–24; Chan, *This Bittersweet Soil*, pp. 54–55, 62–63, 68–69; and idem, "Exclusion of Chinese Women," p. 107. I would favor the higher figures for 1860 and 1880 given by Sucheng Chan, in which she took unlisted prostitutes into consideration by looking closely at household composition. Whenever single women between the ages of fifteen and forty-five were shown living in all-female households, she coded them as "probable prostitutes" ("Exclusion," p. 141). Although the accuracy of U.S. census statistics, particularly for a group that is primarily non-English-speaking like the Chinese, is questionable, the manuscript census is one of the few sources available that provides information on household composition and the socioeconomic background of Chinese women.

51. Megumi Dick Osumi, "Asians and California's Anti-Miscegenation Laws," in *Asian and Pacific American Experiences: Women's Perspectives*, ed. Nobuya Tsuchida (Minneapolis: Asian/Pacific American Learning Resource Center and General College, University of Minnesota, 1982), p. 6.

52. In contrast, Chinese men were able to intermarry in British Malaya, North Borneo, Sarawak, the Dutch East Indies, the Philippines, Hawaii, Mexico, Guatemala, Peru, Siberia, and Australia; as a result, prostitution was not as widespread in these places as it was in the continental United States. See Ching Chao Wu, "Chinese Immigration in the Pacific Area" (Master's thesis, University of Chicago, 1926), pp. 26–28; and idem, "Chinatowns: A Study of Symbiosis and Assimilation" (Ph.D. diss., University of Chicago, 1928), chap. 4.

53. Hirata, "Free, Indentured, Enslaved," pp. 8–29. Prostitution in general

at this time was just as lucrative for everyone. As Barnhart points out in chapter 6 of *The Fair but Frail*, a wide sector of society profited from prostitution, including business people such as dressmakers, jewelers, doctors, liquor salesmen, and theater managers, as well as judges and other municipal officers who took bribes.

54. Eng Ying Gong and Bruce Grant, *Tong War!* (New York: Nicholas L. Brown, 1930), pp. 14–23.

55. Also known as Chinese Consolidated Benevolent Association, the Chinese Six Companies was formed in 1882 to protect the general interests of the Chinese on the Pacific Coast. It originally consisted of six *huiguan* (united clans of people from the same region or district in China): Ning Yung, Hop Wo, Kong Chow, Young Wo, Sam Yup, and Yan Wo. See Him Mark Lai, "Historical Development of the Chinese Consolidated Benevolent Association/*Huiguan* System," *Chinese America: History and Perspectives 1987*, pp. 13–51.

56. Ashbury, *Barbary Coast*, pp. 170–71.

57. According to Sue Gronewold in *Beautiful Merchandise: Prostitution in China, 1860–1936* (New York: Harrington Park Press, 1985), pp. 30–34, the hierarchy of prostitution in China was very similar to that in San Francisco. Prostitutes in China were categorized into three classes: courtesans who worked in luxurious establishments that catered to high officials, wealthy merchants, scholars, and artists; singing girls and prostitutes in wine houses, restaurants, or taverns frequented by lower officials and middle-level scholars and merchants; and prostitutes in sparsely furnished rooms who provided cheap, quick sex to poor men, soldiers, and young scholars. As a prostitute's beauty faded, she was sold downward to lower-class brothels where her life was shortened considerably owing to physical abuse and disease. For another depiction of organized prostitution in China, see Gail Hershatter, "The Hierarchy of Shanghai Prostitution, 1870–1949," *Modern China* 15, no. 4 (October 1989): 463–98.

58. Ashbury, *Barbary Coast*, pp. 154–55.

59. Ibid., p. 259; *Nell Kimball*, p. 223.

60. Richard Symanski, *Immoral Landscape: Female Prostitution in Urban Society* (Toronto: Butterworth, 1981), p. 130. Symanski uses the "geopolitical sink" principle in this work to explain discrimination against minorities—that is, the idea that public opinion and political action combine to confine immoral institutions to areas that have the least political clout, namely ethnic ghettos. According to Symanski, it is no accident that San Francisco's red-light district encompassed both Chinatown and Little Chile in the nineteenth century and that these communities were singled out for moral condemnation and legal suppression.

61. See, for example, John A. Davis, *The Chinese Slave Girl: A Story of Woman's Life in China* (Philadelphia: Presbyterian Board of Publications, [ca. 1880]); Gibson, *Chinese in America;* Helen F. Clark, *The Lady of the Lily Feet and Other Stories of Chinatown* (Philadelphia: Griffith & Rowland Press, 1900); Augustus W. Loomis, "Chinese Women in California," *Overland Monthly* 2 (April 1869): 344–46; Edholm, "Stain on the Flag," pp. 159–70; "Her Back Was Burnt With Irons," *San Francisco Call*, July 23, 1897, p. 12; and "Taken Out of a Den of Slaves," *San Francisco Call*, July 27, 1897, p. 7.

62. Albert S. Evans, *A la California: Sketches of Life in the Golden Gate* (San

Francisco: A. L. Bancroft, 1873), p. 285; and *Facts upon the Other Side of the Chinese Question: With a Memorial to the President of the United States from Representative Chinamen in America*, 1876, p. 21.

63. *Chinatown Declared a Nuisance!* (San Francisco), March 10, 1880, p. 12. In another municipal report, a physician estimated that nine-tenths of venereal disease cases in San Francisco were contracted in that city ("Condition of the Chinese Quarter," p. 171).

64. Quoted in Barnhart, *Fair but Frail*, p. 47; emphasis in the original.

65. Ibid., pp. 48-49; Pillors, "Criminalization of Prostitution," pp. 113-15; and Chan, "Exclusion of Chinese Women," pp. 97-105. Organized Japanese prostitution, although lesser in degree, was similar to Chinese prostitution in that Japanese women were also sold, kidnapped, or lured into the trade. According to Yuji Ichioka, *The Issei: The World of the First Generation Japanese Immigrants, 1865-1924* (New York: Free Press, 1988), p. 29, the number of Japanese prostitutes in San Francisco ranged from thirty to seventy-one in the 1890s. They worked mainly in Japanese brothels near Chinatown, although Japanese prostitutes were also found in Chinese brothels and Chinatown cribs. Concerned with America's image of Japan and the Japanese people and fearful that Japanese prostitution would be used as a pretext to exclude Japanese immigration (as happened to the Chinese), Japanese government officials instructed the Japanese Consulate in San Francisco to cooperate with American immigration officials in apprehending Japanese prostitutes at the port of entry, thus nipping the problem in the bud before Japanese prostitution became widespread.

66. See George Anthony Peffer, "Forbidden Families: Emigration Experience of Chinese Women Under the Page Law, 1875-1882," *Journal of American Ethnic History* 6 (1986): 28-46.

67. My calculations are based on statistics given in appendix table 2.

68. M. Culbertson, "Report of Chinese Mission Home," *Women's Occidental Board of Foreign Missions, Annual Report*, 1890, p. 26. In another similar case, sixteen-year-old Lee Yow Chun, suspecting that she had been sold into prostitution instead of marriage as promised, refused to be landed upon arrival in the United States. As she testified from a rescue home, "When word came from the collector that I could land, not being able to do anything else I fell in a lump on the floor and cried loudly, saying I did not want to be landed by those people [the procurers]; that I would jump into the sea rather than be taken by them. Somehow the fact that I cried reached the ears of the official interpreter, who came and said the collector had allowed me to go to a rescue home and there to remain until the next returning boat to China" (Ching Chao Wu, "Chinatowns," p. 105).

69. Quoted in Curt Gentry, *The Madams of San Francisco* (New York: Doubleday, 1964), p. 52.

70. Benard de Russailh, *Last Adventure*, pp. 88-89.

71. *San Francisco Examiner*, January 23, 1881, p. 1.

72. McLeod, *Pigtails and Gold Dust*, pp. 175-77; Gentry, *Madams of San Francisco*, pp. 50-59; Gunther Barth, *Bitter Strength: A History of the Chinese in the United States, 1850-1870* (Cambridge, Mass.: Harvard University Press, 1964), pp. 84-85; William Bode, *Lights and Shadows of Chinatown* (San Fran-

cisco: Crocker Co., 1896), n.p.; *San Jose Mercury Herald*, February 2, 1928, p. 8; and *San Francisco Examiner*, February 2, 1928, p. 8.

73. *San Francisco Call*, April 2, 1899, p. 25; and Ashbury, *Barbary Coast*, p. 178.

74. For a discussion of how linkages among race, class, and gender can create privilege or subordination between different groups of women, see Maxine Baca Zinn, "Feminist Rethinking from Racial-Ethnic Families," in *Women of Color in U. S. Society*, ed. Maxine Baca Zinn and Bonnie Thornton Dill (Philadelphia: Temple University Press, 1994), pp. 303–14; Judith Rollins, *Between Women: Domestics and Their Employers* (Philadelphia: Temple University Press, 1985); and James Francis Warren, "Chinese Prostitution in Singapore: Recruitment and Brothel Organization," in Jaschok and Miers, eds., *Women and Chinese Patriarchy*, pp. 77–107.

75. Gibson, *Chinese in America*, p. 207.

76. For an in-depth study of the activities and influence of Protestant missionary women in San Francisco Chinatown, see Peggy Pascoe, *Relations of Rescue: The Search for Female Moral Authority in the American West, 1874–1939* (New York: Oxford University Press, 1990).

77. See Gibson, *Chinese in America*, chap. 9.

78. Martin, *Chinatown's Angry Angel*, p. 87. According to the Mission Home's annual reports and "Register of Inmates," a total of 392 Chinese women and girls found refuge there between 1874 and 1893. See Sarah Refo Mason, "Social Christianity, American Feminism, and Chinese Prostitutes: The History of the Presbyterian Mission Home, San Francisco, 1874–1935," in Jaschok and Miers, eds., *Women and Chinese Patriarchy*, pp. 205–6.

79. See Martin, *Chinatown's Angry Angel*, chaps. 3 and 4; Gibson, *Chinese in America*, chap. 9; Laurene Wu McClain, "Donaldina Cameron: A Reappraisal," *Pacific Historian* 27, no. 3 (fall 1983): 25–35; Hirata, "Free, Indentured, Enslaved," pp. 25–28; and Pascoe, *Relations of Rescue*, chap. 3. Pascoe finds the number of Chinese women who married from the Mission Home impressive, estimating that 266 such marriages occurred between 1874 and 1928 (p. 157). Because of the skewed sex ratio, legal constraints against interracial marriage, the economic difficulties in sending for a bride from China, and the acceptability of former prostitutes as brides, there was no shortage of suitors at the Presbyterian Mission Home. In her study of the home, Sarah Refo Mason found that the staff did not insist on non-Christian residents marrying Christians. However, they were adamant that the women not become second wives. By 1889, there were forty-six families on the West Coast that had been established by marriages of women from the Mission Home ("Social Christianity," pp. 206–9).

80. See Pascoe, *Relations of Rescue*, chaps. 3 and 5.

81. John W. Stephens, "A Quantitative History of Chinatown San Francisco, 1870 and 1880," in *The Life, Influence, and the Role of the Chinese in the United States, 1776–1960* (San Francisco: Chinese Historical Society of America, 1976), p. 73. Most likely, many *mui tsai* were listed as "daughters" in the manuscript census. According to Lucie Cheng Hirata's examination of the manuscript censuses ("Free, Indentured, Enslaved," p. 21), in 1860 more native-born girls lived

in brothels than not; in 1870 an even number lived in brothels and outside; and in 1880 more lived outside brothels than in them. Hirata suspects that these girls were the daughters of prostitutes and that they somehow managed to escape the clutches of brothel owners by 1880, since only seven of the prostitutes were listed as native born in the 1880 manuscript census.

82. See Maria Jaschok, *Concubines and Bondservants* (London: Zed Books, 1988); Gronewold, *Beautiful Merchandise*; Royal Mui Tsai Commission, *Mui Tsai in Hong Kong and Malaya* (London: His Majesty's Stationery Office, 1937); Lai Ah Eng, *Peasants, Proletarians, and Prostitutes: A Preliminary Investigation into the Work of Chinese Women in Colonial Malaya* (Singapore: Institute of Southeast Asian Studies, 1986); and Suzanne Miers, "Mui Tsai Through the Eyes of the Victim: Janet Lim's Story of Bondage and Escape," in Jaschok and Miers, eds., *Women and Chinese Patriarchy*, pp. 108–21.

83. Salinger, *Labor and Indentured Servants*, p. 100.

84. The following account is derived from Kathleen Wong, "Quan Laan Fan: An Oral History" (student paper, Asian American Studies Library, University of California, Berkeley, 1974).

85. The following account is taken from Victor Nee and Brett de Bary Nee, *Longtime Californ': A Documentary Study of an American Chinatown* (New York: Pantheon Books, 1972), pp. 83–90. There, Wu Tien Fu is given the pseudonym Lilac Chen. Her story also appears in Martin, *Chinatown's Angry Angel*; and Pascoe, *Relations of Rescue*.

86. For other rescue accounts of abused *mui tsai*, see Margarita Lake, "A Chinese Slave Girl in America," *Missionary Review of the World* 26 (July 1903): 532–33; and Martin, *Chinatown's Angry Angel*.

87. In Hong Kong during this same time period, the *mui tsai* system was said to be a main supplier of prostitutes. See Elizabeth Sinn, "Chinese Patriarchy and the Protection of Women in 19th-Century Hong Kong," in Jaschok and Miers, eds., *Women and Chinese Patriarchy*, p. 148.

88. My calculations are based on statistics given in Stephens, "Quantitative History of Chinatown," p. 77, and on my tally from the 1900 manuscript census of population for San Francisco (see appendix table 4).

89. Judging from the household composition in the manuscript censuses and missionary and newspaper accounts, we can assume that polygamy was practiced by the merchant class in Chinatown. Although illegal and considered immoral in America, polygamy was not so regarded in China, where it symbolized a man's wealth and was often practiced to ensure a progeny of sons.

90. Sui Seen Far, "The Chinese Woman in America," *Land of Sunshine* 6, no. 2 (January 1897): 62. Sui Seen Far was the pen name of Edith Maud Eaton, a Eurasian who identified strongly with her Chinese heritage and who wrote about Chinese life in America. Her stories were published in various popular magazines and later collected in *Mrs. Spring Fragrance* (Chicago: A. C. McClurg, 1912). For more information on her and her writings, see Amy Ling, *Between Worlds: Women Writers of Chinese Ancestry* (New York: Pergamon Press, 1990), pp. 21–55.

91. The following account is taken from the *San Francisco Chronicle*, October 1, 1893, p. 2.

92. Stephens, "Quantitative History of Chinatown," p. 79; and Hirata, "Free, Indentured, Enslaved," p. 23.

93. Quoted in Connie Young Yu, "From Tents to Federal Projects: Chinatown's Housing History," in *The Chinese American Experience*, ed. Genny Lim (San Francisco: Chinese Historical Society of America, 1983), p. 132.

94. Quoted in ibid., p. 133.

95. *Chinatown Declared a Nuisance!* p. 2.

96. Quoted in Charles Loring Brace, *The New West; or, California in 1867–1868* (New York: G. P. Putnam, 1869), p. 212.

97. *Facts upon the Other Side of the Chinese Question*, pp. 30–31.

98. Richard Dillon, *The Hatchet Men: San Francisco's Chinatown in the Days of the Tong Wars, 1880–1906* (New York: Ballantine Books, 1972), pp. 152–53.

99. Hirata, "Chinese Immigrant Women," p. 237; Stephens, "Quantitative History of Chinatown," p. 73. According to Evelyn Nakano Glenn in "Split Household, Small Producer, and Dual Wage Earner: An Analysis of Chinese-American Family Strategies," *Journal of Marriage and Family* 45, no. 1 (February 1983): 35–48, until the 1920s Chinatown remained a bachelor society of "split-household families," a situation where production (wage earning) was separated from other family functions and carried out by the husband overseas, while reproduction, socialization, and family consumption (supported by the husband's remittances) were carried out by the wife or other relatives in the home village. The nuclear family structure, though, was prevalent among Chinatown families where wives were present.

100. As Margery Wolf points out in "Chinese Women: Old Skills in a New Context," in *Women, Culture, and Society*, ed. Michelle Zimbalist Rosaldo and Louise Lamphere (Stanford: Stanford University Press, 1974), pp. 157–72, only when a Chinese woman attained the status of mother-in-law was she able to wield any power. Veneration for her age and motherhood gave the mother-in-law respect and authority to rule the household—and particularly the daughter-in-law—with an iron fist. Many tyrannized the daughter-in-law as compensation for their own former suffering and in an effort to maintain control over the son, the one person who could serve as their "political front" in domestic and public affairs.

101. Coolidge, *Chinese Immigration*, p. 437.

102. See *Overland Monthly* 32 (July 1898): 16 and (September 1898): 324.

103. "Report of House-to-House Visitations Among Heathen Families," *Foreign Mission Board of the Presbyterian Church, Annual Report*, 1880, p. 43. On the history of Protestant missionary work in San Francisco, see Wesley Woo, "Protestant Work Among the Chinese in the San Francisco Bay Area, 1850–1920" (Ph.D. diss., University of California, Berkeley, 1983).

104. Emma R. Cable, "House to House Visitation," *Foreign Mission Board of the Presbyterian Church, Annual Report*, 1887, p. 56.

105. "House to House Visitation," *Foreign Mission Board of the Presbyterian Church, Annual Report*, 1892, p. 25.

106. *San Francisco Chronicle*, April 29, 1893.

107. Quoted in Carl T. Smith, "The Gillespie Brothers: Early Links Between Hong Kong and California," *Chung Chi Bulletin* 47 (December 1969): 28. See also Tin-Yuke Char, *The Sandalwood Mountains: Readings and Stories of the Early*

Chinese in Hawaii (Honolulu: University Press of Hawaii, 1975), pp. 42–44.

108. Dobie, *San Francisco's Chinatown*, pp. 25–27.

109. *San Francisco Morning Call*, November 23, 1892, p. 12. See also Mc-Cunn, *Chinese American Portraits*, pp. 40–45.

110. Quoted in Victor Low, *The Unimpressible Race: A Century of Educational Struggle by the Chinese in San Francisco* (San Francisco: East/West, 1982), p. 66; see pp. 59–73 for a discussion of *Tape v. Hurley*.

111. *Alta*, April 16, 1885, p. 1.

112. See discussion above, and note 13.

113. Him Mark Lai, "History of the Bing Lai Family," Him Mark Lai private collection; and McCunn, *Chinese American Portraits*, pp. 106–17.

2.   Unbound Feet

1. *San Francisco Chronicle*, November 3, 1902, p. 7.

2. See Jean Chesneaux, Marianne Bastid, and Marie-Claire Bergère, *China from the Opium Wars to the 1911 Revolution*, trans. Anne Destenay (New York: Pantheon Books, 1976); and Charlotte L. Beahan, "The Women's Movement and Nationalism in Late Ch'ing China" (Ph.D. diss., Columbia University, 1976). The Chinese concept of the "new woman" is similar to the American concept prevalent during this same period. Often referred to in the Chinese press as *ziyounü* (a liberated woman), she was—in marked contrast to traditional gender roles—an educated, self-supporting woman who worked in some urban occupation, assumed a modern lifestyle, and was involved in social and political affairs.

3. *Chung Sai Yat Po* (hereafter cited as *CSYP*), November 3, 1902; *San Francisco Examiner*, November 3, 1902, p. 7.

4. See Roxane Witke, "Transformation of Attitudes Towards Women During the May Fourth Era of Modern China" (Ph.D. diss., University of California, Berkeley, 1970); Beahan, "Women's Movement"; Kazuko Ono, *Chinese Women in a Century of Revolution, 1850–1950* (Stanford: Stanford University Press, 1989); and Leslie Eugene Collins, "The New Women: A Psychological Study of the Chinese Feminist Movement from 1900 to the Present" (Ph.D. diss., Yale University, 1976). For a critique of the Orientalist assumption that Chinese women were not on the road to "liberation" until Westerners arrived to start them on their way, see Li Yu-ning, "Historical Roots of Changes"; Ko, *Teachers of the Inner Chambers;* and Mann, "Learned Women."

5. *CSYP*, August 31, 1901; *San Francisco Examiner*, October 23, 1902, p. 2; and *San Francisco Chronicle*, March 1, 1903, p. 2.

6. See Beahan, "Women's Movement." This difference in lines of argument is also discussed by Bernadette Li in "Chinese Feminist Thought at the Turn of the Century," *St. John's Papers*, no. 25 (Jamaica, N.Y.: St. John's University, 1978), p. 5: "Thus, from the beginning, the basic argument for the liberation of Chinese women was different from that used in the West. The feminist movement in the West had its origin in the basic belief in the equality of all human beings, without regard for differences in sex, as we see for example in the writ-

ings of Mary Wollstonecraft. In contrast, the emancipation of Chinese women was inseparable from the national cause. Women were still expected to play secondary roles. Better health and better education would enable them to perform their traditional roles of wives and mothers in a better way." For a further discussion of how feminist movements in Third World countries are inevitably colored by nationalism, see Kumai Jayawardena, *Feminism and Nationalism in the Third World* (London: Zed Books, 1986).

7. *San Francisco Chronicle*, November 3, 1902, p. 7.

8. *San Francisco Examiner*, November 2, 1902, p. 41.

9. *CSYP*, October 12, 1903.

10. According to Louise Leung Larson's autobiography, *Sweet Bamboo: Saga of a Chinese American Family* (Los Angeles: Chinese Historical Society of Southern California, 1989), pp. 51–52, Sieh King King left San Francisco and went to Los Angeles, where she stayed with the family of Tom Leung, an active Baohuanghui member. She was allegedly in the United States to plot the assassination of the Empress Dowager, but the empress died in 1908 before the plan could be realized. Sieh King King later graduated from the University of Chicago, married a fellow student, and returned to China, where her husband started a chain of banks.

11. In a similar way, gender roles for American women changed each time the United States became engaged in war. See Sara M. Evans, *Born for Liberty: A History of Women in America* (New York: Free Press, 1989).

12. See Judy Yung, "The Social Awakening of Chinese American Women as Reported in *Chung Sai Yat Po*, 1900–1911," in *Unequal Sisters: A Multicultural Reader in U.S. Women's History*, ed. Ellen Carol DuBois and Vicki L. Ruiz (New York: Routledge, 1990), pp. 195–207.

13. See Chesneaux, Bastid, and Bergère, *China From the Opium Wars to the 1911 Revolution*; and Jean Chesneaux, Françoise Le Barbier, and Marie-Claire Bergère, *China From the 1911 Revolution to Liberation*, trans. Paul Auster and Lydia Davis (New York: Pantheon Books, 1977).

14. Quoted in Ono, *Chinese Women*, p. 141.

15. Kung, *Chinese in American Life*, pp. 33, 93.

16. Rose Hum Lee, *The Chinese in the United States of America* (Hong Kong: Hong Kong University Press, 1960), pp. 34–37.

17. Ching Chao Wu, in "Chinatowns," p. 236, noted that while 24,782 Chinese men were listed as married in the 1920 U.S. census, only 3,046 Chinese women were so listed. In other words, most Chinese wives had been left behind in China. In another study published in the *Chinese Times*, May 16, 1929, 55 percent of the Chinese men surveyed in San Francisco were unmarried, 35 percent had wives in China, and 10 percent had wives with them in America. The study also indicated that a large percentage of the men who had wives in China returned home for visits once every ten to fifteen years.

18. Many more Chinese women were immigrating to British Malaya than to the United States. According to Lai Ah Eng in *Peasants, Proletarians and Prostitutes*, p. 15, there was a great influx of Chinese immigrant women from Guangdong Province to Malaya in the 1920s and 1930s. Many were widows and single women escaping economic depression, famine, and the impending

war with Japan. Similar to the situation in Hawaii in the nineteenth century, Malaya wanted Chinese immigrant women to help stabilize the Chinese male work force as well as to provide cheap labor. Consequently, women were exempt from Malaya's Aliens Ordinance of 1933, which restricted overall immigration. According to statistics presented by Ching Chao Wu in "Chinese Immigration in the Pacific Area," pp. 23–26, Malaya had the largest Chinese immigrant population and the highest percentage of Chinese immigrant women in the world in the 1920s. There were 1,173,354 Chinese in Malaya in 1921, as compared to 61,639 in the United States in 1920. In those same years, 38.4 percent of the Chinese population in Malaya were women, as compared to 12.5 percent in the United States.

19. See U.S. House, *Admission of Wives of American Citizens of Oriental Ancestry: Hearings Before the Committee on Immigration and Naturalization on H.R. 6544,* 69th Cong., 1st sess., 1926; and U.S. Senate, *Admission as Nonquota Immigrants of Certain Alien Wives and Children of United States Citizens: Hearing Before a Subcommittee of the Committee on Immigration on S. 2271,* 70th Cong., 1st sess., 1928.

20. As Sucheng Chan notes in "Exclusion of Chinese Women," pp. 129–32, there was a noticeable increase in the numbers of Chinese women who immigrated as daughters of U.S. citizens after passage of the 1924 Act prevented wives from coming. They were considered derivative or statutory U.S. citizens according to section 1993 of the U.S. Revised Statutes.

21. Ibid., p. 125. According to Weili Ye, "Crossing the Cultures: The Experiences of Chinese Students in the United States of America, 1900–1925" (Ph.D. diss., Yale University, 1989), the first four Chinese female students in the United States came with the support of missionaries to study medicine in the late nineteenth century. Then, in 1907, Chinese women began coming on government scholarships, and in 1911, on private funds. In 1925 there were approximately 300 women among 1,400 Chinese students in the United States.

22. See Vincente Tang, "Chinese Women Immigrants and the Two-edged Sword of Habeas Corpus," in *The Chinese American Experience,* ed. Genny Lim (San Francisco: Chinese Historical Society of America, 1983), pp. 48–56; and Him Mark Lai, Genny Lim, and Judy Yung, *Island: Poetry and History of Chinese Immigrants on Angel Island, 1910–1940* (Seattle: University of Washington Press, 1991).

23. "Social Document of Pany Lowe," Survey of Race Relations Collection, Hoover Institution on War, Revolution, and Peace, Stanford University. Similar sentiments were expressed in an interview with Chin Yen, also an American-born Chinese ("Life History as a Social Document of Mr. Chin Yen," Survey of Race Relations Collection, Hoover Institution on War, Revolution, and Peace, Stanford University): "My wife is still in China. I have not seen her for ten years. You wonder why I don't bring my wife here? Well, that is the question. Because my wife come over and you Americans cause her lots of trouble."

24. Wong Ah So, "Story of Wong Ah So—Experiences as a Prostitute," in *Orientals and Their Cultural Adjustment,* Social Science Source Documents, no. 4 (Nashville: Social Science Institute, Fisk University, 1946), p. 31.

25. Ibid.

26. Quoted in Donaldina Cameron, "The Story of Wong So," *Women and Mission* 2, no. 5 (August, 1925): 170.

27. "Story of Wong Ah So," p. 31.

28. Quoted in Cameron, "Story of Wong So," p. 170.

29. The following account is from Law Shee Low, interview with author, October 20, 1988.

30. Jane Kwong Lee, "A Chinese American" (unpublished autobiography), pt. I, p. 3.

31. Ibid., p. 95.

32. Ibid., p. 151.

33. Ibid., p. 169.

34. Ibid., p. 203.

35. *CSYP*, June 10, 1903. Mai's speech is significant not only as an indictment of discriminatory treatment, but also as an early example of the sentiments of an outspoken immigrant woman. She concluded her speech by calling on her compatriots to work together to make China strong, and to women in the audience she said, "My dear sisters, we must take heart. We are human beings, not to be compared to animals and goods. We must work together so that we can stand in equality and liberty."

36. David M. Brownstone, Irene M. Franck, and Douglass L. Brownstone, *Island of Hope, Island of Tears* (New York: Penguin Books, 1986), pp. 168–70.

37. To compare the ordeal suffered by Chinese immigrants at Angel Island and that of European immigrants at Ellis Island, see Lai, Lim, and Yung, *Island;* and Brownstone, Franck, and Brownstone, *Island of Hope.*

38. During the early years of the Exclusion period, immigration authorities discriminated against Chinese students, merchants, and other exempt classes. A 1905 boycott of American goods in China was spurred in part by discriminatory treatment of the exempt classes. See Shih-shan Henry Tsai, *China and the Overseas Chinese in the United States, 1868–1911* (Fayetteville: University of Arkansas Press, 1983), chap. 6.

39. The following account is from my interview with Law Shee Low.

40. Wen-Hsien Chen, "Chinese Under Both Exclusion and Immigration Laws" (Ph.D. diss., University of Chicago, 1940), p. 107.

41. Lai, Lim, and Yung, *Island*, p. 111.

42. Ibid., p. 16; Woo, "Protestant Work Among the Chinese," pp. 65–66; and *San Francisco Chronicle*, June 24, 1951, p. 10S.

43. Unfortunately, because the administration building that housed Chinese women was destroyed in the 1940 fire, no poems by Chinese women survive at Angel Island.

44. Ruth Chan Jang, interview with author, July 8, 1994.

45. Lai, Lim, and Yung, *Island*, p. 74.

46. Law Shee Low, interview with author.

47. See Florence Worley Chinn, "Religious Education in the Chinese Community of San Francisco" (Master's thesis, University of Chicago, 1920), pp. 28–31; Whitfield, "Public Opinion," chap. 3; Ivan Light, "From Vice District to Tourist Attraction: The Moral Career of American Chinatowns, 1880–1940," *Pacific Historical Review* 43, no. 3 (August 1974): 367–94; and Philip P. Choy,

"San Francisco's Chinatown Architecture," *Chinese America: History and Perspectives 1990*, pp. 37–66.

48. Whitfield, "Public Opinion," pp. 65–71. A "Survey of Social Work Needs of the Chinese Population of San Francisco" published by the Community Chest of San Francisco in 1930 (hereafter cited as Community Chest 1930 Survey) concluded that "health conditions among the Chinese of San Francisco are bad . . . [because of] poor housing, poor sanitation, lack of sun, light and air, poor recreation facilities and inadequate social opportunities," accounting for a death rate among the Chinese that was almost three times as great as among the general population of the City. The leading causes of death for the Chinese were diseases of the heart and circulatory system and tuberculosis (p. 3).

49. See L. Ling-chi Wang, "An Overview of Chinese American Communities During the Exclusion Era, 1883–1943" (unpublished paper); and Helen Virginia Cather, "The History of San Francisco's Chinatown" (Master's thesis, University of California, Berkeley, 1932), chap. 4.

50. Started by the Presbyterian minister Ng Poon Chew in 1900, *CSYP* favored reform in China and advocated equal rights for all Chinese Americans, including women. The daily newspaper enjoyed a wide circulation among Chinese Americans until its decline in the 1930s. See Him Mark Lai, "The Chinese American Press," in *The Ethnic Press in the United States: A Historical Analysis and Handbook*, ed. Sally M. Miller (New York: Greenwood Press, 1987), pp. 27–43; Corinne K. Hoexter, *From Canton to California: The Epic of Chinese Immigration* (New York: Four Winds Press, 1976); and Yung, "Social Awakening."

51. "Story of Wong Ah So," p. 31.

52. Cameron, "Story of Wong So," p. 171.

53. Wong Ah So, letter to her mother, file 260, Cameron House, San Francisco.

54. Cameron, "Story of Wong So," p. 171.

55. "Story of Wong Ah So," pp. 32–33.

56. Wong Ah So, letter to Donaldina Cameron, October 24, 1928, file 258, Cameron House, San Francisco; Pascoe, *Relations of Rescue*, pp. 163–65.

57. Donaldina Cameron, "New Lives for Old in Chinatown," *Missionary Review of the World* 57 (July–August 1934): 329.

58. Hirata, "Free, Indentured, Enslaved," p. 24. The figures for 1900, 1910, and 1920 are based on my computations from the U.S. National Archives, Record Group 29, "Census of U.S. Population" (manuscript), San Francisco, California (hereafter cited as 1900, 1910, or 1920 manuscript census). There were 280 prostitutes listed in 1900, and another 59 women were probably also prostitutes, judging from their living arrangements—three or more single young women living in all-female households. No prostitutes were listed as such in the 1910 census, but I suspect 92 were prostitutes again based on their living arrangements (see appendix table 6). I am indebted to Sucheng Chan for sharing her data on Chinese women in San Francisco from the 1900 and 1910 manuscript schedules. Any computational errors are mine.

59. Martin, *Chinatown's Angry Angel*, pp. 256–61; and Mason, "Social Christianity," pp. 216–18.

60. Richard Kock Dare, "The Economic and Social Adjustment of the San

Francisco Chinese for the Past Fifty Years" (Master's thesis, University of California, Berkeley, 1959), p. 23; Martin, *Chinatown's Angry Angel*, p. 239.

61. *San Francisco Call*, November 23, 1895, p. 7.

62. *San Francisco Chronicle*, January 2, 1905, p. 16.

63. See Pascoe, *Relations of Rescue*; Martin, *Chinatown's Angry Angel*; and Carol Green Wilson, *Chinatown Quest: One Hundred Years of Donaldina Cameron House, 1874–1974* (San Francisco: California Historical Society, 1974).

64. Martin, *Chinatown's Angry Angel*, pp. 193–94.

65. Donaldina Cameron, "Report of the Mission Home Superintendent," *Women's Occidental Board of Foreign Missions, Annual Report*, 1908–9, p. 76.

66. For different assessments of Donaldina Cameron, see McClain, "Donaldina Cameron"; Martin, *Chinatown's Angry Angel*; Pascoe, *Relations of Rescue*; and Mason, "Social Christianity."

67. Wilson, *Chinatown Quest*, pp. 19–25; Martin, *Chinatown's Angry Angel*, pp. 55–59; Howard A. Zink, "Cast of Characters," Kum Quey file, Palo Alto Historical Association; *Palo Alto Times*, April 27, 1900; *CSYP*, March 24, April 2, 3, 5, 13, 14, 16, 25, 28, 30, May 7, 8, 14, 1900; *San Francisco News*, March 17, 1937, p. 17.

68. *CSYP*, August 8, 1907. For an overview of *CSYP*'s coverage of women's issues, see Yung, "Social Awakening."

69. Ashbury, *Barbary Coast*, pp. 169–72.

70. See David J. Pivar, *Purity Crusade: Sexual Morality and Social Control, 1868–1900* (Westport, Conn.: Greenwood Press, 1973).

71. O. Edward Janney, *The White Slave Traffic in America* (New York: National Vigilance Committee, 1911), p. 13. Although white slavery, as opposed to black slavery, referred to European American women by definition, Chinese women who had been forced into prostitution were implicated.

72. See M. G. C. Edholm, "Traffic in White Girls," *Californian Illustrated Magazine* 2 (June–November 1892): 825–38; Janney, *White Slave Traffic*; Francesco Cordasco, *The White Slave Trade and the Immigrants: A Chapter in American Social History* (Detroit: Blaine Ethridge Books, 1981); Howard B. Woolston, *Prostitution in the United States* (New York: Century Co., 1921), pp. 159–78; Pillors, "Criminalization of Prostitution," pp. 140–45; and Rosen, *Lost Sisterhood*, pp. 112–35.

73. See Ashbury, *Barbary Coast*, chap. 12; Issel and Cherny, *San Francisco*, pp. 106–9; Neil Larry Shumsky and Larry M. Springer, "San Francisco's Zone of Prostitution, 1880–1934," *Journal of Historical Geography* 7, no. 1 (1981): 71–89; Pillors, "Criminalization of Prostitution," pp. 146–63; and Symanski, *Immoral Landscape*, pp. 129–35.

74. Pillors, "Criminalization of Prostitution," pp. 164–69.

75. See Jerry Flamm, *Good Life in Hard Times: San Francisco's 1920s and 1930s* (San Francisco: Chronicle Books, 1978), chap. 6.

76. The figures for 1880 are from Stephens, "Quantitative History," pp. 71–88; and Hirata, "Free, Indentured, Enslaved." Figures for 1900, 1910, and 1920 are based on my computation of data from the manuscript censuses.

77. According to the 1920 manuscript census, 38 percent of Chinese husbands were merchants or managers. Some of these, however, may in fact have

been posing as such so that their wives could come from China and join them in America. If these men were actually laborers, their wives likely had to engage in wage work.

78. Housing conditions in Chinatown were congested and unsanitary, according to the Community Chest 1930 Survey. Of the 153 families surveyed, only 19 had bathtubs, 49 had private kitchens, and 33 had private toilets. Family size averaged 6.1 persons, and most families occupied two small rooms, half of which had no windows.

79. Law Shee Low, interview with Sandy Lee, May 2, 1982, Chinese Women of America Research Project, Chinese Culture Foundation of San Francisco.

80. Segregation had the same effect on the acculturation of Italian and Mexican women; see Cohen, *Workshop to Office;* and George J. Sanchez, *Becoming Mexican American: Ethnicity, Culture, and Identity in Chicano Los Angeles, 1900–1945* (New York: Oxford University Press, 1993).

81. For a study of changing clothing and hairstyles as indicators of acculturation, see Ginger Chih, "Immigration of Chinese Women to the U.S.A." (Master's thesis, Sarah Lawrence College, 1977).

82. At one point, Law gave this alternative a shot: "We tried to pick shrimps and decided it was easier to sew. My older daughter brought home ten pounds and we picked at home. Our shoulders hurt and our nails hurt and we gave up. Only made $1 that day for the ten pounds." The following account is derived from my interview with Law Shee Low, except as noted.

83. Law Shee Low, interview with Sandy Lee.

84. Most women who sewed at home were averaging $1 a day, according to Elsa Lissner in 1922; see "Investigation into Conditions in the Chinese Quarter in San Francisco and Oakland," Survey of Race Relations Collection, Hoover Institution on War, Revolution, and Peace, Stanford University.

85. J. C. Geiger et al., *The Health of the Chinese in an American City: San Francisco* (San Francisco: Department of Public Health, 1939), p. 25.

86. See H. Hartmann, "Capitalism, Patriarchy, and Job Segregation"; see also E. Glenn, "Racial Ethnic Women's Labor," for an argument on why this framework does not apply to women of color.

87. For a discussion of women's survival as resistance, see Patricia Hill Collins, *Black Feminist Thought: Knowledge, Consciousness, and the Politics of Empowerment* (London: HarperCollins Academic, 1990), chap. 7; and Bettina Aptheker, *Tapestries of Life: Women's Work, Women's Consciousness, and the Meaning of Daily Experience* (Amherst: University of Massachusetts Press, 1989), chap. 5.

88. See Bonnie Thornton Dill, "Our Mother's Grief: Racial Ethnic Women and the Maintenance of Families," *Journal of Family History* 13, no. 4 (1988): 415–31; and E. Glenn, "Racial Ethnic Women's Labor."

89. Law Shee Low, interview with author. Law Shee Low's frequent references to both the Christian God and Chinese gods (as represented by "heaven") are another indication of her pragmatic approach to life: cover all the bases.

90. *CSYP*, April 2, 1907.

91. See Yung, "Social Awakening."

92. I am indebted to Peggy Pascoe for sharing with me her extensive files

on past inmates of the Presbyterian Mission Home (name changed to Cameron House in 1942) and to the Gum Moon Women's Residence for allowing me to review the case files of the Methodist Mission Home. For a fuller account and interpretation of the Presbyterian records, see Pascoe, *Relations of Rescue*.

93. Caroline Chew, "Development of Chinese Family Life in America" (Master's thesis, Mills College, 1926), pp. 22–23; and Ching Chao Wu, "Chinatowns," pp. 248–50.

94. Chew, "Development of Chinese Family Life," p. 30; and Ching Chao Wu, "Chinatowns," pp. 245–46.

95. Elaine Tyler May, *Great Expectations: Marriage and Divorce in Post-Victorian America* (Chicago: University of Chicago Press, 1980), p. 85.

96. Ching Chao Wu, "Chinatowns," p. 235; Pascoe, *Relations of Rescue*, pp. 38, 160; and Dare, "Economic and Social Adjustment," p. 90.

97. *San Francisco Call*, January 5, 1921, p. 14. In another case, reported in the *San Francisco Chronicle*, July 3, 1924, p. 6, "fervid love letters, written by a white woman to Harry, a Chinese, and from Harry to the white woman, won a divorce for Minnie, Harry's wife, yesterday when produced before Superior Judge Michael J. Roche."

98. Pascoe, *Relations of Rescue*, p. 160.

99. Dare, "Economic and Social Adjustment," p. 90.

100. See Rosaldo, "Woman, Culture, and Society."

101. See Dorothy O. Helly and Susan M. Reverby, eds., *Gendered Domains: Rethinking Public and Private in Women's History* (Ithaca: Cornell University Press, 1992).

102. J. Lee, "A Chinese American," pt. II, p. 10.

103. Jane Kwong Lee, interview with author, October 22 and November 2, 1988.

104. For a comparison of work patterns among different groups of women, see Louise A. Tilly and Joan W. Scott, *Women, Work, and Family* (New York: Holt, Rinehart & Winston, 1978); Alice Kessler-Harris, *Out to Work: A History of Wage-earning Women in the United States* (Oxford: Oxford University Press, 1982); Cohen, *Workshop to Office*; Laura Anker, "Family, Work, and Community: Southern and Eastern European Immigrant Women Speak from the Connecticut Federal Writers' Project," in Helly and Reverby, eds., *Gendered Domains*, pp. 303–21; and E. Glenn, *Issei, Nisei, Warbride*.

105. See Issel and Cherny, *San Francisco*, pp. 76–77; Alex Yamato, "Socioeconomic Change Among Japanese Americans in the San Francisco Bay Area" (Ph.D. diss., University of California, Berkeley, 1986), chap. 4; and Albert S. Broussard, *Black San Francisco: The Struggle for Racial Equality in the West, 1900–1954* (Lawrence: University Press of Kansas, 1993), chap. 2.

106. Chinn, ed., *History of the Chinese in California*, pp. 53–54; Dean Lan, "Chinatown Sweatshops," in *Counterpoint: Perspectives on Asian America*, ed. Emma Gee (Los Angeles: Asian American Studies Center, University of California, 1976), pp. 347–58; and Dare, "Economic and Social Adjustment," pp. 15–16, 66.

107. Community Chest 1930 Survey, p. 8. When Chinese men dominated the trade, there were three Chinese guilds to regulate hours, wages, and work

conditions. These guilds, which did not allow women members, became defunct after women entered the trade. Women workers remained unorganized until 1938, when they formed their own local under the auspices of the International Ladies' Garment Workers' Union.

108. Lissner, "Investigation into Conditions."

109. Whitfield, "Public Opinion," p. 45.

110. Lissner, "Investigation into Conditions."

111. See S. Glenn, *Daughters of the Shtetl.*

112. See "Miscellaneous Accounts," Survey of Race Relations Collection, Hoover Institution on War, Revolution, and Peace, Stanford University.

113. Diane Mei Lin Mark and Ginger Chih, *A Place Called Chinese America* (Dubuque: Kendall/Hunt, 1982), p. 67.

114. Ibid., pp. 68–69.

115. Lissner, "Investigation into Conditions," p. 2. A similar work environment for Jewish women is described in S. Glenn, *Daughters of the Shtetl:* "The informal authority of the boss, the small size of the shop, and the shared ethnic background of the work force created a relatively unstructured environment. Few rules governed shop life. Hard work was expected, but any form of social behavior that encouraged it was usually tolerated. As a result, singing, talking, smoking, drinking, eating, and other 'merry makings' were a regular part of the routine in these shops" (p. 135).

116. See Patricia Zavella, *Women's Work and Chicano Families: Cannery Workers of the Santa Clara Valley* (Ithaca: Cornell University Press, 1987), for a similar analysis of how outside work affected family roles and relationships for Chicanas employed in canneries.

117. California State Emergency Relief Administration, "Survey of Social Work Needs of the Chinese Population of San Francisco, California," 1935 (hereafter cited as CSERA 1935 Survey), p. 32. My own mother's former boss, who ran a Chinatown sewing factory for over fifty years, gained the friendship and loyalty of my mother and many other workers through her willingness to assist them with personal problems, her fairness in delegating work assignments, and her generosity in hosting luncheons for the workers during the Chinese New Year, Thanksgiving, and Christmas holidays. Despite her illegal practice of paying her workers below the minimum wage, none of her employees reported her, and two women stayed with her for over forty years.

118. Jane Kwong Lee, interview.

119. See Gerda Lerner, *The Majority Finds Its Past: Placing Women in History* (Oxford: Oxford University Press, 1979), chap. 5.

120. See ibid., chap. 6; Anne Firor Scott, *Natural Allies: Women's Associations in American History* (Urbana: University of Illinois Press, 1991); Karen J. Blair, *The Clubswoman as Feminist: True Womanhood Redefined, 1868–1914* (New York: Holmes & Meier, 1980); Paula Giddings, *When and Where I Enter: The Impact of Black Women on Race and Sex in America* (New York: William Morrow, 1984); and Evelyn Brooks Higginbotham, *Righteous Discontent: The Women's Movement in the Black Baptist Church, 1880–1920* (Cambridge, Mass.: Harvard University Press, 1993).

121. *San Francisco Chronicle*, January 18, 1903, p. 2.

122. Woo, "Protestant Work," pp. 231, 264.

123. Dora Lee Wong, interview with author, October 5, 1982.

124. Ira M. Condit, *The Chinaman as We See Him and Fifty Years of Work for Him* (Chicago: Fleming H. Revell Co., 1900), pp. 209–10; Hoexter, *From Canton to California*; and *CSYP*, May 25 and 28, 1911.

125. King Yoak Won Wu, interview with Genny Lim, October 27, 1982, Chinese Women of America Research Project, Chinese Culture Foundation of San Francisco.

126. I am indebted to Teresa Wu of the Chinese YWCA, historian and architect Philip P. Choy of the Chinese Historical Society of America, and Yee Ling Fong of the International Institute of San Francisco for sharing past correspondence, board minutes, and staff reports of the Chinese YWCA with me.

127. According to Giddings, *When and Where I Enter*, pp. 155–58, black women in the South resented the discriminatory policies of the national board, particularly the lack of black women on the board and local black input on the establishment and running of YWCA branches in the South.

128. See Alison R. Drucker, "The Role of the YWCA in the Development of the Chinese Women's Movement, 1890–1927," *Social Services Review*, September 1979, pp. 421–40; Mary S. Sims, "The Natural History of a Social Institution: The Y.W.C.A." (Ph.D. diss., New York University, 1935); Jean McCown, "Women in a Changing China: The Y.W.C.A." (April 5, 1970), YWCA of the U.S.A., National Board Archives, New York; Emma Sarepta Yule, "Miss China," *Scribner's* 71 (January 1922): 66–79; and Kwok Pui-lan, *Chinese Women and Christianity, 1860–1927* (Atlanta: Scholars Press, 1992), pp. 126–32.

129. *CSYP*, September 28, 1929.

130. Florence Chinn Kwan, interview with author, October 12, 1988.

131. For an analysis of the baby contest in the larger context of maternal and infant care in the United States, see Alisa Klaus, *Every Child a Lion: The Origins of Maternal and Infant Health Policy in the United States and France, 1890–1920* (Ithaca: Cornell University Press, 1993).

132. *CSYP*, May 4, 1907.

133. *CSYP*, April 21, May 12, 17, 1911.

134. Zeng Bugui, "Sun Zhongshan yu Jiujinshan nü Tongmenghui yuan" (Sun Yat-sen and the women members of San Francisco's Tongmenghui), in *Zhongshan xiansheng yishi* (Anecdotes of Sun Yat-sen) (Beijing: Zhongguo Wenshi Chubanshe, 1986), pp. 141–42.

135. See Lilly King Gee Won, "My Recollections of Dr. Sun Yat-sen's Stay at Our Home in San Francisco," *Chinese America: History and Perspectives 1990*, pp. 67–82.

136. *San Francisco Call*, February 13, 1911, p. 1; October 29, 1911, p. 34; and *CSYP*, May 25, November 21, 27, 1911; January 12, 1912.

137. See Mary Backus Rankin, "The Emergence of Women at the End of the Ch'ing: The Case of Ch'iu Chin," in *Women in Chinese Society*, ed. Margery Wolf and Roxane Witke (Stanford: Stanford University Press, 1975), pp. 39–66; and L. Collins, "New Women," pp. 351–60.

138. Quoted in Croll, *Feminism and Socialism*, pp. 68–69.

139. *CSYP*, August 22, 31, September 9, 11, 12, 13, 16, 17, 1907.

140. Zeng, "Sun Zhongshan," p. 141; *San Francisco Call*, October 29, 1911, p. 34.

141. Jane Kwong Lee, "Chinese Women in San Francisco," *Chinese Digest*, June 1938, p. 8.

142. Levy, *Chinese Footbinding*, pp. 275–80; Dora Lee Wong, interview; Florence Chinn Kwan, interview; Fred Schulze, interview with author, January 26, 1989; Clara Lee, interview with author, October 2, 1986; Connie Young Yu, "The World of Our Grandmothers," in *Making Waves: Anthology of Writings By and About Asian American Women*, ed. Asian Women United (Boston: Beacon Press, 1989), pp. 33–42.

143. Rose Hum Lee, "The Growth and Decline of Chinese Communities in the Rocky Mountain Region" (Ph.D. diss., University of Chicago, 1947), pp. 252–53.

144. *San Francisco Examiner*, May 10, 1914, p. 78.

145. *San Francisco Examiner*, July 26, 1915, p. 6.

146. *San Francisco Chronicle*, February 8, 1914, p. 5.

147. The Chinese Native Sons of the Golden State changed its name to the Chinese American Citizens Alliance in 1928 after the Native Sons of the Golden West refused to give them affiliated status. See Sue Fawn Chung, "The Chinese American Citizens Alliance: An Effort in Assimilation, 1895–1965," *Chinese America: History and Perspectives 1988*, pp. 30–57.

148. *San Francisco Chronicle*, February 8, 1914, p. 5.

149. Ibid.

150. *Sai Gai Yat Po*, August 22, 1913.

151. Clara Lee, interview with author, July 31, 1989.

152. The daughter of liberal parents Rev. Chan Hon Fun and Ow Muck Gay, Clara Lee was born in 1886. The family moved to Oakland before the 1906 earthquake, and Clara remained there after her marriage to Dr. Charles Lee, the first Chinese licensed dentist in California. She had just turned 100 when I interviewed her in 1986. Clara Lee passed away in 1993 at the age of 106.

3.   First Steps

1. See Park, *Race and Culture*.

2. See Milton M. Gordon, *Assimilation in American Life* (New York: Oxford University Press, 1964); and Omi and Winant, *Racial Formation*.

3. Ching Chao Wu, "Chinatowns," p. 290. Park attracted a number of Chinese American students to study sociology at the University of Chicago. Among those who chose to research and write about Chinese Americans were Rose Hum Lee ("The Growth and Decline of Chinese Communities in the Rocky Mountain Region," Ph.D. diss., 1947), Beulah Ong Kwoh ("Occupational Status of the American-born Chinese College Graduates," Master's thesis, 1947), Liang Yuan ("The Chinese Family in Chicago," Master's thesis, 1951), and Paul C. P. Siu ("The Chinese Laundryman," Ph.D. diss., 1953).

4. The following account is derived from an interview I conducted with Alice Sue Fun on February 28, 1982.

5. Many working-class immigrant daughters had their schooling cut short because of traditional values and economic constraints; see, for example, Cohen, *Workshop to Office*, chap. 4; and S. Glenn, *Daughters of the Shtetl*, chap. 2.

6. Florence Chinn Kwan, interview with author, October 12, 1988. Chinese Christian families were the first in Chinatown to dress in Western clothing. Clara Lee, whose father, Chan Hon Fun, was also a minister, recalls feeling conspicuous when she first wore a Western dress in Chinatown: "When I walked down from Stockton Street to go to the store, I was all dressed up and so proud. Then some Chinese man said, 'Yun ng yun, gwai ng gwai, do ng gee jo muk yeh?' [It doesn't appear to be human or devil; what is it?). And of course I cried" (Clara Lee, interview with author, October 2, 1986).

7. Florence Chinn Kwan, "Some Rambling Thoughts on Why I Am a Christian" (unpublished paper, November 1966).

8. Florence Chinn Kwan, interview with author, October 7, 1988.

9. Ibid.

10. To compare how Mexican American and Japanese American women experienced acculturation and responded to cultural conflicts, see Sanchez, *Becoming Mexican American*; Vicki L. Ruiz, "'Star Struck': Acculturation, Adolescence, and Mexican American Women, 1920–1950," in *Small Worlds: Children and Adolescents in America, 1850–1950*, ed. Elliott West and Paul Petrik (Lawrence: University Press of Kansas, 1992), pp. 61–80; Mei Nakano, *Japanese American Women: Three Generations, 1890–1990* (Berkeley, Calif.: Mina Press, 1990); and Valerie Matsumoto, "Desperately Seeking 'Deirdre': Gender Roles, Multicultural Relations, and Nisei Women Writers of the 1930s," *Frontiers: A Journal of Women Studies* 12, no. 1 (1991): 19–32.

11. Ching Chao Wu, "Chinatowns"; Kit King Louis, "A Study of American-born and American-reared Chinese in Los Angeles" (Master's thesis, University of Southern California, 1931); and Marjorie Lee, "*Hu-Jee*: The Forgotten Second Generation of Chinese America, 1930–1950" (Master's thesis, University of California, Los Angeles, 1984).

12. I am indebted to Colleen Fong and Marjorie Lee for calling my attention to Karl Mannheim's "The Problem of Generations," in *Essays on the Sociology of Knowledge by Karl Mannheim*, ed. Paul Keeskemeti (London: Routledge & Kegan, 1959), pp. 276–320. According to Mannheim, there are three aspects to the sociology of generations: generational status, that is, being born within the same historical and cultural context; actual generation, that is, participating in the common destiny of the historical and social unit; and generational unit, that is, sharing the same response to sociohistorical forces. By studying generational units we acknowledge the importance of historical location rather than birth order in understanding the diversity of political perspectives within an actual generation. Mannheim's contention is that one unit's perspective generally comes to dominate, speaking for and influencing the entire generation. Jade Snow Wong's perspective of cultural fusion, also found in the autobiographical writings of her peers, can be said to be that dominant view for her generation.

13. The following works were also useful in my analysis of Jade Snow Wong's life story: Lowell Chun-Hoon, "Jade Snow Wong and the Fate of Chinese-American Identity," *Amerasia Journal* 1 (1971): 52–63; Elaine H. Kim, *Asian*

American Literature: An Introduction to the Writings and Their Social Context (Philadelphia: Temple University Press, 1982), pp. 58–90; and Marjorie Lee, "*Hu-Jee*," pp. 64–79.

14. J. Wong, *Fifth Chinese Daughter*, p. 2.

15. Ibid., p. vii. Jade Snow Wong does not follow this practice in her second autobiography, *No Chinese Stranger* (New York: Harper & Row, 1975). That book begins in the third person singular, but she switches to first person midway through, after the death of her father—as a sign of her readiness to be the head of her own family.

16. J. Wong, *Fifth Chinese Daughter*, pp. 2–3.

17. Ibid., pp. 14–15.

18. Ibid., p. 35.

19. Ibid., p. 69.

20. Ibid., pp. 113–14.

21. Ibid., pp. 109–10.

22. Ibid., p. 128.

23. Ibid., p. 246.

24. "Story of a Chinese College Girl (The Conflict Between the Old and the Young)," Survey of Race Relations Collection, Hoover Institution on War, Revolution, and Peace, Stanford University.

25. Ibid., p. 3.

26. According to another interview in the Survey of Race Relations Collection, "Miss Wong says there are two kinds of girls in Chinatown, the old-fashioned Chinese girl and the modern Chinese girl. A man who wants a real Chinese wife marries the old-fashioned girl, who can keep house, will be willing to stay at home and who will not spend too much on paint and clothes" ("Esther Wong, Native-born Chinese, San Francisco, July 1, 1924," p. 1).

27. "Story of a Chinese College Girl," p. 8.

28. Ibid., p. 3.

29. See Paula Fass, *The Damned and the Beautiful: American Youth in the 1920s* (New York: Oxford University Press, 1977); and John D'Emilio and Estelle Freedman, *Intimate Matters: A History of Sexuality in America* (New York: Harper & Row, 1988).

30. Judy Chu, "Anna May Wong," in *Counterpoint: Perspectives on Asian America*, ed. Emma Gee (Los Angeles: Asian American Studies Center, University of California, 1976), pp. 284–88; and *San Francisco Chronicle*, June 3, 1928, p. 13.

31. *San Francisco Examiner*, May 1, 1922, p. 8.

32. "Interview with Flora Belle Jan, Daughter of Proprietor of the 'Yet Far Low,' Chop Suey Restaurant, Tulare St. and China Alley, Fresno," Survey of Race Relations Collection, Hoover Institution on War, Revolution, and Peace, Stanford University.

33. "Chinatown Sheiks" appeared in the *San Francisco Examiner*, March 27, 1924, p. 9. "Old Mother Grundy" was mentioned by Flora Belle Jan in the Survey of Race Relations interview, but I have been unable to locate a copy of it.

34. I am indebted to Flora Belle Jan's daughters, whose names have been withheld by request, for sharing some of the letters written by their mother to her friend, Ludmelia Holstein.

35. Flora Belle Jan, letter to Ludmelia Holstein, July 17, 1921.

36. Ibid., September 3, 1918; August 17, 1921; June 28, 1920.

37. Ibid., August 20, 1920.

38. Ibid., July 17, 1921.

39. For a history of discrimination against Chinese students in the San Francisco public schools, see Low, *Unimpressible Race.*

40. Liu Pei Chi, *A History of the Chinese in the United States of America*, vol. 2 (in Chinese) (Taipei: Liming Wenhua Shiye Gongsi, 1981), p. 363.

41. *CSYP*, February 17, 1903.

42. *CSYP*, February 17, 1913.

43. F. Chinn, "Religious Education," p. 40. In 1906, the San Francisco school board changed the name of the school from Chinese Primary School to Oriental Public School to accommodate Japanese and Korean students. Under pressure from the Chinese American Citizens Alliance, which found "Oriental" derogatory, the name was subsequently changed to Commodore Stockton School in 1924. See Low, *Unimpressible Race*, pp. 112–15.

44. Mary Bo-Tze Lee, "Problems of the Segregated School for Asiatics in San Francisco" (Master's thesis, University of California, Berkeley, 1921).

45. Low, *Unimpressible Race*, pp. 115–23.

46. Liu Pei Chi, *History*, p. 364.

47. Shih Hsien-ju, "The Social and Vocational Adjustment of the Second Generation Chinese High School Students in San Francisco" (Ph.D. diss., University of California, Berkeley, 1937), pp. 36–54.

48. Eva Lowe, interview with Genny Lim, July 15, 1982, Chinese Women of America Research Project, Chinese Culture Foundation of San Francisco.

49. J. Wong, *Fifth Chinese Daughter*, pp. 68–69.

50. Thomas W. Chinn, *Bridging the Pacific: San Francisco's Chinatown and Its People* (San Francisco: Chinese Historical Society of America, 1989), p. 248.

51. "Story of a Chinese College Girl," p. 4.

52. Shih, "Social and Vocational Adjustment," pp. 56–64.

53. Janie Chu, "The Oriental Girl in the Occident," *Women and Mission* 3, no. 5 (August 1926): 175.

54. See Kwoh, "Occupational Status."

55. "The cream" is taken from Grace W. Wang's "A Speech on Second-Generation Chinese in U.S.A.," presented to the Chinese Women's Association in New York: "These college and high school students are sometimes referred to as the cream of Second Generation Chinese, for only a few members of the average Chinese community are students seeking higher learning" (*Chinese Digest*, August 7, 1936, p. 6).

56. Florence Chinn Kwan, interview with author.

57. Christopher Chow and Russell Leong, "A Pioneer Chinatown Teacher: An Interview with Alice Fong Yu," *Amerasia Journal* 5, no. 1 (1978): 77. See also Katie Choy, "Alice Fong Yu: Remembrances of a Chinese Pioneer," *Prism* 11, no. 2 (December 1974): 5–8.

58. Bessie Jeong, interview with Suellen Cheng and Munson Kwok, December 17, 1981, Southern California Chinese American Oral History Project, Chinese Historical Society of Southern California, Los Angeles.

59. *San Francisco Chronicle*, May 14, 1914, p. 8.

60. Edwin Owyang, interview with author, September 10, 1987.

61. Mrs. William Z. L. Sung, "A Pioneer Chinese Family," in *The Life, Influence, and the Role of the Chinese in the United States, 1776–1960* (San Francisco: Chinese Historical Society of America, 1976), p. 291.

62. See E. Glenn, "Split Household, Small Producer."

63. May Kew Fung, interview with Jeffrey Ow, March 25, 1990, Jeffrey Ow private collection.

64. According to Mickey Lee, the first Chinese girls to take jobs at the 1915 Exposition at Treasure Island were called *gee yow nu* (liberated women) because they had broken with tradition and left home to work (Mickey Lee, interview with author, November 1, 1989).

65. Quoted in Louis, "Study of American-born and American-reared Chinese," p. 85. His reference to "the Americans" as exclusively the white dominant group was common during this period, and even today most Chinese, regardless of where they were born, do not feel they are a part of America or that they are Americans.

66. Community Chest 1930 Survey, pp. 22–23.

67. Eliot Grinnell Mears, *Resident Orientals on the American Pacific Coast: Their Legal and Economic Status* (Chicago: University of Chicago Press, 1928), p. 200.

68. Donaldina Cameron, "Salvaged for Service," *Women and Mission* 4, no. 5 (August 1927): 65.

69. Pascoe, *Relations of Rescue*, pp. 166–71. For a comparative analysis of how and why Japanese American women became concentrated in domestic work, see E. Glenn, *Issei, Nisei, Warbride*.

70. William Carlson Smith, *Americans in Process: A Study of Our Citizens of Oriental Ancestry* (Ann Arbor: Edwards Bros., 1937), pp. 92–93, 301.

71. Gladys Ng Gin, interview with author, November 4, 1988.

72. Rose Yuen Ow, interview with Philip P. Choy and Him Mark Lai, September 9, 1970, Him Mark Lai private collection.

73. "Savings Development," *Bulletin, Financial Advertisers Association*, May 1941, p. 269.

74. Ibid.

75. "Our Chinatown Branch," *Bank American*, January, 1956, p. 7.

76. *Chinese Digest*, April 10, 1936, pp. 10, 14.

77. Ruth Fong Chinn, "Square and Circle Club of San Francisco: A Chinese Women's Culture" (Senior thesis, University of California, Santa Cruz, 1987), pp. 29–43; Mrs. Choy Lee, interview with Him Mark Lai and Helen Lai, March 2, 1975, Him Mark Lai private collection; and Cameron, "Salvaged for Service," p. 70.

78. During the 1910s, with the assistance of the female-dominated Telephone Operators Union, thousands of women across the country walked off their jobs to protest the industry's autocratic methods and to demand better hours, wages, and benefits. Although significant, their resistance and union militancy were short-lived. See Stephan H. Norwood, *Labor's Flaming Youth: Telephone Operators and Worker Militancy, 1878–1923* (Urbana: University of Illinois Press, 1990).

79. See Broussard, *Black San Francisco,* chap. 2; and Elizabeth Higginbotham, "Employment for Professional Black Women in the Twentieth Century," paper prepared for the Albany Conference, Ingredients for Women's Employment Policy, April 19–20, 1985.

80. J. Wong, *Fifth Chinese Daughter,* p. 188.

81. Ibid., p. 234.

82. K. Choy, "Alice Fong Yu," p. 7.

83. Mickey Fong Lee, interview with Ernest Chann, February 23, 1982, Ernest Chann private collection.

84. Bessie Jeong, interview.

85. Margaret Chung, "TV Summary," unpublished autobiography, Asian American Studies Library, University of California, Berkeley.

86. *Chinese Hospital Medical Staff Archives, 1978–1981* (San Francisco: Chinese Hospital, 1982), pp. 8–9.

87. J. Wong, *Fifth Chinese Daughter,* p. 95.

88. Alice Fong Yu, interview with Gordon Chang, November 21, 1986, Gordon Chang private collection.

89. Flora Belle Jan's daughters (names withheld by request), interview with author, August 6, 1989.

90. Flora Belle Jan, letter to Ludmelia Holstein, December 1944.

91. Ibid., July 16, 1947.

92. R. Lee, *Chinese in the United States,* p. 124.

93. Barbara Sickerman, ed., *Notable American Women: The Modern Period* (Cambridge, Mass.: Harvard University Press, 1980), pp. 414–15.

94. See Fass, *Damned and the Beautiful;* D'Emilio and Freedman, *Intimate Matters,* chap. 11; and Mary P. Ryan, *Womanhood in America: From Colonial Times to the Present* (New York: Franklin Watts, 1983), chap. 5.

95. Chingwah Lee, "The Second Generation of the Chinese," *Hospital Social Service* 21, no. 3 (March 1930): 193.

96. Janie Chu, "Oriental Girl," p. 175.

97. Other minority women experienced the same predicament. See Ruiz, "'Star Struck'"; and Matsumoto, "Desperately Seeking 'Deirdre.'"

98. Chinese YWCA, "Annual Report," 1926.

99. *CSYP,* August 23, 1915.

100. Sexual exploitation becomes more pronounced when beauty contests turn into bathing suit contests in the post–World War II period. See Judy Yung, "Miss Chinatown USA and the Representation of Beauty," paper presented at the Ninth National Conference of the Association of Asian American Studies, San Jose, Calif.: May 30, 1992.

101. *San Francisco Examiner,* March 27, 1924, p. 9.

102. Flora Belle Jan, letter to Ludmelia Holstein, November 27, 1925.

103. Florence Lee Loo, interview with June Quan, January 6, 1982, Chinese Women of America Research Project, Chinese Culture Foundation of San Francisco.

104. In 1935, five denominational institutions provided for the care and welfare of Chinese children: Presbyterian Girls Home, Methodist Home (for girls), Ming Quong Home (established by Presbyterians for girls), Chung Mei Home

(established by Baptists for boys), and Mei Lun Yuen Home (established by Presbyterians for infants). See CSERA 1935 Survey, pp. 47–52.

105. F. Chinn, "Religious Education," pp. 49–50; Community Chest 1930 Survey, pp. 17–18; CSERA 1935 Survey, pp. 53–58; and Him Mark Lai, *Cong huaqiao dao huaren* (From overseas Chinese to Chinese American) (Hong Kong: Joint Publishing Co., 1992), pp. 138–49.

106. F. Chinn, "Religious Education," p. 46; and Chinese YWCA, correspondence, board minutes, and staff reports.

107. *CSYP*, November 4, 1928.

108. R. Chinn, "Square and Circle Club," pp. 46–47; T. Chinn, *Bridging the Pacific*, pp. 129–30; and *San Francisco Examiner*, March 12, 1975, p. 22.

109. *San Francisco Daily News*, September 17, 1924.

110. See Linda Gordon, "Black and White Visions of Welfare: Women's Welfare Activism, 1890–1945," in *Unequal Sisters: A Multicultural Reader in U.S. Women's History*, 2d ed., ed. Vicki L. Ruiz and Ellen Carol DuBois (New York: Routledge, 1994), pp. 157–85.

111. I am indebted to Rosemary Chan for giving me access, with the permission of the Square and Circle Club, to the club's past minutes and scrapbooks.

112. Had they passed, the Dickstein Nationality Bill would have denied citizenship to foreign-born children of Chinese Americans, and the Anti-Alien Land Bill would have barred aliens ineligible to citizenship (Chinese, Japanese, Koreans, and Asian Indians) from owning property in Texas.

113. R. Chinn, "Square and Circle Club," p. 54.

114. *Chinese Digest*, October 23, 1936, p. 11.

115. Louis, "Study of American-born and American-reared Chinese," p. 127.

116. See Sanchez, *Becoming Mexican American;* and Bill Hosokawa, *Nisei: The Quiet Americans* (New York: William Morrow, 1969).

117. The Ging Hawk Club, an organization of young Chinese American women in New York, was founded in 1929 under the auspices of the International Institute of the YWCA. The club's name meant "Striving for Learning," and its purpose was "to absorb the best of American culture without losing their Chinese heritage." See Lorraine Wong, "Chinese All American Girl," *Record,* January 1935, p. 21.

118. Robert Dunn, "Does My Future Lie in China or America?" *Chinese Digest,* May 15, 1936, pp. 3, 13.

119. Kaye Hong, "Does My Future Lie in China or America?" *Chinese Digest,* May 22, 1936, pp. 3, 14.

120. Jane Kwong Lee, "The Future of Second Generation Chinese Lies in China and America," *Chinese Digest,* June 5, 1936, p. 5.

121. *Chinese Digest,* May 1937, p. 8.

122. *Chinese Digest,* July 3, 1936, p. 14.

123. *CSYP,* June 25, 1935.

124. *CSYP,* March 3, 1937.

125. J. Wong, *Fifth Chinese Daughter,* pp. 134–35.

126. It is uncertain how many Chinese Americans actually went to China

for work in the 1920s and 1930s. Rose Hum Lee, in her article "Chinese Dilemma," *Phylon* 10, no. 2 (1949): 140, indicated that "many Chinese-Americans have journeyed to the land of their forefathers to pursue their professional and occupational careers. China's need for leadership has opened avenues of expression which the society here did not offer. Since many are the first-generation born on American soil, they are bi-lingual and had a knowledge of the ideographic language. Their adjustment there was notable, and the Chinese-American group was a sizeable one in any port city of importance, with California, of course, sending the largest contingent." According to Kum Pui Lai, in "Attitudes of the Chinese in Hawaii Toward Chinese Language Schools," *Sociology and Social Research* 20, no. 2 (November 1935): 140–44, 741 Chinese Americans from Hawaii were in China, mainly teaching in universities and colleges like Lingnam University, St. John's Shanghai University, Peking Union Medical College, and Yenjing University. Another article, "California-educated Chinese Rebuild Canton" by Julean Arnold, in the *Chinese Christian Student*, May–June 1934, pp. 8–9, 34, noted that only about 60 Chinese Americans had gone to China; most of them, Arnold stated, were alumni of the University of California who lived and worked in Shanghai and Canton as bankers, businesspeople, engineers, and government officials.

127. *CSYP*, May 18, 23, 1918.

128. *San Francisco Chronicle*, October 18, 1919, p. 12; and December 22, 1919, p. 2.

129. The following account is derived from my interview with Eva Lowe.

130. Li Yauguang, "World Famous Chinese American Aviatrix Ouyang Ying" (in Chinese), *Huaxing*, June 23, 1989.

131. *San Francisco Call and Post*, November 12, 1919, p. 1.

132. See also Guan Zhongren, *Study on Chinese Women Aviators* (in Chinese) (Canton: Zhongshan Library of Guangdong Province, 1988), pp. 78–81.

133. *Linking Our Lives: Chinese American Women of Los Angeles* (Los Angeles: Chinese Historical Society of Southern California, 1984), pp. 72–73; Guan, *Study on Chinese Women Aviators*, pp. 105–14.

134. Liu Pei Chi, "Chinese Americans and the National Salvation Through Aviation Movement" (in Chinese), *Guangdong Wenxian* 10, no. 2 (1980): 5; Guan, *Study on Chinese Women Aviators*, pp. 115–118.

135. *San Francisco Bulletin*, November 22, 1911, p. 4.

136. *San Francisco Call*, May 19, 1912, p. 63.

137. Ibid.

138. Bessie Mae Ferina, "The Politics of San Francisco's Chinatown" (Master's thesis, University of California, Berkeley, 1949), pp. 55–58; W. Smith, *Americans in Process*, p. 122; Dare, "Economic and Social Adjustment," p. 63.

139. Lim P. Lee, "The Chinese Citizens Alliance: Its Activities and History," *Chinese Digest*, October 30, 1936, p. 15.

140. *CSYP*, July 22, 1926.

141. Community Chest 1930 Survey, p. 23.

142. *San Francisco Chronicle*, October 2, 1931, p. 4.

143. Weatherford, *Foreign and Female*, pp. 223–24.

144. The following account is derived from Bessie Jeong, "Story of a Chi-

nese Girl Student," Survey of Race Relations Collection, Hoover Institution on War, Revolution, and Peace, Stanford University; and from Suellen Cheng and Munson Kwok's interview with Bessie Jeong.

145. Newspaper accounts and the records of the Presbyterian Mission Home attest to a number of Chinese American women who, like Bessie Jeong, resisted undesirable arranged marriages by seeking refuge at the Mission Home; see *CSYP*, January 25, 1918; *San Francisco Examiner*, July 14, 1922, p. 1; Donaldina Cameron, "Orientals in the United States," *Women and Mission* 9, no. 10 (January 1935): 340–41; Pascoe, *Relations of Rescue*, pp. 161–62.

146. Chingwah Lee, "Remember When?" *Chinese Digest*, January 17, 1936, p. 8.

147. Rose Fong evidently got her way, as the newspaper also reported that her parents finally approved of her marriage to Tsoa Min after the two eloped. See *San Francisco Examiner*, May 12, 1909, p. 11.

148. Caroline Chew, "Development of Chinese Family Life in America" (Master's thesis, Mills College, 1926), p. 24.

149. King Yoak Won Wu, interview with Genny Lim, October 27, 1982, Chinese Women of America Research Project, Chinese Culture Foundation of San Francisco.

150. *San Francisco Call*, July 30, 1913, p. 5.

151. T. Chinn, *Bridging the Pacific*, pp. 250–52. See J. Wong, *Fifth Chinese Daughter*, pp. 138–46, for a similar description of a Chinese American wedding.

152. Chew, "Development of Chinese Family Life in America," p. 31.

153. Act of September 22, 1922, 42 United States Statutes at Large, 1021.

154. Kathryn M. Fong, "Asian Women Lose Citizenship," *San Francisco Journal*, December 29, 1976, p. 12; and Chan, "Exclusion of Chinese Women," pp. 128–29.

155. Kathryn M. Fong, "Pioneer Recalls Earthquake and Schools," *San Francisco Journal*, January 5, 1977, p. 6.

156. Flora Belle Jan, letter to Ludmelia Holstein, 1932.

157. Flora Belle [Jan], folder 2070/174, Chinese Departure Case Files, Chicago District Office, Immigration and Naturalization Service, National Archives, Chicago.

158. Tye Leung Schulze, "Tiny," Louise Schulze Lee private collection.

159. Fred Schulze, interview with author, January 26, 1989; Louise Schulze Lee, interview with author, November 7, 1988.

160. Fred Schulze, interview.

161. Chew, "Development of Chinese Family Life in America," p. 31.

162. *San Francisco Examiner*, January 25, 1923, p. 15.

163. *San Francisco Chronicle*, November 24, 1928, p. 6.

164. Chew, "Development of Chinese Family Life in America," p. 29.

165. Daisy Wong Chinn, interview with Genny Lim, July 29, 1982, Chinese Women of America Research Project, Chinese Culture Foundation of San Francisco.

166. J. Wong, *No Chinese Stranger*, pp. 38–39.

167. Fred Schulze, interview.

168. Gladys Ng Gin, interview.

169. Flora Belle Jan, letter to Ludmelia Holstein, January 1934.

170. *San Francisco Chronicle*, January 29, 1927, p. 10.

171. Fred Schulze, interview.

172. Ibid.

173. J. Wong, *No Chinese Stranger*, pp. 365–66. Ming Choy is Jade Snow Wong's younger son. Earlier in the autobiography (p. 193) she translates one of the Chinese school lessons he brings home titled "The Foolish Old Man Moving a Mountain." The lesson tells of an old man who was determined to remove a 700-foot mountain that obstructed his doorway. People thought him foolish for trying, but he replied that as long as he kept at it and his sons and grandsons kept at it, the mountain could be moved.

4. Long Strides

1. See William E. Leuchtenburg, *Franklin D. Roosevelt and the New Deal, 1932–1940* (New York: Harper & Row, 1963); and Robert S. McElvaine, *The Great Depression America, 1929–1941* (New York: Times Books, 1982).

2. See Studs Terkel, *Hard Times: An Oral History of the Great Depression* (New York: Pantheon Books, 1970); John Steinbeck, *The Grapes of Wrath* (New York: Viking Press, 1939); Andrea Fisher, *Let Us Now Praise Famous Women: Women Photographers for the U.S. Government, 1935 to 1944* (New York: Pandora Press, 1987); and PBS's "The Great Depression" (Blackside, Inc., 1993).

3. For studies on women during the Great Depression, see Susan Ware, *Holding Their Own: American Women in the 1930s* (Boston: Twayne, 1982); Kessler-Harris, *Out to Work*, chap. 9; Lois Scharf, *To Work and to Wed: Female Employment, Feminism, and the Great Depression* (Westport, Conn.: Greenwood Press, 1980); Jeane Westin, *Making Do: How Women Survived the '30s* (Chicago: Follett, 1976); Julia Kirk Blackwelder, *Women of the Depression: Caste and Culture in San Antonio, 1929–1939* (College Station, Tex.: A & M University Press, 1984); and Jacqueline Jones, *Labor of Love, Labor of Sorrow: Black Women, Work, and the Family from Slavery to the Present* (New York: Random House, 1985), chap. 6. For studies on how specific minority groups weathered the depression, see Harvard Sitkoff, *A New Deal for Blacks: The Emergence of Civil Rights as a National Issue*, vol. 1: *The Depression Decade* (New York: Oxford University Press, 1978); John B. Kirby, *Black Americans in the Roosevelt Era: Liberalism and Race* (Knoxville: University of Tennessee Press, 1980); Raymond Wolters, *Negroes and the Great Depression: The Problem of Economic Recovery* (Westport, Conn.: Greenwood Press, 1970); Abraham Hoffman, *Unwanted Mexican Americans in the Great Depression: Repatriation Pressures, 1929–1939* (Tucson: University of Arizona Press, 1974); Sanchez, *Becoming Mexican American*, chap. 10; Camille Guerin-Gonzales, *Mexican Workers and American Dreams: Immigration, Repatriation, and California Farm Labor, 1900–1939* (New Brunswick, N.J.: Rutgers University Press, 1994); and Donald L. Parman, *The Navajos and the New Deal* (New Haven: Yale University Press, 1976).

4. Lynn Simross, "Yees Remember the Struggles and Celebrate Their Success," *View* sec., *Los Angeles Times*, August 26, 1981, p. 2.

5. Wong Wee Ying, interview with author, May 7, 1982.

6. Helen Hong Wong, interview with author, June 17, 1982.

7. See Broussard, *Black San Francisco,* chap. 6. That segment of the Chinese male population which worked in these same sectors outside Chinatown suffered similar hardships.

8. According to Davis McEntire, *The Labor Force in California: A Study of Characteristics and Trends in Labor Force Employment of Occupations in California, 1900–1950* (Berkeley: University of California Press, 1952), the Chinese and Japanese in California experienced less than the average rate of unemployment owing to the intragroup economic and social support system each group had developed. For example, in 1940, the Japanese had an extraordinarily low unemployment rate of 3.3 percent, compared to the general rate of 14.4 percent (p. 66).

9. Nee and Nee, *Longtime Californ',* pp. 100–101.

10. *CSYP,* March 23, 1931. These statistics are much higher than those reported in the U.S. censuses, and without knowing how the Shiyi Hui conducted its survey, it is difficult to determine which figures are more accurate. The U.S. Bureau of the Census, *Fifteenth Census of the United States: 1930, Unemployment,* vol. 1 (Washington, D.C.: GPO, 1931), p. 156, reported 21,448 persons out of work in San Francisco: 20,327 whites, 168 blacks, 262 Mexicans, and 691 members of other races (half of whom were Chinese). In 1937, according to the U.S. Bureau of the Census, *Final Report on Total and Partial Unemployment for California* (Washington, D.C.: GPO, 1938), table 1, p. 1, the unemployed in San Francisco increased to 29,506: 28,118 whites, 459 blacks, and 929 members of other races.

11. CSYP, January 26, February 1, March 24, 29, April 25, 27, May 21, 1931. On January 24, 1933, *CSYP* also reported that the Huaren Shiyi Hui had sent representatives to participate in a statewide hunger march on Sacramento to demand state aid, unemployment insurance, and a stop to the deportation of unemployed Chinese aliens. For a discussion of Huaren Shiyi Hui and the Chinese Marxist left in the United States, see Him Mark Lai, "To Bring Forth a New China, to Build a Better America: The Chinese Marxist Left in America to the 1960s," *Chinese America: History and Perspectives 1992,* pp. 3–82.

12. William Mullins, *The Depression and the Urban West Coast, 1929–1933* (Bloomington: Indiana University Press, 1991). The major effort made by San Francisco to take care of its unemployed is substantiated by other statistical reports. According to David Bryant, *Summary Report: Civil Works Administrative Statistics, State of California, November 27, 1933, to March 29, 1934* (San Francisco: Civil Works Administration, 1934), p. 110, $4,212,630 was spent on relief in San Francisco from July 1933 to March 1934. Of this amount, the city contributed 45 percent; the federal government, 31 percent; and the state, 24 percent.

13. CSERA 1935 Survey, p. 40; Mullins, *Depression,* p. 102; *CSYP,* April 1, August 23, 1933.

14. Ethel Lum, "Chinese During the Depression," *Chinese Digest,* November 22, 1935, p. 10.

15. Lim P. Lee, interview with author, October 31, 1989.

16. Lum, "Chinese During the Depression." State statistics indicate that the

Chinese in California received their fair share of relief. In 1939, the Chinese, who made up 0.7 percent of California's population in 1930, accounted for 0.6 percent of the state relief rolls. Other minority groups received larger proportions: Mexicans and black Americans, who made up 6.5 percent and 1.4 percent of the state's population, respectively, accounted for 25.2 percent and 4.3 percent of the state relief rolls. See H. Dewey Anderson, "Who Are on Relief in California?" in *Miscellaneous Publications* (San Francisco: California State Relief Administration, 1939), p. 2.

17. *CSYP*, January 6, 1934.

18. Lim P. Lee, interview.

19. Ethel Lum, "The W.P.A. and Chinatown," *Chinese Digest*, January 10, 1936, pp. 10, 15.

20. See Frances Fox Piven and Richard A. Cloward, *Regulating the Poor: The Functions of Public Welfare* (New York: Pantheon Books, 1971), chap. 3.

21. Qutoted in Nee and Nee, *Longtime Californ'*, p. 101.

22. McEntire, *The Labor Force in California*, p. 67.

23. Lum, "W.P.A. and Chinatown," p. 15.

24. According to U.S. Bureau of the Census, *Final Report*, table 3, p. 12, 72 percent of racial minorities employed in federal emergency jobs performed semiskilled or unskilled labor, as compared to 45 percent of white workers.

25. Nee and Nee, *Longtime Californ'*, pp. 101–2. Blacks also condemned the NRA as "Negro Run Around" and "Negro Ruined Again" under President Roosevelt's first administration because it excluded the bulk of black labor and failed to stop labor unions and employers from discriminating against blacks (Sitkoff, *New Deal*, p. 55).

26. U.S. Bureau of the Census, *Final Report*, p. 12.

27. J. Wong, *No Chinese Stranger*, p. 8.

28. *CSYP*, August 22, 1934.

29. *CSYP*, February 5, 1935.

30. CSERA 1935 Survey, p. 8.

31. *CSYP*, October 18, 1936.

32. *Chinese Digest*, June 1937, pp. 15–16.

33. See Hoffman, *Unwanted Mexican Americans;* Sanchez, *Becoming Mexican American,* chap. 10; and Guerin-Gonzales, *Mexican Workers,* chap. 4.

34. Carey McWilliams, *Brothers Under the Skin* (Boston: Little, Brown, 1944), pp. 240–43.

35. *Chinese Digest*, July 1938, p. 6; June 1937, p. 11. An editorial in the *Chinese Digest*, June 1937, p. 2, remarked that the presence of Chinese picketers in the San Francisco hotel strike was "epoch-making in its implications. On the one hand it shows that organized labor's anti-Chinese predilections are on the wane, at least in this particular locality. On the other hand, interpreting the matter sociologically, it indicates the gradual integration of the Chinese into the American system of economic life."

36. H. Mark Lai, "A Historical Survey of the Chinese Left in America," in *Counterpoint: Perspectives on Asia America,* ed. Emma Gee (Los Angeles: Asian American Studies Center, University of California, 1976), p. 68.

37. For example, on October 31, 1936, *CSYP* reported that three unions

representing fishermen, maritime stewards, and culinary workers held a meeting to solicit Chinese membership. Then on November 7, 1937, the newspaper reported that more than two hundred Chinese and white workers picketed the Japanese consulate's office to protest Japanese aggression in China.

38. *Chinese Digest,* January 31, 1936, p. 14.

39. Nee and Nee, *Longtime Californ',* p. 105.

40. William Hoy, "The Passing of Chinatown: Fact or Fancy," *Chinese Digest,* January 31, 1936, p. 11.

41. *Chinese Digest,* December 1937, p. 16.

42. According to William H. Chafe, *The American Woman: Her Changing Social, Economic, and Political Roles, 1920–1970* (London: Oxford University Press, 1972), the depression fostered a wave of reaction against any change in gender roles. At the height of the depression, over 80 percent of the American people opposed married women entering the labor market (pp. 135, 148). As Philip Foner also points out in *Women and the American Labor Movement* (New York: Free Press, 1980), pp. 257–58, competition for jobs only intensified male enmity toward working women, and government legislation was passed at all levels to discourage if not prevent women from entering the labor market. For a further discussion of the controversy, see Kessler-Harris, *Out to Work,* pp. 255–58.

43. Ruth Milkman, "Women's Work and the Economic Crisis: Some Lessons from the Great Depression," in *A Heritage of Her Own: Toward a New Social History of American Women,* ed. Nancy F. Cott and Elizabeth Pleck (New York: Simon & Schuster, 1979), pp. 510–11; and U.S. Bureau of the Census, *Final Report,* p. 142. Following Milkman's example, I have combined unemployment classes A ("persons out of a job, able to work, and looking for a job") and B ("persons having jobs but on layoff without pay, excluding those sick or voluntarily idle") in computing the unemployment rates of males and females in San Francisco.

44. Milkman, "Women's Work," pp. 510–20; and Kessler-Harris, *Out to Work,* pp. 259–61.

45. U.S. Bureau of the Census, *Final Report,* p. 107; and Emily Huntington, *Unemployment Relief and the Unemployed in the San Francisco Bay Region, 1929–1934* (Berkeley: University of California Press, 1939), pp. 31–36.

46. Lum, "Chinese During the Depression."

47. CSERA 1935 Survey, pp. 31–34.

48. Ibid., pp. 13–26.

49. See Linda Gordon, "The New Feminist Scholarship on the Welfare State," in *Women, the State, and Welfare,* ed. Linda Gordon (Madison: University of Wisconsin Press, 1990), pp. 9–34.

50. According to Huntington, *Unemployment Relief and the Unemployed,* p. 36, the subsistence rate in 1929 was $130 a month.

51. Law Shee Low, interview with author, October 30, 1989.

52. Wong Shee Chan, interview with author, March 5, 1982.

53. CSERA 1935 Survey, p. 12; and Pardee Lowe, "The Good Life in Chinatown: Further Adventures of a Chinese Husband and His American Wife Among His Own People," *Asia* 37 (February 1937): 128.

54. See Jones, *Labor of Love,* pp. 196–97; Lois Rita Helmbold, "Beyond the

Family Economy: Black and White Working-Class Women During the Great Depression," *Feminist Studies* 13, no. 3 (fall 1987): 636; Scharf, *To Work and to Wed*, pp. 115–16; and McEntire, *Labor Force in California*, p. 143.

55. See Westin, *Making Do;* Milkman, "Women's Work," pp. 520–28; Jones, *Labor of Love*, pp. 221–30; and Rosalinda M. Gonzalez, "Chicanas and Mexican Immigrant Families, 1920–1940: Women's Subordination and Family Exploitation," in *Decades of Discontent: The Women's Movement, 1920–1940*, ed. Lois Scharf and Joan M. Jensen (Westport, Conn.: Greenwood Press, 1983), p. 70.

56. See Helmbold, "Beyond the Family Economy."

57. Jones, *Labor of Love*, pp. 224–26.

58. *CSYP*, April 30, 1933; January 17, June 9, August 29, September 25, 1934; March 19, 1937; *Chinese Times*, August 8, 1936; March 19, 1937.

59. Wong Shee Chan, interview.

60. Penny Chan Huey, interview with author, November 21, 1988.

61. Jane Kwong Lee, "A Resume of Social Service," *Chinese Digest*, December 20, 1935, p. 10.

62. On how the New Deal discriminated against women and racial minorities, see Scharf, *To Work and to Wed*, chap. 6; Kessler-Harris, *Out to Work*, pp. 262–71; Jones, *Labor of Love*, chap. 6; Blackwelder, *Women of the Depression*, chap. 7; and Gwendolyn Mink, "The Lady and the Tramp: Gender, Race, and the Origins of the American Welfare State," in *Women, the State, and Welfare*, ed. Linda Gordon (Madison: University of Wisconsin Press, 1990), pp. 111–14.

63. Lum, "Chinese During the Depression"; and CSERA 1935 Survey, pp. 40–41.

64. *CSYP*, July 11, 1933; July 11, 1934; March 13, 1935; March 6, 1939; *Chinese Times*, February 16, 17, 1936; and *San Francisco News*, April 26, 1936, p. 1.

65. See CSERA 1935 Survey.

66. Ibid., p. 17. Similarly, Pardee Lowe wrote in 1937 that "in striking, almost bewildering contrast to the preearthquake period, practically all of Chinatown's women are permitted to and do find employment outside of the home" ("Good Life," p. 128).

67. Frank J. Taylor, "The Bone Money Empire," *Saturday Evening Post*, December 24, 1933, p. 48.

68. *CSYP*, November 13, 1933.

69. *CSYP*, May 31, June 1, 1935.

70. J. Lee, "A Chinese American," pt. II, p. 81.

71. Ibid., p. 91.

72. *CSYP*, August 15, 1936.

73. J. Lee, "A Chinese American," pt. II, pp. 92–93.

74. Ibid., p. 87.

75. Alice Sue Fun, interview with author, February 28, 1982.

76. *Chinese Digest*, May 29, 1936, p. 14.

77. Gladys Ng Gin, interview with author, November 4, 1988.

78. Lim P. Lee, "The Postal Chinese Club of San Francisco," *Asian Week*, January 27, 1984, p. 7.

79. Dare, "Economic and Social Adjustment," pp. 68–69; Lowe, "Good

Life," p. 128; and *Chinese Digest*, November 13, 1936, p. 7; March, 1937, p. 14.

80. Ethel Lum, "Young Woman, Are You Looking for a Job?" *Chinese Digest*, March 27, 1936, p. 11.

81. *Chinese Times*, July 29, 1936.

82. Jones, *Labor of Love*, pp. 206–7.

83. Scharf, *To Work and to Wed*, p. 114.

84. *Chinese Digest*, March 27, 1936, p. 11.

85. Broussard, *Black San Francisco*, p. 122.

86. *Chinese Digest*, October 16, 1936, p. 10.

87. CSYP, March 29, 1934.

88. CSYP, November 5, 7, 1935; and *Chinese Digest*, December 13, 1935, p. 5.

89. *Chinese Digest*, February 14, 1936, p. 2.

90. Gladys Ng Gin, interview.

91. Quoted in *Forbidden City, U.S.A.: World Premiere Benefit* (San Francisco, 1989).

92. Quoted in Dexter Waugh, "Forbidden City," *Image* sec., *San Francisco Examiner*, October 29, 1989, p. 20.

93. Bertha Hing, interview with Kirk Fong and Valerie Fong, March 1991, Kirk Fong private collection.

94. Quoted in Lorraine Dong, "The Forbidden City Legacy and Its Chinese American Women," *Chinese America: History and Perspectives 1992*, p. 138.

95. Ibid., p. 140.

96. Bertha Hing, interview.

97. Waugh, "Forbidden City," pp. 19–24, 34; and Jim Marshall, "Cathay Hey-Hey!" *Collier's*, February 28, 1942, pp. 13, 53.

98. *Business Week*, March 12, 1938, p. 28.

99. *Chinese Christian Student*, April 1939, p. 5; *Chinese Digest*, May–June 1939, p. 3.

100. Jane Kwong Lee, interview with author, October 22, 1988.

101. CSERA 1935 Survey, p. 9.

102. Eva Lowe, interview with Genny Lim.

103. Henriette Horak, "New Chinatown: Modernity Creeping Into Section," *San Francisco Chronicle*, July 9, 1936, p. 7.

104. Lowe, "Good Life," p. 128. In this article, Lowe provides detailed notes of the bicultural lifestyle he found in San Francisco Chinatown but makes no mention of any poverty conditions caused by the depression.

105. Jane Kwong Lee, "Chinese Women in San Francisco," *Chinese Digest*, June 1938, p. 9.

106. See Sanchez, *Becoming Mexican American*, chap. 11.

107. Eva Lowe, interview with Genny Lim.

108. According to Him Mark Lai, "To Bring Forth a New China," pp. 12–14, the Chinese Students Association supported the Guomindang left faction and was strongly against any foreign domination in China. In 1929 the group was raided by the San Francisco Chinatown Police Squad and closed down for alleged Communist activities.

109. Eva Lowe, interview with author, July 15, 1982.

110. Eva Lowe, interview with Genny Lim.

111. The following account is derived from my interview with Alice Fong Yu, March 31, 1986.

112. *Chinese Times,* March 16, 1936.

113. Alice Fong Yu, interview with Gordon Chang, June 29, 1987.

114. *Chinese Digest,* March 13, 1936, p. 11; "A Summary of Proceedings of the Sixth Annual Chinese Young People's Christian Conference Held at Zephyr Point, Lake Tahoe, August 1–14, 1938," Him Mark Lai private collection; and Alice Fong Yu, interview.

115. *CSYP,* April 1, 1938; and *Chinese Digest,* July 1937, pp. 14, 19.

116. *CSYP,* April 11, 1935. As government pressure mounted against Chinatown factories that violated NRA codes, other articles appeared in *CSYP* beseeching owners to consolidate and improve working conditions in Chinatown (e.g., March 18, 22, 1936).

117. *Time,* March 28, 1938, pp. 54, 56.

118. In other words, the employer was underreporting the hours that employees worked in order to pay them at the piece rate and giving work to women who sewed at home even though homework was illegal. Sue Ko Lee, interview with author, October 26, 1989.

119. "Jennie Matyas and the ILGWU," oral history conducted 1955 by Connie Gilb, Regional Culture History Project, Bancroft Library, University of California, Berkeley, 1957, p. 172 (hereafter cited as Matyas interview).

120. *Chinese Digest,* July 1937, p. 19.

121. Sue Ko Lee, interview.

122. See Rose Pesotta, *Bread upon the Waters* (New York: Dodd, Mead, 1944), chap. 6; titled "Subterranean Sweatshops in Chinatown," the chapter describes her investigation of conditions in Chinatown garment factories and how she comes to understand the difficulties involved in organizing Chinese workers.

123. *San Francisco Chronicle,* May 17, 1934, p. 1; *Chinese Times,* February 16, 1936; *CSYP,* March 13, 15, 22, 1936; and *San Francisco News,* April 26, 1936, p. 1.

124. Pesotta, *Bread upon the Waters,* pp. 74–76.

125. Him Mark Lai, "To Bring Forth a New China," pp. 10–20; and Matyas interview, pp. 127–28, 173–74.

126. Sue Ko Lee, interview.

127. Kessler-Harris, *Out to Work,* p. 262; and Scharf, *To Work and to Wed,* pp. 130–32.

128. Ware, *Holding Their Own,* p. 42; Jones, *Labor of Love,* p. 212; Blackwelder, *Women of the Depression,* pp. 135–39; and Sanchez, *Becoming Mexican American,* pp. 232–35.

129. Matyas interview, pp. 163–77; "Good News!!! Chinese Workers Are in the Union!" Sue Ko Lee scrapbook (in my possession); *Chinese Digest,* March 1938, p. 15; and Jennie Matyas, letter to William Green, President of the American Federation of Labor, March 7, 1938, Labor Archives and Research Center, San Francisco State University.

130. *Chinese Digest,* April 1938, pp. 10–12; Jennie Matyas, "History and

Background of Dispute Between Chinese Ladies' Garment Workers, Local 341, and Dollar Stores," Labor Archives and Research Center, San Francisco State University; and *San Francisco Chronicle*, February 27, 1938, p. 4.

131. "A Letter to the Public Regarding the Strike," February 26, 1938, Sue Ko Lee scrapbook.

132. "A Statement to the Public Regarding the Damages Done to Business by the Chinese LGWU Strike Against National Dollar Store," March 2, 1938, Sue Ko Lee scrapbook.

133. "Another Letter to the Public from Local 341, the Chinese Chapter of the ILGWU," March 5, 1938, Sue Ko Lee scrapbook.

134. "A Statement by Golden Gate Company," March 7, 1938, Sue Ko Lee scrapbook.

135. "An Explanation Regarding the Strike Against National Dollar Stores by Workers of the Golden Gate Company," Sue Ko Lee scrapbook.

136. "A Letter to Fellow Union Members by Local 341, the Chinese Chapter of the ILGWU," Sue Ko Lee scrapbook.

137. Ware, *Holding Their Own*, p. 42; Scharf, *To Work and to Wed*, pp. 132–33; and Elaine Leeder, *The Gentle General: Rose Pesotta, Anarchist and Labor Organizer* (Albany: State University of New York Press, 1993), pp. 53–57. See Dana Frank, *Purchasing Power: Consumer Organizing, Gender, and the Seattle Labor Movement, 1919–1929* (Cambridge: Cambridge University Press, 1994), pp. 117–26, for a discussion of the sexual division of labor in the Seattle trade union movement; and Vicki L. Ruiz, *Cannery Women, Cannery Lives: Mexican Women, Unionization, and the California Food Processing Industry, 1930–1950* (Albuquerque: University of New Mexico Press, 1987), for an example of a union formed and run by Mexican women workers.

138. Sue Ko Lee, interview.

139. Matyas interview, pp. 183–84.

140. Sue Ko Lee, interview.

141. According to Him Mark Lai, "A Historical Survey of Organizations of the Left Among the Chinese in America," *Bulletin of Concerned Asian Scholars* 4, no. 3 (fall 1972): 10–20, organizations such as Ping Sheh and Chinese Workers Mutual Aid Association developed in the 1920s and 1930s as part of a leftist movement among Chinese Americans committed to supporting the Chinese revolution and fighting exploitation and discrimination in America. Ping Sheh was an anarchist organization that advocated worker solidarity through the publication of pamphlets, a monthly magazine, and leaflets it distributed in support of workers' struggles in Chinatown. The Chinese Workers Mutual Aid Association was established in 1937 following a successful strike against the Alaskan Packers Association to unite Chinese workers for the purposes of improving working conditions and raising their status in labor unions.

142. "A Letter to the Public Regarding the Strike," February 26, 1938; "Another Letter to the Public From Local 341, the Chinese Chapter of the ILGWU," March 5, 1938; and "The Opportunity for Chinese Workers' Liberation Has Arrived," February 27, 1938; all in Sue Ko Lee scrapbook.

143. Sue Ko Lee, interview.

144. Matyas interview, pp. 190–92.

145. Sue Ko Lee, interview.

146. Matyas interview, pp. 184–91; Matyas, "History and Background of Dispute"; and "Labor Strike in Chinatown Official Statements."

147. None of the strikes by Chinese laborers in San Francisco prior to the 1938 National Dollar Stores strike lasted more than a week or two: construction workers at the Parrot building (1852), garment workers (1875), shoemakers (1877), cigarmakers (1884), and laundry workers (1929).

148. "Local 341 Letter to the Public Regarding Strike Settlement," June 11, 1938, "The Chinese Local Extends Greetings," Sue Ko Lee scrapbook; and Agreement Between Golden Gate Manufacturing Company and ILGWU, Chinese Ladies' Garment Workers, Local No. 341," June 8, 1938, Labor Archives and Research Center, San Francisco State University.

149. David Dubinsky, president of ILGWU, telegram to Jennie Matyas, May 31, 1938, Labor Archives and Research Center, San Francisco State University.

150. Matyas interview, p. 192.

151. Handwritten note, Labor Archives and Research Center, San Francisco State University.

152. Sue Ko Lee, interview.

153. G. N. Wong Low, Golden Gate Mfg. Co., letter to International Ladies' Garment Workers Union, Chinese Ladies' Garment Workers Local No. 341, May 6, 1939, Labor Archives and Research Center, San Francisco State University.

154. Sue Ko Lee interview; and Matyas interview, pp. 193–204, 289.

155. Patricia M. Fong, "The 1938 National Dollar Strike," *Asian American Review* 2, no. 1 (1975): 196. Douglas Monroy makes a similar argument about the 1933 Mexican Dressmakers' Strike in Los Angeles: "Consistent with its corporate ideology, the ILGWU leadership was not so much interested in assisting Mexican workers in establishing their own strength in the dress factories, as it was interested in establishing its own strength in the garment industry"; see Monroy, "La Costura en Los Angeles, 1933–1939: The ILGWU and the Politics of Domination," in *Mexican Women in the United States: Struggles Past and Present*, ed. Magdalena Mora and Adelaida R. Del Castillo (Los Angeles: Chicano Studies Research Center, University of California, Los Angeles, 1980), p. 176.

156. Sue Ko Lee, interview.

157. Jennie Matyas, "Chinatown Turns Union," Sue Ko Lee scrapbook. At the time, the ILGWU had been dismissed from the American Federation of Labor (AFL) and San Francisco Labor Council for supporting the Congress of Industrial Organizations. In 1940, the union reaffiliated with the AFL. See Matyas interview, pp. 291–306.

158. Sue Ko Lee, interview.

159. Ibid.

160. "Statement in Support of the Strike by Employees of the Emporium and Other Department Stores," September 21, 1938, "Chinese Local Carrying on Battle for Economic Freedom Against Odds," "Boycott Japanese Goods," Sue Ko Lee scrapbook; and *Chinese Times*, December 24, 1938.

5. In Step

1. See Chafe, *American Woman*; Ruth Milkman, *Gender at Work: The Dynamics of Job Segregation by Sex During World War II* (Urbana: University of Illinois Press, 1987); Margaret Randolph Higonnet et al., eds., *Behind the Lines: Gender and the Two World Wars* (New Haven: Yale University Press, 1987); Leila Rupp, *Mobilizing Women for War: German and American Propaganda, 1939–1945* (Princeton: Princeton University Press, 1978); Karen Anderson, *Wartime Women: Sex Roles, Family Relationships, and the Status of Women During World War II* (Westport, Conn.: Greenwood Press, 1981); D'Ann Campbell, *Women at War With America* (Cambridge, Mass.: Harvard University Press, 1984); Susan Hartmann, *The Home Front and Beyond: American Women in the 1940s* (Boston: Twayne, 1982); and Sheila Tropp Lichtman, "Women at Work, 1941–1945: Wartime Employment in the San Francisco Bay Area" (Ph.D. diss., University of California, Davis, 1981).

2. See Jones, *Labor of Love*, chap. 7.

3. See Nakano, *Japanese American Women*, chaps. 5, 7, and 8.

4. *San Francisco Chronicle*, March 13, 1932, p. 8A; *Chinese Times*, December 29, 1939; Liu Pei Chi, *History*, pp. 566–73; and Wu Jianhung, "The Chinese American Patriotic Movement Before and After the 9-18 Incident" (in Chinese), paper presented at the First International Conference on Overseas Chinese Studies, Peking, 1978. San Francisco Chinatown was full of conflicts between political parties, social classes, religious organizations, and different generations. Moreover, when the Communists split from Chiang Kai-shek's Guomindang Party in 1927, a similar split between the left and right factions occurred in the Chinese American community.

5. Wu Jianhung, "Chinese American Patriotic Movement," p. 9.

6. *San Francisco Chronicle*, September 28, 1931, p. 7. The Kellogg-Briand peace pact of 1928 pledged that the United States would back any effort to renounce war as an instrument of national policy.

7. Wu Jianhung, "Chinese American Patriotic Movement," p. 7.

8. Ibid., p. 18. According to Wu's calculations, the Chinese in the United States gave more to the Nineteenth Route Army than Chinese in other parts of the world (p. 13). Joe Shoong of the National Dollar Stores alone gave $30,000 (p. 9).

9. *CSYP*, August 19, 1936.

10. Liu Pei Chi, *History*, pp. 566–73; Wu Jianhung, "Chinese American Patriotic Movement"; and *San Francisco Chronicle*, March 13, 1932, p. 8A.

11. Lowe, "Good Life," p. 130; and Tsai, *Chinese Experience*, p. 111.

12. *Chinese Digest*, September 1937, p. 10.

13. Liu Pei Chi, *History*, pp. 569–70; and *Chinese Digest*, September 1937, pp. 9–10.

14. Liu Pei Chi, *History*, pp. 577–83.

15. *Chinese Digest*, September 1937, p. 9; July 1938, pp. 12–13, 19; and *San Francisco Chronicle*, May 1, 1939, p. 9.

16. *Chinese Digest*, December 1937, pp. 14, 23; Y. K. Chu, *History of the Chinese People in America* (in Chinese) (New York: China Times, 1975), pp. 125–27; and *CSYP*, October 25, 1939.

17. Lim P. Lee, interview; Ira Lee, interview with author, November 1, 1989; and District Intelligence Office, Twelfth Naval District, Commandant's Office, "Chinese Situation in the San Francisco Bay Area," General Correspondence, folder A8-5, National Archives, San Bruno, Calif., 1945, pp. 20–21. See also Norman Bock, "Chameleon Cloaks, Flying Tigers, and Missionary Ladies: The Oral History and Political Economy of Baltimore Chinatown and the China Relief Movement, 1937–41" (B.A. thesis, Harvard College, 1976), chap. 5; and Mei Zheng, "Chinese Americans in San Francisco and New York City During the Anti-Japanese War: 1937–1945" (Master's thesis, University of California, Los Angeles, 1990), pp. 62–63.

18. *CSYP*, October 25, 1939.

19. Liu Pei Chi, *History*, p. 579.

20. *Chinese Digest*, November 1937, p. 15.

21. Him Mark Lai, "Sprouting Wings on the Dragon: Some Chinese Americans Who Contributed to the Development of Aviation in China," in *The Annals of the Chinese Historical Society of the Pacific Northwest* (Bellingham, Wash.: Chinese Historical Society of the Pacific Northwest, 1984), p. 182.

22. *CSYP*, January 15, 1932.

23. *Chinese Times*, May 23, 1939. Similar editorials often appeared on March 8, International Women's Day: e.g., *CSYP*, March 8, 1942; and *Chinese Times*, March 8, 1942, 1944, 1945.

24. Quoted in *Chinese Digest*, November 1937, p. 11.

25. For a further discussion of women's role in the War of Resistance in China, see Ono, *Chinese Women*, pp. 161–70; Croll, *Feminism and Socialism*, chap. 6; Esther S. Lee Yao, *Chinese Women: Past and Present* (Mesquite, Tex.: Ide House, 1983), pp. 137–42; and Edith Hsiao, "Women's Activities in War-torn China," *Chinese Christian Student* 30, nos. 3 (January 1940): 1, 4; and 4 (February 1940): 4.

26. On "the process of social change," see Sherna Berger Gluck, *Rosie the Riveter Revisited: Women, the War, and Social Change* (New York: New American Library, 1987), p. 260: "Rather than debating the *degree* of change resulting from the wartime experiences, the life stories of these former aircraft workers encourage, instead, a study of the *process* of change."

27. Signed by the United States at the Washington Naval Conference following World War I, the Nine-Power Treaty pledged respect for the sovereignty, independence, and territorial integrity of China.

28. Both letters and the history of New York's Chinese Women's Association are in *The Chinese Women's Association Fifth Anniversary Special Issue* (New York: Chinese Women's Association, 1937), microfilm, New York Public Library.

29. *CSYP*, March 16, 1932. A sister of Soong Mei-ling (Madame Chiang Kai-shek), Soong Ching-ling chose to side with the Chinese Communist Party.

30. Ibid. Liang Hongyu, the wife of the Sung general Han Shizhong, stopped the advancing Tartars in a decisive battle by beating the drums to arouse the morale of her husband's troops. Hong Xuanjiao lived during the time of the Taiping Rebellion and was related to Hong Xiuquan, leader of the rebellion. For a description of the activities of the Women's Patriotic Club, see *CSYP*, February 7, March 11, 1932; February 5, 1933; December 8, 1934; March 6, April

27, 29, August 17, 1935; March 9, 1936; September 19, October 10, 1937; November 28, 1938; and February 15, 1942.

31. Emily Lee Fong, interview with Him Mark Lai and Gilbert Woo, March 1, 1975, Him Mark Lai private collection; *CSYP*, May 23, 1939; and Liu Pei Chi, *History*, p. 255.

32. Emily Lee Fong, interview; King Yoak Won Wu, interview with Genny Lim; and *CSYP*, August 2, 5, December 14, 1939; December 28, 1940; January 5, March 16, 1941; August 16, 1942; January 10, August 21, 1943; August 21, 1944.

33. *CSYP*, September 20, 26, 27, October 2, 8, 17, 1937; January 21, July 24, December 28, 1938; January 4, 12, October 8, 1939; and October 7, 1940.

34. *Chinese Times*, July 4, 1936; and *CSYP*, September 25, 1938; January 23, 1939; June 22, August 12, 1940; May 2, 1941.

35. Lorena How, interview with Sandy Lee, May 1, 1982, Chinese Women of America Research Project, Chinese Culture Foundation of San Francisco.

36. *CSYP*, September 26, 1931; February 22, 1932; and *Chinese Digest*, September 1937, p. 10.

37. Lorena How, interview.

38. *CSYP*, April 2, 3, 8, 11, 30, May 6, 7, and 15, 1939.

39. *CSYP*, May 2, 1940.

40. J. Lee, "A Chinese American," pt. II, p. 110.

41. Ibid., chaps. 9 and 10; and "Lianzhen chu ji" (Collection of plays by Lianzhen) (unpublished collection).

42. *CSYP*, February 6, 1938; October 16, 1939; January 11, 1940; and Square and Circle Club minutes, 1932–41.

43. Quoted in Mark and Chih, *A Place Called Chinese America*, p. 84; and T. Chinn, *Bridging the Pacific*, p. 238.

44. *CSYP*, February 17, 1939.

45. Y. K. Chu, *History of the Chinese People*, p. 124; and *Chinese Digest*, October 1937, p. 3.

46. *Chinese Digest*, March 1938, p. 10; May 1938, p. 9; Square and Circle Club minutes, September 17, 1937; January 21, June 22, 1938; *CSYP*, September 30, 1937; and *Chinese Times*, September 29, 1937.

47. *Chinese Digest*, November 1938, p. 6.

48. *Chinese Digest*, February 1938, p. 9.

49. Zheng, "Chinese Americans in San Francisco," p. 40.

50. *CSYP*, February 5, 1932.

51. Community Chest 1930 Survey, p. 13; Stanley Lee, interview with author, July 26, 1985; *CSYP*, April 26, February 5, 1932; March 16, 1933; December 3, 1938, February 22, 1944; and *Chinese Times*, September 8, 1937.

52. *Chinese Digest*, March 1938, p. 3.

53. *San Francisco Chronicle*, June 17, 1938, p. 1.

54. *Chinese Digest*, July 1938, pp. 12–13, 19; *San Francisco Chronicle*, June 18, 1938, p. 1; and *California Chinese Press*, May 2, 1941, p. 2.

55. William Hoy, "S.F. Chinatown's 'Bowl of Rice' Pageant," *Chinese Digest*, July 1938, pp. 12, 19.

56. *CSYP*, February 9–12, 1940; May 2–5, 1941; *California Chinese Press*,

May 2, 1941, p. 2; and *San Francisco Chronicle*, February 10–12, 1940; May 3–6, 1941.

57. Dare, "Economic and Social Adjustment," p. 78; and *CSYP*, February 12, 1940.

58. Lim P. Lee, "Chinatown Goes Picketing," *Chinese Digest*, January 1939, pp. 10–11.

59. *CSYP*, December 19, 1938.

60. *Chinese Digest*, January 1939, pp. 10–11; February 1939, p. 7; *San Francisco Chronicle*, December 20, 21, 1938; and Zheng, "Chinese Americans in San Francisco," pp. 34–37.

61. Liu Pei Chi, *History*, pp. 254–55.

62. *Chinese Digest*, December 1937, pp. 14, 23; and *CSYP*, December 2, 1937.

63. Liu Pei Chi, *History*, pp. 552–63.

64. *San Francisco Chronicle*, March 1, 1932, p. 3.

65. *Chinese Digest*, November 1937, p. 1; and December 1937, pp. 14, 23.

66. *Chinese Digest*, October 1937, p. 11; February 1938, p. 12; and *CSYP*, January 14, 1941; February 4, 1942.

67. *San Francisco Chronicle*, September 18, 1937, p. 11.

68. *San Francisco Chronicle*, September 15, 1937, p. 2; and *Chinese Digest*, November 1937, p. 13.

69. Margaret Chung, "TV Summary of Margaret Chung's Life" (unpublished autobiography, Asian American Studies Library, University of California, Berkeley, ca. 1945).

70. *CSYP*, October 2, November 9, 1938.

71. J. Lee, "A Chinese American," pt. II, p. 132.

72. *CSYP*, November 9, 1938.

73. *CSYP*, April 27, 1939; Ruth Brown Reed, "Career Girl, Chinese Style," *Independent Women*, September 1942, pp. 260, 286; and Guan, *Study on Chinese Women Aviators*, pp. 120–28.

74. *San Diego Union*, April 17, 1939, p. 3.

75. *CSYP*, May 2, 1939.

76. *CSYP*, February 8, 1941.

77. For a report of Madame Chiang's visit to San Francisco, see Chen Yueh, *Madame Chiang Kai-shek's Trip Through the United States and Canada* (San Francisco: Chinese Nationalist Daily, 1943), pp. 76–106; *CSYP*, March 26–31, 1943; and *Chinese Press*, April 2, 1943, p. 2.

78. Chen Yueh, *Madame Chiang Kai-shek*, p. 80; and *CSYP*, March 31, 1943. The six key groups included the Women's Council, Women's Patriotic Club, New Life Association, Chinese YWCA, Square and Circle Club, and Fidelis Coteri. The Refugee Relief Committee was omitted most likely because it was an auxiliary of the CWRA.

79. *CSYP*, June 17, 1945.

80. *Chinese Christian Student*, November–December 1933, p. 11.

81. *CSYP*, June 16, 1945.

82. *San Diego Union*, April 17, 1939, p. 3.

83. *Chinese Times*, March 8, 1945.

84. Lonnie Quan, interview with Genny Lim, August 10, 1982, Chinese Women of America Research Project, Chinese Culture Foundation of San Francisco.

85. For a discussion of the differential impact of World War II on the various Asian ethnic groups owing to politics and foreign relations, see Ronald Takaki, *Strangers from a Different Shore: A History of Asian Americans* (New York: Little, Brown, 1989), chap. 10.

86. Jules Archer, *The Chinese and the Americans* (New York: Hawthorne Books, 1976), p. 106; and J. Lee, "A Chinese American," pt. II, p. 169.

87. Helen Pon Onyett, interview with author, January 9, 1983.

88. *Time*, March 1, 1943, p. 23.

89. *Life*, March 1, 1943, p. 26.

90. *Time*, March 1, 1943, p. 23.

91. *Chinese Press*, April 2, 1943, p. 2.

92. Fred W. Riggs, *Pressure on Congress: A Study of the Repeal of Chinese Exclusion* (New York: Columbia University Press, 1950), p. 111.

93. *San Francisco Chronicle*, October 12, 1943, p. 4.

94. For a discussion of the negligible impact of repeal on Chinese Americans, see L. Ling-chi Wang, "Politics of Assimilation and Repression: History of the Chinese in the United States, 1940–1970," chap. 5 (typescript, Asian American Studies Library, University of California, Berkeley).

95. Rose Hum Lee, "Chinese in the United States Today: The War Has Changed Their Lives," *Survey Graphic: Magazine of Social Interpretation* 31, no. 10 (October 1942): 444.

96. Lonnie Quan, interview.

97. Although internment disrupted family and community life and was an equally negative experience for Japanese American women as for men, women did gain some advantages by it. For the first time in their hardworking lives, *issei* (first generation) women found leisure time to pursue educational classes and hobbies, while *nisei* (second generation) women were able to work in nontraditional positions of authority in the camps. In addition, *nisei* women who resettled outside the camps before the end of the war benefited from their travel, work, and educational experiences. See Valerie Matsumoto, "Japanese American Women During World War II," *Frontiers: A Journal of Women Studies* 8, no. 1 (1984): 6–14.

98. Tsai, *Chinese Experience*, p. 117; L. Wang, "Politics of Assimilation," pp. 156–57; "Veterans Survey Report," *Bulletin, Chinese Historical Society of America* 17, no. 7 (September 1982): 2; Y. K. Chu, *History of the Chinese People*, p. 129; and R. Lee, "Chinese in the United States Today," p. 444.

99. *Buckley Armorer*, February 4, 1944, pp. 1, 4.

100. Midway through the war, the U.S. Army decided to induct Americans of Japanese ancestry into an all-Japanese combat team. Approximately 25,000 *nisei* ended up serving in the military, 18,000 in the 442nd Regimental Combat Team. In contrast, Chinese American G.I.'s were not segregated except for the all–Chinese American 407th Air Service Squadron of the Fourteenth Air Force (Flying Tigers), which served in the China-Burma-India theater of war. See Christina Lim and Sheldon Lim, "In the Shadow of the Tiger: The 407th

Air Service Squadron," and Peter Phan, "Familiar Strangers: The Fourteenth Air Service Group Case Study of Chinese American Identity During World War II," *Chinese America: History and Perspectives 1993*, pp. 25–74, 75–107, respectively.

101. "Veterans Survey"; and Tsai, *Chinese Experience*, p. 117.

102. Except for a detachment of *nisei* Wacs in the intelligence corps, the approximately three hundred Japanese American women who volunteered for service were assigned to bases all over the country as well as in Germany and Japan. See Nakano, *Japanese American Women*, p. 170.

103. See Susan Hartmann, "Women in the Military Service," in *Clio Was a Woman: Studies in the History of American Women*, ed. Mabel Deutrich and Virginia Purdy (Washington, D.C.: Howard University Press, 1980), pp. 195–205, Campbell, *Women at War*, chaps. 1 and 2; Hartmann, *Home Front and Beyond*, chap. 3; Jones, *Labor of Love*, chap. 7; and Mattie Treadwell, *United States Army in World War II, Special Studies; The Women's Army Corps* (Washington, D.C.: Department of the Army, 1954), chap. 30.

104. Campbell, *Women at War*, p. 49. Spars (from *Semper Paratus*, the motto of the U.S. Coast Guard) were members of the Coast Guard women's reserve.

105. See ibid., chap. 2; and Hartmann, *Home Front and Beyond*, chap. 3.

106. The following account is derived from my interview with Helen Pon Onyett.

107. The following account is from my interview with Jessie Lee Yip, November 2, 1989.

108. Ruth Chan Jang, who enlisted in the WAC in 1944, said she initially had no intention of joining the service because her parents read in the Chinese newspapers that "servicewomen go in there only to serve the men" (interview with author, July 8, 1994).

109. *CSYP*, January 6, April 29, October 22, 29, November 12, 1943; and *Chinese Press*, March 26, April 16, October 8, 22, 29, 1943.

110. Charlotte Sexton, interview with author, August 17, 1982.

111. Maggie Gee, interview with author, February 25, 1990.

112. Maggie Gee, slide presentation at Chinese Historical Society of America, San Francisco, May 17, 1991.

113. For a history of the WASP, see Sally Van Wagenken Keil, *Those Wonderful Women in Their Flying Machines* (New York: Rawson, Wade, 1979); and Vera S. Williams, *WASPs: Women Airforce Service Pilots of World War II* (Osceola, Wis.: Motorbooks International, 1994).

114. Maggie Gee, interview.

115. Maggie Gee, slide presentation.

116. Helen Pon Onyett, interview.

117. Jessie Lee Yip, interview.

118. May Lew Gee, interview with author, June 25, 1994.

119. Marietta Chong Eng, slide presentation at Chinese Historical Society of America, San Francisco, May 17, 1991; and interview with Genny Lim, September 13, 1982, Chinese Women of America Research Project, Chinese Culture Foundation of San Francisco.

120. Ruth Chan Jang, interview.

121. On the impact of World War II upon women in the labor force, see Chafe, *American Woman*, chap. 6; Milkman, *Gender at Work*, chap. 4; Campbell, *Women at War*, chaps. 4 and 5; Hartmann, *Home Front and Beyond*, chaps. 4 and 5; Charles Wollenberg, *Marinship at War: Shipbuilding and Social Change in Wartime Sausalito* (Berkeley, Calif.: Western Heritage Press, 1990), chaps. 6 and 7; Rupp, *Mobilizing Women*, chap. 6; and Gluck, *Rosie the Riveter*, chap. 1.

122. See Jones, *Labor of Love*, chap. 7.

123. Quoted in Gluck, *Rosie the Riveter*, p. 42.

124. On the demobilization of women in the labor force at the end of World War II, see Chafe, *American Woman*, chap. 8; Campbell, *Women at War*, chap. 8; Rupp, *Mobilizing Women*, chap. 6; and Milkman, *Gender at Work*, chap. 7.

125. Louise Purwin, "Chinese Daughters of Uncle Sam," *Independent Woman* 23 (November 1944): 337, 353.

126. Lucy Lee, interview with author, May 17, 1982.

127. The six shipyards included the Kaiser yards in Richmond, Mare Island Navy Yard in Vallejo, Naval Drydocks at Hunter's Point in San Francisco, Marinship in Sausalito, Moore Dry Dock Company in Oakland, and Bethlehem Steel in Alameda and South San Francisco.

128. L. Wang, "Politics of Assimilation," p. 135. For sample ads, see *Chinese Press*, January 1, 1943; and *Chinese Times*, October 6, November 2, 1942.

129. *Chinese Press*, August 21, 1942, p. 1; Tsai, *Chinese Experience*, p. 116.

130. Broussard, *Black San Francisco*, p. 145; and Shirley Ann Moore, "The Black Community in Richmond, California, 1910–1963" (Ph.D. diss., University of California, Berkeley, 1989), p. 86.

131. *San Francisco Chronicle*, December 24, 1942, p. 1.

132. *Fore 'n Aft*, December 31, 1942.

133. *Fore 'n Aft*, April 7, 1944.

134. *Marin-er*, June 26, 1943.

135. Ibid.

136. Letter quoted in ibid.

137. Ibid.

138. See Moore, "Black Community," pp. 93–96; Broussard, *Black San Francisco*, pp. 158–65; and Wollenberg, *Marinship at War*, chap. 7. All three sources discuss the landmark case of *James v. Marinship*, in which a black welder, Joseph James, won a discrimination suit against the Boilermakers' Union for segregating blacks into an auxiliary union.

139. See Lichtman, "Women at Work," chap. 2.

140. Katherine Archibald, *Wartime Shipyard* (Berkeley: University of California Press, 1947), pp. 100–109.

141. *San Francisco Chronicle*, December 24, 1942, p. 1.

142. Frances Jong, interview with author, February 12, 1990.

143. Maggie Gee, interview.

144. May Lew Gee, interview.

145. Rena Jung Chung, interview with author, June 30, 1994.

146. J. Wong, *Fifth Chinese Daughter*, pp. 194–95; *CSYP*, April 21, 1943.

147. See Campbell, *Women at War*, chap. 4; Hartmann, *Home Front*, chap. 5; Chafe, *American Woman*, chap. 7; and Lichtman, "Women at Work," chap. 3.

148. Dare, "Economic and Social Adjustment," p. 69; and R. Lee, "Chinese in the United States Today," p. 419.

149. *Chinese Press,* May 28, 1943, p. 6; and June 4, 1943, p. 2.

150. Gladys Ng Gin, interview.

151. J. Lee, "A Chinese American," pt. II, p. 167.

152. *CSYP,* June 3, 1942; February 27, March 26, 1943; April 11, 1944; February 11, 1945; and *Chinese Press,* April 2, 1943, p. 6.

153. *Chinese Press,* May 29, 1942, p. 6.

154. Margaret Woo, interview with author, February 24, 1983.

155. Lonnie Quan, interview.

156. Broussard, *Black San Francisco,* pp. 146–65.

157. Lonnie Quan, interview.

158. Campbell, *Women at War,* pp. 66–71.

159. *San Francisco Chronicle,* August 7, 1942, p. 8.

160. Chung, "TV Summary."

161. Ibid.; Purwin, "Chinese Daughters of Uncle Sam," p. 337; *CSYP,* October 31, 1944; Gertrude Atherton, *My San Francisco* (Indianapolis: Bobbs-Merrill, 1946), pp. 272–77; and *San Francisco Chronicle,* June 5, 1945, p. 5; January 6, 1959, pp. 1, 4.

162. *Chinese Press,* March 27, 1942, p. 1.

163. Quoted in *Chinese Press,* December 26, 1941, p. 1.

164. *Chinese Press,* January 30, 1942, p. 1.

165. J. Lee, "A Chinese American," pt. II, p. 173.

166. *Chinese Press,* August 20, 1943, p. 1; October 29, 1943, pp. 1–2; and *CSYP,* January 3, December 8, 22, 1943; March 14, December 24, 1944.

167. *Chinese Press,* January 16, 1942, p. 1.

168. *Chinese Press,* January 16, 1942, p. 1.

169. *Chinese Press,* August 13, 1943, p. 1; *CSYP,* May 15, 1943; and Alice Fong Yu, interview with author, March 31, 1986.

170. *Chinese Press,* January 16, March 30, April 10, September 4, November 13, 1942; April 9, 1943; Emily Lee Fong, interview with Carey Mark Huang, April 12, 1982, Chinese Women of America Research Project, Chinese Culture Foundation of San Francisco; and Stanley Lee, interview.

171. *San Francisco Chronicle,* April 6, 1942, p. 12; and R. Lee, "Chinese in the United States Today," p. 444. On the nationally coordinated effort at wartime fund-raising as carried out in San Francisco, see Leni Cahn, "Community Interpretation of Foreign Groups Through Foreign War Relief Agencies in San Francisco" (Master's thesis, University of California, Berkeley, 1946).

172. Liu Pei Chi, *History,* p. 580.

173. Martha Taam, interview with author, November 27, 1989.

174. Purwin, "Chinese Daughters of Uncle Sam," p. 327; and *CSYP,* November 6, 9, 1942.

175. *CSYP,* December 5, 1942; May 17, 1943; December 23, 1945; and *San Francisco Chronicle,* June 19, 1944, p. 9; July 8, 1944, p. 1.

176. *CSYP,* August 14, 15, 19, 1945.

177. Margaret Woo, interview.

178. Lorena How, interview.

179. *CSYP,* August 19, and September 8, 1945.

Epilogue

1. The following account is derived from Jew Law Ying, interview with author, September 7, 1982.

2. The actual transcript of her interrogation ran ten pages (single-spaced) and included many details regarding family history, village and home life, her wedding celebration, and the time she spent with my father in Hong Kong before he departed for the United States. See Jew Law Ying, folder 40766/11-13, CDCF-SFDO.

3. As someone who helped my mother calculate her earnings every month, I was aware of the "doctoring" of time sheets that her employer required of her. Throughout her working life as a seamstress in Chinatown, my mother was paid at a piece rate and not by an hourly wage, in violation of state laws and union regulations. Like many other Chinatown seamstresses, she was a victim of paternalism at work and union tokenism; and she felt powerless to do anything about it. For an analysis of the difficulties in organizing Chinatown seamstresses, see Chalsa Loo, *Chinatown: Most Time, Hard Time* (New York: Praeger, 1991), pp. 189–211.

4. For a discussion of the postwar period and supporting statistical evidence, see Judy Yung, *Chinese American Women: A Pictorial History* (Seattle: University of Washington Press, 1986), pp. 80–95, 123–24.

5. For a discussion of the basic tenets of the Asian American movement within the context of the civil rights movement, see William Wei, *The Asian American Movement* (Philadelphia: Temple University Press, 1993).

Glossary

Ah Kum　亞琴
Anti-Japanese Chinese Salvation
　Society　華僑拒日後授會
Atoy　亞彩
Bak Heong　逼鄉
Baohuanghui　保皇會
"Blood Stains Rivers and Moun-
　tains"　《血濺河山》
Boxer Rebellion　義和團動亂
"Boycott Silk Stockings"　《抵制絲
　襪》
Canton　廣州
Chan Hon Fun　陳翰芬
Chan, May　陳繼成夫人
Chang, H. Y.　張康仁
Chen Yue　陳越
cheong sam　長衫
Cheung, Katherine　張瑞芬
Chew, Caroline　伍瓊蘭
Chew, Rose　伍秋梅
"Chi Lai" ("March of the Volun-
　teers")　《起來》
Chiang Kai-shek　蔣介石
Chick Char Musical Club　叱咤音
　樂社
Chin Lung (Chin Hong Dai)　陳龍
　（陳康大）
Chin Suey Kum　陳瑞琴
Chin Suey Ngon　陳瑞顏

Chin Wing　陳社榮
Chinese American Citizens Alliance
　同源會
Chinese Chamber of Commerce
　中華總商會
Chinese Consolidated Benevolent
　Association　中華總會館
Chinese Hospital　東華醫院
Chinese Independent Baptist
　Church　華人獨立浸信會
Chinese Ladies' Garment Workers'
　Union　華人婦女車衣工會
Chinese Nationalist League of
　America　駐美中國國民黨
Chinese Women's Needlework
　Guild　華人婦女雲錦針黹會
Chinese Six Companies　中華總會
　館
Chinese Students Association　中國
　學生會
Chinese Times　《金山時報》
Chinese War Relief Association
　旅美華僑總一義捐救國總會
Chinese Women's Association (New
　York)　紐約華僑婦女愛國會
Chinese Women's Jeleab Association
　旅美中國女界自立會
Chinese Workers Mutual Aid
　Association　加省華工合作會

359

Ching Ming　清明
Chinn, Daisy Wong　黃杏玉
Chinn, Florence　陳奇馨
Chinn, Ruth Fong　鄺九愛
Chinn, Thomas W.　陳參盛
Chow, Theodore　周敬
Christian Union　基督教聯會
Chu, Y. K.　朱夏（朱耀渠）
Chun Fah　春花
Chung Mei Home　中美學校
Chung, Margaret　張瑪珠
Chung, Rena Jung　張美玉
Chung Sai Yat Po　《中西日報》
Chungshan District　中山縣
Dai Fow　大埠
dai kum　大衿
dim sum　點心
Dragon Boat Festival　端午節
Dupont Street　都板街
Eng, Marietta Chong　張惠英
erh hu　二胡
Eu, March Fong　江月桂
Fa, Angie　法安琪
fan gwai jai　番鬼仔
Fee, Ben　張恨棠
Fidelis Coteri Club　婦女誠志會
Fong, B. S.　鄺炳舜
Fong, Emily Lee　李彩瓊
Fong, Marian　方玉清
Fong, Martha　方美娟
Fong, Mickey　方雪球
Fun, Alice Sue　蘇翠嵐
Funü Ju Ri Jiuguo Tuan (Women's Patriotic Club)　婦女拒日救國團
Funü Xie Hui (Women's Council)　婦女協會
Funü Xinyun Hui (New Life Association)　婦女新運會
Funü Zhanqu Nanmin Chouzhen Hui (Women's War Zone Refugee Relief Committee)　婦女戰區難民籌賑會
gamsaanpo　金山婆
Gee, Charles　曾慧初
Gee, Dolly　曾荷珠
Gee, Maggie　朱美嬌
Gee, May Lew　劉彩美

gee yow nu　自由女
Gin, Gladys Ng　伍玉娥
Ging Hawk Club　競學社
Ginling Women's College　金陵女子大學
Girls' Day　乞巧節
Go, Willie (Go Quai Sing)　高桂成
Golden Gate Manufacturing Company　金門製造公司
Goong, Rose　龔金鳳
Guangdong Province　廣東省
Guomindang　中國國民黨
Han Shizhong　韓世忠
Hangzhou　杭州
Hankow　漢口
He Bing　賀冰
Heilongjiang　黑龍江
Hip Yee Tong　協義堂
ho ga gow　好家教
hoi fan　開飯
Hong Kong　香港
Hong Xiuquan　洪秀全
Hong Xuanjiao　洪宣嬌
Hop Sing Tong　合勝堂
Hop Wo Association　合和會館
How, Lorena　陳瑞球
Hua Mulan　花木蘭
"Huan Xing Xiongsi"　《喚醒雄獅》
Huaren Shiyi Hui　華人失業會
Huey, Penny Chan　陳娉嬋
Jan, Flora Belle　鄭容金
Jang, Ruth Chan　陳月紅
Jean, Lily K.　呂蓮
Jesus woman　耶穌婆
Jew Law Ying　趙羅英
Jew Yee Yuet　趙以越
Jong, Frances　鍾迎春
Kai Gok village　谿角村
Kang Youwei　康有為
Kin Kuo Chinese School　建國中學校
Kingston, Maxine Hong　湯婷婷
Kong Chow　岡州
Kum Quey　金貴
Kwan, Florence Chinn　陳奇馨
Kwong Dock Tong　廣德堂
Lai Chun-chuen　黎春泉

Lai, Him Mark　麥禮謙
Lai Yee Kai　黎如桂
Lai Yun Oi　黎潤愛
Law Shee Low (Law Yuk Tao)
　劉羅氏（羅玉桃）
Lee, Ann　李妙齡
Lee, Charles　李肇榮
Lee, Chingwah　李華清
Lee, Choy (Mrs.)　陳瑞彩
Lee, Clara　陳意妙
Lee, Edwar　李華鎮
Lee, Hazel Ying　李月英
Lee, Ira　李群樾
Lee, Ivy　李妙琴
Lee, Jane Kwong　鄺蓮眞
Lee, Jennie　李彩英
Lee Jow Hing　李祖慶
Lee, Lim P.　李泮霖
Lee, Rose Hum　譯金美
Lee, Sue Ko　蕭修
Lee Ya Ching　李霞清
Leong, Charles　梁普禮
Leong Shee (Leong Kum Kew)
　梁氏（梁琴嬌）
Leung, Faith So　梁細蘇
Li Ruzhen　李汝珍
Li Yauguang　李耀光
Liang Hongyu　梁紅玉
"Lianzhen Chu Ji"　《蓮眞劇集》
ling gok　菱角
Liu Pei Chi　劉伯驥
Liu Yilan　劉義蘭
lo mo　老母
Loo, Florence Lee　李雲娣
Lowe, Eva　陳君綺
Lui Chen Shee　雷陳氏
Lugouqiao　蘆溝橋
Lum, Emma　林娉娉
Ma Zhanshan　馬占山
Macao　澳門
mah-jongg　麻將
Mai Zhouyi　麥灼儀
Manchu　滿族
Manchuria　東北（東三省）
Mao Qiling　毛奇齡
"March of the Volunteers"　《義勇
　軍進行曲》

Marco Polo Bridge　蘆溝橋
May Fourth Movement　五四運動
Mei Fang Girls' Middle School
　梅芳中學
Mei Lun Yuen　美鄰園
Mid-Autumn Festival　中秋節
Ming Quong Home　明光女學校
mui tsai　妹仔
Mukden Incident　瀋陽事變
Nanhai District　南海縣
Nanking　南京
National Dollar Stores　中興公司
Ng Poon Chew　伍盤照
9-18 Humiliation Day　九一八國
　恥紀念日
1911 Revolution　辛亥革命
Ning Yung Association　寧陽會館
Nü'er-Ching　女兒經
1-28 Humiliation Day　一二八國
　恥紀念日
Onyett, Helen Pon　陳玉珠
Op Lee Jeu village　鴨脷嘴村
Opium Wars　鴉片戰爭
Ouyang Ying　歐陽英
Ow Muck Gay　區麥基
Ow, Rose Yuen　阮妹
Panyu District　番禺縣
Peace Society　和平總會
Pearl River Delta　珠江三角洲
Peking　北京
Ping Sheh　平社
Punti-Hakka feud　土客械鬥
Qing dynasty　清朝
Qiu Jin　秋瑾
Quan, Lonnie　黃美蘭
Red Turban uprising　紅巾起事
Rice Bowl movement　一碗飯運動
Sai Gai Yat Po　《世界日報》
sai yun　西人
Sam Yup　三邑
sausaanggwai　守生寡
see mun　斯文
Schulze, Tye Leung　梁亞娣
See Heong　思鄉
Self-Governing Association　自治
　會
7-7 Incident　七七事變

Shandong Province　山東省

Shanghai　上海

Shoong, Joe　周崧

shuqi　梳起

Shunde District　順德縣

Sieh King King　薛錦琴

Sing Kee　生記

Sing, Lillian　甄郭麗蓮

"Sing Loy"　《醒來》

Soo Hoo Nam Art　司徒南達

Soong Ching-ling (Mme Sun Yat-sen)　宋慶齡(孫中山夫人)

Soong Mei-ling (Mme Chiang Kai-shek)　宋美齡(蔣介石夫人)

Square and Circle Club　方圓社

Suey Sing Tong　萃勝堂

Sui Seen Far　水仙花

Sun, Hoo Joe　周燊

Sun Yat-sen　孫中山

Sung dynasty　宋朝

Taam, Martha (Mrs. T. T. Taam)　譯祖鈿夫人

Taiping Rebellion　太平天國起義

Taiwan　台灣

Tang dynasty　唐朝

Tang, Julie　鄧孟詩

Tape, Joseph　趙洽

Tape, Mary　趙洽夫人

Tartar　韃靼

Teng, Mabel　鄧式美

Tientsin　天津

"To the Front"　《向前線去》

Toishan District　台山縣

Tom Fat Kwong　譯發光

Tom Leung　譯良

Tom Yip Jing　譯業精

tong (secret society)　堂號

Tongmenghui　同盟會

True Light Seminary　眞光學校

True Sunshine Chinese School　聖公會中文學校

Tsai Ting-kai　蔡廷鍇

Tung Chee　同治

Uncle Haw　賀大舅(越成賀)

Uncle Lurt　律二舅(越成律)

United Service Organization (USO)　慰勞華裔軍人會

wan fan　挽飯

War of Resistance Against Japan　抗日戰爭

Wei Kim Fong　衞劍芳

Winter Solstice　冬至

Won Hongfei　溫雄飛

Won King Yoak　溫瓊玉

Won, Lilly King Gee　溫瓊珠(溫徵德)

Wong Ah So　黃亞蘇

Wong, Anna May　黃柳霜

Wong, Bessie　黃瓊香

Wong, Daisy K.　黃碧琴

Wong, Daisy L.　黃杏玉

Wong, Dora Lee　王彼珍

Wong, Esther　黃玉燕

wong gaa　皇家

Wong, G. N.　王官梧

Wong, Helen Hong　阮蘭香

Wong Ho　黃好

Wong, Jade Snow　黃玉雪

Wong, Ruth　黃玉蓮

Wong, Virginia　黃桂燕

Wong Shee Chan　陳黃氏(黃煥桂)

Wong Wee Ying　黃衞英

Woo, Margaret　蔡玉卿

Wu, Daniel　伍智清

Wu Jianxiong　吳劍雄

Wu Minchi　吳敏墀

Wu Tien Fu　伍天福

Wu Yifang　吳貽芳

Xiang Dingrong　項定榮

Xinhui District　新會縣

Yan Wo Association　人和會館

Yang Hueimin　楊惠敏

Yangtze River　長江

Yip, Jessie Lee　李琦仙

Yoke Choy Club　育才社

Young Wo Association　陽和會館

Yu, Alice Fong　方玉屛

Yu Zhengxie　俞正燮

Yuan Mei　袁枚

Yue Fei　岳飛

Yung Hin Sen　楊庭順

Yung Ung　楊棟

Yung, Judy　楊碧芳

Yung, Patricia　楊碧貞

Yung, Sandra　楊思鄉
Yung, Sharon　楊碧香
Yung, Virginia　楊碧琦
Yung, Warren Tom　楊劍華
Zeng Bugui　曾步規
Zhao Shaoping　趙小平
Zhang Zhujun　張竹君

Zhejiang　浙江
Zhigongtang　致公堂
zishunü　自梳女
ziyounü　自由女
"Zong Dongyuan"　《總動員》
Zuo Xueli　左學禮

Bibliography

Manuscripts and Archival Collections

Chinese Departure Case Files [CDCF]. San Francisco District Office, Immigration and Naturalization Service. Record Group 85. National Archives, San Bruno, Calif.

Chinese Hospital Medical Staff Archives, 1978–81. Chinese Hospital, San Francisco.

The Chinese Women's Association Fifth Anniversary Special Issue. New York: Chinese Women's Association, 1937. Microfilm, New York Public Library.

Chinese Young People's Christian Conference. Proceedings and minutes, 1938–47. Him Mark Lai private collection.

Chinese YWCA files (correspondence, board minutes, staff reports, photographs), 1916–45. Chinese YWCA, San Francisco; and Philip P. Choy private collection.

Chung, Margaret. Private papers, scrapbooks, photographs. Asian American Studies Library, University of California, Berkeley.

International Institute of San Francisco files (scrapbooks, board minutes, staff reports, case files), 1918–50. International Institute, San Francisco.

International Ladies' Garment Workers' Union (ILGWU) collection. Labor Archives and Research Center, San Francisco State University.

Jan, Flora Belle. Letters to Ludmelia Holstein, 1918–50. In possession of daughter (name withheld by request).

Lee, Jane Kwong. "A Chinese American." Unpublished autobiography (in my possession).

Lee, Sue Ko. Scrapbook of clippings, leaflets, and photographs (in my possession).

Methodist Mission Home (Gum Moon Women's Residence) case files, 1903–34. Gum Moon Women's Residence, San Francisco.

Schulze, Tye Leung. "Tiny." Louise Schulze Lee private collection.

Square and Circle Club files (scrapbooks, minutes of meetings, photographs), 1924–46. Square and Circle Club, San Francisco.

Survey of Race Relations collection (oral histories and research papers),

1923–25. Hoover Institution on War, Revolution, and Peace, Stanford University.

U.S. District Intelligence Office, Twelfth Naval District, Commandant's Office. "Chinese Situation in the San Francisco Bay Area," 1945. General Correspondence, folder A8-5. National Archives, San Bruno, Calif.

Women's Occidental Board of Foreign Missions. Annual Reports, 1874–1920. San Francisco Theological Seminary, San Anselmo, Calif.

Oral Histories

Chin Yen. "Life History as a Social Document of Mr. Chin Yen." Survey of Race Relations Collection, Hoover Institution on War, Revolution, and Peace, Stanford University.

Chinn, Daisy Wong. Interview with Genny Lim, July 29, 1982, Chinese Women of America Research Project, Chinese Culture Foundation of San Francisco.

Chung, Rena Jung. Interview with author, June 30, 1994.

Eng, Marietta Chong. Interview with Genny Lim, September 13, 1982, Chinese Women of America Research Project, Chinese Culture Foundation of San Francisco.

Fong, Emily Lee. Interview with Him Mark Lai and Gilbert Woo, March 1, 1975, Him Mark Lai private collection; interview with Carey Mark Huang, April 12, 1982, Chinese Women of America Research Project, Chinese Culture Foundation of San Francisco.

Fun, Alice Sue. Interview with author, February 28, 1982.

Fung, May Kew. Interview with Jeffrey Ow, March 25, 1990, Jeffrey Ow private collection.

Gee, Maggie. Interview with author, February 25, 1990.

Gee, May Lew. Interview with author, June 25, 1994.

Gin, Gladys Ng. Interview with author, November 4, 1988.

Hing, Bertha. Interview with Kirk Fong and Valerie Fong, March, 1991, Kirk Fong private collection.

How, Lorena. Interview with Sandy Lee, May 1, 1982, Chinese Women of America Research Project, Chinese Culture Foundation of San Francisco.

Huey, Penny Chan. Interview with author, November 21, 1988.

Hung, Bessie. Interview with author, June 30, 1989.

Jan, Flora Belle. "Interview with Flora Belle Jan, Daughter of Proprietor of the 'Yet Far Low' Chop Suey Restaurant, Tulare St. and China Alley, Fresno." Survey of Race Relations Collection, Hoover Institution on War, Revolution, and Peace, Stanford University.

Jang, Ruth Chan. Interview with author, July 8, 1994.

Jeong, Bessie. Interview with Suellen Cheng and Munson Kwok, December 17, 1981, Southern California Chinese American Oral History Project, Chinese Historical Society of Southern California, Los Angeles.

Jew Law Ying. Interview with author, September 7, 1982, and January 14, 1987.

Jong, Frances. Interview with author, February 12, 1990.

Kwan, Florence Chinn. Interview with author, October 7 and 12, 1988.
Lee, Clara. Interview with author, October 2, November 4, 1986; and July 31, 1989.
Lee, Ira. Interview with author, November 1, 1989.
Lee, Jane Kwong. Interview with author, October 22 and November 2, 1988.
Lee, Lim P. Interview with author, October 31, 1989.
Lee, Louise Schulze. Interview with author, November 7, 1988.
Lee, Lucy. Interview with author, May 17, 1982.
Lee, Mickey Fong. Interview with Ernest Chann, February 23, 1982, Ernest Chann private collection; interview with author, November 1, 1989.
Lee, Mrs. Choy. Interview with Him Mark Lai and Helen Lai, March 2, 1975, Him Mark Lai private collection.
Lee, Stanley. Interview with author, July 26, 1985.
Lee, Sue Ko. Interview with author, October 26, 1989.
Loo, Florence Lee. Interview with June Quan, January 6, 1982, Chinese Women of America Research Project, Chinese Culture Foundation of San Francisco.
Law Shee Low. Interview with author, October 20, 1988; interview with Sandy Lee, May 2, 1982, Chinese Women of America Research Project, Chinese Culture Foundation of San Francisco.
Lowe, Eva. Interview with Genny Lim, July 15, 1982, Chinese Women of America Research Project, Chinese Culture Foundation of San Francisco.
Lowe, Pany. "Social Document of Pany Lowe." Survey of Race Relations Collection, Hoover Institution on War, Revolution, and Peace, Stanford University.
Matyas, Jennie. "Jennie Matyas and the ILGWU." Oral history conducted 1955 by Connie Gilb, Regional Cultural History Project, The Bancroft Library, University of California, Berkeley, 1957.
Mock, May. Interview with author, July 17, 1993.
Onyett, Helen Pon. Interview with author, January 9, 1983.
Ow, Rose Yuen. Interview with Philip P. Choy and Him Mark Lai, September 9, 1970, Him Mark Lai private collection.
Owyang, Edwin. Interview with author, September 10, 1987.
Quan, Lonnie. Interview with Genny Lim, August 10, 1982, Chinese Women of America Research Project, Chinese Culture Foundation of San Francisco.
Schulze, Fred. Interview with author, January 26, 1989.
Sexton, Charlotte. Interview with author, August 17, 1982.
Taam, Martha. Interview with author, November 27, 1989.
Wong, Dora Lee. Interview with author, October 5, 1982.
Wong, Esther. "Native-born Chinese." Survey of Race Relations Collection, Hoover Institution on War, Revolution, and Peace, Stanford University.
———. "Story of a Chinese College Girl (The Conflict Between the Old and the Young)." Survey of Race Relations Collection, Hoover Institution on War, Revolution, and Peace, Stanford University.
Wong, Helen Hong. Interview with author, June 17, 1982.
Wong Shee Chan. Interview with author, March 5, 1982.
Wong Wee Ying. Interview with author, May 7, 1982.

Woo, Margaret. Interview with author, February 24, 1983.
King Yoak Won Wu. Interview with Genny Lim, October 27, 1982, Chinese
    Women of America Research Project, Chinese Culture Foundation of San
    Francisco.
Yip, Jessie Lee. Interview with author, November 2, 1989.
Yu, Alice Fong. Interview with author, March 31, 1986; interview with
    Gordon Chang, November 21, 1986, and June 29, 1987, Gordon Chang
    private collection.

Newspapers and Journals

California Chinese Press, 1940–45.
Chung Sai Yat Po, 1900–45.
Chinese Christian Student, 1929–45.
Chinese Digest, 1935–40.
Chinese Students' Monthly, 1906–31.
Chinese Times, 1928–45.
Fore 'n Aft, 1942–46.
Marin-er, 1943–45.
San Francisco Call, 1883–1913.
San Francisco Chronicle, 1869–1945.
San Francisco Examiner, 1881–1945.
Women and Mission, 1924–46.

Government Documents

Act of September 22, 1922, 42 United States Statutes at Large, 1021.
Anderson, H. Dewey. "Who Are on Relief in California?" *Miscellaneous
    Publications*. San Francisco: California State Relief Administration, 1939.
Bryant, David. *Summary Report: Civil Works Administrative Statistics, State of
    California, November 27, 1933, to March 29, 1934*. San Francisco: Civil
    Works Administration, 1934.
California State Emergency Relief Administration (CSERA). "Survey of
    Social Work Needs of the Chinese Population of San Francisco, Califor-
    nia." 1935.
Case of the Chinese Wife, 21 Federal Reporter 785 (1884).
*Chinese Immigration: The Social, Moral, and Political Effect of Chinese
    Immigration. Testimony Taken Before a Committee of the Senate of the State
    of California, Appointed April 3d, 1876*. Sacramento: State Printing Office,
    1876.
Community Chest of San Francisco. "Survey of Social Work Needs of the
    Chinese Population of San Francisco." 1930.
"Condition of the Chinese Quarter." *San Francisco Municipal Reports for the
    Fiscal Year 1884–85, Ending June 30, 1885*. San Francisco: Board of
    Supervisors, 1885.
Geiger, J. C., et al. *The Health of the Chinese in an American City: San
    Francisco*. San Francisco: Department of Public Health, 1939.

In re Ah Quan, 21 Federal Reporter 182 (1884).

In re Chung Toy Ho and Wong Choy Sin, 42 Federal Reporter 398 (1890).

Royal Mui Tsai Commission. *Mui Tsai in Hong Kong and Malaya*. London: His Majesty's Stationery Office, 1937.

U.S. Bureau of the Census. *Fifteenth Census of the United States: 1930*.

——. *Final Report on Total and Partial Unemployment for California,* 1938.

——. *Fourteenth Census of the United States: 1920 Population*.

——. *Seventeenth Census of the United States. Census of the Population:* 1950.

——. *Sixteenth Census of the United States. Population: 1940*.

——. *Thirteenth Census of the United States. Population: 1910*.

——. *Twelfth Census of the United States. Population: 1900*.

U.S. House. *Admission of Wives of American Citizens of Oriental Ancestry: Hearings Before the Committee on Immigration and Naturalization on H.R. 6544*. 69th Cong., 1st sess., 1926.

U.S. National Archives. Record Group 29. "Census of U.S. Population" (manuscript), San Francisco, California, 1900, 1910, and 1920.

U.S. Senate. *Admission as Nonquota Immigrants of Certain Alien Wives and Children of United States Citizens: Hearing Before a Subcommittee of the Committee on Immigration on S. 2271*. 70th Cong., 1st sess., 1928.

United States v. Gue Lim. 88 Federal Reporter 136 (1897).

Secondary Sources

Anderson, Karen. *Wartime Women: Sex Roles, Family Relationships, and the Status of Women During World War II*. Westport, Conn.: Greenwood Press, 1981.

Anker, Laura. "Family, Work, and Community: Southern and Eastern European Immigrant Women Speak from the Connecticut Federal Writers' Project." In *Gendered Domains: Rethinking Public and Private in Women's History*, edited by Dorothy O. Helly and Susan M. Reverby, pp. 303–21. Ithaca: Cornell University Press, 1992.

Anzaldua, Gloria, ed. *Making Face, Making Soul, Haciendo Caras: Creative and Critical Perspectives by Women of Color*. San Francisco: Aunt Lute Foundation, 1990.

Aptheker, Bettina. *Tapestries of Life: Women's Work, Women's Consciousness, and the Meaning of Daily Experience*. Amherst: University of Massachusetts Press, 1989.

——. *Woman's Legacy: Essays on Race, Sex, and Class in American History*. Amherst: University of Massachusetts Press, 1982.

Archer, Jules. *The Chinese and the Americans*. New York: Hawthorne Books, 1976.

Archibald, Katherine. *Wartime Shipyard*. Berkeley: University of California Press, 1947.

Arnold, Julean. "California-educated Chinese Rebuild Canton." *Chinese Christian Student*, May–June 1934, pp. 8–9, 34.

Ashbury, Herbert. *The Barbary Coast: An Informal History of the San Francisco Underground.* New York: Alfred A. Knopf, 1933.

Atherton, Gertrude. *My San Francisco.* Indianapolis, N.Y.: Bobbs-Merrill, 1946.

Barnhart, Jacqueline Baker. *The Fair but Frail: Prostitution in San Francisco, 1849–1900.* Reno: University of Nevada Press, 1986.

Barth, Gunther. *Bitter Strength: A History of the Chinese in the United States, 1850–1870.* Cambridge, Mass.: Harvard University Press, 1964.

Beahan, Charlotte L. "The Women's Movement and Nationalism in Late Ch'ing China." Ph.D. diss., Columbia University, 1976.

Beckwith, Holmes. "The Chinese Family, with Special Relation to Industry." Master's thesis, University of California, Berkeley, 1909.

Benard de Russailh, Albert. *Last Adventure, San Francisco in 1851.* San Francisco: Westgate, 1931.

Blackwelder, Julia Kirk. *Women of the Depression: Caste and Culture in San Antonio, 1929–1939.* College Station, Tex.: A & M University Press, 1984.

Blair, Karen J. *The Clubswoman as Feminist: True Womanhood Redefined, 1868–1914.* New York: Holmes & Meier, 1980.

Blauner, Robert. *Racial Oppression in America.* New York: Harper & Row, 1972.

Bock, Norman. "Chameleon Cloaks, Flying Tigers, and Missionary Ladies: The Oral History and Political Economy of Baltimore Chinatown and the China Relief Movement, 1937–41." B.A. thesis, Harvard College, 1976.

Bode, William. *Lights and Shadows of Chinatown.* San Francisco: Crocker Co., 1896.

Bodnar, John. *The Transplanted: A History of Immigration in Urban America.* Bloomington: Indiana University Press, 1985.

Brace, Charles Loring. *The New West; or, California in 1867–1868.* New York: G. P. Putnam, 1869.

Broussard, Albert S. *Black San Francisco: The Struggle for Racial Equality in the West, 1900–1954.* Lawrence: University Press of Kansas, 1993.

Brownstone, David M., Irene M. Franck, and Douglass L. Brownstone. *Island of Hope, Island of Tears.* New York: Penguin Books, 1986.

Burchell, R. A. *The San Francisco Irish, 1848–1880.* Manchester: Manchester University Press, 1979.

Butler, Anne. *Daughters of Joy, Sisters of Misery: Prostitution in the American West, 1865–90.* Urbana: University of Illinois Press, 1985.

Cahn, Leni. "Community Interpretation of Foreign Groups Through Foreign War Relief Agencies in San Francisco." Master's thesis, University of California, Berkeley, 1946.

Cameron, Donaldina. "New Lives for Old in Chinatown." *Missionary Review of the World* 57 (July–August 1934): 327–31.

———. "Orientals in the United States." *Women and Mission* 9, no. 10 (January 1935): 340–41.

———. "Salvaged for Service." *Women and Mission* 4, no. 5 (August 1927): 168–70.

———. "The Story of Wong So." *Women and Mission* 2, no. 5 (August 1925): 169–72.

Campbell, D'Ann. *Women at War With America*. Cambridge, Mass.: Harvard University Press, 1984.

Cather, Helen Virginia. "The History of San Francisco's Chinatown." Master's thesis, University of California, Berkeley, 1932.

Chafe, William H. *The American Woman: Her Changing Social, Economic, and Political Roles, 1920–1970*. London: Oxford University Press, 1972.

Chan, Sucheng. *Asian Americans: An Interpretive History*. Boston: Twayne, 1991.

———. "Chinese American Entrepreneur: The California Career of Chin Lung." *Chinese America: History and Perspectives 1987*, pp. 73–86.

———. "European and Asian Immigration into the United States in Comparative Perspective, 1820s to 1920s." In *Immigration Reconsidered: History, Sociology, and Politics*, edited by Virginia Yans-McLaughlin, pp. 37–75. New York: Oxford University Press, 1990.

———. "The Exclusion of Chinese Women, 1870–1943." In *Entry Denied: Exclusion and the Chinese Community in America, 1882–1943*, edited by Sucheng Chan, pp. 94–146. Philadelphia: Temple University Press, 1991.

———. *This Bittersweet Soil: The Chinese in California, 1860–1910*. Berkeley and Los Angeles: University of California Press, 1986.

Char, Tin-Yuke. *The Sandalwood Mountains: Readings and Stories of the Early Chinese in Hawaii*. Honolulu: University Press of Hawaii, 1975.

Chen, Helen. "Chinese Immigration into the United States: An Analysis of Changes in Immigration Policies." Ph.D. diss., Brandeis University, 1980.

Chen, Wen-Hsien. "Chinese Under Both Exclusion and Immigration Laws." Ph.D. diss., University of Chicago, 1940.

Chen Yueh. *Madame Chiang Kai-shek's Trip Through the United States and Canada*. San Francisco: Chinese Nationalist Daily, 1943.

Chesneaux, Jean, Françoise Le Barbier, and Marie-Claire Bergère. *China from the 1911 Revolution to Liberation*. Translated by Paul Auster and Lydia Davis. New York: Pantheon Books, 1977.

Chesneaux, Jean, Marianne Bastid, and Marie-Claire Bergère. *China from the Opium Wars to the 1911 Revolution*. Translated by Anne Destenay. New York: Pantheon Books, 1976.

Chew, Caroline. "Development of Chinese Family Life in America." Master's thesis, Mills College, 1926.

Chih, Ginger. "Immigration of Chinese Women to the U.S.A." Master's thesis, Sarah Lawrence College, 1977.

Chinatown Declared a Nuisance! (San Francisco). Pamphlet written and distributed by an investigative committee of the Anti-Chinese Council, W.P.C. Haggin Museum, Stockton, Calif. March 10, 1880.

Chinn, Florence Worley. "Religious Education in the Chinese Community of San Francisco." Master's thesis, University of Chicago, 1920.

Chinn, Ruth Fong. "Square and Circle Club of San Francisco: A Chinese Women's Culture." Senior thesis, University of California, Santa Cruz, 1987.

Chinn, Thomas W. *Bridging the Pacific: San Francisco's Chinatown and Its People*. San Francisco: Chinese Historical Society of America, 1989.

————, ed. *A History of the Chinese in California: A Syllabus.* San Francisco: Chinese Historical Society of America, 1969.

Chow, Christopher, and Russell Leong. "A Pioneer Chinatown Teacher: An Interview with Alice Fong Yu." *Amerasia Journal* 5, no. 1 (1978): 77.

Choy, Katie. "Alice Fong Yu: Remembrances of a Chinese Pioneer." *Prism* 11, no. 2 (December 1974): 5–8.

Choy, Philip P. "San Francisco's Chinatown Architecture." *Chinese America: History and Perspectives 1990,* pp. 37–66.

Chu, Janie. "The Oriental Girl in the Occident." *Women and Mission* 3, no. 5 (August 1926): 174–75.

Chu, Judy. "Anna May Wong." In *Counterpoint: Perspectives on Asian America,* edited by Emma Gee, pp. 284–88. Los Angeles: Asian American Studies Center, University of California, 1976.

Chu, Y. K. *History of the Chinese People in America* (in Chinese). New York: China Times, 1975.

Chun-Hoon, Lowell. "Jade Snow Wong and the Fate of Chinese-American Identity." *Amerasia Journal* 1 (1971): 52–63.

Chung, Margaret. "TV Summary of Margaret Chung's Life." Unpublished autobiography. Asian American Studies Library, University of California, Berkeley, [ca. 1945].

Chung, Sue Fawn. "The Chinese American Citizens Alliance: An Effort in Assimilation, 1895–1965." *Chinese America: History and Perspectives 1988,* pp. 30–57.

Cinel, Dino. *From Italy to San Francisco: The Immigrant Experience.* Stanford: Stanford University Press, 1982.

Clark, Helen F. *The Lady of the Lily Feet and Other Stories of Chinatown.* Philadelphia: Griffith & Rowland Press, 1900.

Cohen, Miriam. *Workshop to Office: Two Generations of Italian Women in New York City, 1900–1950.* Ithaca: Cornell University Press, 1992.

Collins, Leslie Eugene. "The New Women: A Psychological Study of the Chinese Feminist Movement from 1900 to the Present." Ph.D. diss., Yale University, 1976.

Collins, Patricia Hill. *Black Feminist Thought: Knowledge, Consciousness, and the Politics of Empowerment.* London: HarperCollins Academic, 1990.

Condit, Ira M. *The Chinaman as We See Him and Fifty Years of Work for Him.* Chicago: Fleming H. Revell Co., 1900.

Coolidge, Mary Roberts. *Chinese Immigration.* New York: Henry Holt, 1909.

Cordasco, Francesco. *The White Slave Trade and the Immigrants: A Chapter in American Social History.* Detroit: Blaine Ethridge Books, 1981.

Croll, Elizabeth. *Feminism and Socialism in China.* New York: Schocken Books, 1980.

Dare, Richard Kock. "The Economic and Social Adjustment of the San Francisco Chinese for the Past Fifty Years." Master's thesis, University of California, Berkeley, 1959.

Davis, Angela. *Women, Race, and Class.* New York: Random House, 1981.

Davis, John A. *The Chinese Slave Girl: A Story of Woman's Life in China.* Philadelphia: Presbyterian Board of Publications, [ca. 1880].

D'Emilio, John, and Estelle Freedman. *Intimate Matters: A History of Sexuality in America*. New York: Harper & Row, 1988.

Dill, Bonnie Thornton. "Our Mother's Grief: Racial Ethnic Women and the Maintenance of Families." *Journal of Family History* 13, no. 4 (1988): 415–31.

Dillon, Richard. *The Hatchet Men: San Francisco's Chinatown in the Days of the Tong Wars, 1880–1906*. New York: Ballantine Books, 1972.

Diner, Hasia R. *Erin's Daughters in America: Irish Immigrant Women in the Nineteenth Century*. Baltimore: Johns Hopkins University Press, 1983.

Dobie, Charles Caldwell. *San Francisco's Chinatown*. New York: D. Appleton–Century, 1936.

Dong, Lorraine. "The Forbidden City Legacy and Its Chinese American Women." *Chinese America: History and Perspectives* 1992, pp. 125–48.

Drucker, Alison R. "The Role of the YWCA in the Development of the Chinese Women's Movement, 1890–1927." *Social Services Review*, September 1979, pp. 421–40.

Dunn, Robert. "Does My Future Lie in China or America?" *Chinese Digest*, May 15, 1936, pp. 3, 13.

Edholm, M. G. C. "A Stain on the Flag." *Californian Illustrated Magazine* 1 (February 1892): 159–70.

———. "Traffic in White Girls." *Californian Illustrated Magazine* 2 (June–November 1892): 825–38.

Evans, Albert S. *A la California: Sketches of Life in the Golden Gate*. San Francisco: A. L. Bancroft, 1873.

Evans, Sara M. *Born for Liberty: A History of Women in America*. New York: Free Press, 1989.

Ewen, Elizabeth. *Immigrant Women in the Land of Dollars: Life and Culture on the Lower East Side, 1890–1925*. New York: Monthly Review Press, 1985.

Facts upon the Other Side of the Chinese Question: With a Memorial to the President of the United States from Representative Chinamen in America. 1876. Pamphlet written and distributed by members of the Chinese Six Companies. Bancroft Library, University of California.

Fass, Paula. *The Damned and the Beautiful: American Youth in the 1920s*. New York: Oxford University Press, 1977.

Ferina, Bessie Mae. "The Politics of San Francisco's Chinatown." Master's thesis, University of California, Berkeley, 1949.

Fisher, Andrea. *Let Us Now Praise Famous Women: Women Photographers for the U.S. Government, 1935 to 1944*. New York: Pandora Press, 1987.

Flamm, Jerry. *Good Life in Hard Times: San Francisco's 1920s and 1930s*. San Francisco: Chronicle Books, 1978.

Foner, Philip. *Women and the American Labor Movement*. New York: Free Press, 1980.

Fong, Kathryn M. "Asian Women Lose Citizenship." *San Francisco Journal*, December 29, 1976, p. 12.

———. "Pioneer Recalls Earthquake and Schools." *San Francisco Journal*, January 5, 1977, p. 6.

Fong, Patricia M. "The 1938 National Dollar Strike." *Asian American Review* 2, no. 1 (1975): 183–200.

Forbidden City, U.S.A.: World Premiere Benefit. San Francisco, 1989.

Frank, Dana. *Purchasing Power: Consumer Organizing, Gender, and the Seattle Labor Movement, 1919–1929.* Cambridge: Cambridge University Press, 1994.

Gaw, Kenneth. *Superior Servants: The Legendary Cantonese Amahs of the Far East.* Oxford: Oxford University Press, 1988.

Gentry, Curt. *The Madams of San Francisco.* New York: Doubleday, 1964.

Gibson, Otis. *The Chinese in America.* Cincinnati: Hitchcock & Walden, 1877.

Giddings, Paula. *When and Where I Enter: The Impact of Black Women on Race and Sex in America.* New York: William Morrow, 1984.

Glenn, Evelyn Nakano. *Issei, Nisei, Warbride: Three Generations of Japanese American Women in Domestic Service.* Philadelphia: Temple University Press, 1986.

———. "Racial Ethnic Women's Labor: The Intersection of Race, Gender, and Class Oppression." *Review of Radical Political Economics* 17, no. 3 (1985): 86–108.

———. "Split Household, Small Producer, and Dual Wage Earner: An Analysis of Chinese-American Family Strategies." *Journal of Marriage and Family* 45, no. 1 (February 1983): 35–48.

Glenn, Susan. *Daughters of the Shtetl: Life and Labor in the Immigrant Generation.* Ithaca: Cornell University Press, 1990.

Gluck, Sherna Berger. *Rosie the Riveter Revisited: Women, the War, and Social Change.* New York: New American Library, 1987.

Gong, Eng Ying, and Bruce Grant. *Tong War!* New York: Nicholas L. Brown, 1930.

Gonzalez, Rosalinda M. "Chicanos and Mexican Immigrant Families, 1920–1940: Women's Subordination and Family Exploitation." In *Decades of Discontent: The Women's Movement, 1920–1940,* edited by Lois Scharf and Joan M. Jensen, pp. 59–84. Westport, Conn.: Greenwood Press, 1983.

Gordon, Linda. "Black and White Visions of Welfare: Women's Welfare Activism, 1890–1945." In *Unequal Sisters: A Multicultural Reader in U.S. Women's History,* 2d ed., edited by Vicki L. Ruiz and Ellen Carol DuBois, pp. 157–85. New York: Routledge, 1994.

———. "The New Feminist Scholarship on the Welfare State." In *Women, the State, and Welfare,* edited by Linda Gordon, pp. 9–34. Madison: University of Wisconsin Press, 1990.

———, ed. *Women, the State, and Welfare.* Madison: University of Wisconsin Press, 1990.

Gordon, Milton M. *Assimilation in American Life.* New York: Oxford University Press, 1964.

Gronewold, Sue. *Beautiful Merchandise: Prostitution in China, 1860–1936.* New York: Harrington Park Press, 1985.

Guan Zhongren. *Study on Chinese Women Aviators* (in Chinese). Canton: Zhongshan Library of Guangdong Province, 1988.

Guerin-Gonzalez, Camille. *Mexican Workers and American Dreams: Immigration, Repatriation, and California Farm Labor, 1900–1939*. New Brunswick, N.J.: Rutgers University Press, 1994.

Hartmann, Heidi. "Capitalism, Patriarchy, and Job Segregation by Sex." *Signs: Journal of Women in Culture and Society* 1, no. 3 (spring 1976): 137–70.

Hartmann, Susan. *The Home Front and Beyond: American Women in the 1940s*. Boston: Twayne, 1982.

———. "Women in the Military Service." In *Clio Was a Woman: Studies in the History of American Women*, edited by Mabel Deutrich and Virginia Purdy, pp. 195–205. Washington, D.C.: Howard University Press, 1980.

Helly, Dorothy O., and Susan M. Reverby, eds. *Gendered Domains: Rethinking Public and Private in Women's History*. Ithaca: Cornell University Press, 1992.

Helmbold, Lois Rita. "Beyond the Family Economy: Black and White Working-Class Women During the Great Depression." *Feminist Studies* 13, no. 3 (fall 1987): 629–55.

Hershatter, Gail. "The Hierarchy of Shanghai Prostitution, 1870–1949." *Modern China* 15, no. 4 (October 1989): 463–98.

Higginbotham, Elizabeth. "Employment for Professional Black Women in the Twentieth Century." Paper prepared for the Albany Conference, Ingredients for Women's Employment Policy, April 19–20, 1985.

Higginbotham, Evelyn Brooks. "African-American Women's History and the Metalanguage of Race." *Signs: Journal of Women in Culture and Society* 17, no. 2 (1992): 251–73.

———. *Righteous Discontent: The Women's Movement in the Black Baptist Church, 1880–1920*. Cambridge, Mass.: Harvard University Press, 1993.

Higonnet, Margaret Randolph, Jane Jenson, Sonya Michel, and Margaret Collins Weitz, eds. *Behind the Lines: Gender and the Two World Wars*. New Haven: Yale University Press, 1987.

Hing, Bill Ong. *Making and Remaking Asian America Through Immigration Policy, 1850–1990*. Stanford: Stanford University Press, 1993.

Hirata, Lucie Cheng. "Chinese Immigrant Women in Nineteenth-Century California." In *Women of America: A History*, edited by C. R. Berkin and M. B. Norton, pp. 223–44. Boston: Houghton-Mifflin, 1979.

———. "Free, Indentured, Enslaved: Chinese Prostitutes in Nineteenth-Century America." *Signs: Journal of Women in Culture and Society* 5, no. 1 (autumn 1979): 3–29.

Hoexter, Corinne K. *From Canton to California: The Epic of Chinese Immigration*. New York: Four Winds Press, 1976.

Hoffman, Abraham. *Unwanted Mexican Americans in the Great Depression: Repatriation Pressures, 1929–1939*. Tucson: University of Arizona Press, 1974.

Hom, Marlon K. *Songs of Gold Mountain: Cantonese Rhymes from San Francisco Chinatown*. Berkeley and Los Angeles: University of California Press, 1987.

Hong, Kaye. "Does My Future Lie in China or America?" *Chinese Digest*, May 22, 1936, pp. 3, 14.

hooks, bell. *Feminist Theory: From Margin to Center.* Boston: South End Press, 1984.

Horak, Henriette. "New Chinatown: Modernity Creeping into Section." *San Francisco Chronicle*, July 19, 1936, p. 7.

Hosokawa, Bill. *Nisei: The Quiet Americans.* New York: William Morrow, 1969.

Hoy, William. "The Passing of Chinatown: Fact or Fancy?" *Chinese Digest*, January 31, 1936, p. 11.

Hsiao, Edith. "Women's Activities in War-torn China." *Chinese Christian Student* 30, nos. 3 (January 1940): 1, 4; and 4 (February 1940): 4.

Huntington, Emily. *Unemployment Relief and the Unemployed in the San Francisco Bay Region, 1929–1934.* Berkeley: University of California Press, 1939.

Ichioka, Yuji. *The Issei: The World of the First Generation Japanese Immigrants, 1865–1924.* New York: Free Press, 1988.

Issel, William, and Robert Cherny. *San Francisco, 1865–1932: Politics, Power, and Urban Development.* Berkeley and Los Angeles: University of California Press, 1986.

Janney, O. Edward. *The White Slave Traffic in America.* New York: National Vigilance Committee, 1911.

Jaschok, Maria. *Concubines and Bondservants.* London: Zed Books, 1988.

Jaschok, Maria, and Suzanne Miers, eds. *Women and Chinese Patriarchy: Submission, Servitude, and Escape.* Hong Kong: Hong Kong University Press, 1994.

Jayawardena, Kumai. *Feminism and Nationalism in the Third World.* London: Zed Books, 1986.

Johnson, Kay Ann. *Women, the Family, and Peasant Revolution in China.* Chicago: University of Chicago Press, 1983.

Jones, Jacqueline. *Labor of Love, Labor of Sorrow: Black Women, Work, and the Family from Slavery to the Present.* New York: Random House, 1985.

Keil, Sally Van Wagenken. *Those Wonderful Women in Their Flying Machines.* New York: Rawson, Wade, 1979.

Kessler-Harris, Alice. *Out to Work: A History of Wage-earning Women in the United States.* Oxford: Oxford University Press, 1982.

Kim, Elaine H. *Asian American Literature: An Introduction to the Writings and Their Social Context.* Philadelphia: Temple University Press, 1982.

Kimball, Nell. *Nell Kimball: The Life as an American Madam by Herself.* Edited by Stephen Longstreet. New York: Macmillan, 1970.

Kingston, Maxine Hong. *The Woman Warrior: Memoirs of a Girlhood Among Ghosts.* New York: Alfred A. Knopf, 1976.

Kirby, John B. *Black Americans in the Roosevelt Era: Liberalism and Race.* Knoxville: University of Tennessee Press, 1980.

Klaus, Alisa. *Every Child a Lion: The Origins of Maternal and Infant Health Policy in the United States and France, 1890–1920.* Ithaca: Cornell University Press, 1993.

Ko, Dorothy. "Pursuing Talent and Virtue: Education and Women's Culture in Seventeenth- and Eighteenth-Century China." *Late Imperial China* 13, no. 1 (June 1992): 9–39.

———. *Teachers of the Inner Chambers: Women and Culture in Seventeenth-Century China*. Stanford: Stanford University Press, 1994.

Kulp, Daniel Harrison. *Country Life in South China: The Sociology of Familism*. New York: Columbia University Press, 1925.

Kung, S. W. *Chinese in American Life: Some Aspects of Their History, Status, Problems, and Contributions*. Westport, Conn.: Greenwood Press, 1973.

Kwan, Florence Chinn. "Some Rambling Thoughts on Why I Am a Christian." Unpublished paper (in my possession), November 1966.

Kwoh, Beulah Ong. "Occupational Status of the American-born Chinese College Graduates." Master's thesis, University of Chicago, 1947.

Kwok Pui-lan. *Chinese Women and Christianity, 1860–1927*. Atlanta: Scholars Press, 1992.

Lai Ah Eng. *Peasants, Proletarians, and Prostitutes: A Preliminary Investigation into the Work of Chinese Women in Colonial Malaya*. Singapore: Institute of Southeast Asian Studies, 1986.

Lai Chun-chuen. *Remarks of the Chinese Merchants of San Francisco upon Governor John Bigler's Message and Some Common Objectives, with Some Explanations of the Character of the Chinese Companies and the Laboring Class in California*. San Francisco: Office of the Oriental, Whitton, Town, and Co., 1855.

Lai, Him Mark. "The Chinese American Press." In *The Ethnic Press in the United States: A Historical Analysis and Handbook*, edited by Sally M. Miller, pp. 27–43. New York: Greenwood Press, 1987.

———. *Cong huaqiao dao huaren* (From overseas Chinese to Chinese American). Hong Kong: Joint Publishing Co., 1992.

———. "Historical Development of the Chinese Consolidated Benevolent Association/*Huiguan* System." *Chinese America: History and Perspectives 1987*, pp. 13–51.

———. "A Historical Survey of the Chinese Left in America." In *Counterpoint: Perspectives on Asia America*, edited by Emma Gee, pp. 63–80. Los Angeles: Asian American Studies Center, University of California, 1976.

———. "A Historical Survey of Organizations of the Left Among the Chinese in America." *Bulletin of Concerned Asian Scholars* 4, no. 3 (fall 1972): 10–20.

———. "History of the Bing Lai Family." Him Mark Lai private collection.

———. "Sprouting Wings on the Dragon: Some Chinese Americans Who Contributed to the Development of Aviation in China." In *The Annals of the Chinese Historical Society of the Pacific Northwest*, pp. 179–83. Bellingham, Wash.: Chinese Historical Society of the Pacific Northwest, 1984.

———. "To Bring Forth a New China, to Build a Better America: The Chinese Marxist Left in America to the 1960s." *Chinese America: History and Perspectives 1992*, pp. 3–82.

Lai, Him Mark, Genny Lim, and Judy Yung. *Island: Poetry and History of Chinese Immigrants on Angel Island, 1910–1940*. Seattle: University of Washington Press, 1991.

Lai, Kum Pui. "Attitudes of the Chinese in Hawaii Toward Chinese Language Schools." *Sociology and Social Research* 20, no. 2 (November 1935): 140–44.

Lake, Margarita. "A Chinese Slave Girl in America." *Missionary Review of the World* 26 (July 1903): 532–33.

Lan, Dean. "Chinatown Sweatshops." In *Counterpoint: Perspectives on Asian America,* edited by Emma Gee, pp. 347–58. Los Angeles: Asian American Studies Center, University of California, 1976.

Larson, Louise Leung. *Sweet Bamboo: Saga of a Chinese American Family.* Los Angeles: Chinese Historical Society of Southern California, 1989.

Lee, Chingwah. "The Second Generation of the Chinese." *Hospital Social Service* 21, no. 3 (March 1930): 192–97.

———. "Remember When?" *Chinese Digest,* January 17, 1936, p. 8.

Lee, Jane Kwong. "Chinese Women in San Francisco." *Chinese Digest,* June 1938, pp. 8–9.

———. "The Future of Second Generation Chinese Lies in China and America." *Chinese Digest,* June 5, 1936, p. 5.

———. "A Resume of Social Service." *Chinese Digest,* December 20, 1935, pp. 10, 14.

Lee, Lim P. "Chinatown Goes Picketing." *Chinese Digest,* January 1939, pp. 10–11.

———. "The Chinese American Citizens Alliance: Its Activities and History." *Chinese Digest,* October 30, 1936, pp. 11, 15.

———. "The Postal Chinese Club of San Francisco." *Asian Week,* January 27, 1984, p. 7.

Lee, Mary Bo-Tze. "Problems of the Segregated School for Asiatics in San Francisco." Master's thesis, University of California, Berkeley, 1921.

Lee, Marjorie. "*Hu-Jee*: The Forgotten Second Generation of Chinese America, 1930–1950." Master's thesis, University of California, Los Angeles, 1984.

Lee, Rose Hum. "Chinese Dilemma." *Phylon* 10, no. 2 (1949): 137–40.

———. *The Chinese in the United States of America.* Hong Kong: Hong Kong University Press, 1960.

———. "Chinese in the United States Today: The War Has Changed Their Lives." *Survey Graphic: Magazine of Social Interpretation* 31, no. 10 (October 1942): 419, 444.

———. "The Growth and Decline of Chinese Communities in the Rocky Mountain Region." Ph.D. diss., University of Chicago, 1947.

Leeder, Elaine. *The Gentle General: Rose Pesotta, Anarchist and Labor Organizer.* Albany: State University of New York Press, 1993.

Lerner, Gerda. *The Majority Finds Its Past: Placing Women in History.* Oxford: Oxford University Press, 1979.

Leuchtenburg, William E. *Franklin D. Roosevelt and the New Deal, 1932–1940.* New York: Harper & Row, 1963.

Levy, Howard S. *Chinese Footbinding: The History of a Curious Erotic Custom.* New York: Walton Rawls, 1966.

Li, Bernadette. "Chinese Feminist Thought at the Turn of the Century." *St. John's Papers,* no. 25. Jamaica, N.Y.: St. John's University, 1978.

Li Yauguang. "World Famous Chinese American Aviatrix Ouyang Ying" (in Chinese). *Huaxing,* June 23, 1989.

Li Yu-ning. "Historical Roots of Changes in Women's Status in Modern China." In *Chinese Women Through Chinese Eyes*, edited by Li Yu-ning, pp. 102–22. Armonk, N.Y.: M. E. Sharpe, 1992.

Liang Yuan. "The Chinese Family in Chicago." Master's thesis, University of Chicago, 1951.

Lichtman, Sheila Tropp. "Women at Work, 1941–1945: Wartime Employment in the San Francisco Bay Area." Ph.D. diss., University of California, Davis, 1981.

Light, Ivan. "From Vice District to Tourist Attraction: The Moral Career of American Chinatowns, 1880–1940." *Pacific Historical Review* 43, no. 3 (August 1974): 367–94.

Lim, Christina, and Sheldon Lim. "In the Shadow of the Tiger: The 407th Air Service Squadron." *Chinese America: History and Perspectives 1993*, pp. 25–74.

Ling, Amy. *Between Worlds: Women Writers of Chinese Ancestry*. New York: Pergamon Press, 1990.

Linking Our Lives: Chinese American Women of Los Angeles. Los Angeles: Chinese Historical Society of Southern California, 1984.

Lissner, Elsa. "Investigation into Conditions in the Chinese Quarter in San Francisco and Oakland." Survey of Race Relations Collection, Hoover Institution on War, Revolution, and Peace, Stanford University, 1922.

Liu, Fu-ju. "A Comparative Demographic Study of Native-born and Foreign-born Chinese Populations in the United States." Ph.D. diss., School of Graduate Studies of Michigan, 1953.

Liu Pei Chi. "Chinese Americans and the National Salvation Through Aviation Movement" (in Chinese). *Guangdong Wenxian* 10, no. 2 (1980): 1–7.

———. *A History of the Chinese in the United States of America*. Vol. 2. Taipei: Liming Wenhua Shiye Gongsi, 1981.

Locke, Mary Lou. "Out of the Shadows and into the Western Sun: Working Women of the Late Nineteenth-Century Urban Far West." *Journal of Urban History* 16, no. 2 (February 1990): 175–204.

Loo, Chalsa. *Chinatown: Most Time, Hard Time*. New York: Praeger, 1991.

Loomis, Augustus W. "Chinese Women in California." *Overland Monthly* 2 (April 1869): 344–46.

Louis, Kit King. "A Study of American-born and American-reared Chinese in Los Angeles." Master's thesis, University of Southern California, 1931.

Low, Victor. *The Unimpressible Race: A Century of Educational Struggle by the Chinese in San Francisco*. San Francisco: East/West, 1982.

Lowe, Pardee. "The Good Life in Chinatown: Further Adventures of a Chinese Husband and His American Wife Among His Own People." *Asia* 37 (February 1937): 127–31.

Lum, Ethel. "Chinese During the Depression." *Chinese Digest*, November 22, 1935, p. 10.

———. "The W.P.A. and Chinatown." *Chinese Digest*, January 10, 1936, pp. 10, 15.

———. "Young Woman, Are You Looking for a Job?" *Chinese Digest*, March 27, 1936, p. 11.

McClain, Charles J. *In Search of Equality: The Chinese Struggle Against Discrimination in Nineteenth-Century America.* Berkeley and Los Angeles: University of California Press, 1994.

McClain, Laurene Wu. "Donaldina Cameron: A Reappraisal." *Pacific Historian* 27, no. 3 (fall 1983): 25–35.

McCown, Jean. "Women in a Changing China: The Y.W.C.A." YWCA of the U.S.A., National Board Archives, New York, April 5, 1970.

McCunn, Ruthanne Lum. *Chinese American Portraits: Personal Histories, 1828–1988.* San Francisco: Chronicle Books, 1988.

McElvaine, Robert S. *The Great Depression America, 1929–1941.* New York: Times Books, 1982.

McEntire, Davis. *The Labor Force in California: A Study of Characteristics and Trends in Labor Force Employment of Occupations in California, 1900–1950.* Berkeley: University of California Press, 1952.

McLeod, Alexander. *Pigtails and Gold Dust.* Caldwell, Idaho: Caxton Printers, 1948.

McWilliams, Carey. *Brothers Under the Skin.* Boston: Little, Brown, 1944.

Mann, Susan. "Learned Women in the Eighteenth Century." In *Engendering China: Women, Culture, and the State,* edited by Gail Hershatter, Lisa Rofel, and Christina Gilmartin, pp. 27–47. Cambridge, Mass.: Harvard University Press, 1994.

Mannheim, Karl. "The Problem of Generations." In *Essays on the Sociology of Knowledge by Karl Mannheim,* edited by Paul Keeskemeti, pp. 276–320. London: Routledge & Kegan, 1959.

Mark, Diane Mei Lin, and Ginger Chih. *A Place Called Chinese America.* Dubuque: Kendall/Hunt, 1982.

Marshall, Jim. "Cathay Hey-Hey!" *Collier's,* February 28, 1942, pp. 13, 53.

Martin, Mildred Crowl. *Chinatown's Angry Angel: The Story of Donaldina Cameron.* Palo Alto: Pacific Books, 1977.

Mason, Sarah Refo. "Social Christianity, American Feminism, and Chinese Prostitutes: The History of the Presbyterian Mission Home, San Francisco, 1874–1935." In *Women and Chinese Patriarchy: Submission, Servitude, and Escape,* edited by Maria Jaschok and Suzanne Miers, pp. 198–220. Hong Kong: Hong Kong University Press, 1994.

Matsumoto, Valerie. "Desperately Seeking 'Deirdre': Gender Roles, Multicultural Relations, and Nisei Women Writers of the 1930s." *Frontiers: A Journal of Women Studies* 12, no. 1 (1991): 19–32.

———. "Japanese American Women During World War II." *Frontiers: A Journal of Women Studies* 8, no. 1 (1984): 6–14.

May, Elaine Tyler. *Great Expectations: Marriage and Divorce in Post-Victorian America.* Chicago: University of Chicago Press, 1980.

Mears, Eliot Grinnell. *Resident Orientals on the American Pacific Coast: Their Legal and Economic Status.* Chicago: University of Chicago Press, 1928.

Mei, June. "Socioeconomic Origins of Emigration: Guangdong to California, 1850 to 1882." In *Labor Migration Under Capitalism: Asian Workers in the United States Before World War II,* edited by Lucie Cheng Hirata and Edna Bonacich, pp. 219–47. Berkeley and Los Angeles: University of California Press, 1984.

Miers, Suzanne. "Mui Tsai Through the Eyes of the Victim: Janet Lim's Story of Bondage and Escape." In *Women and Chinese Patriarchy: Submission, Servitude, and Escape*, edited by Maria Jaschok and Suzanne Miers, pp. 108–21. Hong Kong: Hong Kong University Press, 1994.

Milkman, Ruth. *Gender at Work: The Dynamics of Job Segregation by Sex During World War II.* Urbana: University of Illinois Press, 1987.

———. "Women's Work and the Economic Crisis: Some Lessons from the Great Depression." In *A Heritage of Her Own: Toward a New Social History of American Women*, edited by Nancy F. Cott and Elizabeth Pleck, pp. 507–41. New York: Simon & Schuster, 1979.

Mink, Gwendolyn. "The Lady and the Tramp: Gender, Race, and the Origins of the American Welfare State." In *Women, the State, and Welfare*, edited by Linda Gordon, pp. 92–122. Madison: University of Wisconsin Press, 1990.

Mohanty, Chandra Talpade, Ann Russo, and Lourdes Torres, eds. *Third World Women and the Politics of Feminism.* Bloomington: Indiana University Press, 1991.

Monroy, Douglas. "La Costura en Los Angeles, 1933–1939: The ILGWU and the Politics of Domination." In *Mexican Women in the United States: Struggles Past and Present*, edited by Magdalena Mora and Adelaida R. Del Castillo, pp. 171–78. Los Angeles: Chicano Studies Research Center, University of California, Los Angeles, 1980.

Moore, Shirley Ann. "The Black Community in Richmond, California, 1910–1963." Ph.D. diss., University of California, Berkeley, 1989.

Morris, Richard B. *Government and Labor in Early America.* New York: Columbia University Press, 1946.

Mullins, William. *The Depression and the Urban West Coast, 1929–1933.* Bloomington: Indiana University Press, 1991.

Nakano, Mei. *Japanese American Women: Three Generations, 1890–1990.* Berkeley, Calif.: Mina Press, 1990.

Nee, Victor, and Brett de Bary Nee. *Longtime Californ': A Documentary Study of an American Chinatown.* New York: Pantheon Books, 1972.

Ng, Franklin. "The Sojourner, Return Migration, and Immigration History." *Chinese America: History and Perspectives 1987*, pp. 53–71.

Norwood, Stephan H. *Labor's Flaming Youth: Telephone Operators and Worker Militancy, 1878–1923.* Urbana: University of Illinois Press, 1990.

Omi, Michael, and Howard Winant. *Racial Formation in the United States from the 1960s to the 1980s.* New York: Routledge & Kegan Paul, 1986.

Ong, Paul. "Chinese Labor in Early San Francisco: Racial Segmentation and Industrial Expansion." *Amerasia Journal* 8, no. 1 (spring/summer 1981): 69–92.

Ono, Kazuko. *Chinese Women in a Century of Revolution, 1850–1950.* Stanford: Stanford University Press, 1989.

Osumi, Megumi Dick. "Asians and California's Anti-Miscegenation Laws." In *Asian and Pacific American Experiences: Women's Perspectives*, edited by Nobuya Tsuchida, pp. 1–37. Minneapolis: Asian/Pacific American Learning Resource Center and General College, University of Minnesota, 1982.

"Our Chinatown Branch." *Bank American,* January 1956, pp. 6–7.

Park, Robert E. *Race and Culture.* New York: Free Press, 1950.

Parman, Donald L. *The Navajos and the New Deal.* New Haven: Yale University Press, 1976.

Pascoe, Peggy. *Relations of Rescue: The Search for Female Moral Authority in the American West, 1874–1939.* New York: Oxford University Press, 1990.

Peffer, George Anthony. "Forbidden Families: Emigration Experience of Chinese Women Under the Page Law, 1875–1882." *Journal of American Ethnic History* 6 (1986): 28–46.

Pesotta, Rose. *Bread upon the Waters.* New York: Dodd, Mead, 1944.

Phan, Peter. "Familiar Strangers: The Fourteenth Air Service Group Case Study of Chinese American Identity During World War II." *Chinese America: History and Perspectives 1993,* pp. 75–107.

Pillors, Brenda Elaine. "The Criminalization of Prostitution in the United States: The Case of San Francisco, 1854–1919." Ph.D. diss., University of California, Berkeley, 1982.

Pivar, David J. *Purity Crusade: Sexual Morality and Social Control, 1868–1900.* Westport, Conn.: Greenwood Press, 1973.

Piven, Frances Fox, and Richard A. Cloward. *Regulating the Poor: The Functions of Public Welfare.* New York: Pantheon Books, 1971.

Purwin, Louise. "Chinese Daughters of Uncle Sam." *Independent Woman,* November 1944, pp. 337, 353.

Rankin, Mary Backus. "The Emergence of Women at the End of the Ch'ing: The Case of Ch'iu Chin." In *Women in Chinese Society,* edited by Margery Wolf and Roxane Witke, pp. 39–66. Stanford: Stanford University Press, 1975.

Reed, Ruth Brown. "Career Girl, Chinese Style." *Independent Woman,* September 1942, pp. 260, 286.

Riggs, Fred W. *Pressure on Congress: A Study of the Repeal of Chinese Exclusion.* New York: Columbia University Press, 1950.

Rollins, Judith. *Between Women: Domestics and Their Employers.* Philadelphia: Temple University Press, 1985.

Rosaldo, Michelle Zimbalist. "Woman, Culture, and Society: A Theoretical Overview." In *Woman, Culture, and Society,* edited by Michelle Zimbalist Rosaldo and Louise Lamphere, pp. 17–42. Stanford: Stanford University Press, 1974.

Rosen, Ruth. *The Lost Sisterhood: Prostitution in America, 1900–1918.* Baltimore: Johns Hopkins University Press, 1982.

Ruiz, Vicki L. *Cannery Women, Cannery Lives: Mexican Women, Unionization, and the California Food Processing Industry, 1930–1950.* Albuquerque: University of New Mexico Press, 1987.

———. "'Star Struck': Acculturation, Adolescence, and Mexican American Women, 1920–1950." In *Small Worlds: Children and Adolescents in America, 1850–1950,* edited by Elliott West and Paul Petrik, pp. 61–80. Lawrence: University Press of Kansas, 1992.

Ruiz, Vicki L., and Ellen Carol DuBois, eds. *Unequal Sisters: A Multicultural Reader in U.S. Women's History.* New York: Routledge, 1994.

Rupp, Leila. *Mobilizing Women for War: German and American Propaganda, 1939–1945.* Princeton: Princeton University Press, 1978.

Ryan, Mary P. *Womanhood in America: From Colonial Times to the Present.* New York: Franklin Watts, 1983.

Salinger, Sharon V. *"To Serve Well and Faithfully": Labor and Indentured Servants in Pennsylvania, 1682–1800.* Cambridge: Cambridge University Press, 1987.

Sanchez, George J. *Becoming Mexican American: Ethnicity, Culture, and Identity in Chicano Los Angeles, 1900–1945.* New York: Oxford University Press, 1993.

Sankar, Andrea Patrice. "The Evolution of the Sisterhood in Traditional Chinese Society: From Village Girls' Houses to Chai T'angs in Hong Kong." Ph.D. diss., University of Michigan, 1978.

"Savings Development." *Bulletin, Financial Advisors Association,* May 1941, pp. 269–70.

Saxton, Alexander. *The Indispensable Enemy: Labor and the Anti-Chinese Movement in California.* Berkeley and Los Angeles: University of California Press, 1971.

Scharf, Lois. *To Work and to Wed: Female Employment, Feminism, and the Great Depression.* Westport, Conn.: Greenwood Press, 1980.

Scharf, Lois, and Joan M. Jensen. *Decades of Discontent: The Women's Movement, 1920–1940.* Westport, Conn.: Greenwood Press, 1983.

Scott, Anne Firor. *Natural Allies: Women's Associations in American History.* Urbana: University of Illinois Press, 1991.

Seller, Maxine Schwartz. *Immigrant Women.* Philadelphia: Temple University Press, 1981.

———. *To Seek America: A History of Ethnic Life in the United States.* Englewood, N.J.: J. S. Ozer, 1977.

Shih, Hsien-ju. "The Social and Vocational Adjustment of the Second Generation Chinese High School Students in San Francisco." Ph.D. diss., University of California, Berkeley, 1937.

Shumsky, Neil Larry, and Larry M. Springer. "San Francisco's Zone of Prostitution, 1880–1934." *Journal of Historical Geography* 7, no. 1 (1981): 71–89.

Sickerman, Barbara, ed. *Notable American Women: The Modern Period.* Cambridge, Mass.: Harvard University Press, 1980.

Simross, Lynn. "Yees Remember the Struggles and Celebrate Their Success." *View* sec., *Los Angeles Times,* August 26, 1981, pp. 1–3.

Sims, Mary S. "The Natural History of a Social Institution: The Y.W.C.A." Ph.D. diss., New York University, 1935.

Sinn, Elizabeth. "Chinese Patriarchy and the Protection of Women in 19th-Century Hong Kong." In *Women and Chinese Patriarchy: Submission, Servitude, and Escape,* edited by Maria Jaschok and Suzanne Miers, pp. 141–70. Hong Kong: Hong Kong University Press, 1994.

Sitkoff, Harvard. *A New Deal for Blacks: The Emergence of Civil Rights as a National Issue.* Vol. 1: *The Depression Decade.* New York: Oxford University Press, 1978.

Siu, Paul C. P. "The Chinese Laundryman." Ph.D. diss., University of Chicago, 1953.

Smith, Arthur. *Village Life in China: A Study in Sociology.* New York: Fleming H. Revell, 1899.

Smith, Carl T. "The Gillespie Brothers: Early Links Between Hong Kong and California." *Chung Chi Bulletin* 47 (December 1969): 23–28.

Smith, William Carlson. *Americans in Process: A Study of Our Citizens of Oriental Ancestry.* Ann Arbor: Edwards Bros., 1937.

Steinbeck, John. *The Grapes of Wrath.* New York: Viking Press, 1939.

Stephens, John W. "A Quantitative History of Chinatown San Francisco, 1870 and 1880." In *The Life, Influence, and the Role of the Chinese in the United States, 1776–1960,* pp. 71–88. San Francisco: Chinese Historical Society of America, 1976.

Stockard, Janice. *Daughters of the Canton Delta: Marriage Patterns and Economic Strategies in South China, 1860–1930.* Stanford: Stanford University Press, 1989.

Sui Seen Far. "The Chinese Woman in America." *Land of Sunshine* 6, no. 2 (January 1897): 59–62.

———. *Mrs. Spring Fragrance.* Chicago: A. C. McClurg & Co., 1912.

Sung, Mrs. William Z. L. "A Pioneer Chinese Family." In *The Life, Influence, and the Role of the Chinese in the United States, 1776–1960,* pp. 287–92. San Francisco: Chinese Historical Society of America, 1976.

Symanski, Richard. *Immoral Landscape: Female Prostitution in Western Societies.* Toronto: Butterworth, 1981.

Takaki, Ronald. *Strangers from a Different Shore: A History of Asian Americans.* Boston: Little, Brown, 1989.

———. "They Also Came: The Migration of Chinese and Japanese Women to Hawaii and the Continental United States." *Chinese America: History and Perspectives 1990,* pp. 3–19.

Tang, Vincente. "Chinese Women Immigrants and the Two-Edged Sword of Habeas Corpus." In *The Chinese American Experience,* edited by Genny Lim, pp. 48–56. San Francisco: Chinese Historical Society of America, 1983.

Taylor, Frank J. "The Bone Money Empire." *Saturday Evening Post,* December 24, 1933, pp. 24, 47–48.

Terkel, Studs. *Hard Times: An Oral History of the Great Depression.* New York: Pantheon Books, 1970.

Tilly, Louise A., and Joan W. Scott. *Women, Work, and Family.* New York: Holt, Rinehart & Winston, 1978.

Topley, Marjorie. "Marriage Resistance in Rural Kwangtung." In *Women in Chinese Society,* edited by Margery Wolf and Roxane Witke, pp. 67–88. Stanford: Stanford University Press, 1975.

Treadwell, Mattie. *United States Army in World War II, Special Studies; The Women's Army Corps.* Washington, D.C.: Department of the Army, 1954.

Tsai, Shih-shan Henry. *China and the Overseas Chinese in the United States, 1868–1911.* Fayetteville: University of Arkansas Press, 1983.

———. *The Chinese Experience in America.* Bloomington: Indiana University Press, 1986.

"Veterans Survey Report." *Bulletin, Chinese Historical Society of America* 17, no. 7 (September 1982): 2.

Wakeman, Frederic, Jr. *Strangers at the Gate: Social Disorder in South China,*

1839–1861. Berkeley and Los Angeles: University of California Press, 1966.

Wang, Grace W. "A Speech on Second-Generation Chinese in U.S.A." *Chinese Digest*, August 7, 1936, pp. 6, 14.

Wang, L. Ling-chi. "An Overview of Chinese American Communities During the Exclusion Era, 1883–1943." L. Ling-chi Wang private collection.

———. "Politics of Assimilation and Repression: History of the Chinese in the United States, 1940–1970." Typescript. Asian American Studies Library, University of California, Berkeley.

Wang, Sing-wu. *The Organization of Chinese Emigration, 1848–1888*. San Francisco: Chinese Materials Center, 1978.

Ware, Susan. *Holding Their Own: American Women in the 1930s*. Boston: Twayne, 1982.

Warren, James Francis. "Chinese Prostitution in Singapore: Recruitment and Brothel Organization." In *Women and Chinese Patriarchy: Submission, Servitude, and Escape*, edited by Maria Jaschok and Suzanne Miers, pp. 77–107. Hong Kong: Hong Kong University Press, 1994.

Watson, Rubie S. "Girls' Houses and Working Women: Expressive Culture in the Pearl River Delta, 1900–1941." In *Women and Chinese Patriarchy: Submission, Servitude, and Escape*, edited by Maria Jaschok and Suzanne Miers, pp. 25–44. Hong Kong: Hong Kong University Press, 1994.

Waugh, Dexter. "Forbidden City." *Image* sec., *San Francisco Examiner*, October 29, 1989, pp. 19–24, 34.

Weatherford, Doris. *Foreign and Female: Immigrant Women in America, 1840–1930*. New York: Schocken Books, 1986.

Wei, William. *The Asian American Movement*. Philadelphia: Temple University Press, 1993.

Westin, Jeane. *Making Do: How Women Survived the '30s*. Chicago: Follett, 1976.

Whitfield, Ruth Hall. "Public Opinion and the Chinese Question in San Francisco, 1900–1947." Master's thesis, University of California, Berkeley, 1947.

Williams, Vera S. *WASPs: Women Airforce Service Pilots of World War II*. Osceola, Wis.: Motorbooks International, 1994.

Wilson, Carol Green. *Chinatown Quest: One Hundred Years of Donaldina Cameron House, 1874–1974*. San Francisco: California Historical Society, 1974.

Witke, Roxane. "Transformation of Attitudes Towards Women During the May Fourth Era of Modern China." Ph.D. diss., University of California, Berkeley, 1970.

Wolf, Margery. "Chinese Women: Old Skills in a New Context." In *Women, Culture, and Society*, edited by Michelle Zimbalist Rosaldo and Louise Lamphere, pp. 157–72. Stanford: Stanford University Press, 1974.

Wollenberg, Charles. *Marinship at War: Shipbuilding and Social Change in Wartime Sausalito*. Berkeley, Calif.: Western Heritage Press, 1990.

Wolters, Raymond. *Negroes and the Great Depression: The Problem of Economic Recovery*. Westport, Conn.: Greenwood Press, 1970.

Won, Lilly King Gee. "My Recollections of Dr. Sun Yat-sen's Stay at Our Home in San Francisco." *Chinese America: History and Perspectives 1990*, pp. 67–82.

Wong Ah So. "Story of Wong Ah So—Experiences as a Prostitute." *Orientals and Their Cultural Adjustment*. Social Science Source Documents, No. 4, pp. 31–35. Nashville: Social Science Institute, Fisk University, 1946.

Wong, Jade Snow. *Fifth Chinese Daughter*. New York: Harper & Bros., 1950.

———. *No Chinese Stranger*. New York: Harper & Row, 1975.

Wong, Kathleen Wong. "Quan Laan Fan: An Oral History." Student paper, Asian American Studies Library, University of California, Berkeley, 1974.

Wong, Lorraine. "Chinese All American Girl." *Record*, January 1935, pp. 21, 26.

Woo, Wesley. "Protestant Work Among the Chinese in the San Francisco Bay Area, 1850–1920." Ph.D. diss., University of California, Berkeley, 1983.

Woolston, Howard B. *Prostitution in the United States*. New York: Century Co., 1921.

Wu, Ching Chao. "Chinatowns: A Study of Symbiosis and Assimilation." Ph.D. diss., University of Chicago, 1928.

———. "Chinese Immigration in the Pacific Area." Master's thesis, University of Chicago, 1926.

Wu Jianhung. "The Chinese American Patriotic Movement Before and After the 9-18 Incident" (in Chinese). Paper presented at the First International Conference on Overseas Chinese Studies, Peking, 1978.

Yamato, Alex. "Socioeconomic Change Among Japanese Americans in the San Francisco Bay Area." Ph.D. diss., University of California, Berkeley, 1986.

Yans-McLaughlin, Virginia. *Family and Community: Italian Immigrants in Buffalo, 1880–1930*. Ithaca: Cornell University Press, 1971.

Yao, Esther S. Lee. *Chinese Women: Past and Present*. Mesquite, Tex.: Ide House, 1983.

Ye, Weili. "Crossing the Cultures: The Experiences of Chinese Students in the United States of America, 1900–1925." Ph.D. diss., Yale University, 1989.

Young, Ludwig J. "The Emancipation of Women in China Before 1920, with Special Reference to Kwangtung." Master's thesis, Columbia University, 1965.

Yu, Connie Young. "From Tents to Federal Projects: Chinatown's Housing History." In *The Chinese American Experience*, edited by Genny Lim, pp. 130–39. San Francisco: Chinese Historical Society of America, 1983.

———. "The World of Our Grandmothers." In *Making Waves: Anthology of Writings by and About Asian American Women*, edited by Asian Women United, pp. 33–42. Boston: Beacon Press, 1989.

Yule, Emma Sarepta. "Miss China." *Scribner's* 71 (January 1922): 66–79.

Yung, Judy. *Chinese American Women: A Pictorial History*. Seattle: University of Washington Press, 1986.

———. "Miss Chinatown USA and the Representation of Beauty." Paper presented at the Ninth National Conference of the Association of Asian American Studies, San Jose, Calif., May 30, 1992.

———. "The Social Awakening of Chinese American Women as Reported in *Chung Sai Yat Po*, 1900–1911." In *Unequal Sisters: A Multicultural Reader in U.S. Women's History*, edited by Ellen Carol DuBois and Vicki L. Ruiz, pp. 195–207. New York: Routledge, 1990.

Zavella, Patricia. *Women's Work and Chicano Families: Cannery Workers of the Santa Clara Valley*. Ithaca: Cornell University Press, 1987.

Zeng Bugui. "Sun Zhongshan yu Jiujinshan nü Tongmenghui yuan" (Sun Yat-sen and the women members of San Francisco's Tongmenghui). In *Zhongshan Xiansheng yishi* (Anecdotes of Sun Yat-sen), pp. 141–42. Beijing: Zhongguo Wen-shi Chubanshe, 1986.

Zheng, Mei. "Chinese Americans in San Francisco and New York City During the Anti-Japanese War: 1937–1945." Master's thesis, University of California, Los Angeles, 1990.

Zink, Howard A. "Cast of Characters." Kum Quey file, Palo Alto Historical Association.

Zinn, Maxine Baca. "Feminist Rethinking from Racial-Ethnic Families." In *Women of Color in U.S. Society*, edited by Maxine Baca Zinn and Bonnie Thornton Dill, pp. 303–14. Philadelphia: Temple University Press, 1994.

Zinn, Maxine Baca, and Bonnie Thornton Dill, eds. *Women of Color in U. S. Society*. Philadelphia: Temple University Press, 1994.

Zo Kil Young. "Chinese Emigration into the United States, 1850–1880." Ph.D. diss., Columbia University, 1971.

Index

Judy Yung is a second-generation Chinese American born and raised in San Francisco Chinatown. She has served as a librarian, as a journalist, and as director of the Chinese Women of America Research Project in San Francisco. She is currently Assistant Professor of American Studies at the University of California, Santa Cruz. Her earlier books include *Chinese Women of America: A Pictorial History* and *Island: Poetry and History of Chinese Immigrants on Angel Island, 1910–1940*. (Cindy Chow-Sravely photo)

Compositor:	ICS; glossary by Birdtrack Press
Text:	10/13 Galliard
Display:	Galliard
Printer:	Edwards Bros.
Binder:	Edwards Bros.